Intercultural Communication
for Everyday Life

Intercultural Communication for Everyday Life

Second edition

John R. Baldwin, Alberto González, Nettie Brock,
Ming Xie, and Chin-Chung Chao

WILEY Blackwell

Registered Offices
John Wiley & Sons, Inc., 111 River Street, Hoboken, NJ 07030, USA
John Wiley & Sons Ltd, The Atrium, Southern Gate, Chichester, West Sussex, PO19 8SQ, UK

For details of our global editorial offices, customer services, and more information about Wiley products visit us at www.wiley.com.

Wiley also publishes its books in a variety of electronic formats and by print-on-demand. Some content that appears in standard print versions of this book may not be available in other formats.

Library of Congress Cataloging-in-Publication Data
Names: Baldwin, John R., 1960- author.
Title: Intercultural communication for everyday life / John R Baldwin, Alberto González, Nettie Brock, Ming Xie, and ChinChung Chao.
Description: Second edition. | Hoboken, NJ : John Wiley & Sons, 2024. | Includes bibliographical references and index.
Identifiers: LCCN 2023003260 (print) | LCCN 2023003261 (ebook) | ISBN 9781119897903 (paperback) | ISBN 9781119897910 (ebook) | ISBN 9781119897927 (epub)
Subjects: LCSH: Communication--Philosophy. | Intercultural communication.
Classification: LCC P90 .I5545 2024 (print) | LCC P90 (ebook) | DDC 302.23--dc23
LC record available at https://lccn.loc.gov/2023003260
LC ebook record available at https://lccn.loc.gov/2023003261

Cover image: © toos/Getty Images
Cover design by Wiley

Set in 9.5/12pt MinionPro by Integra Software Services Pvt. Ltd, Pondicherry, India

Brief contents

Contents

Part two Elements 69

Part three Messages 133

Contents

Preface

Living in a world of uncertainty

The years since the first edition of this text (2014) have seen many changes, and these have often bought increased tension and uncertainty. This tension augments the fact that many young adults were struggling with anxiety and depression in the United States and other cultures even before recent times. In the last years, we have seen protests across many cultures for racial justice, women's rights, LGBTQ+ rights, and the right to public expression. Some countries are accused of suppressing Muslim, Kurdish, or other minority groups, seeking to force them to conform to dominant cultures. We have seen a growing frequency of climate-related changes, such as increased storms in some areas, rising sea levels, shrinking ice caps, and resulting changes in food supplies. The number of refugees from local strife and from climate-related issues has risen drastically. At the time of this writing, there is open conflict in Ukraine, Ethiopia, and Yemen, but also refugees fleeing Syria, Venezuela, and other countries. And then there was that whole COVID-19 virus thing. Surrounding all of these, many of our countries are seeing a rise in political polarization, which hints at political instability.

Our need has grown for interconnections with those around the world to understand others and to reach hands across borders to seek resolutions for world problems that affect people in their everyday life. Our hope for this text is that you will learn about culture, but specifically, that the outcome of the book is that you will become a more informed and prepared world citizen.

Grand-scale problems require complex solutions, and these solutions require the synergy of efforts of people with different cultural perspectives. But even if we do not see the connection of global issues to our own lives or ever travel abroad, culture touches our lives. We live in a multicultural, global economy, where, to survive, most large businesses employ, buy, and sell across cultural and national lines. Many of us, regardless of our country of residence, have doctors, teachers, bosses, students, or employees from "cultures" besides our own. With new and interactive media, we might play online games, chat, or develop friendships or romances with people in other lands without leaving our own borders. Besides this, we each live within and are influenced and sometimes constrained by our own cultures. The more we know about our own culture, the more effective we will be where we live, the more we can engage in issues and problems within our own community (which have cultural elements), and the more we will see the strengths and limits of our own culture. As we see these strengths and limits, we will have more likelihood of being able to make choices and change those cultures. Rather than a "problem," we should see the interconnections with people from other groups and cultures not just as a challenge but as a strength. As our lives and cultures intertwine with the lives, experiences, and values of those of people from other cultures, our diverse and yet interconnected exepriences can weave together a rich fabric of diverse perspectives and solutions. We can weave our differences into a strong, vibrant, and colorful fabric, like that illustrated on the front cover of this text.

Whether we are discussing world-level crises or community issues, there is a bright spot as we talk about social issues, and that is the rise of involvement of citizens in the public sphere—at least in some ways. Kim Parker and Ruth Igielnik (2020), from the Pew Research Center, in a news article appropriately titled, "On the Cusp of Adulthood and Facing an Uncertain Future," describe what they see as characteristics of the youngest adult generation in the United States. This generation is, overall, more comfortable with aspects of diversity, is higher in education than any previous generation, is more likely to believe that climate change is at least partly due to human activity, and sees "societal change as a good thing." As we look at images of protests from around the world—including but far from limited to Iran, Bangladesh, India, Sweden, and Israel—the images are often of young adults seeking to change their world. Engagement and duty are both impacted by things such as level of education, racial background, and religiosity. Increasingly, companies are encouraging their employees to participate in the community, and universities are promoting civic and political engagement.

There seems to be a fresh wind in the air as students in secondary schools, colleges, and universities seek to give back to the community. Volunteerism had risen to a high point in 2017, according to Tobi Johnson (2020), with about 30% of people over 15 years of age volunteering in Australia and the United States, 38% in Great Britain, and 44% in Canada. Ironically, Johnson wrote in March 2020, just before the worldwide COVID-19 crisis. While some sources, such as the United Nations (n.d.) report a surge of volunteerism around the world in response to COVID, Theresa Wu, a volunteering advocate, reports that volunteering dropped 93% during covid and has only rebounded up to 50% of what it was before the crisis. Volunteering trends, according to Wu (2021), include digital media and corporate social responsibility, both things we will discuss in this book. In sum, there is a need for us to be engaged in our societies, in whichever country we find ourselves.

Why another intercultural text?
(Features of this book)

The need for solutions for community, as well as the growing interest in community engagement, is a driving force for the present book. We have three main goals in writing this text. First, we want to provide responsible knowledge of things cultural. Many introductory textbooks present simple explanations of things for the student new to cultural issues. We believe students are capable of deep thought, so, where possible, we introduce basic ideas, but then challenge students to critical thought about those ideas. Our second goal is for readers to be able to take something practical from the text for their own workplaces, relationships, and schooling, the traditional focus of intercultural studies. But the third goal is to bring an imagination of possibilities for community engagement—civic or political. We want to encourage readers, and ourselves as authors, to find ways to make the knowledge practical for making people's lives better, to address social issues, and to meet the personal needs of people in our lives and in our classrooms. With this in mind, this book has several distinctive features:

→ The authors write for introductory readers, with clear definition of terms, but use original frameworks and introduce theories in a way that does not condescend to the reader.

→ We treat culture complexly. While we sometimes discuss national cultures, through most of the book we see cultures as distinct from national boundaries. Some cultures cross national boundaries, and a single city might have people of many different cultures within it. There are regional, urban–rural, or other cultural differences within nations; even organizations have cultures.

→ We construct a vision of culture that uses examples from around the world as much as possible, seeking to remove some of our own U.S.-centric bias as authors, and we use examples that relate to a variety of types of diversity, including age, sex, race, religion, and sexual orientation. While these, in and of themselves, do not constitute cultures, they often contain cultural elements, and there are cultural constructions of how a society treats different groups that deserve our attention as engaged citizens.

→ As authors, we have different cultural backgrounds, but also different focuses within communication—rhetoric, media, and face-to-face communication studies—we (re)introduce notions to the study of intercultural communication not present in many books, including large sections on intercultural ethics and chapters on media (traditional and social media), rhetoric, and political communication.

→ Throughout the book, we promote civic engagement with cues toward individual intercultural effectiveness and giving back to the community in socially relevant ways; we do this throughout the chapters and with discussion questions and engagement activities at the end of each chapter.

→ We weave pedagogy throughout the text with student-centered examples, thought (or "text") boxes, applications, critical thinking questions, a glossary of key terms, and online resources for students and instructors. These online resources include sample syllabi, test questions, glossary terms, power points, and class exercise options.

Focus and direction of this book

With these goals in mind, our text begins with a discussion of the foundations of intercultural communication. In Chapter 1, we introduce several reasons why it is important to study intercultural communication, with updated situations and examples of world and community diversity. In Chapter 2, we introduce our central concepts of political and civic engagement and discuss the importance and nature of ethical intercultural communication and cultural research. We then turn to different ways to define culture (Chapter 3).

The second portion of the book focuses on elements that inform the intercultural communication process, starting with the foundation upon which all communication rests—values, beliefs, and worldview (Chapter 4). We consider the view we have of ourselves as that relates to the groups to which we belong—identity (Chapter 5)—and then look at our attitudes towards those of other identities (Chapter 6).

In the third part of our book, we look at the exchange of messages through different channels. We begin with verbal communication—that is, face-to-face communication as it relates to the use of words in interaction (Chapter 7). We next consider the various channels of face-to-face communication that do not use words—nonverbal communication (Chapter 8). This includes a discussion of things such as space, time, touch, eye contact, and gesture. We examine messages given by speakers or in texts to persuade—rhetoric (Chapter 9). We then look at aspects of mediated communication, in terms of how we mediate identity and culture (Chapter 10). We finally consider social media specifically (Chapter 11) and how it is used differently around the world and can be used for culture- and group-related civic engagement.

Our final section contains issues and contexts of intercultural communication, starting with crosscultural adaptation and intercultural communication competence (Chapter 12), then moving to intercultural relations, conflict, and negotiation (Chapter 13), political communication (Chapter 14), and finally the organizational context (Chapter 15).

The order is intended to be flexible for the instructor. As we have used drafts of this text in our own teaching, we find that, after the foundational chapters, each chapter stands on its own; we can choose the chapters that best meet our needs, for example, with a special unit on media (or leaving media out), or skipping over the section on personal relationships. We encourage the student reading this preface to start each chapter you read by looking at the objectives at the top of each chapter—those are things that we, the authors, felt were most important as we wrote. Then read the discussion questions at the end. As you read, start with an understanding of the larger structure and bolded terms in the chapter, before you try to learn specific details.

In each area, there are areas for practical applications of culture to work and school, ways in which knowledge of culture will teach us about ourselves and give us more freedom over our choices, and aspects that will allow us to be more effective and engaged citizens in our communities.

Changes from the first edition

Much has happened since the first edition of this book, as noted in our introductory paragraph. It is simply time for a new edition. We have changed our focus from simply needing to be aware of differences to specifically seeing this awareness as crucial because of the uncertainty of our times. We keep our focus on civic engagement and activism. But this book has some changes.

Several chapters have been revised with updated examples from popular culture and the civic world around us (e.g., Chapters 1, 14). We have also restructured Chapter 6 for more clarity and a great discussion of views regarding structural inequities that impact communication. The chapters on identity (Chapter 5), media (Chapter 10), and organization (Chapter 15) are mostly totally revised, including up-to-date research on cultural differences in some of the aspects from around the world. We have removed our chapter on globalization, as globalization permeates much of the book, and replaced it with a chapter that focuses specifically on social media.

Throughout the text, we have sought to provide balance to some debates, showing strengths and limitations, though throughout, you will no doubt sense the authors' concern with social justice. We hope that you benefit from this book by reading it as much as we have by writing it.

References

COVID-19 response. (n.d.) *United Nations*. Accessed December 9, 2022, at https://www.un.org/en/coronavirus/covid-19-drives-global-surge-volunteering

Johnson, T. (2020, March 12). Recruitment for volunteers: Key trends & what to do about them. *Toby Johnson & Associates*. Accessed December 9, 2022, at https://tobijohnson.com/recruitment-for-volunteers

Parker, K., & Igielnik, R. (2020, May 14). On the cusp of adulthood and facing an uncertain future: What we know about Gen Z so far. *PewResearchCenter*. Accessed December 9, 2022, at https://www.pewresearch.org/social-trends/2020/05/14/on-the-cusp-of-adulthood-and-facing-an-uncertain-future-what-we-know-about-gen-z-so-far-2

Wu, T. (2021, November 18). 2021 volunteering trends and how to optimize the relaunch of your volunteer program. *Civic Champs*. Accessed December 9, 2021, at https://www.civicchamps.com/post/2021-volunteering-trends-and-how-to-optimize-the-relaunch-of-your-volunteer-program

Acknowledgments

Each of the co-authors thanks the other authors for their contributions and feedback on chapters. But we are especially grateful to the people we have worked with at Wiley, especially Nicole Allen and Laura Matthews, for their motivation and collaboration in bringing this second edition to fruition. Thank you also to Rosie Hayden, Radhika Raheja Sharma, and Ed Robinson (copy and cover), and especially to Sindujaabirami "Abi" Ravichandiran (who did wonders finding images and permissions), Jayavel "Jay" Radhakrishnan and Christy Michael (final page proofs). These fine people have been a constant encouragement to us in the writing of this second edition. They believed in us and checked on us, sometimes with polite reminders to "get it in gear." We also thank the anonymous reviewers who provided comments on earlier versions of this text. You have made this a better text than it would have been with only our own efforts.

As it has come to revisions, we thank those who have helped us with different concepts. We appreciate the help of our colleagues Sandra Metts, Joe Blaney, Lance Lippert, and Steve Hunt (Illinois State University) for giving us insight on different aspects of the book, from face to media to civic engagement. A special thanks to Joe Zompetti, who has given us constant insight on everything semiotic, postmodern, postcolonial, and otherwise critical. And we thank our students, from whom we always learn so much, as we ourselves continue to be "students" of culture.

Finally, we thank our families and partners for putting up with the hours of work that the task has entailed, and for their support in the process. With family and connection in mind, John dedicates this book to his wife and life-long partner, Dr. Kim Baldwin, who provides inspiration and is a sounding board for many of his ideas. Al acknowledges the assistance of Dr. Carol A. Engler. He dedicates this 2nd edition to the undergraduate and graduate interculturalists at BGSU. Nettie would like to thank her partner, Josh Carey, for putting up with her as she struggled through this process, and her parents and siblings for always supporting her through academia. And Chin-Chung (Joy) wishes to express her greatest appreciation to John's efforts and leadership on this project; without him, this book would not be possible. In addition, Chin-Chung's thanks would like to go to Ming Xie who has squeezed time out her busy schedule for co-authoring and providing helpful feedback.

About the Companion Website

This text has a comprehensive companion website which features the following resources for instructors:

→ Powerpoint slides to accompany each chapter

→ Sample syllabi for both undergraduate and graduate courses

→ Testbank, containing problems for each chapter, along with answers

→ Glossary

→ Exercises for all chapters, along with a resource list and some general assignments.

Please visit http://www.wiley.com/go/baldwin2e to access the materials.

Walk through

Part opening page The book is divided into four parts. Each part opens with a list of the chapters it contains, followed by a short introduction summarizing the purposes of each chapter.

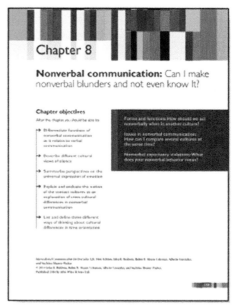

Chapter opening page Each chapter opens with a list of the main chapter objectives and the chapter table of contents.

End-of-chapter pedagogy Each chapter ends with a summary, a listing of the key terms in the chapter, discussion questions, action points, details of further resources under the heading "For More Information," and references.

Key terms and glossary Key terms are introduced in bold and clearly defined both in the text and in a complete glossary at the end of the book.

On the net This feature provides students with an activity based on visiting a website that ties into the text discussion.

Break it down These exercises encourage students to engage in civic action and apply their knowledge to the world at large.

What do you think? These boxes ask the reader to think critically on an issue or examine their own opinions on a subject.

Pop culture This feature uses examples from the media and pop culture as jumping-off points for the reader to apply their knowledge.

Foundations

f you try to build a structure of some sort, you know that you need certain materials to make it—bricks, wood, plastic, metal—and some plan for the structure—a blueprint. As you consider these things, you will need to think of how the building will be used. Will it be a restaurant? A bank? A hockey rink? But before you lay the first brick, you must make sure that your building is on firm footing: you need a good foundation.

In the same way, in the later sections of this book, we describe the things that make up intercultural communication (part two), the ways we use it (part three), and the different functions we can use it for (part four). We provided a general road map to the book at the end of the Preface. But before we do any of that, we need to lay a groundwork—a foundation—of some basic principles. That is the purpose of the first part of the book.

In Chapter 1, we provide a rationale for studying intercultural communication. Throughout the world, people are facing uncertain time. Wars, climate change, hate crimes and prejudice, and joblessness all increase our uncertainty, but these combine in complex ways with things such as our use of social media and interpersonal contact with others. Even before a recent rise in political polarization in many countries, protests for racial justice, women's rights, or the rights of other groups in many countries, or the ongoing COVID-19 pandemic, younger adults were already experiencing higher anxiety and depression than before. We need to build cross-cultural connections to address these challenges and better understand differences within our own cultures for greater inclusion and treatment of diverse groups. Beyond these vital needs, intercultural communication can also help us have better relationships and be better students or organizational members. Even though there are many benefits of studying intercultural com-

Intercultural Communication for Everyday Life, Second Edition. John R. Baldwin, Alberto González, Nettie Brock, Ming Xie, and Chin-Chung Chao.
© 2024 John Wiley & Sons Ltd. Published 2024 by John Wiley & Sons Ltd.
Companion Website: http://www.wiley.com/go/baldwin2e

munication, there are also some limitations, which we also address. Finally, we speak briefly about the history of the study of intercultural communication. We speak of it because it gives us context for what we study, and context is important to understanding what we do and why we do it. We treat it briefly, as we want to keep our focus primarily practical.

Chapter 2 introduces what we feel are the most important principles for practicing and researching intercultural communication. We could, here, discuss what it means to be a "competent" communicator across cultures, but we need to know more about sending and receiving messages first. It is important that we be aware of what it means to be ethical in our communication, so we discuss different ethical approaches in depth. It is an ethical position by the authors that leads us to feel that communication—and intercultural communication especially—should be related to civic and political action, so we introduce these terms and their relationship to intercultural communication. Finally, as much of what we understand about culture involves research of some sort, we introduce different ways of seeing the world as they relate to studying culture and communication.

Finally, in Chapter 3, we introduce a definition of culture. But defining culture is not that easy, because people from different disciplines often see culture in different and opposing ways. We discuss some of these ways and provide our own tentative definition. We describe some of the key components of culture, such as values, norms, and beliefs, and then provide a model to help explain the influences that might be present, to greater or lesser degrees, in any communication, but especially in intercultural or intergroup communication.

With these foundations—a reason to study culture and communication, an understanding of ethical communication and civic engagement, and a view of the nature of culture—we will be able to look more closely at the components that impact the creation and interpretation of messages between and within cultures. Combined, these should build a foundation for helping us understand our complex world and hopefully become better local and world citizens.

Chapter 1

Intercultural communication for uncertain times: Why should we know about other cultures?

Chapter objectives

After this chapter, you should be able to:

→ Provide several reasons, with evidence, as to why it is important to study intercultural communication

→ Describe possible limitations of studying intercultural communication

→ Summarize briefly the history of intercultural communication as a field of research

Building a rationale: Why do we need to know about intercultural communication? 5

The history and focus of intercultural communication: Where did the discipline come from? 16

Intercultural Communication for Everyday Life, Second Edition. John R. Baldwin, Alberto González, Nettie Brock, Ming Xie, and Chin-Chung Chao.
© 2024 John Wiley & Sons Ltd. Published 2024 by John Wiley & Sons Ltd.
Companion Website: http://www.wiley.com/go/baldwin2e

W̶e live in a world of uncertainty, as we travel through uncertain times. Since the writing of the first edition of this book, ten years ago, there have been astounding changes, both within single countries and across the world. Many countries have seen the rise of right-wing "populist" movements. These movements are "populist" in that they appeal to and receive support from the "common person" who feels their needs have been ignored by previous regimes or political systems. But they are right-wing in that they often oppose social change and immigration, providing a conservative call to return to some notion of a nostalgic past. Countries including the United States, Brazil, Austria, and India have elected populist leaders in the recent past. Indeed, Annalisa Merelli (2019) lists 20 nations with governments supported by "right-wing" populist parties, with such parties also making great inroads in countries such as France, Italy, Lebanon, South Korea, Belgium, and several countries in Scandinavia.

In addition, often in opposition to such movements, social advocacy groups including those surrounding cultural politics have become more prominent than before. On May 25, 2020, George Floyd, a Black man, was killed in Minneapolis, a major U.S. city, by a police officer, giving added impetus to the growing Black Lives Matter movement. But other movements have also grown over the last years, including the #Me Too movement, which began in 2006, but went viral in 2017, expanding to receive worldwide focus (Chicago Tribune, 2021). An article on NPR's website ("The 2010s," 2019) outlines protests in over 30 nations. These include Occupy Wallstreet, against economic inequality, the Arab Spring protests beginning in Tunisia and spreading to Libya and Bahrain; protests for women's rights in Argentina, with similar protests around the world (see Figure 1.1); and protests against homophobia and transphobia in Russia. In many countries, the struggle between conservatism and diversity of different sorts has led to debates, political and personal, surrounding "identity politics."

Figure 1.1 People in Iran protest for women's rights in 2022 after the death of Mahsa Amini [Or similar world protest image with caption and call out].
Source: Gregorio Borgia/AP Photo.

Addressing uncertainty: Why do we need to know about intercultural communication?

We must add to these changes the expansive cultural transition brought about by the COVID-19 epidemic in many areas of personal, social, and organizational life. At the initial drafting of this paragraph, COVID has claimed 6,320,599 deaths (WHO Coronavirus Dashboard, 2022), with nearly one out of six of those being in the United States (Ortiz, 2022), with resulting anxiety and depression linked to job or income loss, loss of loved ones, and the lifestyle restrictions necessitated by COVID precautions. In the educational setting, COVID brought about unpredictability as students first moved online for a year or more, and then face-to-face again, facing uncertainty at each stage. Researchers have explored the potential negative impact of COVID on primary and secondary students' learning of basic academic skills in the United States (Wyse et al., 2020); on loss of class time, academic performance, and loss of learning due to COVID interruption of early childhood teaching (McCoy et al., 2021) in over 60 countries; on sexual violence in Canada (van Rensburg & Smith, 2021); and on general levels of anxiety and depression in the Republic of Ireland (Hyland et al., 2020) and Japan (Ueda et al., 2020), especially for those who are economically advantaged, who face the impacts of COVID more severely.

Change is natural in all cultures, as we will note in Chapter 3, but the rapid and often unsettling changes in the last decade can lead to great uncertainty for today's college students and world citizens and a need to address that uncertainty. Uncertainty is not a new concept in the field of intercultural communication.

Building on uncertainty reduction theory (Berger & Calabrese, 1975), William Gudykunst and Young Yun Kim (2003) noted that in intercultural communication, we try to explain the behavior of the "stranger" and anticipate their future actions. Gudykunst (2005) calls this cognitive or thought-based attempt to mentally explain the other **uncertainty.** He adds to this the notion of **anxiety**, an emotional or "affective" reaction to interacting with others, in which we feel "uneasy, tense, worried, or apprehensive about what might happen" (p. 287). Walter and Cookie Stephan (1985) describe how encounters with individuals from different "groups" (we will explore "group" versus "culture" in Chapter 3) can lead to different types of anxiety, such as fearing negative evaluations by those of the other or our own groups when we interact with people from other cultures. For our discussion, we will treat uncertainty and anxiety together.

Personal uncertainty. These notions of uncertainty and anxiety are useful but need expansion in today's world of cultural change. In terms of culture and communication, we experience uncertainty and anxiety in at least three ways. First, we must deal with uncertainty at the personal level. It is not just intercultural encounters that can provoke uncertainty, but the cultural changes that societies around the world are facing. Research suggests that in the United States, college students are facing anxiety and uncertainty at a greater level than ever. Rates of anxiety, depression, self-injury, and suicidality among college students increased steadily from 2011 to 2018 (Duffy et al., 2019). This trend was only made worse by the COVID crisis, with transition difficulties to and from on-line, increased arguments, and increased loneliness (Hyland et al., 2020; Ueda et al., 2020).

Interpersonal uncertainty. We experience uncertainty, as noted above, simply when we engage in meaningful encounters with people who are culturally different. But the changes noted above also introduce into our lives uncertainty regarding interaction even with those we love—our friends and family—as we engage with each other on group- and cultural-identity topics, be that through social media or sitting around the table.

International uncertainty. At the international level, we are faced with continued crises that require the work of cross-national collaboration. This includes issues such as global conflict, global warming, population control and food shortages, and major disasters—earthquakes, tsunamis, or other disasters that require us to join hands across nations to provide aid or to seek solutions. In this chapter, we will introduce several such issues.

But before we begin, we should define some key terms briefly, though we will discuss them in more detail in Chapter 3. We define **culture** simply as the way of life of a group of people, including symbols, values, behaviors, artifacts, and other shared aspects. Culture continually evolves as people share messages, and, often, it is the result of struggle between different groups who share different perspectives, interests, and power relationships (Hecht et al., 2006). For our purposes, **communication** is the process of creating and sending symbolic behavior and the interpretation of behavior between people. And **intercultural communication** occurs when culture impacts the communication between two or more people enough to make a difference. This differs from **international communication**, which focuses on media systems. Communication between diplomats and international politicians is intercultural, but this is a special type of communication as the communicators represent not only their own interests but also those of larger organizations or nations. This last form of communication might take place for economic advancement or for the addressing of world problems. UNESCO, in its 2009 World Report executive summary, highlights the need for dialogue across many areas of social and global development. In its closing recommendations, it advocates the development of guidelines for cross-cultural dialogue, the creation and distribution of audio-visual (mediated) materials that are culturally sensitive, the promotion of (cross-cultural) media literacy, the development of minority–majority member dialogues within national cultures, and the creation of "real and virtual forums" for the development of "cultural intelligence" in the business and marketing world (UNESCO, 2009, p. 35). In fact, the name of the UNESCO report involves "cultural diversity" and "intercultural dialogue." But as we shall see, addressing global problems is only one reason to study intercultural communication—there are other motives.

The personal growth motive

The first motive to address has to do with the benefit to you, as a person, of learning about other cultures. While there are many personal benefits to learning about other cultures, we will focus on three: worldmindedness, self-awareness, and personal empowerment.

First, learning about cultures and intercultural communication helps us better understand others in the world. Bradford "J." Hall (2003) lists "freedom from ignorance" as one of the benefits of studying intercultural communication (p. 22). Knowing about other cultures helps us to be more responsible employees, travelers, consumers and producers of media, and world citizens, bringing to each interaction an increased awareness of others and competence. Hall states, "As we are freed from ignorance and negative attributions, we are able to build better relationships… with a wide variety of people" (p. 22). Communication and contact over time can bring us, in both our face-to-face and socially mediated interactions, from a state of ethnocentrism, where we feel that our way is best, to a state where we see the value in the perspectives and ways of living of others. The greatest benefit will come from both education and contact, as these can help us to appreciate cultural differences within our own nation and across borders (see Chapter 5), making us better world citizens.

As we learn more about other cultures, we also learn more about our own cultures and about ourselves. The more people study other languages, the more they learn about their own language; much the same is true when studying cultures. If you grow up in a culture that makes arguments through deductive, linear logic ("If A is true, and B is true, then C must be true"), you may never be aware of that approach to argumentation until you study or live in a culture in which one makes an argument through an extended, even circular story.

Finally, knowledge of and extended experience with other cultures make us more flexible as individuals. Young Yun Kim and Brent Ruben (1988) suggest that learning new cultures gives us new ways to think, feel, and act. We might, over time, become "intercultural persons," able to move freely between cultures, or at least to understand different cultural perspectives more easily. This knowledge shows us that the things that we often assume are "natural," are, in fact, cultural. The ways we think about friendship, success, beauty, family, or democracy are in fact something that our culture has defined for us. Often such concepts are not evolving naturally within a culture, but are manipulated by corporations, advertisers, politicians, and citizens who benefit from particular views of the world. Knowledge of cultures gives us increased agency to choose between different ways of being a friend or being successful. It "gives us a broader view of our own lives and the problems we face" (Hall, 2003, p. 22), even if our choices are constrained by social, political, and economic circumstances.

The social responsibility motive

We are not simply isolated individuals—we live in contact with others, and we have responsibility to live together peaceably and ethically (see Chapter 2). Marshall McLuhan (1962) suggested that the world is a Global Village, in that our communities become more interconnected because of increased technology, media, and ease of travel. In addition, more and more people share this planet with its limited space and resources. As well, a complex web of changing labor relations, social policies, tribal and international conflicts, religious fervor, and other things lead to an increase in social problems. Some of these come from the growing stress on the environment brought about by an increase in both people and industry. As we face global environmental change (and debate the causes of that change), there is an increased need for global discussion among leaders for policies that are equitable to nations and that can seek to preserve and improve the environment. One such effort was the Kyoto Protocol (2012), an initiative by the United Nations Framework Convention on Climate Change, aimed at encouraging 37 industrialized nations to work more actively to reduce greenhouse gasses.

What do you think? The UN Framework Convention on Climate Change lists 191 nations that have ratified the Kyoto Protocol, established over twenty years ago, in 1997, to reduce greenhouse emissions: https://treaties.un.org/Pages/ViewDetails.aspx?src=TREATY&mtdsg_no=XXVII-7-a&chapter=27&clang=_en. Is your nation among those that have ratified it? Go onto websites such as https://worldpopulationreview.com/country-rankings/co2-emissions-by-country to see where your country ranks in total and per capita emissions. What are some of the reasons that some of the countries with the highest production of greenhouse gasses might not ratify an agreement such as the Kyoto Protocol? What are the implications for such choices for citizens of the countries involved?

Of course, the environment is only one of the issues that demand global cooperation. A global population clock (Current world population, n.d.) gives the population of the world, at the writing of this paragraph, as 7,995,919,828. According to the World Bank (2022), the number of those living in poverty (defined here as less than $U.S.1.90 income per person per day) had been steadily declining for the last few years, reaching 8.6% in 2018, with great varieties based on region of the world (Castaneda Aguilar et al., 2022). However, COVID-19 interrupted this decrease, with greater impact on women, children, and low-wage, urban workers. Continued impacts of COVID, the 2022 war in Ukraine, and inflation may work against efforts to decrease poverty. The World Bank (2022) notes that in low-income countries, people spend about two thirds of their income on food, whereas in higher-income countries, the cost is only one fourth of their income. But how we address poverty requires a "dialogic" approach (Martin et al., 2002), in which we talk with people within the situation to understand their own view of poverty and how to address it (see Chapter 2). Developmental approaches must take into account local cultural perspectives to be successful. This holds true for issues such as human trafficking, drug trafficking, child soldiers, violence against women, and the search for cures for illnesses such as HIV/AIDS, cancer, or heart disease.

Some might include within this discussion social class inequalities. For example, the World Population Review (World Ineqality by Country 2022) ranks countries based on how great the difference is between poorest and richest families, based on what is called the Gini Index, with Southern African nations, Suriname, and Brazil, being at the unequal end of the spectrum, and Iceland, Azerbaijan, Ukraine, and Belgium having the most equality in incomes. Based on this report, the more "equal" nations, mostly in Europe, differ, for example, from the United States. The latter is a "market economy," where "market forces control other areas of society such as education, health, and wages," leading to greater health inequality. Ventura noted that, as COVID was contributing to the deaths of 21,000 people daily around the world, the world's 10 richest billionaires "more than doubled their wealth to an astounding $1.5 trillion." Such discrepancies led to the 2011 Occupy Wall Street movement and the protest for economic justice for the "99%." U.S. CEOs don't consider the contrast to worker pay or even to their cross-national peers, to be important. Rather, they consider their pay comparable to peers in other high-producing industries.

In addition to social issues, wars and armed conflicts are occurring throughout the world. The International Crisis Group, in 2022, is tracking 70 "conflicts and crises" around the world, including the Koreas, Ukraine, Colombia, Burkina Faso, Eritrea and Ethiopia, the Democratic Republic of the Congo, Tajikistan, and Egypt (for a fuller list, see Wars in the World, 2022). Websites such as Wars in the World (2022) and the Council on Foreign Relation's Global Conflict Tracker (n.d.) identify wars and conflicts around the world. In many cases, struggles are not armed, but are battled over prestige, social status, and social capital within nations, as groups strive to gain recognition and equal opportunity within their own countries, from the Roma in Hungary and other European nations to the Ainu of Japan. This includes struggles for equality for groups of different races, sexes, sexual orientations, and religious affiliations.

What do you think? Do your own Internet research on your own country and region. What is the average discrepancy between CEOs of organizations and the average employee? How does this compare to discrepancies in other countries or regions? What are arguments for or against the existence of such discrepancies?

The economic motive

Even though movements like Occupy Wall Street claim economic injustice, in part, at the hands of big business, we could not exist without corporations, and they have made contributions to societies worldwide. Most students work for some organization at some point in their lives, and it is the business context that provides our next motive for the study of intercultural communication. It is now commonplace for major companies to cross cultural borders that such figures are hard to determine. Aside from potential between international teachers or supervisors and their students or subordinates, even major companies can make cultural errors at the grand level. While Walmart's now well-known pull-out of Germany happened in 2006, it illustrates well how cultural failures go beyond the many online examples of marketing and product-naming blunders. Analysts suggest Walmart culture failed in Germany for (at least) three reasons—asking employees to smile at strangers, having employees do sports-like (and thus out-of-place) cheers at the beginning of each workday, and asking employees to report on each other for engaging in inappropriate employee behavior (McDonald, 2017). The company eventually sold off its 85 German outlets at a loss of nearly $U.S. 1 billion.

It should come as no surprise to us that such difficulties occur, with an ever-expanding and ever-more-interconnected international economy. Multinational corporations continue to grow, constituting an increasing piece of the world economy. A comparison of the earnings shows that the world's most profitable companies (Saudi Aramco, Apple, Berkshire Hathaway, Microsoft, Samsung, etc.) make more than the 100 countries listed lower than the Democratic Republic of the Congo in annual GDP (Companies Ranked by Earnings, 2022; GDP Ranked by Country, 2022). Such statistics evidence the role of global business. Statistics suggest that currently (as of 2020) over 50% of the total GDP in the world is related to foreign trade (Trade (% of GDP), n.d.).

Both the OECD and current CEOs (in an interview study of 1500 CEOs worldwide by an IBM "CEO Study") see a coming shift in global economic power from developed nations to developing nations (Radjou & Kalpa, August 6, 2010). Such a shift in world economics drives a need for what Navi Radjou and Prassad Kalpa (August 6, 2010) call "polycentric" organizations—those that leverage potential of new employees both from the Millennial generation and from around the world. Still, only 23% of the CEOs interviewed felt that globalization would have a major impact on their organization in the next five years. And, while Western CEOs see more than 50% of their future growth as coming from world markets like India and China, only 2% have senior leadership from those areas. Statistics such as these, as well as the growing involvement with major corporations in world politics, has led Thomas McPhail (2019) to suggest that large and powerful nations have ceded their leadership of the world to the new giants—multinational corporations.

Although we see the benefit in local jobs and economies of world trade and globalization, we realize that these are not neutral forces. One such example is the tension between two world forums: the World Economic Forum and the World Social Forum. The World Economic Forum is an international organization that "engages the foremost political, business, cultural, and other leaders to shape global, regional, and industry agendas" (World Economic Forum, n.d.). The forum, held each year in Davos, Switzerland, is composed of leaders from over 390 firms from over 60 nations who represent many sectors—such as construction, engineering, food and beverage, financial services. One stipulation for membership is that the corporation members must be leaders in their sectors, often with at least $U.S. 5 billion in turnover. Forbes rated Klaus Schwab, the leader of the forum, as number 66 among the world's most powerful people (Forbes.com, 2009).

Over 20 years ago, in open opposition to the World Economic Forum, a group of people began the World Social Forum in Porto Alegre, Brazil. According to a website comparing the two forums:

> The first World Social Forum was held in Porto Alegre, Brazil in January 2001, and was conceived of by the Worker's Party of Brazil and other Brazilian civil society organizations as a counter gathering to the World Economic Forum held for decades in Davos, Switzerland. The Social Forum stands for the ideals of people-centered globalization, with "Another World is Possible!" as its battle cry. (Washington Peace Center, 2013)

The initial forum had 20,000 participants, with delegates from 117 nations. It has fought to develop local policies to resist both the cultural and economic influences of globalization, especially as such forces, according to the forum, tend to benefit the interests of more powerful economic nations and, particularly, big business. While the themes of the WSF change from year to year, common themes are democratic development, human rights, equality and non-discrimination (e.g., sexism, racism, religious sectarianism), the fight against militarization, the environment, and imperialist globalization. Members of the 2022 conference in Mexico included focus on "art and culture for life," "migration and strategies against wars," and "struggles of indigenous, Black, diasporic, and other peoples against racism and for self-determination" (World Social Forum Mexico 2022, n.d.).

Before we assume that the battle between the forums is cut and dried and without debate, we should note that the stated purpose of the World Economic Forum is "improving the state of the world" (Forbes.com, 2009). To that end, leaders are concerned with world crises and situations, but see the response as being in global economic development. So, for example, one frequent participant, Bill Gates, founder of Microsoft, and Melissa French Gates donated $15 U.S. billion in 2021 to their charitable foundation to fight poverty, increase global health development, and "advance equality for women and girls and other marginalized groups" (di Mento, 2022)

The cross-cultural travel motive

In addition to the number of workers traveling abroad and the economic motive, we see, with modern technology, an increased number of international travelers for different reasons. We have noted above the high rates of international workers. However, we also see high numbers of cross-cultural travelers in three other groups—tourists, students, and refugees.

Regarding tourism, the International Monetary Fund (Behsudi, 2020) noted that before the COVID-19 Pandemic, tourism was one of the most vital economic sectors in the world, "accounting for 10 percent of global GDP [Gross Domestic Product] and more than 320 million jobs worldwide." The total amount of GDP spent on tourism worldwide continued to grow up to 2019, when nearly $10 U.S. trillion was spent on tourism (Statista Research Department, 2022). The United Nations World Tourism Organization (UNWTO, 2022) reported $1 U.S. trillion lost in tourism each year of the pandemic (so far), and, although post 2021, tourism is slowly increasing, it is still well below pre-COVID levels. The renewed growth varies by region, for example, with more growth in Europe and the Americas, and in those locations, especially the Southern Mediterranean and Caribbean regions.

These figures speak to the importance of tourism in the world economy, even with the potential for it to lead to the creation of jobs and to sustainable world development in an environmentally conscious manner (World Tourism Organization, 2012). This makes intercultural communication

Break it down

What are the positive and negative aspects of a high degree of tourism on a local culture? What are some of the ways that people within a culture might receive the benefits of cross-cultural tourism while minimizing the negative impacts?

important for those in the tourist industry. But it is also important to consider "cultural" communication—to see the impacts of tourism—both positive and negative—on local cultures. To consider the impact of tourism on culture, we should consider both the number of tourists per size of population, but also the economic impact on the country (Tourism Intelligence Network, n.d.).

Another major source of international travel is international education. Very likely, many readers of this book are reading it in a country outside of their own, or you have had international students in your classes or teachers from other countries than your own. According to the Migration Data Portal, the number of international students worldwide was growing rapidly to 5 million worldwide (International students, 2020, see Figure 1.2), with over half of these being enrolled in the United States, the United Kingdom, Australia, France, Germany, and the Russian Federation. But trends are changing. In the United States, even before the Pandemic, international student numbers began to drop, due in part, according to Elizabeth Redden (2021), to a political environment increasingly hostile to immigrants. Yet, a drop of only 4.4% between 2019

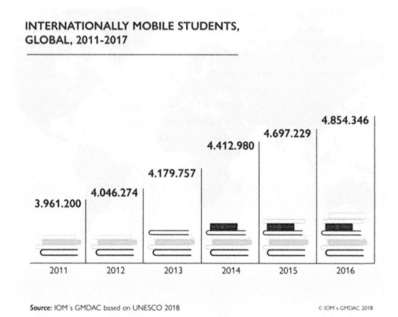

INTERNATIONALLY MOBILE STUDENTS, GLOBAL, 2011-2017

Year	Students
2011	3.961.200
2012	4.046.274
2013	4.179.757
2014	4.412.980
2015	4.697.229
2016	4.854.346

Source: IOM's GMDAC based on UNESCO 2018

© IOM's GMDAC 2018

Figure 1.2 The number of students traveling internationally across the world grew steadily up to the time of the COVID Pandemic. What do you think are the reasons that drive this increase? What are the strengths and challenges of having international students in your classrooms?
Source: International students (June 9, 2020). Migration Data Portal. Retrieved from: https://www.migrationdataportal.org/themes/international-students (accessed 28 June 2022).

and 2020 in the United States led to a loss of \$1.8 U.S. billion and 42,000 U.S. jobs ("The US loses more than 42000 jobs," 2020). Redden (2021) notes that the year following the Pandemic saw a 46% drop in new international students and a 15% drop in total international students in the United States. At the same time, China, a country that long has been one the greatest "exporters" of international students around the world, is now seeking to attract international students from other countries to study in China, with students giving a variety of reasons for choosing China as a study-abroad location (Jiani, 2016). However, as we will not be defining culture as *nation*, but as any group of people with a different set of values, beliefs, norms, and so on, it may be that you have changed "cultures" between regions, or from rural to urban setting (or vice versa), being an "intercultural" student, even if you did not travel abroad!

What do you think? How many study-abroad students are there at your college or university? Which countries do the greatest number come from? Look online to see if you can locate some concrete advantages to studying abroad. What are some challenges to increasing study abroad programs among students at your college?

One group of people travels not by choice but to escape hostile situations. This group consists of refugees and asylum seekers. The United Nations Refugee Agency defines a **refugee** as someone who has traveled outside of her or his country because of a fear of threat to freedom or life based on reasons of group belonging (e.g., race, sex, ethnicity, political affiliation, tribal group), as opposed to the more general **migrant**, who has moved either voluntarily or involuntarily for short or long terms (e.g., agricultural workers). The **asylum seeker** differs slightly in that they are seeking legal protection from the new state, rather than simply moving there because of conditions of strife. Some flee not from threat of a government or ruling party, but from threat of famine (Refugee Facts, 2023).

The United Nations High Commissioner for Refugees (Refugee Facts, 2023) reports that 100 million people forcibly displaced worldwide as of May, 2022, over twice the number in 2011. Of these, 27.1 million are refugees, around half of whom are under the age of 18. Like the groups above, these travelers do not always cross national borders. The Internal Displacement Monitoring Center (Global Report, 2021) reports 40.5 million new internally displaced people in 2020, across 149 countries (see Figure 1.3). Some of these are displaced due to conflict or violence, but others are displaced due to natural disasters and weather changes (see Figure 1.4). A report by the Institute for Economics and Peace (Over One Billion People, 2020) suggests that ecological and climate threat, especially in countries with less resilience to deal with such threats as food insecurity, water stress, and natural disasters, may lead to conflict in many nations. The World Bank (Millions on the Move, 2021) predicts that 216 million people in six regions of the world may be displaced within their own countries due to environmental change by 2050.

The media motive

Another reason to know more about culture in general and intercultural communication specifically is that we are consumers and producers of mediated messages that travel across cultural borders. As in our discussion of cross-cultural travelers above, we should think of such cross-cultural media usage both in terms of national cultures and cultures within national boundaries. First, in

Figure 1.3 Are there refugees or displaced persons in your country? What are the reasons for displacement? What sort of help or support do they need? What policies and conditions lead to refugees in your nation or those that your nation is involved with? Is there anything you can do to aid refugees in your area? https://www.internal-displacement.org/global-report/grid2021/ ©2021, Internal Displacement Monitoring Centre, reproduced with permission.

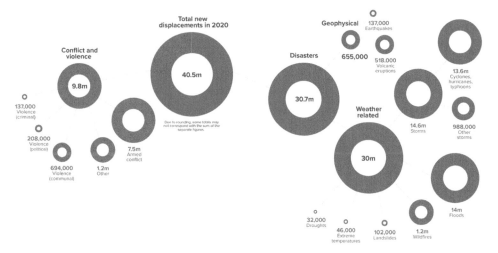

Figure 1.4 Vodafone's "Raising Voices." Source: IMDb.com, Inc./https://www.imdb.com/ / last accessed January 10, 2023.

terms of national cultures, new technology has drastically changed the ways in which we see the world. McPhail (2019) notes how Turner Broadcasting Company's Cable News Network (CNN) changed the way we produce and consume news, with coverage of international events in the 1980s and early 1990s, such as Tiananmen Square and the Gulf War. Like other major networks, such as the British Broadcasting Company (BBC) or Al Jazeera, CNN had international partners all over the world, in places such as Angola, Belize, Greece, and Venezuela. This made news coverage both more immediate—often with live coverage of events—and more internationally focused, something more relevant in the United States perhaps than other countries, as national network news tended to give only brief coverage of international events. In addition, the Turner Network began the rise of global media conglomerates, as Turner sought to increase cable sales with the creation of Nickelodeon, Arts & Entertainment (A&E), USA, Disney, Showtime, HBO, ESPN, and C-Span. McPhail covers giants in several industries—advertising, news services, and the international music industry. International news giants include Deutsche Welle (Germany), Channel News Asia, and Euronews. Music industry giants include Vivendi-Universal (France), Sony (Japan), EMI Group (United Kingdom), Warner (United States), and BMG (Germany).

At any one moment, depending on where we live, we see products advertised by companies in other countries, listen to music made in other countries, see adverts for products made in other countries, or watch news about what has happened in other countries. Especially in the last instance, it is helpful for us to understand the cultures involved to be able to understand what is happening in a particular location. For example, in 2011 National Geographic filmed a special on the troubling conflict between Turkish- and Greek-descended inhabitants of Cyprus, noting the division that resulted from a 1974 conflict. However, Benjamin Broome (2002) notes that Turkish and Greek Cypriots see different major turning points for the centuries-old tensions in Cyprus. The latter date, 1974, is the date of a Greek coup and, more importantly, of the arrival of Turkish troops that led to the current division of the island. This is the date the Greek Cypriots tend to label as the start of the current conflict. Turkish Cypriots, however, trace the conflicts back to the 1960s and Greek Cypriot efforts to join the island (which is off the coast of Türkiye) to Greece. In this case, there are two totally opposing perspectives of the history, and, while the National Geographic program seeks to be balanced, it takes one of the perspectives more prominently. With this in mind, we must realize that any news or information source we read, such as Wikipedia.com, is written from a cultural perspective.

What do you think? Several recent ad campaigns and agencies have fought for women's equality in different spheres, for example, Vodafone's (2018) "Raising Voices"—a video set in London of girls asking tough questions, (see Figure 1.4), or the Malala Fund (n.d.), begun by Malala Yousafzai, a Pakistani activist, and Ziauddin Yousafzai, a Pakistani educator, to promote women's reading and education around the world. Look up one of these or provide your own examples of women's rights movements from different cultures. What specific issues are they addressing within their contexts? What ideas or strategies might transfer to your culture?

The very presence of sources like Wikipedia and YouTube alerts us to another key aspect of media, and that is the rise of computer-mediated communication and social media. The Internet has changed our lives and connected us to the world. In 1995. By 2022, 5.25 billion (66.2% of the world) are on the Internet, an increase of 1,355% over 2000. In 2021, 306 billion emails were sent. The most frequently visited sites are Google, YouTube, Facebook, Twitter, Instagram, Baidu, Wikipedia, Yandex, Yahoo, and Xvideos, and 45% of the people in the world stream an hour or more of video content per day. In China, 1.03 billion people shop online (compared to the second top country—the United States, with 259 million people) (Key Internet Statistics, n.d.). The amount of information available on the Internet continues to grow exponentially.

Two things are apparent with this explosion of new information. First, if we are on the Internet, we will have contact with people from other cultures. We might play *Fortnite* to battle off opponents to be the last person standing, meeting players from other cultures, then browse online news from Xinhua News or the BBC (the biggest news network in the world), then video-chat with or email

---

Break it down

Go to a chat site with positive reputation that has international chat partners available (e.g., Moco Chat, Omegle, or MeetMe) or through a language-practicing app (e.g., HelloTalk, Tandem, or Bilingual). Practice safe chat rules, such as not giving out any personal information! Find out about another person's cultural values or current issues within that culture from the other person's perspective. Don't expect any individual to speak on behalf of their whole culture! What are some strengths and limitations of this exercise?

---

friends or family in another part of the world. Social networking gives us Facebook, VK, WhatsApp, Instagram, WeChat (China), TikTok, or Sina Weibo. Many of us use Twitter, possibly with worldwide feeds. Or we might engage in friendship networks or online random chats like Omegle or MeetMe.

The Internet, and social media specifically, might impact culture, including potentially negative impacts on self-esteem as people across countries adopt the social, sexual, and other ideals they see on Instagram and Twitter (de Lenne et al., 2020). Another impact of the Internet could be the homogenization of cultures, especially among youth. Usman Jimada (2020), for example, borrowing from electronic colonialism theory, suggests that global internet use is homogenizing cultures in Africa. But other research supports the concept of **glocalization**, that despite media's universal spread, cultures use it in distinct ways. One study finds that media content on MSN and Yahoo! Websites is more complicated, with social media often leading to increased cultural diversity (Segev et al., 2007). Other studies find differences in how Chinese and American students present themselves differently on social media (Chu & Choi, 2010) and how people from different ethnic groups within the United States use Facebook differently (deAndrea et al., 2010). We discuss this more in Chapter 11.

The potential impact of social media on culture is supported by the fact that the average user spends 2.5 hours daily on social media but most world social media companies are owned by two major conglomerates—Meta (WhatsApp, Facebook, Instagram, Alphabet, Reddit, Pinterest, Twitter, etc.) and Tencent (QQ, TikTok, WeChat, Baidu, etc., Ang, 2021). The *form* of social media (e.g., focus on self-presentation) might impact other cultures (McPhail, 2019). At the same time cell phones and Twitter are credited with having a major role in Middle Eastern struggles for democracy in the late 2000s.

What do you think? Having considered some of the reasons for studying culture and communication, which do you feel are the most important reasons, and why? How might some of the purposes that people study intercultural communication compete against each other? For example, could studying intercultural communication to promote national and business interests indirectly contribute to situations where one needs to study intercultural communication to help refugees or address the needs of the poor? Is there a way to reconcile such difficulties?

Challenges of studying intercultural communication

Even though there are many benefits of studying intercultural communication, Bradford "J" Hall (2003) summarizes some things to watch out for. One of these is the danger of oversimplifying our understanding of cultures. The UNESCO World Report (2009) advises, for example, against reducing our understanding of culture to national identities and to resist the danger of seeing cultures as stagnant and unchanging. Many cultural identities exist within national cultures, and many cross national boundaries, such as the Ewe tribe in Africa, which can be found in Ghana, Togo, and Benin, or the Basque people, who are found in Spain and France. Some cultures, such as Celtic culture, have left a cultural imprint in many nations, and other groups, such as the Roma in Europe, continue to exist in many places, with similarities among all Roma, yet many differences even within the group. We must recognize that cultures are fluid and constantly changing. Hall warns us against overgeneralizing: While individuals are influenced by their cultures, they are not their cultures and have unique aspects and experiences that distinguish them in some ways from all other members of their culture. Finally, Hall notes, there is a tendency to exaggerate differences. This happens because difference draws our attention more than similarity. It is more interesting to think of how Swiss and Germans may be different than how they are alike (Kopper, 1993). But the film industry and television often magnify the differences in movies such as *Gung Ho, Lost in Translation*, or *Borat*. Finally, even research supports differences: it is much harder to publish research that highlights similarities than research that finds differences.

The history and focus of intercultural communication: Where did we come from?

With an increase in intercultural interaction and recognition of cultural groups within national boundaries, it is no surprise that scholars from the late 20th century onward have dedicated increasing time and effort to the understanding of intercultural communication. But as a field of study, intercultural communication is relatively new. Some writers look to the roots of this field of study in writers such as Charles Darwin and Sigmund Freud (Rogers & Hart, 2002). However, many see the beginning of the modern study of intercultural communication in the works of Edward T. Hall (Figure 1.5) and his colleagues at the Foreign Service Institute in the 1940s and 1950s. Wendy Leeds-Hurwitz (1990) outlines how the focus of the early anthropologists and linguists set the stage for how our discipline first conceived of culture and how it would do research (See Chapter 2). Hall and his colleagues saw culture as patterned and predictable. Beginning with his book *The Silent Language* (1959), Hall provided a great contribution to the study of intercultural communication. He shifted research focus from specific cultures to an examination of interaction between people from different cultures. He developed many frameworks, for space usage (**proxemics**), for time (**chronemics**), and so on, giving us many terms that we still use in the discipline of intercultural communication today.

We see two important aspects for our beginnings in terms of focus and rationale for the study of intercultural communication. First, the disciplinary study of intercultural communication began with the Foreign Service Institute, a branch of the United States government, to help its diplomats be more effective in meeting state goals (Leeds-Hurwitz, 1990). We see an applied, organizational focus that continues in the field today, which relates to the second aspect: Hall's pragmatic focus. Much of the previous sociological and anthropological study of culture had been broad, looking at religion, leisure, family, education, labor, and other systems. But Hall found that his trainees most

Figure 1.5 Edward T. Hall, who wrote a number of books between the 1950s and the 1970s, including *The Silent Language*, *The Hidden Dimension*, and *Beyond Culture*, that form a foundation for the modern study of intercultural communication.
Source: Photo Courtesy of Kathryn Sorrells, 1998.

needed to know how to communicate effectively, so he and his colleagues focused on practical aspects like how close to stand, how much to touch, and how to think of time. Hall produced training methods and extended the study of intercultural communication to business workers, missionaries, and students. Some researchers today might argue that the very discipline was born in relations of power, in terms of advancing U.S. government and organizational interests.

Leeds-Hurwitz (1990) notes that the field of anthropology was not interested in this narrow focus on communication, so the new field of study found itself "homeless." Guo-Ming Chen and William Starosta (1998), provide an excellent, concise summary of what happened over the next few years (see also Baldwin, 2018). There was little academic writing on culture and communication in the 1960s, but the 1970s saw a great growth in the field. Researchers published the first college textbooks on intercultural communication (as well as interracial communication, though that was not considered clearly part of the field at that time). National academic association divisions began in that decade, as well as journals on intercultural communication, including *The International Journal of Intercultural Relations* (a cross-disciplinary, international journal put out by SIETAR), *The Handbook of Intercultural Communication*, and the first issue of *The International and Intercultural Communication Annual*.

We call the 1970s the decade of research, as many scholars were researching a variety of topics. Young Yun Kim (1984) summarizes much research of that time, noting there was a lot of research in the fields of cross-cultural transitions (e.g., culture shock), international business, cross-cultural counseling, and technology transfer.

The 1980s were the decade of theory-building. Scholars had looked at the connection between many variables in the 1970s, but in 1983, the first major theory book came out (Gudykunst, 1983), *Intercultural Communication Theory: Current Perspectives*, an issue of *The International and Intercultural Communication Annual* edited by William Gudykunst. In 1988, Young Yun Kim and Gudykunst published a second volume of the annual on current theories, *Theories in Intercultural Communication* (Kim & Gudykunst, 1988). Richard Wiseman (1995), a colleague of Gudykunst's, published a third issue of the annual, *Intercultural Communication Theory*, in 1995. Many, but not all, of the theories in these books sought to find the variables that predicted certain aspects of intercultural communication, such as conflict outcomes, adjustment, cross-cultural relational development, or effectiveness. Many theories are from a similar perspective, treating communication research as social science and seeking relationships between variables—the causes and effects of culture and communication—or trying to predict differences between cultures on different communication variables.

As early as 1987, scholars were beginning to attempt to "de-Westernize" communication theory. Daniel Kincaid (1987) edited a book compiling writings of different authors from different nations on things such as Chinese rhetoric. New currents were swirling in the discipline. Ethnography of communication—a study of specific cultures largely using observation—had been growing out of sociology into communication during the 1980s, and scholars were clearly seeing the relevance to culture studies; however, this approach treated culture differently (see Chapter 3)—as more fluid and local, for example, the culture of Grateful Dead fans or of a specific Chicago motorcycle gang.

At the same time, informed by Marxist studies, a new approach looked specifically at power relations in society, such as **patriarchy** and **racism**, or the way some definitions (such as success, democracy, freedom, or family) gain power over other ideas. This approach questioned the very content of the intercultural communication field. Theory books and journals, some claimed, kept a particular academic view of what "theory" and "culture" were, excluding other views.

Other writers have also challenged Western ideas of theory. Molefi Kete Asante (1980) promotes an Afrocentric perspective, challenging the ability of Western theory to describe the realities of African and African-descended peoples. More recently, Yoshitaka Miike (2007, 2010) argues that Western theories tend to speak in "totalizing" terms, as if European reality reflects that of all cultures. Western theory "disregards, downplays, or overshadows certain values and elements that have been historically embraced in non-Western cultures" (2010, p. 3). Miike (2007) feels that Western theories often ignore cultural contexts and tend to privilege notions such as individuality and independence, self-enhancement, reason, rights and freedom, and pragmatism and materialism.

The 1990s became a decade of controversy. For example, previous handbooks on intercultural communication (e.g., Asante & Gudykunst, 1989; Gudykunst & Mody, 2002) contained some, but little ethnographic work and almost no critical approaches. But Thomas Nakayama and Rona Halualani (2010) edited an entire handbookfocusing exclusively on critical approaches to culture and intercultural communication that frequently deal with dominant and subordinate cultures, mistreating or misrepresenting people from other cultures, and social inequality. These approaches include feminist theories, Queer theory, anti-racist approaches (including but not limited to critical race theory), and other theories that critique power imbalances in intercultural education, travel, business, and politics. If your library has access to *The International and Intercultural Communication Annual*, you will see that it is always rich, each issue focusing on a specific topic (organizations, identity, relationships, etc.), but with a clear shift in the 1990s to also include issues of empowerment and resistance. However, the older emphases will also be present.

With these changes came a disdain for external frameworks or terms like individualism and collectivism (see Chapter 4) to "categorize" national cultures. In fact, the scholars have challenged the very notion of "national" culture, seeing generalizations of natural culture as **essentialism** (assuming that such-and-such is the "essence" of what it means to be a member of a particular culture)—that is, they tend to treat cultures as "monolithic," as if everyone, or even most people, in a nation are the same, and as "static"—unchanging. The authors critique a "suit-case" model of culture as something simply handed down from parents to children, as this view ignores political and economic forces that seek to change culture. And, with the abandonment of nation as culture, they bring under the "intercultural" umbrella the study of other types of difference—racial, sex or gender, gender orientation, or of "micro-cultures" within larger cultures (Baldwin, 2018). (We will say more about this in Chapter 3.)

Parallel to the changes in content in the field, there has been an increasing growth in the internationalization of researchers. We see three major changes in the last 25 years: a tremendous increase in qualitative and critical research; a great influx of mediated and social media communication; and a rise of international scholars. In fact, authors currently publishing in journals that are focused on intercultural communication come from all over the world. And their focus is on much more than business and foreign travel and culture shock. It includes issues of rhetoric (e.g., public speech), advertising, and small group communication, but also protest and the ways dominant, powerful nations negatively impact nations with growing media economies in terms of cultural flow. The growth of diversity in researchers has also led to new theoretical directions. If anything, the 2000s to the present have become an era of collaboration and division. If you went to a communication conference today, you would find a wide variety of research with many different methods and cultures represented.

Summary

Most people in organizations, at universities, and even in our everyday lives, probably see an awareness of how to communicate with others who are different from us as a central skill. We have seen in this chapter that, although studying culture poses certain risks of overgeneralization, oversimplification, and exaggeration of cultures, it also has many benefits. Some of these benefits are practical: studying culture will help us understand the multicultural workplace. It will aid us as we travel abroad or work with others who travel voluntarily or by force. It will help us to understand the media we see that cover stories from around the world or come from different countries or different cultural groups within our own country.

Each motive has a practical side. How will knowledge of culture help me to have better outcomes? But a newer generation is seeking more than simply knowing how to make more money by knowledge of culture, turning such knowledge into yet another commodity in a capitalist system. It is important and practical, for many reasons, to have good intercultural communication skills; however, there is an increasing need in our world of uncertainty to simply be better relational partners, better citizens, better human beings. Studying intercultural communication gives us more freedom to make informed choices about how we will or will not follow our culture's expectations, but it also helps us to interact in a more respectful way with the person around the world or the person next door.

KEY TERMS

uncertainty, 5
anxiety, 5
culture, 6
communication, 6
intercultural communication, 6
international communication, 6
refugee, 12
migrant, 12

asylum seeker, 12
glocalization, 15
proxemics, 16
chronemics, 16
patriarchy, 18
racism, 18
essentialism, 19
sweatshops, 20

Discussion questions

1   Think about the people around you at your school, in your workplace, or in your neighborhood. How would you describe their level of awareness of domestic and international cultures and identities? How about your own? What are some specific areas in which you would like to develop in terms of your cultural knowledge and skills during this course?

2   In what ways do you feel that the Internet in general, and social media specifically, have changed your culture? What aspects of these changes are useful? Which could be problematic? What strategies does this discussion suggest for your own social media use?

3   There are many possible issues in the world to be concerned about. Alone or in groups, come up with a list of what you think are the top five issues that demand global cooperation. What are the top five issues in your own community?

4   The use of international "**sweatshops**"—factories in developing nations with an inexpensive labor force, or using child labor, is controversial. Some feel that it is abusing people, especially children, in those cultures. Others feel it provides wages that the people might not have otherwise. What do you think are the benefits and disadvantages of sweatshops? Why do they exist? Should we fight to stop them, and if so, what steps would we take?

5   The sweatshop issue (question 4) and others presented in this chapter raise a difficult question. Each issue seems to have two—or several—sides. How can we maintain hope to seek solutions without falling into a despair of not knowing what the action is?

Action points

1   Perform an Internet or library search to understand diversity in your area. What kinds of diversity are there? What are some things that the different groups hold in common? What are some points of difference? Are there particular issues that require dialogue? Brainstorm ways with your friends to start such a dialogue or to join one, if it is already in progress.

2   The Internet joins us in many ways to people from different cultures. Find and join a group specifically related to a specific culture or global issue or visit a SubReddit for the country or issue. See what you can learn about the culture or issue, especially from people within the culture or who have experience with the issue. Share what you find with your classmates or friends.

3 Join a group at your school or in your community that is dedicated toward alleviating some sort of social distress. This might be a known group, like Amnesty International, or it might be a group in your community, for example, to help repair cars for people who do not have money.

For more information

Hofstede, G. J., Pedersen, P.B., & Hofstede, G. (2002). *Exploring culture: Exercises, stories, and synthetic cultures.* Intercultural Press.

Kulich, S. J. (2012). Reconstructing the histories and influences of 1970s intercultural leaders: Prelude to biographies. *International Journal of Intercultural Relations, 36* (6), 744–759. Entire issue provides profiles of early writers in the field of intercultural communication.

Malewski, M. (2011). *GenXPat: The young professional's guide to making a successful life abroad.* Intercultural Press. (e-book).

OECD. (2012). *OECD Factbook 2011–2012: Economic, environmental, and social statistics.* OECD Publishing.

Storti, C. (1994). *Cross-cultural dialogues: 74 brief encounters with cultural difference.* Intercultural Press.

References

Ang, C. (2021, December 6). Ranked: The world's most popular social networks, and who owns them. *VisualCapitalist.* Accessed July 29, 2022, at https://www.visualcapitalist.com/ranked-social-networks-worldwide-by-users

Asante, M. K. (1980). *Afrocentricity: The theory of social change.* Amulefi Publishing.

Asante, M. K., & Gudykunst, W. B. (Eds.). (1989). *Handbook of international and intercultural communication.* Sage.

Baldwin, J. R. (2018). Evolving definitions of culture and intercultural communication for emerging global realities. In W. Jia (Ed.), *Intercultural communication: Adapting to emerging global realities: A reader* (2nd ed., pp. 27–43). Cognella.

Behsudi, A. (December 2020). Wish you were here. *International Monetary Fund.* Accessed February 27, 2023, at https://www.imf.org/en/Publications/fandd/issues/2020/12/impact-of-the-pandemic-on-tourism-behsudi

Berger, C., & Calabrese, R. (1975). Some explorations in initial interaction and beyond. *Human Communication Research, 1*(2), 99–112. DOI: 10.1111/j.1468-2958.1975.tb00258.x

Broome, B. (2002). Views from the other side: Perspectives on the Cyprus conflict. In J. N. Martin, T. K. Nakayama, & L. A. Flores (Eds.), *Readings in intercultural communication* (2nd ed., pp. 101–112). McGraw-Hill.

Castaneda Aguilar, R. A., Eilertsen, A., Fujs, T., Lakner, C., Mahler, D. G., Nguyen, M. C., Schoch, M., Baah, S. K. T., Viveros, M., & Wu, H. (2022, April 08). April 2022 global poverty update from the World Bank. *World Bank.* Accessed July 29, 2022, at https://blogs.worldbank.org/opendata/april-2022-global-poverty-update-world-bank

Chen, G.-M., & Starosta, W. J. (1998). *Foundations of intercultural communication.* Allyn & Bacon.

Chicago Tribune. (2021, February 04). #MeToo: A timeline of events. *Chicago Tribune.* Accessed July 29, 2022, at https://www.chicagotribune.com/lifestyles/ct-me-too-timeline-20171208-htmlstory.html

Chu, S.-C., & Choi, S. M. (2010). Social capital and self-presentation on social networking sites: A comparative study of Chinese and American young generations. *Chinese Journal of Communication, 3*(4), 402–420. https://doi.org/10.1080/17544750.2010.516575

Companies ranked by earnings. (2022). Accessed June 24, 2022, at https://companiesmarketcap.com/most-profitable-companies

CrisisWatch: Tracking conflict worldwide. (2022, May). *International Crisis Group.* Accessed June 23, 2022, at https://www.crisisgroup.org/crisiswatch

Current world population. (n.d.). *Worldometers: Real time world statistics.* Accessed April 23, 2013, at http://www.worldometers.info/world-population

deAndrea, D. C., Shaw, A. S., & Levine, T. R. (2010). Online language: The role of culture in self-expression and self-construal on Facebook. *Journal of

Language and Social Psychology, *29*(4), 425–442. https://doi.org/10.1177/0261927X10377989

de Lenne, O., Vandenbosch, L, Eggermont, S., Karsay, K., & Trekels, J. (2020). Picture-perfect lives on social media: A cross-national study on the role of media ideals in adolescent well-being. *Media Psychology*, *23*(1), 52–78. https://doi.org/10.1080/15213269.2018.1554494

di Mento, M. (2022, January 4). $15B from Gates, French Gates tops 2021 biggest gift list. *AP News*. Accessed June 24, 2022, at https://apnews.com/article/science-business-endowments-bill-gates-melinda-french-gates-cb45fe0a97b8f41c51f44f3226c47218.

Duffy, M. E., Twenge, J. M., & Joiner, T. E. (2019). Trends in mood and anxiety symptoms and suicide-related outcomes among U.S. undergraduates, 2007–2018: Evidence from two national surveys. *Journal of Adolescent Health*, *65*(5), 590–598. https://doi.org/10.1016/j.jadohealth.2019.04.033

Forbes.com. (2009). World's most powerful people: #66 Klaus Schwab. Accessed March 12, 2012, at http://www.forbes.com/lists/2009/20/power-09_Klaus-Schwab_OTWW.html

GDP ranked by country. (2022). *World Population Review*. Accessed June 24, 2022, at https://worldpopulationreview.com/countries/countries-by-gdp

Global Conflict Tracker. (n.d.). *Council on Foreign Relations*. Accessed June 30, 2022, at https://www.cfr.org/global-conflict-tracker

Global report on internal displacement. (2021). *Internal Displacement Monitoring Centre*. Accessed June 28, 2022, at https://www.internal-displacement.org/global-report/grid2021

Gudykunst, W. B. (Ed.). (1983). *Intercultural communication theory: Current perspectives (published as The international and intercultural communication annual)*. Sage.

Gudkyunst, W. B. (2005). An anxiety/uncertainty management (AUM) theory of effective communication: Making the Mesh of the Net Finer. In W. B. Gudkyunst (Ed.), *Theorizing about intercultural communication* (pp. 281–322). Sage.

Gudkyunst, W. B., & Kim, Y. Y. (2003). *Communicating with strangers: An approach to intercultural communication* (4th ed.). McGraw-Hill.

Gudykunst, W. B., & Mody, B. (Eds.). (2002). *Handbook of international and intercultural communication*. Sage.

Hall, B. J. (2003). *Among cultures: The challenge of communication* (2nd ed.). Wadsworth.

Hall, E. T. (1959). *The silent language*. Doubleday.

Hecht, M. L., Baldwin, J. R., & Faulkner, S. L. (2006). The (in)conclusion of the matter: Shifting signs and models of culture. In J. R. Baldwin, S. L. Faulkner, M. L. Hecht, & S. L. Lindsley (Eds.), *Redefining culture: Perspectives across the disciplines* (pp. 53–73). Lawrence Erlbaum Associates.

How George Floyd died, and what happened next. (2022, May 19). *New York Times*. Accessed June 24, 2022, at https://www.nytimes.com/article/george-floyd.html

Hyland, P., Shevlin, M., McBride, O., Murphy, J., Karatzias, T., Bentall, R. P., Martinez, A., & Vallières, F. (2020). Anxiety and depression in the Republic of Ireland during the COVID-19 pandemic. *Acta Psychiatrica Scandinavica*, *142*(3), 249–256. https://doi.org/10.1111/acps.13219

International students. (2020, June 9). *Migration Data Portal*. Accessed June 28, 2022, at https://www.migrationdataportal.org/themes/international-students

Jiani, M. A. (2016). Why and how international students choose Mainland China as a higher education study abroad location. *Higher Education*, *74*(4), 563–579. https://doi.org/10.1007/s10734-016-0066-0

Jimada, U. (2020). Global digital technologies and the homogenization of culture in Africa. *Global Journal of Human Science: C—Sociology and Culture*, *20*(9). ISSN:2249-460x. Online ISSN: 2249-460x & Print ISSN: 0975-587X. Accessed June 29, 2022.

Key internet statistics to know in 2022 (including mobile). (n.d.). Accessed June 29, 2022, at https://www.broadbandsearch.net/blog/internet-statistics

Kim, Y. Y. (1984). Searching for creative integration. In W. B. Gudykunst & Y. Y. Kim (Eds.), *Methods for intercultural communication research* (pp. 13–30). Sage.

Kim, Y. Y., & Gudykunst, W. B. (Eds.). (1988). *Theories in intercultural communication (published as The international and intercultural Communication Annual)*. Sage.

Kim, Y. Y., & Ruben, B. (1988). Intercultural transformation: A systems theory. In Y. Y. Kim & W. B. Gudykunst (Eds.), *Theories in intercultural communication* (pp. 299–321). Sage.

Kincaid, D. L. (Ed.). (1987). *Communication theory: Eastern and Western perspectives*. Academic Press.

Kopper, E. (1993). Swiss and Germans: Similarities and differences in work-related values, attitudes, and behavior. *International Journal of Intercultural Relations*, *17*(2), 167–184. DOI: 10.1016/0147-1767(93)90023-2

Kyoto Protocol. (2012). *United Nations Framework Convention on Climate Change*. Accessed March 14, 2012, at http://unfccc.int/kyoto_protocol/items/2830.php

Leeds-Hurwitz, W. (1990). Notes in the history of intercultural communication: The Foreign Service

Institute and the mandate for intercultural training. *Quarterly Journal of Speech*, 76(3), 262–281. DOI: 10.1080/00335639009383919

Malala Fund. (n.d.). Malala.org. Accessed June 29, 2022.

Martin, J. N., Flores, L. A., & Nakayama, T. K. (2002). Ethical issues in intercultural communication. In J. N. Martin, T. K. Nakayama, & L. A. Flores (Eds.), Readings in intercultural communication (2nd ed., pp. 363–371). McGraw-Hill.

McCoy, D. C., Cuartas, J., Behrman, J., Cappa, C., Heymann, J., López Bóo, F., Lu, C., Raikes, A., Richter, L., Stein, A., & Fink, G. (2021). Global estimates of the implications of COVID-19-related preprimary school closures for children's instructional access, development, learning, and economic well-being. *Child Development*, 92(5), 883–899. https://doi.org/10.1111/cdev.13658

McDonald, D. (2017, March 21). Why Walmart failed in Germany. *The Global Millennial*. Accessed June 24, 2022, at https://medium.com/the-global-millennial/why-walmart-failed-in-germany-f1c3ca7eea65

McLuhan, M. (1962). *The Gutenberg galaxy: The making of typographic man*. University of Toronto Press.

McPhail, T. L. (2019). *Global communication: Theories, stakeholders, and trends* (5th ed.). Wiley-Blackwell.

Merelli, A. (2019, December 30). *The state of global right-wing populism in 2019*. Qz.com. Accessed June 28, 2022, at https://qz.com/1774201/the-global-state-of-right-wing-populism-in-2019

Miike, Y. (2007). An Asiacentric reflection on Eurocentric bias in communication theory. *Communication Monographs*, 74(2), 272–278. DOI: 10.1080/03637750701390093

Miike, Y. (2010). An anatomy of Eurocentrism in communication scholarship: The role of Asiacentricity in de-Westernizing theory and research. *China Media Research*, 6 (1), 1–11.

Millions on the move in their own countries: The human face of climate change. (2021, September 13). *World Bank*. Accessed June 28, 2022, at https://www.worldbank.org/en/news/feature/2021/09/13/millions-on-the-move-in-their-own-countries-the-human-face-of-climate-change

Nakayama, T. K., & Halualani, R. T. (Eds.). (2010). *The handbook of critical intercultural communication*. Wiley-Blackwell.

Ortiz, J. L. (2022, May 17). "We must not grow numb to such sorrow": COVID death toll in the U.S. reaches 1 million. *USA Today*. Accessed June 28, 2022, at https://www.usatoday.com/story/news/nation/2022/05/17/covid-deaths-one-million-united-states/9732932002

Over one billion people at threat of being displaced by 2050 due to environmental change, conflict, and civil unrest. (2020, September 9). *Institute for Economics and Peace*. Accessed June 28, 2022, at https://www.economicsandpeace.org/wp-content/uploads/2020/09/Ecological-Threat-Register-Press-Release-27.08-FINAL.pdf

Radjou, N., & Kalpa, P. (2010, August 6). Do multinationals really understand globalization? The ability of global companies to leverage global opportunities is surprisingly shallow. *Bloomberg Businessweek*. Accessed March 14, 2012, http://www.businessweek.com/globalbiz/content/aug2010/gb2010086_282527.htm

Refugee Facts (2023). *USA for UNHCR*. Accessed February 27 at https://www.unrefugees.org/refugee-facts/

Redden, E. (2021, November 15). International enrollments begin to recover. *Inside Higher Education*. Accessed June 28, 2022, at https://www.insidehighered.com/admissions/article/2021/11/15/international-students-increase-following-pandemic-declines?v2

Rogers, E. M., & Hart, W. B. (2002). The histories of intercultural, international, and development communication. In W. B. Gudykunst & B. Mody (Eds.), *Handbook of international and intercultural communication* (2nd ed., pp. 1–18). Sage.

Segev, E., Ahituv, N., & Barzilai-Nahon, K. (2007). Mapping diversities and tracing trends of cultural homogeneity/heterogeneity in Cyberspace. *Journal of Computer-Mediated Communication*, 12(4), 1269–1297. https://doi.org/10.1111/j.1083-6101.2007.00373.x

Statista Research Department. (2022, May 11). Total contribution of travel and tourism to gross domestic product (GDP) worldwide from 2006 to 2021. *Statista*. Accessed June 28, 2022, at https://www.statista.com/statistics/233223/travel-and-tourism—total-economic-contribution-worldwide

Stephan, W., & Stephan, C. (1985). Intergroup anxiety. *Journal of Social Issues*, 41(3), 157–166. DOI: 10.1111/j.1540-4560.1985.tb01134.x

The 2010s. A decade of protests around the world. (December 31, 2019). *NPR*. Accessed June 28, 2022, at https://www.npr.org/sections/pictureshow/2019/12/31/790256816/the-2010s-a-decade-of-protests-around-the-world

The U.S. loses more than 42,000 jobs and $1.8 billion as students flee for better opportunities. (November 16, 2020). *NAFSA*. Accessed June 28, 2022 at https://www.nafsa.org/about/about-nafsa/

new-nafsa-data-show-first-ever-drop-international-student-economic-value-us#

Tourism Intelligence Network. (n.d.). *Number of tourists or tourism revenues?* Accessed February 14, 2013, at https://veilletourisme.ca/2006/05/16/number-of-tourists-or-tourism-revenues

Trade (% of GDP). (n.d.). *The World Bank.* Accessed June 24, 2022, at https://data.worldbank.org/indicator/NE.TRD.GNFS.ZS

Ueda, M., Stickley, A., Sueki, H., & Matsubayashi, T. (2020). Mental health status of the general population in Japan during the COVID-19 pandemic. *Psychiatry and Clinical Neurosciences, 74*(9), 496–512. https://doi.org/10.1111/pcn.13105

UNESCO. (2009). *UNESCO World Report: Investing in cultural diversity and intercultural dialogue: Executive summary.* Accessed August 5, 2013, at http://unesdoc.unesco.org/images/0018/001847/184755e.pdf

UNESCO. (2021, September 23). Migrants, refugees, or displaced persons. Accessed June 28, 2022, at https://en.unesco.org/news/migrants-refugees-displaced-persons

UNWTO. (2022, June 3). Tourism recovery gains momentum as restrictions ease and confidence returns. *UNWTO.* Accessed June 28, 2022, at https://www.unwto.org/taxonomy/term/347

van Rensburg, M. J., & Smith, H. (2021). Navigating uncertainty, employment, and women's safety during COVID-19. Reflections of sexual assault resistance educators. *Gender, Work & Organization, 28* (S1), 122–136. DOI: 10.1111/gwao.12508

Ventura, L. (Feb 16, 2022). World inequality ranking by country 2022. *Global Finance.* Accessed February 27, 2023 at https://www.gfmag.com/global-data/economic-data/world-inequality-ranking

Vodafone: raising voices. (2018). *Ads of the World.* Accessed June 29, 2022, at https://www.adsoftheworld.com/campaigns/raising-voices

Wars in the World. (2022, June 29). *List of ongoing conflicts.* May 11, 2022. Accessed June 30, 2022, at https://www.warsintheworld.com/?page=static1258254223

Washington Peace Center. (2013). *The world social forum and world economic forum.* Accessed August 20, 2013, at http://washingtonpeacecenter.net/pla_theworldsocialforum

WHO Coronavirus (COVID-19) dashboard. (2022, June 22). *World Health Organization.* Accessed June 28, 2022, at https://covid19.who.int

Wiseman, R. (Ed.). (1995). *Intercultural communication Theory* (published as *The international and intercultural communication annual*). Sage.

World Bank. (2022). *Poverty.* Accessed June 23, 2022, at https://www.worldbank.org/en/topic/poverty/overview

World Economic Forum. (n.d.). Accessed June 24, 2022, at https://www.weforum.org/about/world-economic-forum

World Inequality by country 2022. (2022). *World Population Review.* Accessed June 23, 2022, at https://worldpopulationreview.com/country-rankings/wealth-inequality-by-country

World Social Forum Mexico 2022. (n.d.) wsf2022.org. Accessed June 25, 2022.

World Tourism Organization. (2012) One billion tourists key to creating jobs and stimulating the economy. Accessed March 12, 2012, at http://media.unwto.org/en/press-release/2012-03-05/one-billion-tourists-key-creating-jobs-and-stimulating-economy-unwto-secret

Wyse, A.E., Stickney, E.M., Butz, D., Beckler, A., & Close, C.N. (2020). The potential impact of COVID-19 on student learning and how schools can respond. *Educateional Measurement: Issue and Practice, 39*(3), 60–64.

Chapter 2

Action, ethics, and research: How can I make a difference?

Chapter objectives

After this chapter, you should be able to:

→ Define ethics and morality

→ Describe and evaluate universal ethical approaches and ethical relativism

→ Differentiate between civic engagement and political activism and relate them to culture

→ Outline three approaches (paradigms) to cultural research in communication

→ Distinguish between various research focuses in intercultural communication

Muslim veils in French schools: How can we determine right from wrong in intercultural situations? 27

"Not in our town:" What is the role of intercultural communication in civic engagement? 31

How can we do responsible cultural research? 36

Intercultural Communication for Everyday Life, Second Edition. John R. Baldwin, Alberto González, Nettie Brock, Ming Xie, and Chin-Chung Chao.
© 2024 John Wiley & Sons Ltd. Published 2024 by John Wiley & Sons Ltd.
Companion Website: http://www.wiley.com/go/baldwin2e

Every year more college students, secondary-school students, and working citizens commit themselves to helping others. This help might take the form of "alternative" breaks, in which college students go in groups to cities or regions of their country that need more development or a special service boost, such as a clean-up after a hurricane. In the United States, for example, organizations began creating "alternative spring breaks" for college students in the late 1980s (Alternative Spring Break, n.d.). These gave students the chance to volunteer for service projects over spring break, rather than go to some "party" destination (Figure 2.1). Eventually, other organizations like MTV partnered with colleges to organize breaks (Alternative Spring Break, n.d.). Each year, thousands of students participate in such volunteer opportunities, sometimes with specific organizations, such as the United Way or Habitat for Humanity, and sometimes through their schools. The trend in the United States is not limited to students. AmeriCorps, an agency that promotes service in local communities, reports 77.9 million, or about 30% of U.S. Americans volunteering for some organization in 2019, contributing a total of 5.8 billion hours, "with an economic value of $147 billion" (Schlachter, 2021).

However, Steve Corbett and Brian Fikkert (2009) charge that, often, civic engagement to help the poor does more harm than good. The best-intentioned effort at injecting aid or bringing money into a community can increase dependence, reduce the dignity of local individuals, and harm those who are giving. The givers can demonstrate **paternalism**—showing an intent to help other groups, but with an attitude of superiority—and can stereotype the poor. Such a charge raises difficult questions. When we are interacting with people from other cultures within and outside of our nation, what guidelines, if any, can direct our actions and communication?

Figure 2.1 Students often do service projects as part of alternate spring breaks, mission trips, or other group efforts. Many times, these works provide wonderful service for communities, but they can also have unforeseen ethical implications. Source: Edwin Remsberg/Alamy Stock Photo.

Should we, as citizens, be involved in addressing the needs of people in other cultures? What is our role in the politics or the world around us? Some of us might want to get involved in or give to causes such as Save the Children or Amnesty International. Others of us might ask, "Is that really my responsibility?" or tell ourselves, "Maybe that's something I'll do when I'm older." If we want to do such service projects, how can we best understand local communities and their needs? These questions lead us to three issues that we will consider in this chapter: intercultural communication ethics, civic engagement, and cultural research.

Muslim veils in French schools: How can we determine right from wrong in intercultural situations?

An issue that is dividing much of Europe, and especially France, at the time of writing this text, is the cultural and religious multiculturalism of Europe. One case study from the cultural debate serves to introduce our discussion of ethics: whether the French government should be able to outlaw religious imagery, such as large crosses, yarmulkes, or, perhaps the most controversial, veils for Muslim women (Figure 2.2). On one side of the debate, the French government is concerned with religious division and violence in the schools as well as traditional fears of loss of "French" cultural prestige, as Muslim culture exerts a stronger influence across Europe. On the other side are notions of modesty and decorum held by Muslim women: Many people feel that it is against their religious practices not to cover their heads or portions of their faces. The issue relates to similar questions: Does one nation have the right to tell another nation how to handle its human rights? Should the global feminist movement seek to change the status of women in places where such changes grate against the grain of the culture? Should one offer a "bribe" to a public official to avoid a minor charge or to ensure that some legal process happens in a timely

Figure 2.2 The issue of wearing visual markers of religion, such as the veil, has become a topic of hot political debate in France. In the mid-1990s, these students at Saint-Exupery Secondary School, in France, could still wear veils. Source: Jean-Pierre Rey/ Gamma Rapho/Getty Images.

manner? Or, within a specific culture, is it ethical for a university or business to restrict freedom of speech by limiting "hate speech?" If we remain silent when we see intolerance, such as someone telling a joke that puts down a culture or group of people, is that silence wrong? All of these deal with the notion of ethics.

Ethics and morality

Ethics and morality are linked to notions of right and wrong; while **morality** deals with any behavior that might be considered right or wrong, **ethics** deals specifically with the rightness or wrongness of our interactions with others, that is, the application of moral principles to behavior with others (Wines & Napier, 1992). In some cultures, taking drugs might be considered immoral, as one is (supposedly) only hurting themself, but stealing or lying—as they involve others more directly—are questions of ethics. It is hard enough to determine what is morally or ethically acceptable within a national culture, as people with different political or moral perspectives debate things such as when life begins (and, thus, when or if abortion should be allowed), what the rights of GLBTQ+ persons should be, whether it is ethical to place restrictions on gun and ammunition purchase, or whether the state has the right to execute criminals for certain crimes. It is even more difficult to compare the systems of right and wrong between two cultures or when people from two cultures are interacting, following different moral systems.

We all follow some form of guidelines as we interact with others. Let us imagine that you wish to download your favorite reggae music, illegally, from the Internet. Richard Evanoff (2015) describes two overarching approaches to ethics, each with specific perspectives within it (see also Baldwin et al., 2018). A **universalist ethical approach** assumes that a single ethical approach should be able to apply to all people. Perspectives within this approach propose a **meta-ethic**, an overarching guideline of behavior toward other people that either can or should be applied to people in all cultures. Some base this approach on logic, such as Emmanuel Kant's "deontological ethic" or **categorical imperative**. This approach would determine a universal right or wrong with logical questions. Lying might be (universally) wrong because, "what if everyone did it?" In our digital downloading case, what would happen to our media system if all people just stopped paying for other people's art or other product of labor? A religious approach might apply a single set of scriptures to say that something is inherently right or wrong. Evanoff argues that these approaches tend to fail because there is not a global system of religion or logic, and such approaches assume a "linear" view of cultural development.

Particularistic ethical approaches, on the other hand, "relativize values and norms of particular individuals and/or groups" (Evanoff, 2015, p. 418). That is, there is some notion that ethics might vary based on a given situation ("situational ethics"), in that a given behavior might be ethically acceptable in some situations but not others. Several traditional ethical approaches might fall under this ethical umbrella. **Utilitarianism**, or determining the greatest benefit for the greatest number of people, would lead you to ask who might be helped or hurt by illegal downloading of media content. The **golden mean**, which involves avoiding extremes in decision-making, might suggest that if the music is not obtainable for purchase or if you just want to try it out before you buy, you might download it but not make a steady practice of it. **Ethical egoism** refers to making choices based simply on what seems good or beneficial to us, without a regard for others—you download the music because you want it and can get away with it (Griffin, 2009). Evanoff (2015) sees these particular approaches as related to a more "subjective" way of looking at things (see below), as well as to "postmodernism, the preservation of local culture and ethnic identities, and multilinear model of intercultural development" (p. 418).

Perhaps related to particularist approaches, **moral exclusion** is a common—but perhaps not intentional—practice by which we apply one set of ethical principles to our ingroup (nation, country, religious group, family) but a different set of principles to outgroup members—leading us to treat people from other groups or countries the way we would never accept people from our own group or country to be treated (Opotow, 1990). This relates to a limitation of particularist approaches that some authors have raised: The lack of a single standard can lead to vagueness about the rightness or wrongness of something. Utilitarian, golden mean, and other ethical stances described earlier can inform intercultural communication (Hall, 2003), though each has limitations in actual application. Intercultural writers have dealt with the tension between cultural uniqueness and ethics in different ways.

What do you think? In many nations, today, college students find the things they need in a major chain store. Imagine that you shop at such a store, because it is convenient, and the prices are the lowest in town. But you find out that the organization engages in unfair labor practices. It hires most employees part-time to avoid paying for health insurance. It discriminates against women or minority members by not giving them promotions. Employees are underpaid and easily fired, but the CEOs and owners are very rich. What are the ethical implications of you shopping or not shopping at such a store?

Approaches specific to intercultural communication

Some writers advocate **cultural relativism**, the idea that people in each culture create their own accepted norms about what is right or wrong, with each ethical system being equally as acceptable as any other system. A possible issue with cultural relativism is that all members of a culture could accept a practice that by most standards (e.g., the United Nations Universal Declaration of Human Rights) would be harmful to some members. For example, if most members of a culture believe in bride burning, slavery, torture, or human sacrifice, cultural relativism dictates that those outside the culture should say nothing about it. Ethical relativism has strong implications for human rights activists (e.g., Amnesty International) and initiatives by some national governments to impose a view of human rights on others. Few interculturalists, to our knowledge, take a "cultural relativism" stance; however, Robert Shuter (2000) carefully highlights how different world religious systems treat "communication ethics" differently, such that, in a culture with high value on relationships and interconnectedness, it is logical that relationship overrides a value on "truth" for truth's sake. Western cultures, on the other hand, have tended to place a higher value on freedom of information and "truth," so would be more likely—at least in philosophy—to place "truth" over relationships.

A second perspective promotes a universalistic ethic based on what we call a **derived ethic.** Stella Ting-Toomey (1999) recommends such an approach: We look across cultures to see if they hold ethical principles in common. Once we find ethical stances that overlap, we can combine these for an approach that applies to interaction in any culture (Wines & Napier, 1992). For example, the United Nations Charter on Human Rights puts forth a series of rights agreed upon by people of many nations, such as the "right to life, liberty, and security of person" (United Nations, n.d.). The Charter advocates against all slavery or degrading punishments, and for representation before the law.

Other writers offer universal ethical principles such as the **humaneness principle**, which states that we should not harm others and should treat them well (Hatch, 1994). This is similar to the **peace principle**, which centers the notion of human spirit as the basis for universal ethics: "The guiding principle of any universal code of intercultural communication should be to protect the worth and dignity of the human spirit" (Kale, 2015, p. 424). These principles state that we should not engage in any behavior that has a negative impact on the welfare of others. With this in mind, racism, poverty, and creating human suffering are unethical, and so is ignoring such injustices. David Kale (2015) suggests that with this approach we will treat people of other cultures (and groups) with the same respect that we feel we deserve; we will represent other cultures (and groups) as we feel that they would want to be represented; we will encourage people to express their personal and cultural uniqueness; and we will seek not just to understand others, but to identify with them.

What do you think? **Ethics matters:** Find an ethical case study in the list of business ethics case studies at the McCombs School of Business' "Ethics Unwrapped" (n.d.) website (https://ethicsunwrapped.utexas.edu/case-studies) or John Hendry's (2013) international business case studies. How might different cultures approach the same case differently? What behavior might be appropriate if people in the case took some of the different universal ethical approaches? How might the humaneness or peace principles be useful in the situation?

A second principle that several scholars have suggested in the **communicative** or **dialogic ethic** (Evanoff, 2015) is the idea of speaking *with* people from other groups, not *to* them or *at* them (Martin & Nakayama, 2002). This approach suggests that, as we determine ethics across cultures, we should discuss with the parties involved what sorts of ethical guidelines should be in effect. Evanoff (2015) argues that this approach is practical; it highlights relationships between individuals, and, by learning others' perspectives on their own cultural behaviors, it bridges the gap between universal and particularist approaches. This is in line with Mikhail Bakhtin's (1981) idea of a dialogic imperative, in which there is no monologue, but a comparison of competing perspectives—or Jürgen Habermas' (1998) notion of "communicative freedom" (p. 119), which states that ethical discussion occurs when everyone has the ability to engage in discussion, without coercion or constraint by others, such as through unequal power relations (Niemi, 2008).

For example, an ethical question that has influenced international politics is the degree to which there should be a free flow of media between cultures. Allowing unrestricted importation of international media often harms local artists, musicians, and media systems in developing countries. But restricting its importation limits impacts jobs and economies in the wealthier nations. Most ethical differences are not central to issues of dignity, and intercultural communicators can overlook them (Hatch, 1994). But some differences are important enough to address—questions of human rights, slavery, and genocide (United Nations, n.d.). Before people on either side of an intercultural ethical issue agree to ethical guidelines, they should talk to each other to negotiate an ethical approach that works for both parties, which requires understanding, empathy, and caring.

In sum, we see that ethics are an important part of intercultural communication. It is important to be aware of our own ethical approach. But as we interact with people from other cultures, there are often differences in how we are expected to treat others. Scholars offer different ethical approaches to guide our behavior, including the humanistic and dialogic principles, developed specifically for intercultural communication. Others believe that we can only understand the ethics of each culture uniquely. In most ethical, moral, and religious systems, however, considering the good of others—and working toward that good—seems to be a worthwhile ethical goal.

"Not in our town": What is the role of intercultural communication in civic engagement and political activism?

With a broader conception of culture—viewing culture as ever-negotiated and distinct ways of life, rather than simply as national or ethnic groups—we can see that cultural differences exist in many of the dilemmas that face us in the cities and towns where we live and study. In a world of increasing diversity, we are faced with intolerance toward those of other races, countries, or social class backgrounds. Some individuals in our communities may not have access to the same resources as others. There may be a gap in levels of achievement in our local schools, due in part to a chasm between the culture of the children and the culture of the educational system (García & Guerra, 2006). People on many college campuses call our attention to social issues that often have a cultural component, such as the status of refugees from different countries, or political and religious division in places such as Northern Ireland or the Sudan. And agencies for civil and human rights around the world organize activities that relate to awareness and tolerance. Around the world, citizens strive, often in protest, for human and civil rights.

As one example, the United States values **altruism**, the notion of doing good to someone, even a stranger, and **voluntarism**, the idea of giving one's own time, for no apparent benefit to oneself (Althen et al., 2003). People in the United States give time or money to help tsunami victims or AIDS orphans. They volunteer in organizations like Habitat for Humanity or the American Cancer Foundation (even if they do not know someone with cancer personally). They give money and time to complete strangers, leading some Koreans to think that U.S. Americans treat strangers like friends and friends like strangers (Kohls, 2001).

Many U.S. Americans stand up to prejudice through efforts such as the "Not in Our Town" campaigns that began after intolerance toward Jewish people in Billings, Montana (Not in Our Town, n.d.). At the same time, in response to many efforts toward social change, we say "Not in My Back Yard," a statement so common people refer to it by the acronym NIMBY. For example, many U.S. Americans who disagree with the detainment of prisoners in Guantanamo Bay during since 9–11, might oppose a facility housing those same prisoners in their own community. And we often apply benevolence unequally. Many nations welcomed Ukrainian refugees from the war there that did not welcome refugees from Sudan, Syria, or Ethiopia.

Political activism and civic engagement

There are different ways to get involved in the community. Some involvement has a political motive, and some do not. Involvement that includes participation in the political system is referred to as **political engagement** or **activism**. Political engagement includes working on community problems, serving in organizations with a "stake in political policies or outcomes," supporting or talking to others about political causes, writing letters or blogging about political or social issues, working on campaigns, signing petitions, raising public awareness (e.g., through rallies, protests, street theater, or boycotts), and voting (Colby et al., 2007, pp. 30–31).

Such efforts are "political" not because they are connected to some political party, but because they involve public policy, spending, and socio-political attention. For example, in response to the death of two children hit by a speeding bus in 2019, tens of thousands of Bangladeshis, including many students, protested against unsafe road conditions (Three jailed in Bangladesh, 2019; see Figure 2.3). Efforts at political engagement often involve cross-cultural dialogue and research. A discussion of Haitian workers in the Dominican Republic requires knowledge about Haitian and Dominican cultural differences, Dominican nationalization policy, prejudices between groups, and the intersection of international politics and economies.

At the same time, many people are less concerned about public policy than they are about the everyday wellbeing of others, for example, people who need homes, children who need mentoring, or immigrants and travelers who need to learn the host language. College students might be involved in local children's or history museums, efforts to renovate a downtown or campus area, no-kill animal shelters, and so on. Involvement in the community, regardless of politics, is referred to as **civic engagement**. Civic engagement often leads those involved to feel a sense of responsibility to their community, engaging in civil society, and helping the common good, with activities including learning about diversity, engaging in public problem solving, or assuming leadership roles in organizations (Jacoby, 2009).

To distinguish civic from political engagement, once civic engagement turns to social issues, promoting local and global justice, or taking an active role in the political process, it becomes political engagement, or activism. If a student group raises awareness about the homeless or immigrants, it is political engagement; if the students simply donate time working in a homeless culture or teaching immigrants the host language, it is civic engagement.

People and groups have long promoted voluntarism. One of the founding principles of Harvard College in 1636 was preparing students to engage actively with community life. Social leaders like educator and philosopher John Dewey and U.S. President Franklin Roosevelt promoted connections between universities and the social problems of the day. U.S. President George H. W. Bush passed the National and Community Service Act in 1990 (Jacoby, 2009). Now, many universities focus students' attention on civic and political engagement. Organizations such as the American Democracy Project and the American Association of State Colleges and

Figure 2.3 Tens of thousands of Bangladeshis protest road safety in 2019. Source: BBC/https://www.bbc.com/ last accessed January 10, 2023.

Universities (Jacoby, 2009), as well as specific institutions, such as Illinois State University, Georgetown University, and University of Wisconsin-Madison, support programs to get students involved with the community in some way (Welch, 2009).

Defending civic engagement and political activism among college students

In college, we might be politically involved or see the need to volunteer. However, there are practical and ideological reasons why we may choose not to become engaged or even avoid the discussion of civic or political engagement in the university setting. Practical reasons—those most often in the forefront of students' minds—include logistical issues: "I barely have time to work and do my studies," "I don't know how to get involved," "I'd rather spend my spare time with friends."

There are several responses to these issues. First, in a way, the patterns we establish in college often guide us as we leave college. We are busy with classes, exams, and jobs—but often no busier than when we graduate and have full-time jobs, children, or other commitments. Second, there is a need for someone to reach out and help others—if we do not, who will? Third, there are personal benefits for helping others. If you are from a "collective" culture (see Chapter 4), you might find reward in contributing not only to your family or workgroup, but to the community at large, forging a new, broader sense of group identity. If you are an "individualist," you may find personal reward, a sense of feeling good about yourself, from helping others (Bellah et al., 1996). University life gives us many rewards—friendship, career development, networking opportunities. But involvement in the lives of others gives us a different reward. In fact, John Rogers and Joel Westheimer (2017) argue that "public schools are arguably the institution best situated to educate a large number of citizens and potential civic actors about important matters of contemporary social concern" (p. 1049).

POP CULTURE

Consider the song, *Solo le Pido a Dios*, by Argentine singer, Leon Gieco. How might this song impact its audience in the context of Argentina in 1978? (You may have to do some Internet research to answer this.) How might it translate to the social realities of the over 30 artists who have since covered it, including Bruce Springsteen, U2, and Shakira? What songs have impacted your life as regards helping others or thinking about your social world?

Solo le Pido a Dios (Leon Gieco)

I only ask of God
That I will not be indifferent to the pain
That the dry death will not find me
Empty and alone, without having done enough

I only ask of God
That I will not be indifferent to injustice
That they will not strike my other cheek
After a talon has scratched my destiny

I only ask of God
That I will not be indifferent to war
It is a great monster and steps mightily
Upon all the poor innocence of the people
                                    [Trans. J. Baldwin]

Some people have ideological reasons against teaching civic and political engagement in the classroom. Some claim such teaching indoctrinates students with a specific (supposedly liberal) ideology—it leads them to the left of politics. However, a detailed study of more than 20 courses and programs incorporating Political Engagement Projects (PEPs) at a variety of universities discovered that teaching exercises that created civic and political engagement among students increased their likelihood of being involved in their communities as adults but did not change their political ideology. If they were conservative going into the class, they became involved as conservatives. If they were politically liberal, they engaged in the community in ways true to that political approach (Colby et al., 2007).

POP CULTURE

Some popular music artists, like Rage Against The Machine Gogol Bordello (a Gypsy punk band), U2, or Green Day—or, more recently, Kesha, Beyoncé, Kendrick Lamar, and M.I.A. (See Figure 2.4) make political activism a large part of their musical focus. What popular artists do you know that include social themes in their music? What are some of the issues and values they promote? What are some strengths and limitations of using popular music for social change?

Figure 2.4 M.I.A., a Sri Lankan refugee to England and contemporary hip hop artist, brings social awareness on issues from gun violence to refugees through songs like "Paper Planes" and "Borders." Source: Warscapes Magazine. http://www.warscapes.com/opinion/mia-s-borders-refugees-refugees/ last accessed January 10, 2023.

Another concern critics raise is that the purpose of the college classroom is to teach skills and ideas that help one's career, leaving the instilling of values to the family (Fish, 2008). Colby et al. (2007) respond that "reasonably well-informed, capable, engaged, and public-spirited citizens are essential if a democracy is to flourish" (p. 26). Civic engagement, they argue, leads to citizen participation and to a more informed public, as civic engagement heightens our understanding of the complexities of current social problems. While students have agency to be civic and politically engaged, there are often constraints—political, economic, or cultural—that act upon their ability to be engaged. For example, the political system in Myanmar prohibited the unregistered congregating of more than five people but allowed foreign non-governmental organizations (NGOs) to enter with humanitarian aid.

On the other hand, some people criticize political and civic engagement efforts for not going far enough. We might become engaged in a project, like feeding hungry children, because we see ourselves from a patronizing position—as a cultural (or racial) savior, out of "benevolent" classism or racism (see Chapter 6). Some approaches to civic engagement disempower those receiving the supposed help, leading to dependence on those providing the help. Such efforts hide the unequal access that some groups have to resources and power. John Eby (1998) suggests that most civic engagement ignores larger structural issues, diverts attention from social policy to voluntarism, and leads students to a limited concept of real human needs and how to address them. Colby et al. (2007) respond that civic engagement gives at least some sense of the choices that are possible and may instill a sense of **efficacy** among people—that is, the sense that, with their own work or combined with others, they can accomplish a task to which they set themselves. In this way, people do not just wait for cultural or political elites to make decisions for them; they personally influence the contexts and structures that impact their lives.

Doing civic engagement and political activism

Getting involved matters, but so does *how* we get involved. The humanitarian ethic states that if people are suffering and we do nothing, we are contributing to their suffering. At the same time, the communicative ethic suggests that, as we become engaged, we must participate with those influenced by our actions to determine the goals and the outcomes in a way that empowers them and creates culturally responsible engagement.

The question remains: what would this skeleton of civic engagement that we have provided look like with "flesh and bones" on it? Stephen Hunt and Chad Woolard (2016) outline some good practices for civic engagement education and provide several concrete possibilities, including educating citizens and doing service learning, They add to our understanding also the idea of "democratic engagement," where we work specifically to build and uphold democratic ideals in a society.

We present here three different classroom examples of civic engagement that pertain to culture in some way, based on real exercises used by instructors. In the first case, a group of students could investigate a major women's rights group in your culture (for example, the National Organization of Women (NOW) in the United States or the Women's Rights Advancement and Protection Alternative (WRAPA) in Nigeria). Investigate how the organization relates to the local culture's values, politics, and worldview or how it promotes strategies for change and how effective community members feel those changes are.

In a second case, students could investigate long-standing intergroup tensions in your community (e.g., between Jewish Israelis and Palestinians or between Catholics and Protestants in Ireland). They could explore the various roots of the conflict (see Chapter 6) and look for similarities between the groups and possible ways to promote helpful contact between group members.

Break it down

Look online for local sources in your community for volunteer agencies or see if there is an organization at your school that locates volunteer opportunities for students. Make a list of possible areas of civic engagement or activism *in your community or at your school* that might have some connection to "culture" or group identity.

A third case involves students interviewing people who are different from them on some key aspect of identity (see Chapter 5) as part of audience analysis for a persuasive speech. One student who engaged in such an assignment, a White male named "Henry," interviewed an African American woman, "Sara." Henry was skeptical of the assignment. Joseph Zompetti (2006, para 32) summarizes his speech to the class:

> As Henry told us the story of Sara, he became impassioned with empathy and concern. At times, his eyes clouded up, but his voice remained stern and assertive. Henry sincerely appeared to be moved by his interview with Sara. Given his earlier dislike for discussing identity, the audience, too, was enwrapped in Henry's speech. They seemed amazed at his transformation and appreciated his sincerity. When he concluded his speech, Henry declared, "I've learned that society does treat people differently, and that people have predispositions toward other people … and I've learned it all from Sara." At that moment in time, it seemed as if everyone in the class, particularly Henry, understood the importance of identity and public speaking.

It is important for members in groups, especially groups with privilege, to be **allies** to those in groups with less privilege—to advocate for them or work with them toward social justice. "An ally is an individual who is not only committed to expressing as little prejudice as possible but also invested in addressing social inequality" (Cross, 2021, p. 152). But how one enacts allyship is important and runs several risks, such as the danger of patronizing or unintentionally imposing control on the efforts of a group.

There is both benefit and need for us to look beyond our own desires and careers. We live in a social world, and as such, must be concerned with the needs of the people around us. We can get involved in the lives of others for the sake of making the world a better place, or we can do so at a level that involves public policy and spending.

How can we do responsible cultural research?

Part of being culturally ethical is providing accurate representations of others and of cultural concepts (Evanoff, 2015). One way we may choose to be involved, especially as we gain the skills a college education provides, is by doing research for civic groups. At a minimum, organizations or groups might expect us to understand research. But how can we do or read research effectively? The final section of the chapter introduces approaches to research, and then closes with one last look at ethics as they relate to cultural, cross-cultural, and intercultural research.

Assumptions that guide cultural research

As we look at studies regarding culture and communication, one might be full of statistics; another, observational notes or example quotations from only a few participants; another, an in-depth analysis of a single text (such as a Nelson Mandela speech or a Beyoncé music video). One way to understand the variety of intercultural research is to explore the types of underlying assumptions researchers might have. These assumptions tend to revolve around issues of what is real (at least, what is the reality that we should be considering), what counts as knowledge, and what the role of the researchers' values should be in conducting research. These apply to how scholars do research, but here we will apply them to our own understandings of the world.

Ontology refers to assumptions about the nature of reality. We often take our way of seeing the social world as natural. But in fact, there are several ways to see reality, especially social reality (Miller, 2005, and Potter, 1996, outline some of these differences). For example, we might think of race, sex, or other identities as variables that are either causes or effects of other variables. Or we might believe fundamentally that people have free will. So, regardless of any cultural patterns, each person makes unique choices about how to behave. Or we might think that gender is always changing and that we "create" gender by the way we talk, the jokes we tell, and the images we make.

How we see the world is related to our **epistemology**, or assumptions about knowledge. If we believe that each person has their own reality (e.g., "beauty is in the eye of the beholder"), we will not make predictions or believe in statements that describe how people are alike. Instead, we will talk to individuals to find their own perspectives of reality or perhaps we describe the understandings of a single group of people. But if we believe in internal and external causes for behavior, we will likely use methods that filter out researcher opinion, like experiments or closed-ended surveys, and we might make claims only after we have done research on a large group of people, using statistics.

In addition to our views of reality and knowledge, each of us has assumptions regarding the role of our values as we do research on culture and communication, which is our **axiology**. We might think that research can or should be value-free, or we might think that we really cannot see anything, including research, apart from our own opinions and biases. We could even believe that in a world with social inequalities, we would be wrong not to bring our values to our research, doing research and taking action to address such inequalities (feminist and anti-racist researchers tend to take this stance).

Approaches to studying culture and communication

With these definitions in mind, we can better understand the notion of "paradigms" in the communication field. The three **paradigms**—ways of seeing the (social or empirical) world—most common in communication research—are the scientific, humanistic, and critical paradigms, though some consider postmodernism to be a fourth paradigm. Different approaches to the world are often connected to preferred ways of doing research (Figure 2.5). If you do **social scientific** research, you will likely hold many of these assumptions: (1) Social behavior is predictable because people act based on internal and external causes. (2) Researchers should be systematic and remove personal biases, to understand the universal laws that govern communication behavior. (3) Research might be quantitative, using statistics, but researchers could also use observation or other methods and still believe that they are "uncovering" a world external to themselves. (4) Research is often done to test the relationship between variables in a theory, with a goal to provide better predictions of communication outcomes. We should note that most communication scholars do not believe humans are totally predictable—just similar enough in many ways to make "probable" predictions (Metts, 2004). As an example, you might study whether international travel leads college students or business travelers to have less ethnocentrism or reduced racism.

Figure 2.5 Methods and examples of cultural, cross-cultural, and intercultural research.

Method	Characteristics	Example
Experiment	• two or more conditions with different treatment ("control" and "experimental" group) • observation to see if experimental condition leads to a difference in some variable	A study in Italy (Guizzo & Cadinu, 2021) found that exposure to a sexually objectifying video raised male college students' gender-harassing behavior. Exposure to video from a web campaign against objectification lowered this, as well as their sexual coercion intention and hostile sexism.
Survey (closed-ended)	• Participants answer a list of items with forced choices (e.g, strongly agree to strongly disagree) • Items or groups of items measure "variables." • Researchers see if there are group differences on a variable or relationships between variables	A survey study of Mexican Americans and non-Mexican Latinx Americans in the United States (Figueroa-Caballero & Mastro, 2019) found that participants responded differently, including in terms of preferred label, based on whether they felt shame or anger in response to U.S. media's immigration coverage. Effects were greater for Mexican Latinx participants.
Survey (open-ended)	• Participants answer open-ended questions • Researchers develop themes from answers, with or without counting the responses	Charoensap-Kelly et al. (2020) used an open-ended questionnaire to explore how and why participants revealed their religious identities at work, what happened when they did, and strategies for positive self-disclosure.
Interviews and focus groups	• Researchers talk with participants, often following an unstructured format • A focus group is an interview done with a group of people. • Researchers develop themes from the answers	Hyun (2020) conducted in-depth interviews with ten Thai and ten Korean employees at Korean multinational companies based in Thailand. The findings show cultural communication ideas specific to the two cultures (e.g., Thai concept of *kreng jai*, Korean concept of *ppalli ppallii*).
Observation	• Researchers observe behavior in its natural context. • Research might include interviews, document analysis, and so on. • Research might be quantiative or qualitative	Carbaugh et al. (2006) did fieldwork and observed interaction to discover (and interpret) Finnish understandings of silence (qualitative). Remland et al. (1995) used systematic observation to determine cultural differences between several European countries regarding use of touch, distance, and body angle in conversation (quantitative).
Language analysis	• Researchers record naturally occurring language • Researchers use previous theory or look at the turn-taking and other features of language to understand culture.	Hei (2009) used discourse analysis and face management theory (see Chapter 7) to categorize, from taped everyday conversation, ways Malaysians use direct and indirect ways to refuse requests or offers.

Figure 2.5 (*Continued*)

Method	Characteristics	Example
Textual analysis or media criticism	• Researchers study a single text (e.g., speech, media text), interpreting it. • They might or might not look for ideologies and power structures	Ito and Bisila (2020) analyze how 20 different Japanese *anime* series represent foreigners—that is, as mostly "American," men, and White, with bad accents and "visually sexualized" women.
Media content analysis	• Researchers develop a coding sheet or scheme to measure specific variables in a media text. • Researchers observe many texts of a particular type, counting frequencies or doing statistics	Behm-Morawitz (2017) analyzed 383 U.S. magazine advertisements for video games to see if there were changes in representation, since there have been great increases in women and ethnic minority gamers; her results found little change from previous racial and ethnic stereotypes reproduced in video games.

Note: This list is intended as a list of many of the methods used for research on culture and communication. It is not intended to be exhaustive.

The second paradigm is called **humanistic** or **interpretive**. "Humanistic" implies that humans are unique from other aspects of nature, based on their ability to use symbols or some other aspect of their human essence (Potter, 1996). Research is "interpretive" in that you try to understand (or interpret) individual texts or small groups of individuals or instances. As you research, you might admit your own values as influencing how you see the reality of the people you study. Common assumptions of this view include that (1) People are not (or are less) predictable because they make choices. (2) Researchers should provide an interpretation of a group's reality or of an isolated media text. (3) Research should consider behavior or texts holistically and within larger social contexts. (4) Research should provide an explanation of a specific phenomenon in a culture from that culture's perspective, or an analysis of a speech or media text through application of a set of terms. In this perspective, you might investigate how people on a specific soccer team create a sense of belonging through joke telling and insults. Or you might investigate metaphors in a speech by Kenyan environmental activist Wangari Maathai.

We can see a difference between social scientific and interpretive views of culture in a common distinction some have made between approaches to understanding culture. On one hand, in an **etic approach**, researchers develop some framework of terms or dimensions, such as cultures where people focus more on the individual and those where people focus more on the group, or those where people touch more and stand closer and those where they touch less and stand further apart. Researchers apply the framework to compare people in their cultural behavior, according to terms the researcher has developed. Researchers using an **emic approach** do not want to impose their understandings of meanings or behaviors on a culture but seek to set aside their own understandings. Often using observation or talking to people, they try to discover the categories and meanings people in their own cultures give to their behavior and social reality (Gudykunst & Nishida, 1989)

The third paradigm, **critical** research, seeks to address social injustice in the world or explain how groups with different ideologies about the world struggle with each other to make their views dominant. Unlike the first two paradigms, in critical research, authors deliberately take their values into research. If you take this approach to doing research, you might analyze music videos quantitatively to see if the portrayal of women gives them the same choices and status as men. Or you might study how different groups within your culture struggle over explanations of the causes, treatment, and policy regarding COVID-19, excluding or putting down other views.

Much of critical theory is about ideology and hegemony. **Ideology** here refers to a set of assumptions that we use to interpret the world around us (van Dijk, 1998)—it is different from a paradigm in that it often deals with social structures and power. **Hegemony** is defined as some form or level of control over another group, such as political, cultural, or economic power (Zompetti, 2012). Critical researchers, including most feminists, would now look at gender differences in communication in terms of possible oppression or marginalization of women's communicative styles (Kramarae, 1980), either through media texts or in face-to-face communication, such as through interruptions, topic choice, or slurs people use for men or women.

One branch of critical theory involves **postcolonialism**—a field of study that looks worldwide at problems created by colonization, seeking to bring awareness to these problems and provide empowerment to those harmed by colonial relations (Shome & Hedge, 2002). We can see the imposition of one cultural system from cases as distinct as European colonization of Africa and Asia to more modern forms of economic colonization, with one-way media flows that lead strong media cultures to receive little outside influence, while influencing other cultures greatly. Key notions of postcolonialism include notions of **diaspora**, where people from one culture spread out across many different cultures, and **hybridity**, where cultural elements blend within a culture (we will say more about these in Chapter 3). The dominant group represents diverse groups within its society in different, usually unequal and unfair ways, and there are impacts of postcolonial relations within a society on how subordinate (and dominant) groups see their identity and **agency**, the choices one feels one has. Often, people in subordinated groups, although still having agency, are constrained by the power relations of the dominant group (Shome & Hedge, 2002). At the same time, some writers argue that these power relations are more complicated than they seem at first: the subordinate do have some agency, can represent the dominant group, and have their own bases of power within hybrid relations (García Canclini, 1995).

What do you think? Are there "real" differences between men and women and the way they communicate (and what are they)? Or are these differences socially constructed through communication? If they are socially constructed, are they done in a way that disadvantages women and privileges men (give examples)? Or even in ways that are inconsistent and contradictory?

From critical theory grew an approach called **postmodernism**. Postmodernism involves not a single construction of some aspect of culture, but several. These social constructions place notions, such as "womanhood" or "manhood", together with different concepts. Men are told to be sensitive and to be good fathers or boyfriends but are also told (often indirectly) they should focus on women's body parts and see women as something to be "conquered." That is, there are contradictory discourses, or presentations of ideas, about things such as what it means to be a man or to be truly Japanese, or what counts as success, constitutes "disease," or merits "punishment" in a given culture (Foucault, 1995). Postmodernism rejects much of what modernistic research, including humanistic research stood for, such as linearity, reason, hierarchy of structure, and the search for given meanings or single explanations.

Postmodernists often feel that things such as modern specialization, industrialization, urbanization, and rationalization (focus on reason) serve to sustain systems of domination and control (Best & Kellner, 1991; Rosenau, 1992). The value of analyzing different discourses about things such as illness, crime, masculinity, or democracy, is that it shows us how power works through and between these discourses. If you take a postmodern view as you do research, you would be less likely to make any claim about how a particular group, like Apache U.S. Indians, Japanese *burakumin*, or Black Hondurans, are alike, but would expect there to be different ways of living out each identity. Or you might study how different groups in your culture seek to define notions like "family" or "success" in different ways that would provide power or cultural prominence to one group or another.

Research can be, but does not have to be, linked to social action (political and civic engagement). There is much research needed to make our communities and our world a better place. But many people do research for practical means, such as to improve intercultural business or education, or because of personal interest in some aspect of communication (e.g., do people in southern France use nonverbal communication differently than those in the north of the country?).

But all research has ethical implications. Aside from standard research ethics of being confidential, not manipulating our participants, and so on, in intercultural research, we must be responsible in how we describe other cultures, making sure that our accounts are true to how people in those cultures will see them (Evanoff, 2015). We should be careful not to look at other cultures as strange, quaint, simplistic, or folkloric (there are power relations involved even when we do research). If we make a claim about a culture or about intercultural communication processes, it should be based on sound research, and not just opinion. And we should consider the consequences of anything we present from our research on those we research.

Differences of focus in culture-and-communication studies

Using the methods mentioned, we might look at different aspects of culture and communication. We often use "intercultural communication" as a broad name for all of these, but there are different types of research and communication that involve culture:

Cultural communication research commonly refers to the study or practice of communication in a single culture. Ethnographers in anthropology have taken such an approach for many years. We might study how people in the context of a sports bar use banter with strangers about the game. **Cross-cultural communication** is a term that never describes interaction—only comparisons of two or more cultures. We might compare how members of different national cultural, ethnic, or age groups demonstrate public displays of affection. That is, we would consider how Turks and Thais differ in displays of affection, but not how they communicate with each other.

This last idea more appropriately describes what we can most precisely call **intercultural communication**—defined in Chapter 1 as communication between people of two different cultures, when the culture impacts the communication enough to make a difference. For example, we might consider interaction between Indian and Arab residents of Dubai in the hotel industry. **Co-cultural communication** refers to communication between people of different groups within a larger, dominant culture (what we used to call subcultures). There is a limitation in the notion of co-culture, however, as often the differences between groups within a nation (say, the Hmong community and White young professionals in the northwestern United States) may be more different than differences between different nations (say, Australia and New Zealand). Finally, we will use **intergroup communication** to refer to those instances where group perception and processes (e.g., prejudices, stereotypes) impact communication, even if there are no real cultural differences (Baldwin & Hunt, 2002).

Some scholars look at culture as it relates to communication that is not exclusively face-to-face, but also mediated. **Developmental communication** refers to communicative efforts to bring more development (e.g., water, farming resources, family planning, economic advancement) to communities (though some prefer to call this **communication for social change** because of the condescending implications of the notion of "development"). **International communication** is a vague term. Some use it interchangeably with intercultural communication, though only when referring to cultures as nations. Others use it to refer to national media systems, and finally, others use the term to refer to those situations in which one is speaking for a nation, such as diplomats. In these cases, cultural and personal factors influence the communication process (see Chapter 3), but so does the fact that the person is representing the interests of a larger group.

Summary

In this chapter, we looked at three separate but related issues. We considered ethics, looking at the tension between ethical relativism and the idea of a meta-ethic, a single ethic used to guide behavior regardless of cultures. While we framed our discussion in terms of interpersonal ethical choices, the field of international media entails similar ethical decisions. The ethical stance people take will influence the way they do research. For example, someone might believe that to do research that does not address or highlight social injustice is to be unethical. Another researcher might believe that if one seeks to uncover the social reality of a group, and that group does not believe that its gender relations are oppressive, then to impose this view on the research is unethical.

Related to ethics, we introduced the notions of civic engagement and political activism. We saw that individuals can be politically or civically engaged regardless of political stance. There is a growing need for colleges and universities, in the development of complete citizens, regardless of the country of the student, to promote civic action in a way appropriate to students' culture, and, in some cases, to encourage both students and faculty to strive for cultural change. But we also saw that even an open embracing in the college classroom of civic and political engagement does not have to influence the student's particular political worldview.

Finally, we saw that both ethics and engagement relate to research. As intercultural thinkers, we will gain knowledge and skills that lead us to understand both our own culture and the cultures of others around us better. This knowledge gives us agency and power, within the constraints of our own cultural, political, and social situations. A growing knowledge of culture may equip us more to make a positive influence on the world in a way that is culturally sensitive. And one way that many may choose to do this (or may be forced to, in the context of an intercultural class) is through conducting cultural, cross-cultural, or intercultural research. Hopefully, the ideas here will help us to be better local and global citizens, wherever we find ourselves.

KEY TERMS

paternalism, 26
morality, 28
ethics, 28
universalist ethical approach, 28
meta-ethic, 28
categorical imperative, 28
particularistic ethical approach, 28
utilitarianism, 28
golden mean, 28
ethical egoism, 28
moral exclusion, 29
cultural relativism, 29
derived ethic, 29
humaneness principle, 30
peace principle, 30
communicative/dialogic ethic, 30
altruism, 31
voluntarism, 31
political engagement/activism, 31
civic engagement, 32
efficacy, 35
ally, 36
ontology, 37
epistemology, 37

axiology, 37
paradigms, 37
social scientific, 37
humanistic, 39
interpretive, 39
etic approach, 39
emic approach, 39
critical, 39
ideology, 40
hegemony, 40
postcolonialism, 40
diaspora, 40
hybridity, 40
agency, 40
postmodernism, 40
cultural communication, 41
cross-cultural communication, 41
intercultural communication, 42
co-cultural communication, 42
intergroup communication, 42
developmental communication, 42
communication for social change, 42
international communication, 42

Discussion questions

1   Some people grow discouraged realizing that there are multiple approaches to ethics and morality and find it easier to give up, choosing simply not to think about it. What are some problems with ignoring or giving up on understanding ethics?

2   Some recent sources have critiqued social involvement across cultural borders. Locate and watch Poverty, Inc., a 2014 documentary on such efforts (povertyinc.org) or locate similar texts. Discuss with your classmates, friends, or family, ways that we can "help" across cultural or group lines without "hurting."

3   Writers have tried to make a distinction between civic and political engagement (activism). To what degree do you feel these two can be treated separately? What are the implications, strengths, and limitations of university classes that include a civic or political engagement focus?

4   Imagine a topic for a specific cultural, cross-cultural, or intercultural communication study. What would you want to know? Which method might you choose, and why would it be appropriate for your topic and study goals?

5   Read through the United Nations Universal Declaration of Human Rights (https://www.un.org/en/about-us/universal-declaration-of-human-rights). What are the challenges of creating such a document? In what ways do the rights proclaimed reflect or contradict practices in your culture?

Action Points

1 Look through your local newspaper. Find coverage of a political or social issue. If the article discusses the perspectives of people or organizations involved, see if you can guess what ethical perspective they might be taking. How might a clearer understanding of ethical stances help us as we read about it, or the people in the story as they interact with one another?

2 Consider socially motivated music groups or artists (Greenday, U2, Sting, Nas, Kendrick Lamar, Mary C. Blige, Beyoncé, Talib Kweli, Donald Glover, Petra Glynt, or see this list of socially conscious musicians around the world: https://www.last.fm/tag/socially+conscious/artists) or genres (some rap music). What potential, if any, do you feel this work has for social change?

3 Go to your college's website or visit its student services office. Make a list of all student organizations that are focused in some way on helping others (service organizations) or working for social causes. Which do you find most interesting? Visit a meeting and see what it is about.

4 In groups or pairs, with your instructor's supervision, conduct a small research project in which you either interview or survey people in a group that is involved in the community or about such a group (e.g., you might ask about motivations or the activities of group members, or perceptions of the group by community members). Discuss your findings with the class. What type of knowledge does your study give you? What are some types of knowledge or claims that you could not make from your study?

For more information

Dalton, R. J. (2009). *The good citizen: How a younger generation is reshaping American politics* (rev. ed.). CQ Press.

Fish, S. (2008). *Save the world on your own time.* Oxford University Press.

Fitch, P. (2004). Effects of intercultural service learning on intellectual development and intercultural sensitivity. In M. Welch & S.H. Billig (Eds.), *New approaches to service learning: Research to advance the field* (pp. 107–126). Information Age.

Jacoby, B. (2009). Civic engagement in today's higher education: An overview. In B. Jacoby & Associates (Eds.), *Civic engagement in higher education: Concepts and practices* (pp. 5–30). Jossey-Bass.

Putnam, R. (2000*). Bowling alone: The collapse and revival of American community.* Simon & Schuster.

References

Alternative spring break. (n.d.). *SpringBreak.com.* Accessed July 1, 2022, at https://www.springbreak.com/History/Spring_Break_History_4.html

Althen, G., with Doran A. R., & Szmania, S. J. (2003). *American Ways: A guide for foreigners in the United States* (2nd ed). Intercultural Press.

Bakhtin, M. (1981). *The dialogic imagination: Four essays by M. M. Bakhtin* (M. Holquist, Ed., C. Emerson & M. Holquist, Trans.). University of Texas Press.

Baldwin, J. R., & Hunt, S. K. (2002). Information seeking behavior in intercultural and intergroup communication. *Human Communication Research, 28*(2), 272–286. DOI: 10.1111/j.1468-2958.2002.tb00808.x.

Baldwin, J. R., Ioannidis, I., & Heugel, R. (2018). Ethics, culture, and communication. In J. Nussbaum (Ed.), *Oxford research encyclopedia of communication.* Oxford University Press. http://communication.oxfordre.com/view/10/1093/acrefore/9780190228613.001.0001/acrefore-9780190228613-e-503

Behm-Morawitz, E. (2017). Examining the intersection of race and gender in video game advertising. *Journal of Marketing Communications, 23*(3), 220–239. https://doi.org/10.1080/13527266.2014.914562

Bellah, R. N., Madsen, R., Sullivan, W. M., Swidler, A., & Tipton, S. (1996). *Habits of the heart: Individualism and commitment in American life* (updated ed.). University of California Press.

Best, S., & Kellner, D. (1991). *Postmodern theory: Critical interrogations.* Guilford.

Carbaugh, D., Berry, M., & Nurmikari-Berry, M. (2006). Coding personhood through cultural terms and practices: Silence and quietude as a Finnish "natural way of being". *Journal of Language and Social Psychology, 25*(3), 203–220. https://doi.org/10.1177/0261927X06289422

Charoensap-Kelly, P., Mestayer, C., & Knight, G. B. (2020). Religious talk at work: Religious identity management in the United States Workplace. *Journal of Communication and Religion, 43* (1), 55–74.

Colby, A., Beaumont, E., Ehrlich, T., & Corngold, J. (2007). *Educating for democracy: Preparing undergraduates for responsible political engagement.* Jossey-Bass.

Corbett, S., & Fikkert, B. (2009). *When helping hurts: How to alleviate poverty without hurting the poor and yourself.* Moody Press.

Cross, C. M. (2021). Intergroup dialogue: A pedagogical tool for continuous allyship for Black women. *Women's Studies in Communication, 42*(2),151–155. https://doi.org/10.1080/07491409.2021.1923333

Eby, J. W. (1998). *Why service-learning is bad.* Accessed September 3, 2009, at http://glennblalock.org/~gblalock/glennblalock/wiki/uploads/ACSM1110f09/whySLbad.pdf.

Ethics Unwrapped. (n.d.). McCombs School of Business, University of Texas. Accessed July 2, 2022, at https://ethicsunwrapped.utexas.edu/case-studies.

Evanoff, R. (2015). A communicative approach to intercultural dialogue on ethics. In L. A. Samovar, R. E. Porter, E. R. McDaniel, & C. S. Roy (Eds.), *Intercultural communication: A reader* (14th ed., pp. 417–421). Cengage.

Figueroa-Caballero, A., & Mastro, D. (2019). Does watching this make me feel ashamed or angry? An examination of Latino Americans' responses to immigration coverage. *Journal of Cross-Cultural Psychology, 50*(8), 937–954. https://doi.org/10.1177/0022022119873064

Fish, S. (2008). *Save the world on your own time.* Oxford University Press.

Foucault, M. (1995). *Discipline and punish: The birth of the prison* (A. Sheridan, Trans.). Vintage.

García Canclini, N. (1995). *Hybrid cultures: Strategies for entering and leaving modernity* (C. L. Chiappari & S. L. López, Trans.). University of Minnesota Press.

García, S. B., & Guerra, P. L. (2006). Conceptualizing culture in education: Implications for schooling in a culturally diverse society. In J. R. Baldwin, S. L. Faulkner, M. L. Hecht, & S. L. Lindsley (Eds.), *Redefining culture: Perspectives across the disciplines* (pp. 103–115). Lawrence Erlbaum Associates.

Griffin, E. (2009). *A first look at communication theories* (7th ed.). McGraw-Hill.

Gudykunst, W. B., & Nishida, T. (1989). Theoretical perspectives for studying intercultural communication. In M. K. Asante & W. B. Gudykunst (Eds.), *Handbook of international and intercultural communication* (pp. 17–46). Sage.

Guizzo, F., & Cadinu, M. (2021). Women, not objects: Testing a sensitizing web campaign against female sexual objectification to temper sexual harassment and hostile sexism. *Media Psychology, 24*(4), 509–537. https://doi.org/10.1080/15213269.2020.1756338

Habermas, J. (1998). *Between facts and norms* (W. Rehg, Trans.). MIT Press.

Hall, B. J. (2003). *Among cultures: The challenge of communication* (2nd ed.). Wadsworth.

Hatch, E. (1994). The evaluation of culture. In L. A. Samovar & R. E. Porter (Eds.), *Intercultural communication: A reader* (7th ed., pp. 408–414). Wadsworth.

Hei, K. C. (2009). Moves in refusal: How Malaysians say "no". *Chinese Media Research, 5* (3), 31–44.

Hendry, J. (2013). Short cases in international business ethics. Accessed July 2, 2022, at http://johnhendry.co.uk/wp/wp-content/uploads/2013/05/Short-cases-in-international-business-ethics.pdf

Hunt, S. K., & Woolard, C. E. (2016). Service learning and innovative pedagogies. In S. K. Hunt & C. E. Woolard (Eds.), *Communication and learning* (pp. 527–551). DeGruyter Mouton.

Hyun, Y. (2020). Different cultural conceptualizations underlying intercultural business communication problems between Thais and Koreans. *International Journal of Language & Culture, 7*(2), 215–240. https://doi.org/10.1075/ijolc.18016.hyu

Ito, R., & Bisila, M. (2020). Blond hair, blue eyes, and "bad" Japanese: Representing foreigner stereotypes in Japanese anime. *Language Awareness, 29*(3–4), 286–303. https://doi.org/10.1080/09658416.2020.1786578

Jacoby, B. (2009). Civic engagement in today's higher education. In B. Jacoby & Associates (Eds.), *Civic engagement in higher education: Concepts and practices* (pp. 5–30). Jossey-Bass.

Kale, D. W. (2015). Peace as an ethic for intercultural communication. In L. A. Samovar, R. E. Porter, E. R.

McDaniel, & C. S. Roy (Eds.), *Intercultural communication: A reader* (14th ed., pp. 422–426). Cengage.

Kim, M.-S., Wilson, S. R., Anastasiou, C. A., Oetzel, J., & Lee, H.-R. (2009).The relationship between selfconstruals, perceived face threats, and facework during the pursuit of influence goals. *Journal of International and Intercultural Communication, 2*(4),318–343. DOI: 10.1080/17513050903177326.

Kohls, L. R. (2001). *Learning to think Korean: A guide to living and working in Korea.* Intercultural Press.

Kramarae, C. (1980). *Women and men speaking: Frameworks for analysis.* Newbury House.

Martin, J. N., & Nakayama, T. K. (2002). Ethical issues in intercultural communication. In J. N. Martin, T. K. Nakayama, & L. A. Flores (Eds.), *Readings in intercultural communication* (2nd ed., pp. 363–371). McGraw-Hill.

Metts, S. (2004). Introduction to communication theory. In J. R. Baldwin, S. D. Perry, & M. A. Moffitt (Eds.), *Communication theories for everyday life* (pp. 55–73). Allyn & Bacon.

Miller, K. (2005). *Communication theories: Perspectives, processes, and contexts* (2nd ed.). McGraw-Hill.

Niemi, J. I. (2008). The foundations of Jürgen Habermas's discourse ethics. *The Journal of Value Inquiry, 42*(2), 255–268. https://doi.org/10.1007/s10790-008-9119-7

Not in our town. (n.d.). *Public Broadcasting System.* Accessed September 3, 2009, at http://www.pbs.org/niot/about/index.html

Opotow, S. (1990). Moral exclusion and injustice: An introduction. *Journal of Social Issues, 46*(1), 1–20. DOI: 10.1111/j.1540-4560.1990.tb00268.x.

Potter, W. J. (1996). *An analysis of thinking and research about qualitative methods.* Lawrence Erlbaum Associates.

Rogers, J., & Westheimer, J. (2017). Teaching about economic inequality in a diverse democracy: Politics, ideology, and difference. *Political Science & Politics, 50*(4), 1049–1055. https://doi.org/10.1017/S1049096517001287

Remland, M. S., Jones, T. S., & Brinkman, H. (1995).Interpersonal distance, body orientation, and touch: Effects of culture, gender, and age. *The Journal of Social Psychology, 135*(3), 281–297. DOI: 10.1080/00224545.1995.9713958.

Rosenau, P. M. (1992). *Post-modernism and the social sciences: Insights, inroads, and intrusions.* Princeton University Press.

Schlachter, L. (2021). *Key findings from the 2109 current population survey: Civic engagement and volunteering supplement.* AmeriCorps, Office of Research and Evaluation.

Shome, R., & Hedge, R. S. (2002). Postcolonial approaches to communication: Charting the terrain, engaging the intersections. *Communication Theory, 12*(3), 249–270. DOI: 10.1111/j.1468-2885.2002.tb00269.x.

Shuter, R. (2000). Ethics, culture, and communication: An intercultural perspective. In L. A. Samovar & R. E. Porter (Eds.), *Intercultural communication: A reader* (9th ed., pp. 443–450). Wadsworth.

Three jailed in Bangladesh over crash that sparked mass protests. (2019). *BBC.* Accessed July 2, 2022, at https://www.bbc.com/news/world-asia-50622057

Ting-Toomey, S. (1999). *Communicating across cultures.* Guilford.

United Nations. (n.d.). *Universal Declaration of Human Rights,* Article 1. Accessed July 5, 2022, at http://www.un.org/en/documents/udhr

van Dijk, T. A. (1998). *Ideology: A multidisciplinary approach.* Sage.

Welch, M. (2009). Moving from service-learning to civic engagement. In B. Jacoby (Ed.), *Civic engagement in higher education: Concepts and practices* (pp. 174-195). Jossey-Bass.

What is alternative spring break? (n.d.). *Habitat for Humanity.* Accessed July 1, 2022, at https://www.habitat.org/stories/what-is-alternative-spring-break#:~:text=More%20than%2010%2C000%20high%20school,Habitat%20for%20Humanity%20each%20year

Wines, W. A., & Napier, N. K. (1992). Toward an understanding of cross-cultural ethics: A tentative model. *Journal of Business Ethics, 11*(11), 831–841. DOI: 10.1007/BF00872361.

Zompetti, J. P. (2006). Embracing a critical communication pedagogy: A radical examination of the common communication course. *Radical Pedagogy, 8.* Accessed February 14, 2013, at http://radicalpedagogy.icaap.org/content/issue8_2.

Zompetti, J. P. (2012). The cultural and communicative dynamics of capital: Gramsci and the impetus for social action. *Culture, Theory and Critique, 53*(3), 365–382. DOI: 10.1080/14735784.2012.721628.

Chapter 3

Origins: How can I talk about culture?

Chapter objectives

After this chapter, you should be able to:

→ Compare two different models for how to understand communication and meaning

→ Explain some of the debates concerning the definition of communication

→ Describe different views of the relationship between culture and communication

→ Provide three competing views of how one could define culture

→ List some of the elements that might influence an interaction with someone from another culture or group, applying the model of communication provided in this chapter

eople from one culture, group, or nation sometimes call another group "uncultured." Professors and concerned citizens raise concerns about "culture wars" in different countries. Organizations give training in "cultural sensitivity." Travelers abroad might suffer "culture shock," and some people say there is a "culture clash" between the younger and older generations (Figure 3.1). We see the word "culture" used in many different and sometimes contradictory ways by people in their everyday lives and by researchers from different fields.

These uses of the term culture highlight several issues that are central to our study of culture and communication. First, we must consider what culture even means. In the 19th century, authors like Matthew Arnold (1882/1971, p. 36) defined culture as "a study in perfection." Although few scholars today hold such a definition, it did lead to a commonly used distinction between **high culture**, referring to activities and expressions that represented what people believed to be moral and intellectual refinement (opera, theater, museums), as opposed to **low, or popular culture**, which included the everyday activities and expressions of people. Another issue is whether, just by belonging to a particular racial, age, sex, national or other group, one can be said to have the "culture" of that group. Even if nations should not be considered as cultures, as we suggested in Chapter 1, people debate how large or small a group can be considered a culture—from a couple to an organization to a region of the world.

This chapter introduces possible ways to define culture, some of the building blocks and aspects of culture, and, finally, a model to help us understand intercultural or intergroup communication. But in order even to get to this point, we should first pause to consider the nature of communication itself.

Figure 3.1 Intergenerational communication. Does just being in a different age bracket or cohort (Generation Y, Baby Boomer, etc.) automatically mean that we speak from different "cultures"? Source: Anna Peisl/Corbis.

The relationship between communication and culture: How do they inform each other?

Edward T. Hall (1959, p. 191) said, "Culture is communication, and communication is culture." That is not to say the two are equal, but rather that there is a close connection between communication and culture. If you are studying intercultural communication as part of a degree in some area of communication, you may already have encountered some sort of definition of communication, such as that communication is the transfer of meaning between a sender and a receiver. However, there is much debate as to whether something is or is not communication.

Defining communication

Katherine Miller (2005) summarizes the debate surrounding the notion of communication. She says most scholars agree that we should refer to communication as a process, rather than simply as a single message. We can think of a **message** as a set of symbols—words, sounds, or images—placed together to represent some meaning. While a message might transfer an idea from one person to another, that transfer exists in an ongoing set of messages and ongoing relationships. The concept of **process** refers not just to the message itself, but to how it is intended, sent, received, and interpreted. For example, one standard model of communication (Shannon & Weaver, 1949/1998) describes communication as a message produced intentionally by a source (**sender**) and encoded by a **transmitter**; this made sense as one of the originators of the model was in telecommunications and imagined signals going through wires. The encoded message, now a signal, traveled through a **channel** and was decoded by a **receiver**, so that a message would arrive at a destination. **Noise** can interfere with the passing of the message through the channel (see Figure 3.2).

Such a model applies, for example, to a video-chat discussion between Christelle, a French student, and Guillermo, a friend she has made in Argentina. The Argentinian does not really hear her voice, but sound waves coming through cyberspace, and "noise" can be interference in the transmission, a poor Internet connection, or laughter in the Internet café where she is typing. In face-to-face communication, Christelle's voice and gestures become the transmitter, as she translates her ideas into a message. The channel is airwaves and the receiver, her friends' ears and eyes. In modern applications, noise can be physical or technological, such as whether the room is too cold or you have a poor connection, or it can be psychological, such as if you are bored or hungry.

Figure 3.2 Shannon and Weaver's model of communication is commonly used to explain the communication process.
Source: © Shannon, C., & Weaver, W. 1949/1964. The Mathematical Theory of Communication. Reproduced with permission of the University of Illinois Press.

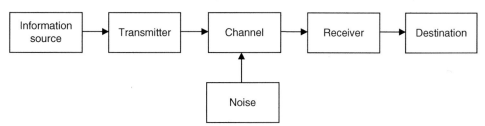

Culture and language differences are a type of noise. If Christelle wants her message to be better understood, she could give the message at a different time, build some (but not too much) repetition into her message, or use more than one channel, like verbal and visual symbols. The partners could decrease cultural noise by finding out more about the others' cultural ways of speaking.

Some suggest that this model is too linear and that, especially in face-to-face communication, both parties send and receive messages at the same time. The idea of **feedback** in the model addresses this criticism to some degree. That is, the receiver later, or even at the same time, gives some verbal or nonverbal response to the sender. Here, we find a second area of agreement regarding the definition of communication, that communication is **transactional**. Communication involves give and take between two or more people, not just of message exchange, but of mutual influence: communicators influence each other, even if they are not aware of the influences. A third area of agreement is that communication is **symbolic**—communicators use words (verbal or printed); images such as photographs or emoticons; sounds such as sighs, grunts, or laughter; and nonverbal behaviors such as a wave of the hand or a wink, to represent something else.

This symbolic focus leads to a view of commuication as meaning-making as it deals with the meaning of words. The symbolic nature of communication shows us that breakdowns in communication are based not only on psychological or physical noise but also on meaning. The Ogden-Richards Triangle of Meaning (Ogden & Richards, 1923/1969) (Figure 3.3) suggests that we connect the words of people in our environment with the reality we experience. For example, we see a little furry animal, and someone says "guinea pig." This links the **reality**, the actual object in our environment, with a **symbol**, a sound or visual representation of the reality. Later, when someone uses the word or image, we sort through the **references**, or thought images in our mind, for the one that links to the symbol we originally heard in regard to that object or action. This is important in cultural communication. First, we realize that the same symbol—"guinea pig"—can be associated with different cultural realities. In each culture, if someone uses the symbol, it links directly to the thought, and if someone sees the object, it links to the thought. But the link between the symbol and what it represents is not exact. A symbol means something

Figure 3.3 Ogden & Richards' Triangle of Meaning: People from different cultures—or even the same family—will have differences in meaning for a word, due to different experiences with the word.
Source: Adapted from Ogden et.al., 1923/1969/The PhilPapers Foundation.

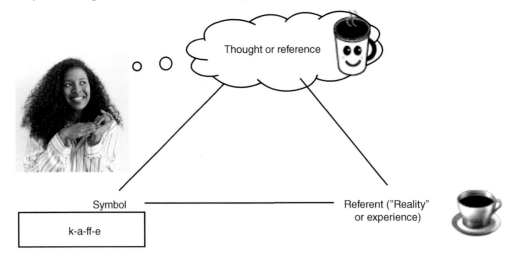

Thought or reference

Symbol

k-a-ff-e

Referent ("Reality" or experience)

different to each person, as no two people have the same experience with an object or with the symbol. One reader might think of a "guinea pig" as a furry pet she had as a child, but a reader in a different culture might think of an animal used in healing rituals or as a tasty snack. The slippery notion of word meaning becomes much more important, however, when we talk about things such as "friendship," "democracy," "freedom," or "sickness" and mistakenly think that our definition is the "real" definition of words that mean different things in different cultures.

What do you think? When people from different cultures work together, there are often different time expectations. One person might want to follow "clock time;" another might want to work out an argument until it is completed, even if it means running late for another appointment. To what degree do you think organizations should make clear expectations for things like time orientations, on which multicultural employees differ?

Communication researchers have debated whether a "sender" must intend some meaning for communication to occur, or whether simply giving meaning to a behavior is communication. While we should study how people from different cultural groups create messages intentionally, it is also important to consider unintentional effects of our messages. For that reason, we consider **communication** to be the process of behaving and interpreting behavior (verbal, nonverbal, mediated) between people.

The relationship between communication and culture

The notion that communication is transactional, which includes the idea that communicators affect each other, leads us to a final consideration regarding communication, and that is its relationship to culture. One possible relationship is that culture is a variable that influences communication. In this view, "culture" or some aspect of identity (such as biological sex, age, or ethnicity) characterizes a group. If this is true, then we will make predictions about people based on culture. For example, Geert Hofstede (2009) argues that people in Austria more often value equality and minimize status, whereas more people in Singapore see status differences as important for society (see Chapter 4). Others have studied how people of different sexes, ages, or ethnicities might differ in terms of communication *within* a single nation, treating sex, race, or age as a variable.

A different view of culture states that people of a particular culture or identity group create values, beliefs, and norms of behavior through communication. This **constitutive approach** says that we socially create meanings and culture (Berger & Luckmann, 1966): Mahatma Gandhi and those who struggled with him reconstructed not only the politics but the self-definition of India. Sandra Metts (2004) suggests that communication both represents and constitutes reality. That is, we can use communication to describe things, much like the semantic triangle in Figure 3.3. But at the same time, cultures are in a constant process of change, some deliberate and some accidental, through the transactional communication of their members. If we use this approach, we would not ask how culture influences people to act, but how groups (regardless of national borders) create "cultures" through their interaction—face-to-face and mediated—with each other.

It might be that even a view that culture and communication change each other through time is too simple. So, there is a third approach—that the social construction of culture is an active process in which groups, with more or less awareness, struggle with one another. Cultural change or

Break it down

The idea that that cultures continue to change and evolve through their communication is useful for civic engagement. We can see how organizational, family, or religious cultures change through time. While outside influences such as natural disasters or epidemics may constrain this change, ultimately, it is how people communicate about these things that leads to change. Think about a culture or identity group to which you belong. Think about the strengths and limitations of some aspect of that group. Make a list of potential actions that individuals or groups could pursue to bring a cultural shift in a direction that is more wholesome or effective for a greater number of members of the culture.

stability is not simply a process of communication, but of intergroup striving—sometimes deliberate and sometimes not—through communication, law, policy, and other efforts, to make a particular cultural view dominant. In sum, the three views of relationship between communication and culture—culture as variable predicting communication; culture as created through ongoing communication; and culture and its creation serving certain power interests—correspond to the scientific, humanistic, and critical views of research (see Chapter 2).

Defining culture: How can we define culture—and what are the implications of our definition?

Traditional definitions of culture

The competing views of the relationship between culture and communication suggest that any definition of culture will represent certain research and theoretical perspectives. Researchers at different times have analyzed the variety of definitions of culture (Baldwin et al., 2006; Kroeber & Kluckhohn, 1952). In contrast to the early definition of culture as moral or intellectual evidence, noted at the beginning of this chapter, today we often treat culture as *a group of people*. We might talk about the Inuit culture of Canada and the United States, or the Ainu of Hokkaido, Japan, thinking not of beliefs or values, but of "the people who share culture" (Winkelman, 1993, p. 86).

Others treat culture as a *structure*: a set of things that exist in a system or pattern, related to each other. This might be a system of meanings—values, norms, and beliefs (e.g., Keesing, 1981) or a whole "way of life" (Williams, 1981, p. 43). Some scholars, including communication scholars, have treated culture as a system of symbols and meanings (Geertz, 1973; Philipsen, 1992). And some place meanings, behaviors, artifacts, and social systems all within a larger set of elements that constitute culture. Culture for these writers is:

> The deposit of knowledge, experience, beliefs, values, attitudes, meanings, hierarchies, religion, notions of time, roles, spatial relations, concepts of the universe, and material objects and possessions acquired by a group of people in the course of generations through individual and group striving. (Samovar & Porter, 2003, p. 8)

Often, these writers focus not only on the structure of culture but also on what it does; that is, on its *function*. It solves some problem for people or helps a group adjust to the stimuli in its environment. We might call this last approach to culture a "suitcase" model of culture, as it treats culture like something that a family, organization, or other group has and passes on to others.

Newer approaches: Culture as fluid, as power, and as discourse

Recent writers have challenged this suitcase model, treating culture with the constitutive view described above. They see cultures as *always in process*–as "variable, open, and dynamic systems, and not as uniform, total, or totalizing entities" (Markus et al., 1996, p. 863). Culture is like a "verb" (Street, 1993)—active and always changing. It both changes and is changed by the messages we create (Figure 3.4).

"Critical" scholars (see Chapter 2) describe culture as a "contested zone in which different groups struggle to define issues in their own interests," with different groups having unequal access to the resources to get their message out to public forums (Moon, 2002, p. 16). In any culture, there is a way of thinking or acting held by most people, but there are also other groups who hold and promote different ways of thinking or acting. Robert Holland (2006) sees the promotion of the idea of a uniform culture (e.g., the "values" that reflect Australia) are created through discourses that are "related to establishment and maintenance, respectively, of political power" (p. 42). This "permits a sense of community within a highly diverse population, while disguising the assumptions underlying its own power" (p. 43). Kent Ono (2010) suggests that seeing culture only as neutrally evolving hides from our understanding the forces that seek to shape it.

Finally, other writers take a more postmodern view, not looking for what makes a group homogenous; instead, they analyze how different sets of ideas compete for attention, such as how different groups in U.S. American society vie to define the meaning of "family" or how there

Figure 3.4 Some views of culture focus on how ongoing communication is constantly creating and recreating your organizational culture. In what ways have the organizations (school, job, social organizations, etc.) changed even over the last five years? Source: https:// amtrustfinancial.com/blog/ small-business/ what-employers-should-know- face-masks

are different ideologies of what it means to be "Black" in the United States. Ramona Hosu (2021) suggests that groups create a "culture" out of a set of **discourses**—practices, messages, and concepts linked together to portray a particular idea. Groups engage "culture" as a *site of struggle*, seeking to make their definition of the group's culture "dominant" over those of other groups. Postmodernists "recognize a radical plurality of general cultural principles and lifestyles within contemporary societies" (Rathje, 2009, p. 36)

What do you think? Think about the culture of your own group (from organization to nation—you decide!), especially if there is some conflict going on in the culture (e.g., new views of how the organization should operate; struggles around new views of the role of men and women in a religious organization). What are dominant cultural premises, ways of action, or meanings? What are some that are "residual" or emerging? In changing cultures, which definition(s) do you find most helpful and why?

It is important how we think and talk about culture or other identities such as sex/gender, race sexual orientation, or age. Much traditional intercultural research has treated and sometimes still treats cultures, sexes, or racial groups as "variables" and tries to describe or predict differences between these groups. This research is useful, as it does provide some general guidelines for us as we travel across national boundaries; but it hides the fact that even within the city of Athens, Greece—or at your college or university—we expect to find several (or many) different cultures. Definitions that focus on the dynamic nature of culture are helpful for they slow down our tendency to think of cultures as unchanging. We often read books or see movies that describe a particular culture, but people from that culture might tell us that it really doesn't represent what their culture is like today. Religious cultures, organizational cultures, and neighborhood cultures are always changing. A critical approach might show how forces actively seek to change cultures to have a more environmental focus, through things such as political lobbying, grassroots campaigns, or online debate, while others offer opposing understandings of things such as global climate change, and environmental issues frequently get mired down in political debates. In a similar way, if we look at growing individualism in Western (and other) cultures, we see that advertisers seek to promote and define that individualism in such a way that we define ourselves by purchasing consumer goods. Cultural notions of beauty support a multibillion-dollar cosmetic industry in the United States and around the world.

Each view of culture has merits. Some research suggests national cultural regularities, such as that, on the average, Russians will likely treat humor differently than Australian Aboriginals. Thus, social scientific research to understand cultures has an important place, especially as we develop organizational, local, and national policy. But we need a view of culture that both sees culture beyond national boundaries and admits its shifting nature. The politics of cultural change are important to admit, and people who hold the more political (critical) definitions of culture usually do not accept the traditional notions of culture. The critical approach shows how different groups try to shape "culture." But dominating or resisting cultural discourses are not always deliberate. Sometimes we tell jokes, make videos, or use communication patterns that simply pass on ways of thinking. Not all of these will be about one group or idea dominating another.

In the end, it is hard to find a definition of culture that covers all perspectives. We define **culture** in this book as the way of life of a group of people, including symbols, values, behaviors, artifacts, and other shared aspects, that continually evolves as people share messages and is often the result of struggle between different groups who share different perspectives, interests, and power relationships.

Elements and characteristics of culture: What is culture like?

Cultures, whether we think of them as a system of elements or as a process of struggle between groups, are made up of certain components and act in certain ways. If someone asked us simply to "describe our culture," we might have difficulty, as culture seems formless and hard to get a hold of. It would be like trying to carry all of our books, pens, and papers to school, but without having a bag of some sort to carry them in! However, a list of aspects of culture gives us a way to organize our thoughts about culture. In this section, we describe elements of culture and then describe what it is like. The elements constitute or make up a culture—its parts, and the characteristics are how it operates, much like the wheels, frame, and cables are parts of a bicycle, but the way they work together to take us from one place to another describe how the bicycle functions.

Elements of culture

Culture consists of a variety of concepts, behaviors, artifacts, and systems. The concepts include things like **values** (ideals or priorities a culture holds to be important), **beliefs** (ideas about the nature of things, with **world view** pertaining to beliefs specifically about humans and their role or place in the cosmos), and **rules**, **norms**, and **mores** (expectations for how one should act in certain situations, with the norms pertaining to whether those expectations have beliefs about the morality of an action and mores being strong enough to bring some social sanction if one does not follow them) (see Chapter 4). In many parts of Brazil, family and time with friends are especially important, and it is important to show hospitality to them (values); and people speak of the future (the "future subjunctive") in a way that suggests a belief in God or in an unpredictable nature of life that may permeate everyday thinking more than in many Western cultures (world view).

Actual behaviors follow these mental patterns (rules, norms, etc.) to a greater or lesser degree. Behaviors may be work-related (functional) rather than symbolic (sending or having meaning for others) and thus not fully part of the communication system. One might take the bus in the big city, simply because it is the only transportation one might have available. Or behaviors can be symbolic—representing some meaning for either the sender or receiver. A complicated class of behaviors and meanings is the **communication system** of a culture—the set of signs and symbols one uses to transfer ideas, emotions, or impressions to others. These include *verbal behaviors*, such as the carrying on of conversation; *nonverbal behaviors*, including everything from how close one stands to whether one has tattoos and facial piercings; *paraverbal behaviors*, which include sounds (laughter, sighs), and sounds of speech that are not words themselves (rate of speech, accent/pronunciation, pauses, intonation); and *mediated messages*, including those created through art, music, mass media, social media, or other mediated forms. (We talk about messages in Chapters 7–11). Language brings together elements of both thought and behavior. Concepts, behavior, and artifacts usually work together, such as the example of money. Money is an artifact with meaning, but we also have cultural ideas about how it should be used, which lead to different spending and saving behaviors in different cultures.

In the Brazilian example, there are many functional behaviors that are just the carrying on of life. In the Amazon city of Manaus, many people take two or three showers a day. However, actions reflect cultural concepts, such as values. It is also polite to offer guests a brief shower before visiting or eating. When eating at someone's house, the host may put a lot of food on the guest's plate, with the idea that it should be more than enough. The guest should show that it is more than enough by leaving some on the plate (behavior reflecting hospitality and connection). People use the *jeito brasileiro*—the "Brazilian way"—building interpersonal connections to cut through the bureaucracy of systems or to help others in a country of social asymmetry (Trigueiro, 2009). And, to reflect a view of the divine in everyday life, many people still say, "*se Deus quiser*" (God willing), when talking about plans for the future.

All of these aspects fit within various **social systems** of culture. Sociologists and anthropologists describe several such systems—economic, educational, family, legal, political, leisure, and so on. To these, we add media systems. These systems provide a context within which cultural and intercultural communication occurs. Context is also a major influence on communication. Certainly, there is the immediate physical and social context of intercultural or intergroup communication that some authors have described (Gudykunst & Kim, 2003). But if we look at communication between the Rohingya and Myanmar populations (and the nationalists and communists) in Myanmar, the Turks and Kurds in Türkiye, or the different factions in Ethiopia or Yemen, we must consider historical tensions as well as social, political, and economic contexts. Both views of context—environmental and social—are important, because relational, historical, and economical contexts, including contexts of warmth or hostility, advantage or disadvantage, influence our communication.

Characteristics of culture

Several authors have outlined some of the ways culture functions and some of the main characteristics of culture (e.g., Brislin, 2006; Condon & LaBrack, 2015; Samovar & Porter, 2004). These authors make important points about what culture is like that can guide our thinking as we consider different "cultures." We will summarize these, with some points of our own.

Culture exists at different, interlocking levels   We can think of culture as existing at different levels (Kim, 1984; see Figure 3.5). At the largest level are macroregional regions, large areas of the world that share cultural similarities, such as Southeast Asia, Latin America, or the Middle East. Regional or national cultures, such as the Australian Outback, or Chinese culture are at the next level. Many authors in intercultural communication have studied differences

Figure 3.5 Levels of Culture. Young Yun Kim describes several levels at which culture might exist. We have modified her figure to include family cultures, but deleted individual culture, as we feel culture is shared. Source: Kim, 1984/Reproduced with permission from SAGE Publications.

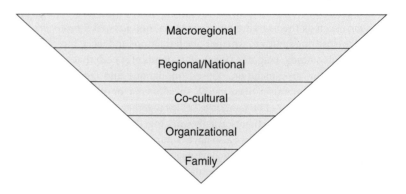

between different national groups. Increasingly, however, researchers are thinking in terms of **co-cultural groups** as cultures as well. These are groups that inhabit a space together, sharing some aspects of a dominant culture, and mixing or blending their cultures to a greater or lesser degree. Smaller cultural groups are organizational cultures, like the airline company Air Emirates, England's Manchester United football club, or the local synagogue, might have their own corporate values (influenced from location to location by regional/national cultures). Kim's smallest level of culture is "individual" culture; but since we believe culture is something that must be shared at some level, we do not see this as a culture. We do believe that there can be family or relational cultures. Carley Dodd and John Baldwin (2002), borrowing from Julia Wood's (1996) idea of relational cultures, suggest that, at a "microcultural" level, even families can have their own expectations, norms, and so on.

These levels inform each other, and co-cultural differences may be greater than national differences. Similar groups, such as farmers in China and in the Pantanal of South America might have more in common which each other than either group has with big-city dwellers in those two regions. The larger group we get, the more cautious we should be with claims. For example, China contains many cultural regions, which, while largely similar, will also pose some differences, and the "Middle East" consists of at least 18 distinct nations, each with various "cultures" within it, and characterized by a variety of languages, religions, and ethnic backgrounds, often within each nation.

Culture is shared   One thing that we determined in our analysis of 313 definitions of culture (Baldwin et al., 2006) is that most authors treat culture as something that is shared—with *someone*. Thus, we can speak of relational cultures—couples, families, or groups of friends—who have their own rituals, understandings, symbols and values, or organizational cultures or city cultures. Where authors disagree is *what part of what is shared* is "culture." There is, as noted above, growing disagreement over the idea that any nation, as a whole, can deeply "share" certain characteristics. Some have critiqued the very notion that there is anything that cultures "share," but they seem to be critiquing the idea when "culture" is applied to a nation (e.g., Morris, 2014). Instead, following the postmodern approach that sees fragmentation within any culture, some argue that the notion of national cultural uniformity is an artifact of the past (Rathje, 2009). It may be, as noted above, that such attempts to frame a national definition of a culture serve those whose power interests are best served by such definitions.

Complicating this notion of the sharedness of a (national) culture is that each of us belongs to multiple, overlapping cultures or groups (Hecht et al., 2005), leading French sociologist Marcel Maffesoli (1996) to reject the concept of a mass society and introduce the idea of **neo-tribes**—groups with shared values and behaviors ("cultures") that surround interest groups, such as fandoms, people with particular hobbies like Dungeons & Dragons or *World of Warcraft* (WOWheads), or interests, such as skateboarding "culture," or sports cultures. People might step in and out of these cultures into the dominant (though perhaps still not "national") cultures where they live the main part of their lives.

Culture is learned and transmitted   As we noted earlier, culture is learned and passed on, either through the generations, or, in younger organizational cultures, through the years. People who study culture note how we learn culture—it is not something that we are born with. We might mistakenly think that because someone is from such-and-such culture, they are naturally aggressive and should be able to hold their alcohol. Even if there is a genetic component to many such traits, behaviors are learned culturally. We learn culture through things such as cultural sayings or proverbs, art, and mass media. We also learn culture from our family, friends, schools, churches, and other social institutions. The process of learning one's own culture is **enculturation**—the process by which people learn their culture of origin. If someone travels to another culture, that person goes through **acculturation**, the process of learning another culture, and **deculturation**, the unlearning of one's own culture (Kim, 2005). We will say more about these processes in Chapter 12.

What do you think? One way to get a glimpse into a culture or co-culture is to look at the proverbs ("A penny saved is a penny earned"; "cleanliness is next to godliness") or sayings ("Look out for number one"). Here are a few examples from Gerd de Ley's (2019) collection of proverbs from around the world:

- It is cruelty to the innocent not to punish the guilty. (Syria)
- If a flea had money, it would buy it's own dog. (Jamaica)
- He who chatters with you will chatter about you. (Egypt)
- What a man says drunk, he has thought sober. (Flanders)
- Those sitting above can easily spit on those below. (Ukraine)

Alone or with a classmate, come up with list of as many cultural sayings as you can think of from your culture (or compare sayings between your cultures). What underlying cultural values do your sayings reflect?

Cultures change and stay the same   Samovar and Porter (2004) note that all cultures are dynamic; that is, they are always changing. They outline three means of change: **invention** or **innovation**, where someone within a culture derives or creates a new artifact (like a cell phone), a new behavioral practice (like text-messaging someone), or a new idea (like communism), which, in turn, changes that culture. Cultures also change through **diffusion**, or the spread of artifacts, behaviors, and ideas across a group or culture or between groups or cultures. Thus, as communism spread from its early roots in the writings of a German philosopher (Marx) to Russia, China, Cuba, and other countries, it "diffused." Environmentalism, feminism, and ideas of civic engagement have spread from culture to culture. Scholars study the spread of the cell phone through Amazonian forest or Gobi desert cultures, and study ways to get a culture with a high HIV + population, as a culture, to adopt safer sex. Finally, cultures can change through **cultural calamity**, a seismic event, often beyond the control of people in the culture, that shapes nearly every aspect of culture. The 2004 Indian Ocean tsunami, the AIDS crisis, and the 9–11 attack on the World Trade Center and Washington, D.C. could be such calamities. A more recent world calamity has been the COVID-19 epidemic, which, according to the WHO Coronavirus dashboard (2022), has killed over 6 million people worldwide (at the writing of this paragraph). Beyond sudden changes through calamity, cultures are changed and change their physical, political, and social environments (e.g., geography, the creation of urban settings and infrastructure). Andean native tribes, like the Aymara, will have cultural aspects that fit the mountain climate, but cultures can also be impacted by the rise of a hardline dictator or endemic intergroup conflict; still, even between and among these groups, we expect nuances of regional and personal similarities and differences. Whereas scholars traditionally thought that some cultures valued stability (and tradition) and others, change, Martin and Nakayama (1999) suggest that, in all cultures, change, and stability—like difference and similarity—wrestle together in tension.

Co-cultures in contact with dominant cultures may change through a process called accul-turation. Different from our first use of the word–how individuals adapt to a new culture–accul-turation here refers to the changing of one group in extensive contact with a group in which it is immersed, such as the Filipino community in Hong Kong or the generations of South Asians in Caribbean countries. This opposes the idea of **assimilation,** by which a co-cultural group (or members of the group) adopts the host culture (see Chapter 12). **Hybridity** refers to the cultural blending between two cultures in contact. This can be in the form of a language that combines elements of two languages (see Chapter 7), new art or music styles (K-pop, or Korean-pop music), or behaviors (using traditional medicine while one also sees a doctor) (Ashcroft et al., 2007). Postcolonial writers such as Jolanta Drzewiecka and Rona Halualani (2002) argue that in hybridity, elements are not blended evenly and what is blended is influenced by power inequali-ties between groups.

What do you think? Many cities have groups that have moved in large numbers from a single homeland to a variety of locations (a **diaspora**). There might be a blend of cultural practices, values, or world views as the two groups live side by side (hybridity). Consider the particular blend of peoples. Consider a major city near you. Describe the elements of each culture that are adopted or considered valid by the other culture. Is the cultural trade bal-anced? What factors do you think might influence whether either group adopts cultural traits of the other? In these cases, is a "melting pot" possible or beneficial? Why or why not?

Culture is closely related to symbolic behavior (communication)

As we noted before, culture is intricately tied to communication. First, communication is the primary means one learns culture. One might also learn through observation. But if culture is the human-made part of our environment (Brislin, 2000), then we would not have any culture if people did not communicate to create it. Thus, culture is created (and changed) through communication.

Culture is mostly invisible to its members

Brislin (2000) notes that most cultural members might have difficulty explaining their culture to others. As we will see in Chapter 4, this is because much of what is actually cultural is beyond our awareness. Our life within our culture is like a fish swimming in water, unaware of what makes up its environment.

Birth and demographics are not culture

We have suggested that culture is shared. This leads to a discussion of differences between terms such as race, ethnicity, and culture, between sex and gender, and so on (see Chapter 5). While each of these identities is cultur-ally constructed (Collier, 2015), some (e.g., ethnicity, gender) are more fluid than others (e.g., race, sex). We suggest, contrary to some authors, that having a particular biological make-up (e.g., sex, race, age, sexual identity, social class, physical disability) does not automatically give one a "culture," but cultures only exist when members of a group (e.g., older adults in a country, people who are hearing impaired) communicate to create a shared sense of identity, values, behavioral expectations, and so on. We see such a difference clearly in the distinction between those who are "deaf" (hard of hearing) and those who see themselves as part of the Deaf community—an identifiable group with expectations for behavior and a sense of group identity.

The aspects of culture are interrelated Samovar and Porter (2004, p. 44) suggest that "culture is an integrated system": If one aspect of a culture changes, that will impact other aspects of the culture. We can see this in the United States after World War II. Many African Americans moved to northern cities to take jobs while White men were at war (though, of course, many African Americans also took part in the war). Beyond the new technology that the war inspired, when the soldiers came home, they took their jobs back. There was a rise in union participation (to remove the Blacks from the jobs so the Whites could have them back), and the women who had also taken jobs were sent back home to take care of children. Black joblessness grew, as did segregation in the urban centers; there was a post-war rise of both Black consciousness and women's rights, and so on.

People may act differently from culture, but that does not mean that culture is not there Gerry Philipsen and his colleagues (2005) point out that every group that has a language "code" also has a unique culture. But these codes of culture are only guidelines, and people have the agency to follow or not follow them. Brislin (2006) states that even though we can think of cultural mistakes cultural members make—exceptions to the cultural rules—the very fact that we realize they are exceptions proves that there is an overall cultural preference for certain attitudes or behaviors. We extend Brislin's idea to argue that these are not always "mistakes and errors," but that many of us seek deliberately to overturn, transgress, or disrupt culture. We saw this in Britain and the United States from the 1970s onward with the Punk Rock movement.

What do you think? Mark Rosenfelder, a "con-langer" (creator of constructed languages and worlds)—"mostly after midnight, with a touch of lime"—has created an extensive web page on aspects of language and culture (http://www.zompist.com). This includes contributed pages on "How to tell if you're American" (or Quebequois, Colombian, Swedish, or Greek). See if there is one on your national culture, and if so, think about the ways it does or does not describe your culture as you see it. Think about ways that you, personally, are like or not like your "culture." If you are different from your culture in some ways, what does that mean for you as you communicate with other people from other places or groups?

People in all cultures are ethnocentric Finally, one thing that all cultures seem to have in common is that they are ethnocentric. **Ethnocentrism** refers to the belief that our culture or group is better than others (see Chapter 6). We may not feel this way intentionally, but because of the invisible nature of culture, we use our cultural framework as a tool with which to judge people from other cultures. We see ethnocentrism in the names we often use for our groups and those of others—Jew and Gentile, Greek and Barbarian. Many names of people groups are translated, literally, "the people" (e.g., Inuit), the "civilized people" (Titska Watich), or the "original people" (Sahnish) (Original Tribal Names of Native North American People, 2007). Maps from different countries often center that country on the map, and some country names, like China's (Figure 3.6) reflect a sense of that country's location in its own esteem of the world. However, we feel that ethnocentrism is not useful for intercultural effectiveness or for moving and adjusting to other cultures and that it is something that we can learn to recognize and even reduce in ourselves and others.

Figure 3.6 The meaning of a name. Zhong-guo is the Chinese name for China (the English name "China" refers back to a specific dynasty of about 2000 years ago). It is comprised of two symbols, meaning "center country." While other countries may not show this centering of themselves in their name, all cultures are to some degree ethnocentric.
Source: Klaus Veitengruber/Adobe Stock.

A model of interaction: How can we best understand intercultural and intergroup communication?

As we have noted, the face-to-face and mediated sharing of messages between people of different cultures is a process of exchange (a transactional process) in which parties bring something to the exchange as producers and consumers of messages. Our question in this section is, with all there is to consider in an intercultural interaction, can we simplify it in such a way that will help us be better communicators? We present here a model of intercultural/intergroup communication. A model of communication is much like a diagram or model of a Vespa, for example, for someone who works on motor scooters. The model should serve to help us make sense of the interaction, but it should also be useful if there is some breakdown in communication to help communicators troubleshoot what has happened in the interaction.

Although race, age, sex, or other group-based identities are not culture, they impact our communication. Awareness of group-based identities represents the first axis of our model, **intergroup communication**. Henri Tajfel and John Turner (1986), in their social identity theory, suggest that we always perceive others on some continuum from interpersonal to intergroup. That is, we see people, at least in part, in terms of the groups to which they belong (see Chapter 6). In the case of war or intergroup conflict, we often see members of the other group only as group members. If we have a spouse or lover, we probably see that person mostly in terms of interpersonal aspects—we interact with them and have expectations of their behavior in terms of our personal knowledge of them. As we get to know people, we move from seeing them only as group members to knowing them more and more as individuals (**interpersonal communication**). Still, at some point, the groups to which we and the others belong are still in the back of our minds.

William Gudykunst and Tae-Sop Lim (1986) modified this to treat interpersonal and intergroup as two separate dimensions (two axes of our model), with both ranging from low to high. Communicators could perceive a given interaction as high in both intercultural and intergroup aspects, such as when two people from different ethnic groups are close friends and understand each other in terms of individual characteristics and validate the groups to which the other belongs. One could be high in intergroup perception but low in interpersonal perception (seeing the person only as a group member), or high only in interpersonal (interacting with the other primarily as an individual). But one could also be low on both factors. This might happen in a culture where role relationships are highly important. We might interact with the cashier at the pharmacy or the person who cleans our building as a "non-person," acting as if they are not even there except to meet functional needs. Here, both group identification and interpersonal perception are low.

Although Gudykunst and Lim's (1986) revision is useful, we add to these two dimensions a third axis—intercultural communication. Since cultures can range from very large ("majority" cultures within nations) to very small (the culture of a gaming group or family), we could say that all communication is inherently intercultural, but then the term "culture" ceases to have any meaning. So, we define **intercultural communication** as communication in which cultural differences are large enough to impact the production or consumption of messages (Collier & Thomas, 1988). Communication can range from very low on the intercultural aspect to extremely high.

In sum, our model contains three axes (Figure 3.7), with three dimensions that can exist from low to high. The three dimensions are unrelated, so we have to imagine the model in three-dimensional space (each dimension is "orthogonal" or perpendicular to the others). The *interpersonal axis* reflects the degree to which we see and treat the person as an individual, and thus relates to similarities or differences in mood, personality, or psychology. This axis is important because it reminds us that, even if we are speaking with (or watching media created by) members of other groups or cultures, we are ultimately speaking with (or watching media created by) *individuals*, who will both reflect and differ from their cultures.

The *intergroup axis* deals with our perception of the other as a group member. It deals with our perceptions of and feelings toward the other group and includes things such as stereotypes and prejudice (see Chapter 6). We might interact with someone in our neighborhood who looks different from us and behave with the assumption that the person is different—even if we are culturally the same.

The third, *intercultural*, axis deals with real differences in things including values and world view, verbal and nonverbal communication, and cultural perceptions of roles and how people should act in those roles (e.g., as teachers and students). If this dimension is high but the intergroup dimension is low, we might talk with someone who looks like us and think that they are from "our" group, but beyond our awareness, cultural differences may impact the conversation. In media and rhetorical communication, the interpersonal dimension is likely low (unless an audience member knows the speaker or media producer), but the cultural dimension may be

Figure 3.7 A three-axis model of communication. Communication with anyone will have three aspects that become more or less important in interaction: perception of the other as an individual, perception of the other as a group member, and real cultural differences.

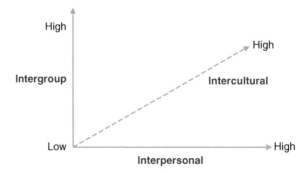

important, and, on the intergroup dimension, someone might discount a speaker or media message simply because of the group that they represent.

All interactions can be thought of in terms of these three dimensions. If Helena, a Peruvian manager from Lima, is talking to Carlos, a representative from his rural district in the south of the country, cultural differences may be present, but not as large as if he were from The Philippines. When they first work together, the interpersonal element will be low but will increase the more direct contact they have. But if Carlos is Asian-Peruvian, each may come to the interaction with stereotypes about the other race (or the other's sex, or the fact that Carlos' rural version of Peruvian Spanish is not the same as Spanish in the big city). In this case, the problem will not be cultural differences—these, in fact, might be minimal—but rather perceived differences. Their interaction would be high in intergroup communication. Likely, all three elements may shift in importance between and even within interactions between the two of them.

Summary

In this chapter we considered the nature of communication and culture and their relationship to each other. Some feel that culture should best be treated as a variable that predicts communication; others see communication as a process that is continually shaping culture. These two views seem to oppose each other, though they do not need to. A constitutive view of communication allows us to consider that communication shapes culture, which in turn shapes communication, and so on. Others see the culture of a group of people as something that people with power (e.g., economic, political) try to shape to their interests. Definitions of culture and communication reflect the same ways of thinking (**paradigms**) that have influenced the fields that look at culture and communication, especially scientific, humanistic, and critical ways of thinking (see Chapter 2). We might think of culture as a suitcase of things (values, beliefs, artifacts, norms) that we pass on to the next generation, as a never-ending process, or as a struggle between groups for power or prestige, and these types of definitions are sometimes contradictory with each other.

We presented some possible elements of culture and finally a model of communication that considers three dimensions—individual, intergroup, and intercultural. This model shows us that we are always communicating with individuals from cultures and groups, not the groups themselves. But it also shows us that as we communicate with someone in another culture, like a Swedish person talking with someone from Tunisia, stereotypes and prejudice, and not only cultural difference, may be present. So also, two people in the same culture might think that there are differences just because the other person looks different or wears a different political or religious name, but in terms of real differences in values, beliefs, and behaviors, the two could be very much the same.

How we think about culture is important for civic and political engagement. If we are engaged, our action shapes the cultures with which we interact, or our own culture. Our action or inaction, at a minimum, reproduces and shapes our culture. But some causes in which we are involved also involve us in ideological struggles within our culture. Gun control is currently a controversial issue in the United States. The right to own guns to protect oneself against a tyrannical government is written into the U.S. constitution. But as we get involved to address bullying in schools, to provide support to those who have been at schools where there are shootings, or to advocate for the continued right to own guns in the face of increasing government restrictions on gun ownership, we engage in a debate that shapes culture. After one recent school shooting, there were calls not to make the issue political, though even silence in the face of such issues provides support for whatever the status quo way of thinking is. Increasingly, more and more such debates are framed in terms of "culture" or group identities—as "culture wars."

The way we think about culture and cultures will shape the way we describe other cultures and groups and the way we work and interact with people from those cultures and groups, in and out of civic engagement efforts. Hopefully, a more complex view of culture and its components will help us to interact with people as individuals informed by their cultures, and it will help us celebrate their cultures--and our own--as complex and dynamic.

KEY TERMS

high culture, 48	rule, 55
low/popular culture, 48	norm, 55
message, 49	more, 55
process, 49	communication system, 55
sender, 49	social system, 56
transmitter, 49	co-cultural group, 57
channel, 49	neo-tribe, 57
receiver, 49	enculturation, 58
noise, 49	acculturation, 58
feedback, 50	deculturation, 58
transactional, 50	invention, 58
symbolic, 50	innovation, 58
reality, 50	diffusion, 58
symbol, 50	cultural calamity, 58
references, 50	assimilation, 59
communication, 51	hybridity, 59
constitutive approach, 51	diaspora, 59
discourse, 54	ethnocentrism, 60
culture, 54	intergroup communication, 61
value, 55	interpersonal communication, 61
belief, 55	intercultural communication, 62
world view, 55	paradigm, 63

Discussion questions

1 Describe a traditional fairy tale in your culture. What values, beliefs, or behaviors does it promote? If you could write a new ending to the tale to reflect cultural change, what would you write?

2 Think about an interaction you have recently had with someone from a different group (in terms of age, culture, ethnicity, etc.). Look at the interaction using the model of culture. Which aspects of communication were most relevant in the interaction (personal, cultural, intergroup) and why?

3   Do you feel that different genres of music in your culture reflect different "cultures?" What other aspects of style (clothing, hair, etc.) or use of the music by listeners (e.g., "fan" behavior) might be part of the culture? Find a video or a song from the type of music you like. Analyze the lyrics and style of music to see if you can determine some things about culture at different levels (national, ethnic, music genre). You could apply the same discussion to other co-cultures, such as an online gaming group.

4   COVID-19 may end up being a "cultural calamity" in that it has deep and lasting impacts on different aspects of culture. Consider different components of culture—organizational and educational behaviors, attitudes, beliefs, norms, and so on. What are some possible ways that COVID has impacted a particular culture? How might changes (or resistance to change) be interrelated? Which elements seem to change, and which seem to remain the same (e.g., do some elements hold stable even while behaviors change?)

Action points

1   Find a copy of your local school or community paper or news website and read through the editorial section (paper editorial and letters to the editors)—or compare national news websites. What are the key issues of the day? What conflict or struggle over cultural meanings, values, or practices do these reflect? Which do you feel are the most important, and why?

2   Volunteer to work in a homeless shelter or soup kitchen, hopefully more than once. Before you go, look up the "culture of poverty" on the Internet—don't forget also to look up criticisms of the idea that there is a culture of poverty. Serve, but also observe people around you. Talk to them if you can and get to know them. How are they similar, but also different from one another? Does simply being poor give one certain cultural characteristics, or vice versa?

3   Interview a politician in your city or an administrator in your school about current issues or debates in your community. Write a short paper or blog post or make a video summarizing the issue—what are the sides? How does the notion of culture (or competing cultures) or group identity inform your understanding of the debate?

For more information

Abu-Lughod, L. (1991). Writing against culture. In R. G. Fox (Ed.), *Recapturing anthropology: Working in the present* (pp. 137–162). School of American Research Press.

Baldwin, J. R. (2018). Evolving definitions of culture and intercultural communication for emerging global realities. In W. Jia (Ed.), *Intercultural communication: Adapting to emerging global realities: A reader* (2nd ed., pp. 27–43). Cognella.

Kroeber, A. L., & Kluckhohn, C. (1952). *Culture: A critical view of concepts and definitions.* Harvard University Press.

Shuter, R. (2000). Revisiting the centrality of culture. In J. N. Martin, T. K. Nakayama, & L. A. Flores (Eds.), *Readings in cultural contexts* (pp. 38–48). Mayfield.

References

Arnold, M. (1882/1971). Culture and anarchy: An essay in political and social criticism. In I. Gregor (Ed.), *Culture and anarchy: An essay in political and social criticism* (pp. 1–176). Bobbs-Merril; [Reprint of London: Smith, Elder, & Co., 1882 version].

Ashcroft, B., Griffiths, G., & Tiffin, H. (2007). *Postcolonial studies: The key concepts* (2nd ed.). Routledge.

Baldwin, J. R., Faulkner, S. L., Hecht, M. L., & Lindsley, S. L. (Eds.). (2006). *Redefining culture: Perspectives across the disciplines.* Lawrence Erlbaum.

Berger, P. L., & Luckmann, T. (1966). *The Social construction of reality: A treatise in the sociology of knowledge.* Doubleday.

Brislin, R. W. (2000). *Understanding culture's influence on behavior* (2nd ed.). Harcourt.

Brislin, R. W. (2006). Culture and behavior: An approach taken in psychology and international business. In J. R. Baldwin, S. L. Faulkner, M. L. Hecht, & S. L. Lindsley (Eds.), *Redefining culture: Perspectives across the disciplines* (pp. 83–90). Lawrence Erlbaum Associates.

Collier, M. J. (2015). Cultural identity and intercultural communication. In L. A. Samovar, R. E. Porter, E. R. McDaniel, & C. S. Roy (Eds.), *Intercultural communication: A reader* (14th ed., pp. 53–61). Cengage.

Collier, M. J., & Thomas, M. (1988). Cultural identity: An interpretive perspective. In Y. Y. Kim & W. B. Gudykunst (Eds.), *Theories in intercultural communication* (pp. 99–120). Sage.

Condon, J., & LaBrack, B. (2015). Definition of culture. In J. M. Bennett (Ed.), *The SAGE encyclopedia of intercultural competence* (pp. 192–195). https://doi. org/10.4135/9781483346267.n70

de Ley, G. (2019). *Proverbs from around the world: A collection of timeless wit, saying, & advice.* Hatherleigh Press.

Dodd, C. H., & Baldwin, J. R. (2002). The role of family and macrocultures in intercultural relationships. In J. N. Martin, T. K. Nakayama, & L. A. Flores (Eds.), *Readings in intercultural communication: Experiences and contexts* (2nd ed., pp. 279–288). McGraw Hill.

Drzewiecka, J. A., & Halualani, R. T. (2002). The structural-cultural dialectic of diasporic politics. *Communication Theory, 12*(3), 340–366. DOI: 10.1111/j.1468-2885.2002.tb00273.x

Geertz, C. (1973). *The interpretation of cultures.* Basic Books.

Gudykunst, W. B., & Kim, Y. Y. (2003). *Communicating with strangers: An approach to intercultural communication* (4th ed.). McGraw Hill.

Gudykunst, W. B., & Lim, T. S. (1986). A perspective for the study of intergroup communication. In W. B. Gudykunst (Ed.), *Intergroup communication* (pp. 1–9). Edward Arnold.

Hall, E. T. (1959). *The silent language.* Doubleday.

Hecht, M. L., Warren, J. R., Jung, E., & Krieger, J. L. (2005). A communication theory of identity: Development, theoretical perspective, and future directions. In W. B. Gudykunst (Ed.), *Theorizing about intercultural communication* (pp. 257–278). Sage.

Hofstede, G. (2009) Cultural dimensions. *Itim International.* Accessed March 2, 2011, at http://www. geert-hofstede.com

Holland, R. (2006). (De-)rationalizing the irrational: Discourse as culture/ideology. *Critical Discourse Studies, 3*(1), 37–59. https://doi. org/10.1080/17405900600589366

Hosu, R. (2021). On cultural ideology and discourse: Concepts and theories. *Studia Universitatis Petrus Maior, Philogia, 9,* 282–289.

Keesing, R. M. (1981). Theories of culture. In R. W. Casson (Ed.), *Language, culture, and cognition* (pp. 42–67). Macmillan.

Kim, Y. Y. (1984). Searching for creative integration. In W. B. Gudykunst & Y. Y. Kim (Eds.), *Methods for intercultural communication research* (pp. 13–30). Sage.

Kim, Y. Y. (2005). Adapting to a new culture: An integrative communication theory. In W. B. Gudykunst (Ed.), *Theorizing about intercultural communication* (pp. 375–400). Sage.

Kroeber, A. L., & Kluckhohn, C. (1952). *Culture: A critical view of concepts and definitions.* Harvard University Press.

Maffesoli, M. (1996). *The time of the tribes: The decline of individualism in mass society* (Sage Publications, Trans.). SAGE. (Original work published 1988) https://doi.org/10.4135/9781446222133

Markus, H. R., Kitayama, S., & Heiman, R. J. (1996). Culture and "basic" psychological principles. In E. T. Higgins & A. W. Kruglanski (Eds.), *Social psychology: Handbook of basic principles* (pp. 857–913). Guilford.

Martin, J. N., & Nakayama, T. K. (1999). Thinking dialectically about culture and communication. *Communication Theory, 6*(1), 1–25. DOI: 10.1111/j.1468-2885.1999.tb00160.x

Metts, S. M. (2004). Introduction to communication theory. In J. R. Baldwin, S. D. Perry, & M. A. Moffitt (Eds.), *Communication theories for everyday life* (pp. 3–20). Allyn & Bacon.

Miller, K. (2005). *Communication theories: Perspectives, processes, and contexts* (2nd ed.). McGraw Hill.

Moon, D. G. (2002). Thinking about 'culture' in intercultural communication. In J. N. Martin, T. K. Nakayama, & L. A. Flores (Eds.), *Readings in intercultural communication: Experiences and contexts* (2nd ed., pp. 13–21). McGraw Hill.

Morris, M. W. (2014). Values as the essence of culture: Foundation or fallacy. *Journal of Cross-Cultural Psychology*, 45 (1), 14–24. https://doi.org/10.1177/0022022113513400

Ogden, C. K., & Richards, I. A. (1923/1969). *The meaning of meaning; A study of the influence of language upon thought and of the science of symbolism*. Routledge.

Ono, K. A. (2010). Reflections on "problematizing 'nation' in intercultural communication research. In T. K. Nayakama & R. T. Halualani (Eds.), *The handbook of critical intercultural communication* (pp. 84–97). Wiley-Blackwell.

Original tribal names of Native North American people. (2007). *Native Languages of the Americas*. Accessed March 2, 2011, at http://www.native-languages.org/original.htm

Philipsen, G. (1992). *Speaking culturally: Explorations in social communication*. State University of New York.

Philipsen, G., Couto, L. M., & Covarrubias, P. (2005). Speech codes theory: Restatement, revisions, and response to criticisms. In W. B. Gudykunst (Ed.), *Theorizing about intercultural communication* (pp. 55–68). Sage.

Rathje, S. (2009). The definition of culture: An application-oriented approach. *Interculture Journal:*

Online-Zeitschrift für Interkulturelle Studien. Accessed July 6, 2022, at https://papers.ssrn.com/sol3/papers.cfm?abstract_id=1533439

Samovar, L., & Porter, R. E. (2003). Understanding intercultural communication: An introduction and overview. In L. A. Samovar & R. E. Porter (Eds.), *Intercultural communication: A reader* (10th ed., pp. 6–17). Wadsworth.

Samovar, L., & Porter, R. E. (2004). *Communication between cultures* (5th ed.). Thompson-Wadsworth.

Shannon, C., & Weaver, W. (1949/1998). *The mathematical theory of communication.* University of Illinois Press.

Street, B. V. (1993). Culture is a verb. In D. Graddol, L. Thompson, & M. Byram (Eds.), *Language and culture* (pp. 23–43). BAAL in association with Multilingual Matters.

Tajfel, H., & Turner, J. C. (1986). The social identity theory of intergroup behavior. In S. Worchel & W. G. Austin (Eds.), *Psychology of intergroup relationships* (2nd ed., pp. 7–24). Nelson-Hall.

Trigueiro, C. (2009). *O "jeito" brasileiro: Um fenômeno cultural [The "jeito brasileiro": A cultural phenomenon]. Romance Notes, 49(2)*, 217–227. DOI: 10.1353/rmc.2009.0009

WHO Coronavirus (COVID-19) dashboard. (2022, July 6). *World Health Organization*. Accessed July 7, 2022, at https://covid19.who.int

Williams, R. (1981). The analysis of culture. In T. Bennett, G. Martin, C. Mercer, & J. Woollacott (Eds.), *Culture, ideology and social process: A reader* (pp. 43–52). Open University.

Winkelman, M. (1993). *Ethnic Relations in the U.S.* West.

Wood, J. T. (1996). Communication and relational culture. In K. M. Galvin & P. Cooper (Eds.), *Making connections* (pp. 11–15). Roxbury.

Elements

n the first section of the book, we looked at the foundation of what culture is, why we should study it, and at least one aspect of what should guide all cultural communication—ethics. In this section, we break down three main aspects that impact how we produce and consume messages: the "ideas" prominent within a culture, our view of ourselves (identity), and our attitudes and treatment toward people of other groups. William Gudykunst and Young Yun Kim (2003) argue that these three aspects influence all messages we send and receive, as these, in turn, are influenced by the contexts of the communication.

While some see culture as the whole "way of life" of a group of people (Williams, 1981, p. 43), others feel that culture is really a set of beliefs, values, and expectations for behavior—but not the behaviors or artifacts themselves. Regardless of how we define culture, it makes sense that the ideas of culture—beliefs, values, and norms—are what drive behavior and the creation of texts and artifacts,which, in turn, produce and reproduce the cultural ideas. In Chapter 4, we review these different components and outline some approaches that scholars have used to try to understand specific cultures and to compare cultures with one another or to understand cultures on their own terms.

Chapter 5 turns to issues of identity. We discuss how we see ourselves as individuals and in terms of the groups to which we belong. We consider the ways identities that are important to us shape the way we communicate. Then we turn to considering different identities as these relate to power structures in society, specifically of race and gender. We consider the ways communication, especially media, deprives or mutes the voices of different groups through notions such as symbolic annihilation, Orientalism, and cultural imperialism. Finally, we suggest thoughts on how to become allies with those who are in underrepresented or mistreated groups.

Intercultural Communication for Everyday Life, Second Edition. John R. Baldwin, Alberto González, Nettie Brock, Ming Xie, and Chin-Chung Chao.
© 2024 John Wiley & Sons Ltd. Published 2024 by John Wiley & Sons Ltd.
Companion Website: http://www.wiley.com/go/baldwin2e

How we think about ourselves and our groups is closely tied to how we see others' groups, so in Chapter 6, we address issues of prejudice, tolerance, and appreciation. We introduce a variety of terms related to prejudice, such as ethnocentrism, xenophobia, and heterosexism. Further, we discuss where types of intolerance such as "racism" lie, that is, whether we should think of them only in individual terms of personal attitude or see them in social structures as well. This discussion is important, because if, as the goal of civic engagement of this book implies, we seek to redress or reduce intolerance and act toward appreciation, we need a better understanding of the problem of intolerance. In that way, our solutions will more effectively address the specific forms of intolerance within our societies.

References

Gudykunst, W. B., & Kim, Y. Y. (2003). *Communicating with strangers: An approach to intercultural communication* (4th ed.). McGraw Hill.

Williams, R. (1981). The analysis of culture. In T. Bennett, G. Martin, C. Mercer, & J. Woollacott (Eds.), *Culture, ideology and social process: A reader* (pp. 43–52). Open University.

Chapter 4

Subjective culture: What is the base upon which cultural communication is built?

Chapter objectives

After this chapter, you should be able to:

→ Explain the difference between subjective and objective aspects of culture

→ Differentiate between norms, rules, values, beliefs, mores, taboos, and laws

→ Produce examples of primary dimensions of culture

→ Compare the emic and etic approaches to understanding subjective culture

→ List some strengths and limitations to each approach to understanding culture

Intercultural Communication for Everyday Life, Second Edition. John R. Baldwin, Alberto González, Nettie Brock, Ming Xie, and Chin-Chung Chao.
© 2024 John Wiley & Sons Ltd. Published 2024 by John Wiley & Sons Ltd.
Companion Website: http://www.wiley.com/go/baldwin2e

The Peace Corps, an agency known around the world for sending workers across borders to help other communities, has produced a video of 15 top cultural mistakes that cross-cultural travelers can commit (Peace Corps, n.d). For example, in Denmark, if you are squeezing past people in a row to find a seat, you should face the people you are passing instead of having your back toward them, in contrast to the practice of facing away from people as you step in front of them, as is the case in many cultures. In Colombia, you should not indicate someone's height by showing your hand at a certain level, as this gesture is only used to describe animals. In Romania and other parts of Eastern Europe, it is great to give flowers to a friend—but hand them with the blossoms down and not up, and be sure to give an odd number of flowers on a happy occasion as even numbers are for funerals. And in Sierra Leone, you cannot just say good-bye to your guest at your door. To be culturally appropriate, you should walk your guest part of the way home, "at least to the first bridge" (and, of course, there could be "cultural" differences between specific groups of people *within* each of these nations, as we discuss in Chapter 3).

The Peace Corps video gives useful hints: learn about the culture from books or natives of the culture before traveling; observe other people in the culture; watch for awkward silences; be direct in addressing misunderstandings and polite in asking questions or making apologies for misbehaviors; inform others helpfully if they make a mistake in your culture; laugh about it, if the blunder is not serious. Even though the behaviors listed in the video are about specific cultures, they teach us about behaviors common in other places. Romanian flower rules help us realize that cultures have intricate gift-giving rules. When do you give gifts? Do you open them in front of the giver? How do you wrap or package them? The Sierra Leone practice of walking to the first bridge is similar to customs in other cultures, such as China. If you are traveling abroad, it is helpful to learn about the details of that culture—etiquette, manners, things that might be offensive.

But there is perhaps a more important hint: Learn the underlying values, world view, and beliefs of the cultural system. Each gaffe mentioned above is based on a deeper foundation of meanings. Harry Triandis (2002) compares this aspect of meaning and thought, which he calls **subjective culture**, from **objective culture**, which refers to the artifacts that a culture produces. Aspects of subjective culture—values, beliefs, and world views—form the deep structure of a culture. Although it is important to understand aspects of verbal and nonverbal communication, organizational etiquette, and–beyond communication–social, political, and religious organizations, one thing that helps us best understand other societies is their subjective culture. This forms the foundation upon which all other elements of communication and society are built.

Basic building blocks of culture: What are the most important things to know?

John Condon and Bruce LeBrack (2015) describe several metaphors writers have used to describe culture. People have described culture as a rainbow, an environment, or a "conversation" that one enters into. The "iceberg" metaphor that many have used to describe culture makes culture like an invisible social blueprint that we follow, usually without thinking about it or knowing it is even there (see Figure 4.1). The idea of the metaphor is that what one sees on the surface of culture are things such as literature, music, food, dance, art, and architecture. The "diversity fairs" we see in many communities include music or food from different ethnic or cultural groups.

But there is an invisible part of culture that includes things such as how we raise our children, what makes a logical argument, how and to whom to show status, and what the pace of life is. Since these things are hidden from view, we often assume them to be natural, rather than

Figure 4.1 The iceberg model of culture shows that much of our culture—and that of others—is beyond our awareness.

Source: AFS Orientation Handbook Vol. 4, p. 41. New York: AFS Intercultural Programs Inc., 1984. https://www.worldcat.org/title/afs-orientation-handbook-volume-iv/oclc/13716656.

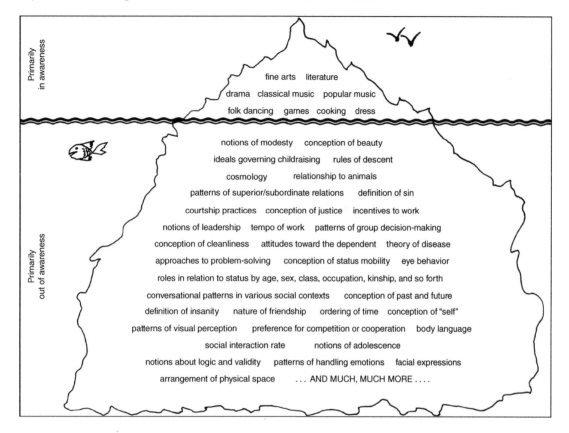

cultural. We think, of course, that everyone knows how to raise children or be a friend—the same way we would! If culture impacts our relationship or communication, it is not likely to be because one of us likes hip hop music and the other, Brazilian *forró*; rather, it is more likely to be over things such as the rules for when to express emotion or what constitutes modesty. Because we are not aware that these unseen things change from culture to culture, we are likely to judge one another negatively when someone does them differently.

Different types of belief form the deep structure of culture. **Beliefs** are assumptions about the nature of something, a thought about the connection between two or more concepts. For example, if you believe that China had printed periodicals and books before 1000 C.E., several hundred years before the Gutenberg Press (Newman, 2019), you would have a belief about printing presses, China, and time periods. Beliefs of different types are interwoven into **belief systems**. Islam, Buddhism, or animism represent such sets of interrelated beliefs. There are more specific types of beliefs within each belief system. For example, religious belief systems contain a **world view**, or beliefs about the connections between humans and the larger elements of the universe. Each system is a set of assumptions or cognitions about things such as the purpose of humans, the nature of deity, and the relative position of humans to nature and the rest of the cosmos.

A **value** is a type of a belief that a thing, idea, or activity is important and should serve as a guide for behavior. For example, the reason for walking a guest part of the way home is so the guest does not have to leave alone. But more than that, the act reflects hospitality toward and connection to others, a core value in some societies. Often, we can express values with single words or phrases, such as honesty, freedom, success, or family. Values are enduring—that is, they do not change easily; and they influence behavior (Rokeach, 1973). Even if surface features of a culture change, values will be much slower to change, like the deep currents of the ocean that sit beneath the changing surface waves. When the majority of members of a cultural group, not just individuals, hold an objective to be important, these become **cultural values**. Finally, **attitudes** describe the way we relate to things, actions, or people. They are more of an emotional (or "affective") reaction to things, influenced by and influencing beliefs, values, and norms.

What do you think? Think about two cultures or co-cultures of which you are a member. For example, if you are a typical college-age student, you might be a member of a late adolescent or young adult culture, but also of a particular national, ethnic, or other culture (e.g., Korean, Latino/a, or Deaf). What are some ways in which the values, world view, beliefs, and attitudes of these two groups are similar or different? How do you find resolution when the values and beliefs of the groups you belong to collide?

Other types of cultural belief involve expectations for behavior. **Rules** are prescriptions for behavior—cultural beliefs about which behaviors are appropriate in certain situations. These refer to things that we can or cannot, should or should not do. For example, in U.S. culture, if professors stand on their head to deliver lectures, they might be weird or out of place, but not necessarily bad people—they are breaking a *rule*. William Gudykunst and Young Yun Kim (2003) define **norms** as expectations for behavior with a moral component. If someone violates a norm, others see the person as bad or immoral. If a teacher lies to give one student privilege over another in grading, the teacher would be seen as violating a norm. If the norm is very strong, with negative social results for violating it, it becomes a **more**. A **taboo** is a cultural more so strong people do not normally even mention it. If a government legalizes what one can or cannot do in terms of behavior, it becomes a **law**. Rules, norms, mores, taboos, and laws are also linked to values, beliefs, and world views.

Values and world views are the bedrock upon which norms and rules, and, in turn, communicative behavior, are built, so we turn now to more detailed consideration of these. Values and world view drive our verbal and communication behavior. At the same time, individuals do not or cannot always act upon their values, beliefs, or world view. Social and structural constraints may work against people's access or ability to enact cultural values or express their beliefs. A fuller understanding of the foundations we present in this chapter would include the situation of people within their social class, ethnic, religious, political and relational group, and other contexts.

We can understand the way the different types of belief relate to each other by considering the cultural notion of beauty. "Beauty" is of high importance (a *value*) in many countries—though some more than others, and people in different cultures may value different types of beauty. The definition of what is "beautiful" reflects a *belief*. What is considered beautiful in terms of weight, the number and location of body piercings, hair styles, and clothing changes through time in a given culture. We

Figure 4.2 Social media selfies reflect our personal beliefs and values, as well as cultural norms. Here, Columbian singer Shakira joins a host of other famous women to post a selfie without make-up to celebrate her 39th birthday. What personal or cultural values do you see in the composition or content of the post (or the fact that people even post selfies).
Source: RAJU SAGI/AGK FIRE INC / https://www.socialnews.xyz/2016/02/03/shakira-celebrates-birthday-with-no-makeup-selfie/ / last accessed January 10, 2023

have beliefs about what tattoos mean and what types of people wear them. A belief that tattoos are "cool" indicates an *attitude* to either like or admire them, or even to get one. But, as with attitudes, beliefs and values about "climate change," "freedom," or "family," forces work to change how we see beauty and who is benefitted by that view of beauty. And we likely "police" who is seen as beautiful (and the consequences of "ugly") in a way that seeks to control or promote different views of group identity. In the end, whether we get tattoos, work out to build our bodies, or cover our skin to keep it pale or to show modesty, our choices will reflect deeper cultural values, like the need to stand out or the need to conform, the need to show social status, or the value of friends (Figure 4.2).

Cultural values: What are some useful frameworks for understanding culture?

Shalom Schwartz (1992), researching values in 20 countries, stated that people in all cultures tend to hold a set of 11 **universal values**. self-direction; stimulation; hedonism; achievement; power; security; conformity; tradition; spirituality; benevolence; and universalism. Schwartz stated that values work together to form a "system of priorities" (p. 143) that guides our actions. He later organized these in terms of three dimensions, answering three social issues, in which people in a culture tended to value one dimension over the other, as these opposed each other (Figure 4.3). The questions involve how people in a culture see boundaries between the self and

Figure 4.3 Schwartz' Universal Values framework.
Source: Schwartz, S. (2006). Used with permission.

the group, how they behave in a way that maintains social order, and how they relate to the natural world (see discussion of world view below).

Milton Rokeach (1973), instead, separated values into two groups—terminal and instrumental values. **Terminal values** represent the end states or desired outcomes of action for individuals. These include things such as a comfortable life, salvation, true friendship, freedom, pleasure, mature love, and self-respect. **Instrumental values** are those characteristics, traits, or "modes of conduct" (p. 7) that people in a culture hold to be important for reaching societal goals—the "means" to the end. They include things such as being polite, cheerful, honest, or courageous. Values intertwine with other values to make "value systems." Researchers have used ideas from Schwartz and Rokeach for years to describe cultural values, with one study (Vauclair et al., 2011) conducting a "meta-analysis" (a study of findings from previous studies) of data from 37 cultures that links the two perspectives. Notably, the study suggests a new value dimension: self- and other-focused. While useful, the value-dimension studies face some limitations. One is that two countries might rank order the values closely (such a 1984 study of of Germany and the United States that found both ranking democracy and true friendship both as higher priority; Reynolds, 1984), while the social understandings of things such as freedom or friendship might vary between the countries. Other authors have challenged specific items, such as Gábor Ittzés et al.'s (2017) study that considered the different dimensions of "religiosity" and found differences on that item between Budapest and the rest of Hungary.

High- and low-context cultures

Edward Hall (1997) proposed high and low context as one dimension by which we can understand cultures. **High-context cultures** are cultures in which meaning tends to be implicit, that is, inside of the communicators—in the background, rules and relationships of the speakers, because they know what to expect based on the circumstance and on role and status relationships. Meaning might be hidden in nuances of word meaning and nonverbal behavior. People in

low-context cultures tend to place more meaning in the "explicit code," that is, in the words themselves, so communicators may be more direct. In this type of culture, people might assume that if a guest needs something, the guest will ask for it (Hall, 1997). People in high-context cultures might seek different sorts of information than low-context cultures when they want to understand someone and might be more likely to ask about your family, university, or home-town (your "context"), where someone from a low-context culture might ask about your personal opinions (Gudykunst & Nishida, 1986). As an example, South Korean culture has the concept of *nunch'i* (Robinson, 2000), in which a host must anticipate the needs of the guest. This reflects a notion common to many high context cultures, in which the guest need not (or should not) voice a request for something ("Hey, can I get a drink of water?") because this would tell the host that they had not met the guest's needs.

While researchers or organizational trainers often speak of low- and high-context cultures as if they existed in a dichotomy, some see cultures on a continuum from very low to very high context. Co-cultures, organizations, or families may also differ in the general level of context people rely on. Some churches might state everything clearly for visitors—now we stand, now we sit, let's say this together; while in others, everyone is just expected to know what to do, with no explicit directions. All cultures have high- and low-context situations, and realistically, individuals are more or less "high context" or even vary in their level of explicitness from context to context. At the same time, there may be cultural preferences toward one mode or the other.

What do you think? Some training organizations use high and low context to describe female-male communication differences in the workplace. In your culture, do you feel that females and males differ in the "context" of their communication? Specifically, do you think males and females differ in how much they look to words and to other aspects for information in interaction? If there are differences, what might be some reasons for those differences?

Hofstede's cultural dimensions

One of the most commonly used frameworks of values across academic disciplines is that developed by Geert Hofstede (1980, 1986), an organizational psychologist from The Netherlands. Hofstede defines a value as a "broad tendency to prefer certain states of affairs over others" (p. 19). In 1980, he published a now-classic work in which he studied employees working from 1967 to 1973 for a large multinational corporation he called HERMES (actually IBM Corporation), collecting initially over 117,000 surveys from 66 nations. Through his survey study, he developed four value dimensions, with each country receiving a score on each dimension; scores are available on his website (Hofstede, 2009). Hofstede sees the impacts of these dimensions, on "general norm[s], family, school, and workplace" (Hofstede & Bond, 1984, p. 37), and "politics and ideas" (Hofstede, 1997, p. 37, 43).

The dimensions   The first dimension, **power distance**, refers to whether people in a culture tend to value status difference and see it as appropriate. As power distance increases, people in a culture—including those of lower status—are more likely to think that it is acceptable that people of different social status (however that is determined) be treated differently (Hofstede & Bond, 1984). In a higher power distance culture, students are more likely to see teachers as experts; there will be a clear hierarchy with deference to superiors in organizations; managers and status elites will expect preferential treatment, and the lower status individuals will feel that this is just and right; governments will more likely be autocratic (e.g., dictator-ships, strong central government); the middle class will be smaller. In low power distance cul-tures, parents and children are more likely to interact like equals (e.g., there will be no "yes, ma'am" or "yes, sir"); bosses will work together with employees to set goals; democracy and majority vote will be common in organizations and society; people will expect equal rights and equal treatment of everyone.

Hofstede (2001) relates the second dimension, **masculinity/femininity**, to male and female emotional rules. People in masculine cultures privilege directness, efficiency, competi-tion, and goal (outcome) orientation; and those in feminine cultures value service, cooperation, modesty, nature, and caring for others. But also, in feminine cultures, there is less sex differen-tiation in tasks—a role fluidity in which men and women share more tasks. In masculine cul-tures, roles are more rigid, with men and women doing separate tasks. A limitation of this dimension is that, since it contains different aspects—directness, task focus, role overlap—a country might seem to be "masculine" in one dimension, but "feminine" in another. Workers in Britain and Italy score considerably higher in masculinity than in Sweden, but they score close to each other. But it is likely that Britain and Italy differ in important ways in gender roles and directness of communication.

The third dimension, **uncertainty avoidance**, pertains to the overall desire for structure and predictability in a culture. In higher uncertainty avoidance cultures, people tend to distrust things or people that violate expectations—what is strange is seen as bad. Countries with lower avoidance of uncertainty, such as Scandinavian countries, are often more flexible in terms of violation of expectations. Strangers might be more welcome, and what is different might actually be seen as good. Uncertainty avoidance (UA) might play out in the classroom in that, in a lower UA culture, a teacher is more likely to say, "I don't know," teachers may seek opinions from par-ents, and classroom learning may be open-ended. In higher UA cultures or situations, students will want more structured learning. Teachers and students may see "truth" as absolute. And children may report lower belief in their ability to accomplish tasks independently (self-efficacy, Hofstede, 2001).

The last dimension, **individualism-collectivism (I/C)**, refers to the links between the per-son and their social network. In more collective societies, people rely more upon social net-works, such as extended family or workplace, to set goals. People make decisions with the group in mind. For example, individuals from Zambia may feel a strong emotional and financial obli-gation not only to nuclear family (father, mother, and children) but to the success of extended family members. In more individualistic cultures, people tend to make decisions based on per-sonal interest and advancement or on the nuclear, rather than extended family. A more individu-alistic culture will probably have more people who change jobs frequently, in terms of how the change addresses personal or nuclear family goals, as opposed to long-term employment (Germany) or even lifetime employment (Japan). Figure 4.4 illustrates where Hofstede's research located several cultures on two of his dimensions. Many researchers see individualism-collectiv-ism as the most important dimension for understanding cultural differences in communication, with some authors, such as cross-cultural psychologist Harry Triandis (1995) and his colleagues (Kim et al., 1994) giving it extensive attention and research. Some see this approach as similar to the GLOBE studies approach by Fons Trompenaars and Charles Hampden-Turner (1998).

Figure 4.4 A comparison of some countries on Hofstede's individualistic/collectivistic and power distance dimensions.
Source: © Geert Hofstede B.V., quoted with permission.

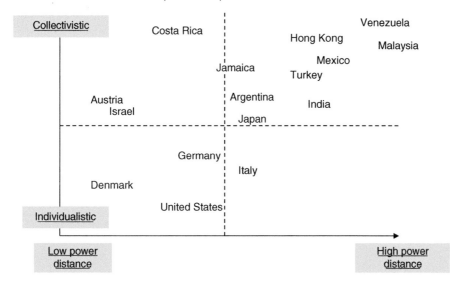

What do you think? Describe a culture that you have visited (or your own), or do a comparison of two cultures in terms of Hofstede's original four dimensions. What behaviors lead you to place the cultures on different places on the dimensions? After you are done, go to Hofstede's website at http://geert-hofstede.com and see how his research places them! (You can compare two specific cultures at https://www.hofstede-insights.com/country-comparison) Do you agree or disagree with his classification? Why or why not?

Critiquing Hofstede's dimensions   Hofstede's value dimensions have received much critical attention in and outside of the communication discipline (Courtright et al., 2011). Cheryl Nakata (2009, p. 3) calls this framework "the dominant cultural paradigm in business studies," with Hofstede among the top-three authors cited in international business. An Internet search of business articles reveals thousands of studies motivated by or using the framework. The framework lists among its strengths the vast database of participants from now over 100 countries and cultures (Hofstede, 2009); the statistical strength of the measure; the simplicity of the framework (Nakata, 2009); and the ability we have to compare national cultures on a specific set of dimensions. The tool is a favorite among those who do organizational training.

One critique is that many scholars treat the dimensions as dichotomies, saying, for example, that cultures are *either* collectivistic or individualistic. In response, Hofstede (1980) emphasized that cultures range in a continuum on any single dimension. If we consider Figure 4.3, we will see that Japan is on the collective side of the average for *all* countries but is much more individualistic than other collectivistic nations. Second, Hofstede suggested that national scores on the dimensions are only average scores. When we speak of cultural differences, say, between Pakistan and Canada, we should recognize that many Pakistanis will score more "individualistic" than some Canadians, and many Canadians will be more "collectivistic" than most Pakistanis.

A second critique is that the number of dimensions is not exhaustive. Michael Bond and his colleagues with the Chinese Culture Connection (1987) introduced **Confucian work dynamism**, which involves respect for tradition, thrift, persistence, and personal steadiness—in essence, a long-term pragmatism that values education and hard work. On Hofstede's (n.d.) "Country Comparison" website, China and other East Asian cultures score high on the dimension he calls **long-term orientation**, whereas many Western cultures score quite low. This is especially surprising, in that the United States, which some authors state places practicality—or pragmatism—among its highest values, leading to a focus on "achievement, action, work, and materialism" (Althen et al., 2003), actually scores quite low on a longer-term pragmatism. This suggests that mainstream U.S. culture, while being practical, prefers short-term solutions, or even "quick fixes." Hofstede (n.d.) later added a sixth dimension, **indulgence-restraint**, with cultures focusing on self-expression and indulging in the moment or seeing life as a duty (rather than "freedom"), related to **propriety**, or engaging in the appropriate behaviors for the situation, context, or relationships. Hofstede (n.d.) now calls the dimensions the "6D Model of National Culture."

Another set of critiques runs deeper to challenge the very idea of making national culture traditions. Some have claimed (and found) that there are other variables that either add to or make better predictions than "national culture" to explain people's behavior, such as economic conditions (Chiang, 2005). Bradley Kirkman and colleagues (2017) suggest other variables, methodological, and other considerations in their 35-year review of work regarding Hofstede's dimensions. And Min-Sum Kim (2005) compares **self-construal**, a psychological notion of how strongly one sees oneself independent from others or connected to others (independent and interdependent self-construals, respectively) to individualism/collectivism. This echoes what scholars and teachers have long said—that *individuals are not cultures*. Thus, just because Cruz is from Guatemala, the country with the lowest individualism score on Hofstede's dimensions, this does not mean they, themself, will reflect collective values. In fact, if they have an "independent" self-construal, they might make quite independent choices.

Finally, as we noted in Chapter 3, many scholars reject the very notion of "national culture." Brendan McSweeney (2002), a strong critic of the dimensions, claims, "Attributing causal power to anything—including 'national culture'—to every level in a society is problematic" (p. 71) and notes how the field of Anthropology has largely abandoned the idea of national culture. Cultures are more dynamic than applying a Hofstede score to a country can capture (Nakata, 2009; Signorini et al., 2009), with some of that change coming through the fluidity and cross-flow of ideas between cultures. This may lead to differences within groups within a culture, such as urban-rural, ethnic co-cultures, or age cohorts. For example, one study of managers among the Nnewi people of Nigeria suggests that participants felt that Nnewi entrepreneurs needed honesty, confidence, and "individual self-help"—that is, individualism (Madichie et al., 2008, p. 292). Younger nationals from the United Arab Emirates are more individualistic than those that are older, though they still value the Islamic work ethic and the use of *wasta*, or interpersonal connection, in the workplace (Whiteoak et al., 2006). Qin Zhang (2007) discusses that Chinese families are evolving and are now just as focused on expressive conversation as American families.

The same strengths and challenges that apply to Hofstede's dimensions may apply to other frameworks that scholars have applied to nations as "cultures," such as the notion of high and low context (described above) or the "value orientations" of Florence Kluckhohn and Fred Strodtbeck (1973), which we describe below under world view.

Culture-specific (emic) approaches

The frameworks above reflect what we call in Chapter 2 an **etic approach**—a set of terms or a theory that researchers develop from outside of any one cultural system, allowing them to compare cultures using the approach. An **emic approach** is quite different, even opposed to, the idea of cultural dimensions—it favors understanding each culture in its own terms (Gudykunst & Nishida, 1989). The first is more preferred by researchers in what we call in Chapter 2 the social scientific approach, and the latter, by those in the humanistic or "interpretive" approach. Scholars from this approach often think that terms universally applied to all cultures, and created from outside of those cultures, hide the nuances and unique elements of each culture. Instead, these authors explain communication behaviors in specific cultures. Clifford Geertz (1973), for example, argues for an "interpretive theory" of culture (p. 3), in which anthropologists travel to cultures and provide rich descriptions of single cultures. The various aspects of a culture—sacred symbols, values, the notions of morality and aesthetics ("ethos"), and the use of symbols, are all intertwined in "webs of meaning," which the researcher unravels. The explanations are not meant to predict anyone's behavior, though the norms, world views, and values *guide* behavior in that cultural members usually tend to follow them.

Robert Bellah and his colleagues (1996) conduct such an analysis of the United States from a sociological perspective. Based on five years of research in four different projects and multiple interviews with more than 200 people across the United States, the authors provide a book-length investigation of individualism in the United States as it relates to American culture. They see everything from governmental systems to romantic feelings and behavior as infused with individualism. Hofstede (1980) listed the United States as the most individualistic of the nations studied; Bellah et al. (1996), in the preface to their revision of their original 1985 study, state boldly: "The consequences of radical individualism are more strikingly evident today than they were even a decade ago" (p. xi), leading, they contend, to increased alienation from others, the "failure of community" (p. xxiii), and a growing loss of "civic membership" in America. Such loss in social capital in a country has the possibility to limit students' engagement in civic or political engagement. This conclusion echoes what Robert Putnam, (2000) in his book *Bowling Alone*, suggests: There is a decline in public involvement and trust, as well as in family values and civility in mainstream United States culture. Increasing individualism, they argue, is leading to a decline in **social capital**—the sense of involvement in one's community, including social organization, trust, networks, a sense of citizenship, and norms.

Many interpretive studies of culture use *ethnography*. This method involves detailed observing, usually involving interaction with people, to understand their lives. Gerry Philipsen and others applied this approach specifically to communication, calling it **ethnography of communication**. Philipsen and his colleagues (2005) outline a theoretical perspective that relies on this approach, **speech codes theory**. In this theory, a **speech code** is the system of symbols, meanings, assumptions, and norms for communication adopted by a group of people. That group of people, a **speech community**, is rarely as big as a nation, but is likely a specific group of people, such as a Harley Davidson motorcycle gang, parents at a Taekwondo studio, or theater majors at a particular university. The theory is "grounded in the observation of communication conduct in particular times and places" (Philipsen et al., 2005, p. 56). The theory proposes that, in any speech community, people can choose or alternate between multiple speech codes. Someone might use one code (variety of speech, norms for speaking, and so on), with friends on the cricket pitch or volleyball court, and quite a different code with instructors. The codes tell us how to act as a "real" member of the community and also who has status and who does not. The codes guide our behavior, but they do not cause us to behave a certain way. Most importantly, the theory argues that each speech community has a way of communicating that is distinct. The theory does not make predictions about how people will communicate in a culture or across cultures. Rather, it provides a framework for analysis that allows us to interpret and gain an understanding of specific types of communication behavior in any culture.

Recognizing the existence of codes and knowing how to interpret them can also help us to be better communicators. If we are aware that the order of actions and types of behaviors may vary on who the participants are in the situation, we can be better observers and learners. For example, we see someone enter an informal close group in Mexico and see that the person greets everyone present, rather than giving a general "hello" to the room. We can determine who does what, in which order, and what the norms of behavior are, to learn the behavior ourselves. But we can also use the framework for social change. For example, if we seek to change a classroom culture that centralizes power with the instructor, with the result that students do not have the resources (training, authority) to raise questions, we can work to change the situation to give students more power.

What do you think? A Jewish Passover Seder has its own set of rules (participants, norms, act sequence), although these will change from one community to another (Figure 4.5). But even our everyday meals have rtuals, often unspoken. Watch the dinner table conversation with your family or friends. Identify a specific genre of behavior (like retelling the day's events, bragging rituals, joke sequences, or children asking parents' permission to do something). How might an ethnographic approach make sense of your "speech code?" Is your code unique, or does it borrow from larger cultural codes?

Studies using ethnography in general, or specifically, "ethnography of communication," demonstrate the diversity of cultures people have analyzed. Donal Carbaugh (2005), in his book *Cultures in Conversation*, summarizes his analysis of specific behaviors in different cultures, such as the use of small talk and "friendliness" behaviors in America and Sweden, the use of

Figure 4.5 In 2009, As U.S. President Barack Obama hosted the first Jewish Passover Seder at the White House (2009), he had to be aware of the proper rules for communication in such an event.
Source: Pete Souza/Wikimedia Commons/Public Domain.

silence and the reluctance to be a polished speaker among Blackfoot Indians, and the negative responses of a public television audience in Russia to Phil Donohue attempting to get them to talk about the assumed problem of teen sex and pregnancy. David Poveda and Beatriz Martín (2004) studied stories told by two small groups of Roma (Gypsy, or *Gitano*) children in Spain, analyzing the communicative gaps between these children, educated first in their home, and the teachers of the Spanish schools they began to attend.

Whereas ethnography has a central focus on observation of some sort, other researchers use methods such as interviews, which also allow in-depth understandings from the perspectives of cultural members. Stephen Croucher (2009) did in-depth interviews with 42 Muslims in France to understand their perceptions and experiences regarding cultural adjustment and assimilation. And Mark Ward, Sr. (2010), after attending 250 worship services in 17 U.S. states, analyzed forms of speech in Fundamentalist Christian churches in the United States. Rona Halualani and Jolanta Drzewiecka (2008) studied Polish and Hawaiian diasporic groups. A **diaspora** is a large group of people that have spread outside of their country or territory of origin, usually maintaining some notion of identity to the homeland. Based on 300 interviews and narratives from Hawaiians compared to an understanding of Polish people living abroad, Halualani and Drzewiecka study the tensions of identity, such as "sameness" and "unity" with the culture of origin and issues of descent, faced by these groups.

World view: What are the beliefs at the center of our "world?"

World view is a key aspect of culture. As we said above, this is a specific set of beliefs about the relationship of humans to one another and to greater elements in the cosmos. Geertz (1973, p. 127) calls the world view of a people "their picture of the way things in sheer actuality are, their concept of nature, of self, of society. It contains their most comprehensive ideas of order." As we noted above, Geertz sees all aspects of culture as interrelated. As he studies the people of Bali, an island in the Pacific, he notes that world view plays out in Balinese notions of time; in the complex set of names, nicknames, family, and status names people have for one another; and in ceremony. In one such ceremony, the Balinese cockfight, men, through their roosters, enact a particular notion of what it means to be a "man" in Bali. World view is connected to communication and ritual, and each of these to our notions of "personhood" and how we enact the different identities that we hold.

Kluckhohn and Strodtbeck (1973), psychological anthropologists, published an analysis of five communities within a 40-mile area in the southwestern United States—a Mormon community, a Texas homestead, a Spanish-American village, and two Native American villages—showing how they differed on several dimensions. Many authors have reproduced this framework, and, while scholars often refer to it as dealing with "value orientations," it really pertains more to world view. The authors suggest that "there is a limited number of common human problems for which all peoples at all times must find some solution" (Kluckhohn & Strodtbeck, 1973, p. 10). Value orientations combine cognitive (thought), affective (feelings), and directive (behavioral) elements to direct human behavior. The values guide us beyond our mere choice, especially since we may often not be aware of them or be able to articulate them. Kluckhohn and Strodtbeck (1973, p. 11) list five basic questions that humans are trying to answer (see Figure 4.6):

1 What is the character of innate human nature?

2 What is the relation of man to nature (and supernature)?

3 What is the temporal focus of human life?

Figure 4.6 Kluckhohn and Strodtbeck's value orientations.
Source: Adapted from Kluckhohn & Strodtbeck, 1973.

Orientation	Postulated Range of Variations		
Human Nature	Evil	Neutral/Good + Evil	Good
Human-(Super) Nature	Subjugation to nature	Harmony with nature	Mastery over nature
Time	Past	Present	Future
Activity	Being	Being-in-becoming	Doing
Relational	Lineality	Collaterality	Individualism

4 What is the modality of human activity?

5 What is the modality of man's relationship with other men?

They pose a framework of different orientations in response to these (Figure 4.5), noting that all value orientations exist in all cultures, but that each culture will rank them differently. Space constraints here do not allow us a full exploration of these, but we can see how they might distinguish cultures in terms of world view in a couple of the dimensions. Some do seem more like values, such as the relational orientation, which includes individualism and two forms of collectivism: lineal, in which the collective might be a tribe or extended family (many African cultures); and collateral, in which the important group would be a workgroup (Japan).

Three of the dimensions especially relate to world view, though the rest do as well, to some degree. In terms of humans' relation to deity (or the supernatural, God, the elements), people in some cultures privilege the idea that we are subject to nature, a sort of fatalism that suggests that humans are at the whims of the gods ("The Devil made me do it!"). In some Latin American cultures, a common saying is "*Así soy yo*"—that's just how I am. Traditionally, a common view was that nature would just "take over" when men and women were alone, which led to very strict supervision of young dating couples. Some years ago, in Brazil, when young men wanted to talk with young women, they used to have to do so through the bars on the front windows, leading to the courtship expression, *comendo grade* (eating grate). People in other cultures see humans as being more in control of nature—they seed the clouds to make it rain and seek to analyze and even control the human genome. And people in yet other cultures tend to seek harmony with nature, seeing themselves working together with the elements ("We eat the buffalo, but then when we die, we feed the grass that feeds the buffalo"). Related to our view of the relationship between humans and the supernatural are our views of human nature (are humans evil, good, or a combination of the two?) and of our activity orientation.

The *doing* orientation, specifically, reflects a culture where the focus is on activity that is often measurable in external accomplishments, a characteristic of U.S. culture, where there seems to be a flurry of activity, with even things like eating ("fast food") geared toward moving us to the next activity. The *being* orientation is characterized by spontaneous expression and living for the impulses of the moment. This represents, perhaps, cultures where "hanging out" or just spending time together, for the sake of the talk and not for some observable purpose, are important. In such a culture, such as many Latin American or African American cultures within the United States, the person you are with may be more important than the schedule on a clock. In *being-in-becoming* cultures, there is a goal, but it is not measurable (as are awards or status or money) but is instead internal. It is the development of the whole person, such as is achieved through some forms of Eastern meditation.

It is easy to want to classify cultures. Scholars say the United States values the future, progress, and pragmatism, and the general view of nature is that it is something to meet human needs (mastery over nature). Asian Indian culture is framed as more fatalistic, with the traditional caste system, a view that humans are subject to the divine; U.S. Indian (Native American) tribes are seen to live in harmony with nature. But each of these borders on cultural stereotypes. We should keep in mind that the same limitations we addressed above, such as rigidly placing cultures into a limited number of boxes or overgeneralizing cultural descriptions to "national" cultures, apply here as well. A closer analysis of any culture, as Kluckhohn and Strodtbeck (1973) themselves said, will reveal elements of all of the dimensions, though there may be preferences for some. Thus, a deeper understanding of the fabric of Indian culture *might* reveal themes of fatalism, but it would have complicated threads of the person impacting her or his own destiny. Ultimately, analyses of the specifics of a culture must rely in strong part on writings by members of the cultures themselves.

We should also note that this is only one framework and that other dimensions or aspects are possible. Carley Dodd (1998), for example, speaks of **guilt cultures**, in which people are motivated by a sense of remorse when they engage in bad behaviors, based on a sense of personal responsibility more common in individualistic cultures. On the other hand, in **shame cultures**, people are motivated by a sense of social obligation, and are more likely to act in a way to protect the honor or "face" of their group than out of a sense of personal responsibility. In **spirit(ual) (or sacred) cultures**, there is a sense of presence of the spiritual or divine in everyday life, and in **secular cultures**, life problems and solutions are seen in terms of science and human ideas. Often, these do not correspond to religious attendance. In many Spanish-speaking South American cultures, if one is planning for the future, one might say, "*Si Dios quiere*"—if God wills, similar to the "*In sh'Allah*" of Arabic-speaking cultures. But in the United States, where church attendance is often higher, people relegate God to certain spheres of life, but do not perceive the divine in the day-to-day workings of life or nature. And cultures that are still traditionally Christian, such as much of Europe, have entered what some have called a post-Christian age, in which atheism is as likely or more likely than faith in a deity.

Break it down

World views and value systems have things that help us progress as a society and things that work against healthy society. Sometimes, even good values, taken to an extreme, can impede progress, community, or other aspects of a culture. With your friends or in a group of classmates, engage in a discussion that considers both the strengths and limitations of the values and/ or world view of your culture (national, organizational, university, co-culture, etc.). What changes could be made in your culture to help it meet multiple goals that are beneficial for the citizens of the culture? What are some concrete things you as a group or individual could do toward bringing about these changes?

Summary

This chapter has been about what we consider to be the deepest foundations of culture—values, beliefs, and world view. These constitute the bedrock upon which behavioral rules and norms—expectations for appropriate behavior in situations, sometimes with implications for morality—are built. Norms and rules, in turn, guide our verbal, nonverbal, and mediated behavior. It is certainly good to learn the etiquette when we travel to other cultures, and there are many good sources that present this sort of information (see the suggested readings in the "For more information" section below). But if we know the underlying structure of a culture—the part that usually lies beneath the surface in the iceberg model of culture—then the rest of the parts of culture may make more sense, and we may be able to act appropriately even in those areas where we do not yet know the specific rules and norms.

We defined key terms regarding the mental frameworks that form the basis upon which cultural and intercultural communication is built. These include values, beliefs, world view, norms, and rules. One approach to understanding these is to develop a framework of terms that can apply to all cultures, such as Hofstede's dimensions, E.T. Hall's notion of high- and low-context cultures, or Kluckhohn and Strodtbeck's value orientations. Other scholars believe that any use of such frameworks forces us to think of cultures in terms that scholars have created and instead seek to understand each culture from the perspective of the people of that culture.

Each approach has strengths and limitations. The first allows for cross-cultural comparisons, as long as we are aware of the limitations of such frameworks. The second allows us to understand cultural behavior in terms of unique cultural histories and contexts. Use of either approach, without care, could lead us to think of cultures as overly uniform and stagnant, as well as to ignore the role of social, economic, and political systems that might work against people's ability to live out their values within a given culture.

As we turn our attention to communication and to political and civic engagement, we must keep in mind that any geographic space has a variety of cultures and co-cultures sharing that space, with fluid and overlapping boundaries, and that cultures are constantly changing through ongoing communication, political, and social, and even geographic and climactic forces. As we engage in civic or political projects, we realize that these always exist within value frameworks, sometimes of cultural values, and sometimes of values of the organization. In some cases, cultural values (like exaggerated individualism) might work against civic engagement—or we might use appeals to personal growth and fulfillment, in such cultures, to motivate participation in engagement, since even the reasons for participating in civic engagement will be influenced by our cultural values and world views. And finally, we may see that in any culture, we may need to strive to change behaviors and messages to bring the groups that we belong to more in line with values, or, a much harder task, seek to change values to be more wholesome and inclusive for all. Regardless of our engagement goals, we recognize that an understanding both of the underlying structure of culture and its ability to change should help us to be better intercultural communicators.

KEY TERMS

subjective culture, 72
objective culture, 72
belief, 73
belief system, 73
world view, 73
value, 74
cultural value, 74
attitude, 74
rule, 74
norm, 74
more, 74
taboo, 74
law, 74
universal value, 75
terminal value, 76
instrumental value, 76
high-context culture, 76
low-context culture, 77
power distance, 77
masculinity/femininity, 78

uncertainty avoidance, 78
individualism-collectivism (I/C), 78
Confucian work dynamism, 80
long-term orientation, 80
indulgence-restraint, 80
propriety, 80
self-construal, 80
etic approach, 81
emic approach, 81
social capital, 81
ethnography of communication, 81
speech codes theory, 81
speech code, 81
speech community, 81
diaspora, 83
guilt culture, 85
shame culture, 85
spirit(ual) (or sacred) culture, 85
secular culture, 85

Discussion questions

1 What do you think are the disadvantages and advantages of each of the two approaches to understanding cultural communication, etic and emic?

2 Martin et al. (2002), suggest that change and stability exist in all cultures in tension with each other. Think of your own culture. What are some things that you see changing, and what are some things that seem to stay the same? Are the things that remain the same on the top or the bottom of the "iceberg" model of culture? Think of how the things that change more or less quickly in a culture relate to each other.

3 As we note in this chapter, some scholars claim that there is a decline in "civility" and social capital in America. If you are in an American classroom, discuss whether you agree or disagree with this notion. If you are not in an American classroom, think of a particular cultural value or ritual that seems to be in transition, and discuss why you think that it is or is not changing—and whether such change is beneficial (or not) to your culture.

4 What seems to be the dominant concepts of world view in your culture? Don't just answer in terms of overall religious belief, but with a deeper discussion of what you think underlying views of reality, knowledge, or the purpose of life is in your culture. What is the general cultural perception of the relationship between individuals, between people and nature, or people and the universe?

5 How do different views of body piercing, tattoos, or other body modifications reflect "cultural differences" *within* your national culture? If you have a body modification—or know someone who does (which may include public figures), what values, meanings, or rules/norms might the modification(s) reflect? You might consider the number, placement, content, theme, or other aspects of the body modifications.

Action points

1 Find a current political issue in a country besides your own. For example, in the writing of this chapter, people are debating the rightness or wrongness of economic embargoes against Iran, the Russian invasion of Ukraine, or the politicization of the Olympics or other sports within and between nations. Discuss this issue with your class or with friends, talking about the underlying value, more/normative, or world view of the culture as these relate to the issue.

2 Go online and view the 20-minute video, "The Story of Stuff" (http://www.storyofstuff.com). Think about your own use of goods and resources. How does this use of resources reflect or contradict your own culture's values? How does your usage impact people in other cultures for good or bad? What changes could you make in your life to use less "stuff?" Also, what are your agreements or disagreements with the idea in the video?

3 The International Youth Foundation (http://www.iyfnet.org) describes stories of young people— teens and young adults changing their world in different ways. Look through the news and videos to find a story on something specific a young person has done. Look at Hart's Ladder of Participation as it relates to involving youth in projects (https://iyfglobal.org/youth-engagement). Take notes and think about what sorts of things young people are doing around the world. What level of "engagement" do the programs that they are involved in reflect? How might such an effort translate to your own community, if someone wanted to do something similar?

For more information

Althen, G., & Bennett, J. (2011). *American ways: A cultural guide to the United States.* Intercultural Press.

Hofstede, G., Hofstede, G. J., & Minkov, M. (2010). *Cultures and organizations: Software of the mind: Intercultural communication and its importance for survival* (3rd ed.). McGraw Hill.

Martin, J. N., Nakayama, T. K., & Flores, L. A. (2002). A dialectical approach to intercultural communication. In J. N. Martin, T. K. Nakayama, & L. A. Flores (Eds.), *Readings in intercultural communication: Experiences and contexts* (pp. 3–13). McGraw Hill.

McSweeney, B. (2002). Hofstede's model of national cultural differences and their consequences: A triumph of faith—a failure of analysis. *Human Relations, 55*(1), 89–118. DOI: 10.1177/0018726702551004

Morrison, T., Conaway, W. A., & Borden, G. A. (1994). *Kiss, bow, or shake hands: How to do business in sixty countries.* B. Adams.

References

Althen, G. with Doran, A. R., & Szmania, S. J. (2003). *American ways: A guide for foreigners in the United States* (2nd ed). Intercultural Press.

Bellah, R. N., Madsen, R., Sullivan, W. M., Swidler, A., & Tipton, S. M. (1996). *Habits of the heart: Individualism and commitment in American life* (updated ed.). University of California Press.

Carbaugh, D. (2005). *Cultures in conversation.* Lawrence Erlbaum Associates.

Chiang, F. (2005). A critical examination of Hofstede's thesis and its application to international reward management. *International Journal of Human Resource Management, 16*(9), 1545–1563. DOI: 10.1080/09585190500239044

Chinese Culture Connection. (1987). Chinese values and the search for culture-free dimensions of culture. *Journal of Cross-Cultural Psychology, 18*(2), 143–164. https://doi.org/10.1177/0022002187018002002

Condon, J., & LeBrack, B. (2014). *Culture, definition of.* In J. M. Bennett (Ed.), *The SAGE encyclopedia of intercultural competence* (pp. 192–195). Sage. https://dx.doi.org/10.4135/9781483346267.n70

Courtright, J. L., Wolfe, R., & Baldwin, J. R. (2011). Intercultural typologies and public relations research: A critique of Hofstede's dimensions. In N. Bardhan (Ed.), *Public relations in global and cultural contexts* (pp. 108–139). Lawrence Erlbaum Associates.

Croucher, S. M. (2009). *Looking beyond the hijab.* Hampton.

Dodd, C. H. (1998). *Dynamics of intercultural communication* (5th ed.). McGraw-Hill.

Geertz, C. (1973). *The interpretation of cultures.* Basic Books.

Gudykunst, W. B., & Kim, Y. Y. (2003). *Communicating with strangers: An approach to intercultural communication* (4th ed.). McGraw Hill.

Gudykunst, W. B., & Nishida, T. (1986). The influence of cultural variability on perceptions of communication behavior associated with relational terms. *Human Communication Research, 13*(2), 147–166. DOI: 10.1111/j.1468-2958.1986.tb00099.x

Gudykunst, W. B., & Nishida, T. (1989). Theoretical perspectives for studying intercultural communication. In M. K. Asante & W. B. Gudykunst (Eds.), *Handbook of international and intercultural communication* (pp. 17–46). Sage.

Hall, E. T. (1997). Context and meaning. In L. A. Samovar & R. E. Porter (Eds.), *Intercultural communication: A reader* (8th ed., pp. 45–54). Wadsworth.

Halualani, R. T., & Drzewiecka, J. (2008). Deploying "descent": The politics of diasporic belonging and intercultural communication. *International and Intercultural Communication Annual, 31*, 59–90.

Hofstede, G. (n.d.) Country comparison. *Hofstede Insights.* Accessed March 4, 2023 at www.hofstede-insights.com/country-comparison

Hofstede, G. (1980). *Culture's consequences: International differences in work-related values.* Sage.

Hofstede, G. (1986). *Culture's consequences: Comparing values, behavior, institutions, and organizations across cultures* (2nd ed.). Sage.

Hofstede, G. (1997). *Cultures and organizations: The software of the mind.* McGraw-Hill.

Hofstede, G. (2001). *Culture's consequences: Comparing values, behaviors, institutions, and organizations across nations.* Sage.

Hofstede, G. (2009). Cultural dimensions. *ITIM International.* Accessed March 28, 2011, at http://geert-hofstede.com

Hofstede, G., & Bond, M. H. (1984). Hofstede's cultural dimensions: An independent validation using Rokeach's Value Survey. *Journal of Cross-Cultural Psychology, 15*(4), 417–433. https://doi.org/10.1177/0022002184015004003

Ittzés, G., Sipos-Bielochradzsky, B., Béres, O., & Pilinszki, A. (2017). Salvation and religiosity: The predictive strength and limitations of a Rokeach Value Survey Item. *European Journal of Mental Health, 12*, 3–24. DOI: 10.5708/EJMH.12.2017.1.1

Kim, M.-S. (2005). Culture-based conversational constraints theory. In W. B. Gudykunst (Ed.), *Theorizing intercultural communication* (pp. 93–117). Sage.

Kim, U., Triandis, H. C., Kâĝitçibaşi, C., Choi, S.-C., & Yoon, G. (Eds.). (1994). *Individualism and collectivism: Theory, method and implications.* Sage.

Kirkman, B.L., Lowe, K.B., & Gibson, C.B. (2017). A retrospective on "Culture's Consequences": The 35-year journey. *Journal of International Business Studies, 48*(1), 12–29. https://www.jstor.org/stable/26169988

Kluckhohn, F. R., & Strodtbeck, F. L. (1973). *Variations in value orientations* (2nd ed.). Greenwood.

Madichie, N. O., Nkamnebe, A. D., & Idemobi, E. I. (2008). Cultural determinants of entrepreneurial emergence in a typical sub-Sahara African context. *Journal of Enterprising Communities, 2*(4), 285–299. https://doi.org/10.1108/17506200810913881

Martin, J. N., Nakayama, T. K., & Flores, L. A. (2002). A dialectical approach to intercultural communication. In J. N. Martin, T. K. Nakayama, & L. A. Flores (Eds.), *Readings in intercultural communication: Experiences and contexts* (pp. 3–13). McGraw Hill.

Nakata, C. (2009). Going beyond Hofstede: Why we need to and how. In C. Nakata (Ed.), *Beyond Hofstede: Culture frameworks for global marketing and management* (pp. 3–15). Palgrave-Macmillan.

Newman, M. S. (June 19, 2019).So, Gutenberg didn't actually invent printing as we know it. Literary Hub.

Accessed March 4, 2023at https://lithub.com/ so-gutenberg-didnt-actually-invent-the-printing-press/.

Peace Corps. (n.d.). *Cultural gaffes at home and abroad. Paul D. Coverdell—Worldwise Schools.* Accessed April 26, 2023, at https://www.youtube.com/ watch?v=qHRcAPTxw0k.

Philipsen, G., Coutu, L. M., & Covarrubias, P. (2005). Speech codes theory: Restatement, revisions, and response to criticisms. In W. B. Gudykunst (Ed.), *Theorizing about intercultural communication* (pp. 55–68). Sage.

Poveda, D., & Martín, B. (2004). Looking for cultural congruence in the education of *gitano* children. *Language in Education, 18*(5), 413–434. DOI: 10.1080/09500780408666892

Putnam, R. D. (2000). *Bowling alone: The collapse and revival of American community.* Simon & Schuster.

Reynolds, B. K. (1984). A cross-cultural study of values of Germans and Americans. *International Journal of Intercultural Relations, 8*(3), 269–278. DOI: 10.1016/0147-1767(84)90027-0

Robinson, J. (2000). Communication in Korea: Playing things by eye. In L. A. Samovar & R. E. Porter (Eds.), *Intercultural communication: A reader* (9th ed., pp. 74–81). Wadsworth.

Rokeach, M. (1973). *The nature of human values.* Free Press.

Schwartz, S. (1992). Universals in the content and structure of values: Theory and empirical tests in 20 countries. In M. Zanna (Ed.), *Advances in experimental social psychology* (Vol. *25*, pp. 1–65). Academic Press.

Schwartz, S. H. (2006). A theory of cultural value orientations: Explication and applications.

Comparative Sociology, 5(2–3). DOI: 10.1163/156913306778667357

Signorini, P., Wiesemes, R., & Murphy, R. (2009). Developing alternative frameworks for exploring intercutlural learning: A critique of Hofstede's cultural difference model. *Teaching in Higher Education, 14*(3), 253–264. DOI: 10.1080/13562510902898825

Triandis, H. C. (1995). *Individualism and collectivism.* Westview.

Triandis, H. C. (2002). Subjective culture.*Online Readings in Psychology and Culture.* Accessed April 26, 2023, at https://scholarworks.gvsu.edu/orpc/vol2/iss2/6/.

Trompenaars, A., & Hampden-Turner, C. (1998). *Riding the waves of culture: Understanding cultural diversity in global business* (2nd ed.). McGraw Hill.

Vauclair, C.-M., Hanke, K., Fischer, R., & Fontaine, J. (2011). The structure of human values at the culture level: A meta-analytical replication of Schwartz' value orientations using the Rokeach Value Survey. *Journal of Cross-Cultural Psychology, 42*(2), 186–205. DOI: 10.1177/0022022110396864

Ward, M., Sr. (2010). "I was saved at an early age": An ethnography of fundamentalist speech and cultural performance. *Journal of Communication and Religion, 33*(1), 108–144.

Whiteoak, J. W., Crawford, N. G., & Mapstone, R. H. (2006). Differences of gender and generational differences in work values and attitudes in an Arab culture. *Thunderbird International Business Review, 48* (1), 77–91. DOI: 10.1002/tie.20086

Zhang, Q. (2007). Family communication patterns and conflict styles in Chinese parent-child relationships. *Communication Quarterly, 55*(1), 113–128. DOI: 10.1080/01463370600998681

Chapter 5

Identity—Struggle, resistance, and solidarity: How can I think about my identity and that of others?

Chapter objectives

After this chapter, you should be able to:

→ Describe sources of your identity

→ Differentiate between personal and social identities

→ Apply the notion that identities are a social construction by giving examples of messages or communication that produce and reproduce your identities

→ Illustrate identity politics – that is, how power defines our own and others' identities

→ Integrate the notions of ideology and hegemony as these apply to identities and how they play out through communication practices of Othering and the symbolic annihilation of race.

Intercultural Communication for Everyday Life, Second Edition. John R. Baldwin, Alberto González, Nettie Brock, Ming Xie, and Chin-Chung Chao.
© 2024 John Wiley & Sons Ltd. Published 2024 by John Wiley & Sons Ltd.
Companion Website: http://www.wiley.com/go/baldwin2e

Every morning, you wake up and make a series of choices. Those choices range from big things—what are you going to finish at work, life changes that need to be decided, etc.—to small things—what to eat, what to wear, how to style your hair. All the outcomes of those choices are based upon who you are as an individual, in other words, your identity. Take clothing. Clothing itself is a means through which we understand other people. Rouse (1993) discusses how "a garment" can be more than just functional, how it "'*says*' something about the wearer" (p. 19, emphasis original). Thus, clothing works as a sort of means of conveying information about ourselves. Rouse (1993) goes on, saying, "You form an impression of that person from the information conveyed to you by their appearance before you speak to them" (p. 22). Think about all the times you have made judgments or assumptions about a person based entirely on how they are dressed. Wilson's (1987) seminal work on fashion, *Adorned in Dreams*, explores the nuances of the roles that clothing can play in culture. She says,

> Fashion, then, is essential to the world of modernity, the world of spectacle and mass communication. It is a kind of connective tissue of our cultural organism. And, although many individuals experience fashion as a form of bondage, as a punitive, compulsory way of falsely expressing an individuality that by its very gesture (in copying others) cancels itself out, the final twist to the contradiction that is fashion is that it often does successfully express the individual. (p. 12)

Her idea that fashion can "express the individual" is not revolutionary, but it is certainly something that people do not frequently consider when thinking about clothes. How do the clothes that you wear express who you are as an individual? This is just one of the many ways that our identities manifest and we communicate those identities with others.

This chapter will discuss the different places that our identities come from, as well as differentiate between personal identities and social ones; we will consider the ways in which identity is a social construct created by those around us. Then, we will look at the role that politics plays in identity through societal ideologies and the dominant hegemony of our culture. Finally, we will bring all these ideas together to consider what identity factors contribute to our understanding of other cultures and people.

Who are you?

In the immortal words of the classic British rock band, The Who (1978): "Who are you? Who? Who?" This is a question that we often ask people when we meet them and that we ask ourselves on a regular basis. It is also a question that is not easily answered. Let's start by simply defining what the question is even asking. According to Barker (2004a), **identity** is "an essence signified through signs of taste, beliefs, attitudes, and lifestyles" that is "constituted" through "social process[es] … without which we would not be persons." In other words, identity is a process by which we express ourselves through aspects of our personality and the things we like; this process is learned through social interactions and the culture we grew up in. Without these identity markers, we are not really people.

We can identify through a variety of means: we can think of ourselves as being part of some particular social category—White, female, heterosexual, etc.; or we can think about what social groups we are a part of—the middle class, college educated, employed, etc. Identity, then, is defined by our "knowing" of ourselves. This knowing means taking an inventory of who we are. Part of that inventory involves our concepts of ourselves as unique individuals, whether, for example, we are shy, athletic, or interested in soccer—our personal identities. However, Larson and Shevchenko (2019) observe that having "positively distinctive" identities is extremely desirable within the social groups we belong to (p. 1190). Thus, part of the inventory involves our role identities (e.g., work or professional roles), relational identities (e.g., enemies, family members, lovers), and our membership in groups (such as national, religious, or political groups, social organizations, or regional identities). These latter, group-based aspects of identity make up our **social identity**. Social identity is where the individual meets later collective bodies, or groups of affiliation. According to Greenaway et al. (2015), "Social identity provides people with a shared framework for understanding the world that increases the enthusiasm and ease with which they engage in communication" (p. 172).

How do we share our identities with others?

But identity is a personal experience and exists in the realm of psychology. This is an intercultural *communication* textbook. So, what does identity have to do with either communication or intercultural communication? Essentially, we communicate our identities constantly—whether through our physical appearance, the actions we take, or the words we speak and write. We also emphasize certain parts of our identities more than others, depending on the situation. Additionally, we receive communications about what other people's identities are and we take that information and utilize it to understand more about them and their culture.

How people identify themselves is a very popular field of communication research and many scholars have proposed different ways in which we construct our identities. One prominent theory that has been considered identity is **Social Identity Theory** (Turner et al., 1979). This theory suggests that: (1) How we see ourselves is closely tied to how we see the groups to which we belong. (2) When we interact with others, we see them in some combination of personal terms and expectations and their membership in groups. (3) When we place people in groups, we tend to compare those groups against our own, usually in a way that makes our groups look better to us (see Figure 5.1). Writers have applied this theory to a wide variety of identities,

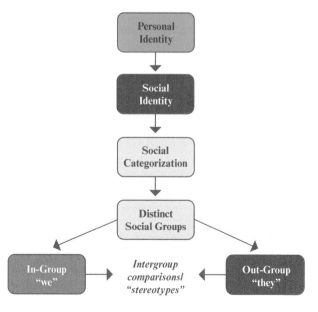

Figure 5.1 Flow chart of Social Identity Theory. Source: Daniel Baxter, 2016/Wikiversity/Public Domain.

including sex, sexual orientation, social class, race, ethnicity, physical ability/disability, and national identity (e.g., Akinci, 2020; Harwood & Giles, 2005), and particularly to how perception of group identities impacts communication (Ng et al., 2004).

Another line of research on identity considers how children grow up to see themselves within a particular identity. Derald Wing Sue and David Sue (2008) outline several models of Black and White identity development, which might transfer in some ways to minority and majority identity development in countries outside of the United States. For example, William Cross (1995) describes the minority development stages of pre-encounter (marked by a desire to assimilate into dominant culture and devalue one's own group), encounter (the person begins to challenge the old way of thinking and reconsider her or his identity), immersion-emersion (the person engages fully in the minority culture, separating from the dominant culture), internalization (the person resolves insecurities between old and new identities), and internalization-commitment (the person makes a decision for social change and civil rights). Janet Helms (1995) outlines a similar model for White (or majority) development that begins with initial contact, a phase in which the majority member is unaware of intolerance, believes in equality of opportunity, and so on; the person then confronts and understands intolerance, perhaps passing through a stage of White (or dominant group) guilt, and moving to a stage that values diversity and encounters it without intimidation or discomfort. Teresa Nance and Anita Foeman (2002) apply these to suggest positive messages that parents can share with biracial children to help them build a wholesome, positive identity.

Some frame identity as something that is constantly changing, because we are always creating and shaping our identities through communication, a view that is more "humanistic;" that is, identities are a **social construction**. They are created through communication in the context of our social world, histories, and relationships. As such, identities are inherently political, with our identity claims and investments not only naming us but at times also affording us more or less power given the context (e.g., "stay-at-home soccer mom" vs. "welfare mother" vs. "career mother"). Michael Hecht and his colleagues (2005) state the complexities of identity well. They argue that identities are not fixed; rather they are dynamic and multiple.

Barker (2004a) reminds us that "no single identity acts as an overarching, organizing identity, rather identities shift according to how subjects are addressed or represented." He goes on to say, "individuals are the unique historically specific articulation of discursive elements that are contingent but also socially determined or regulated." In other words, individual people are each unique because of the social aspects that contribute to their upbringing, but that uniqueness is dependent upon the circumstances. Our identities shift and change as we move from one group or location to another. This happens because the most important part of our identity has changed because of that movement. Kimberlé Crenshaw (1989) discusses the way that identity is often thought of within a "single axis framework" (p. 139). By this, she is referring to the ways that in legal matters, individuals are often thought of as being one part of their identity.

In her essay, Crenshaw (1989) discusses how Black women are frequently thought of as either Black or as Women, but not both at the same time. Because Crenshaw was considering this from a legal perspective, she refers to people in these situations as "multiply-burdened" (p. 140) and by separating people out in this way, they become even more marginalized than they already are. She says, "I argue that Black women are sometimes excluded from feminist theory and antiracist policy discourse because both are predicated on a discrete set of experiences that often does not accurately reflect the interaction of race and gender" (p. 140). If a woman is

Black, Crenshaw suggests that she is often left out of discussions both of feminism and racism as those things cannot include the other. She later dubs the need to look at the ways that multiple identity categories manifest in a single individual as **intersectionality**. A direct result of this essay is that a whole field of critical scholarship appeared, and it is called Intersectionality or Intersectional Studies.

Collins (2015) defines intersectionality as a "critical insight that race, class, gender, sexuality, ethnicity, nation, ability, and age operate not as unitary, mutually exclusive entities, but as reciprocally constructing phenomena that in turn shape complex social inequalities" (p. 2). We all have multiple identities all at the same time, and no one of those identities is more important than any of the others. They all work together to make us who we are, and we cannot simply make some parts of our identity disappear in favor of other parts. We are always our gender, our race, our ethnicity, our sexuality, our age, our nationality, etc. Sometimes we might emphasize certain parts of our identities, but the other parts are still there. They are just less important at this given moment.

Sometimes, people "code-switch" within certain settings because of their identities. Molinsky (2007) defines code-switching as "the act of purposefully modifying one's behavior, in a specific interaction in a foreign setting, to accommodate different cultural norms for appropriate behavior" (p. 623). Most scholars discuss code-switching within the context of linguistics, but it can also apply to behavior. Consider any circumstances where you have to stand up straighter or wear different clothes. With teachers, students often code-switch to a more formal way of speaking and a more professional way of acting. Terhune (2006) looked at the ways that Black women in the Pacific Northwest cope with code-switching. She says, "The burden of always being watched and expected to act as the majority demanded took its tool [sic] on all of the participants" (p. 12) and found that the only solution to this burden was to return to predominantly Black communities to regroup and relax.

Additionally, we need to always remember that intersectionality is true about *everybody*. Therefore, other people are always also going to be more than the first thing you notice about them. A psychological phenomenon called the "primacy effect" causes people to typically remember the first thing they learn better than information gathered later. This is called the "first-impression bias" when discussing people and the ways that we often are heavily influenced by the first time we meet another person (APA, 2022). For us, this means that we need to work even harder to make sure we aren't getting stuck on our first impressions and are able to recognize that other people are just as multi-faceted, just as intersectional as we are.

Break it down

You, and everyone else around you, are made up of multiple identity categories. What are some of yours that you use to define yourself on a regular basis? Do you ever find yourself struggling to balance different parts of your identity? How do you manage to be true to all parts of your identity equally?

What do intersectional identities have to do with power?

At the heart of a lot of the previously discussed issues surrounding intersectional identities is the concept of power. Which identities "matter" the most often depends upon who has the power and the ability to sway people's opinions. Thus, identities matter a lot to how the world works. One way that this manifests is through what we now call **identity politics**. So, what are identity politics, what are some examples, and why are they important? Essentially, identity politics is categorizing groups of people by certain identity markers, usually somehow involved with organized social movements, to politic to specific issues those groups are invested in.

Moran (2018) suggests that until identity became a central role in politics, thus beginning "identity politics," identity didn't really exist as an idea in academic work. It was in the realm of psychology and used in relation to other things, but not important on its own. She further suggests that Raymond Williams' definition of "keywords" as "complex and contested word[s] *whose problems of meaning are inextricably bound up with the problems [they are] used to discuss*" (Moran, 2018, p. 26 emphasis original) is applicable to the word "identity." The word "identity" by this understanding is then always connected to the social and political issues associated with it. Identity and Identity Politics cannot be separated. Thus, we should probably talk about identity politics.

Identity politics center around ideologies. **Ideology** is "the dominant ideas and representations in a given social order" (Durham & Kellner, 2006, p. xiv) and can be found in every one of us. We all have certain beliefs and values that are rooted in our cultures and are a strong part of our identities. These are ideologies. Karl Marx wrote extensively about ideology, suggesting that Western ideologies often stem from the structures of capitalism (Barker, 2004b). Because of the hierarchical ways that capitalism is structured, those in control of production (the upper class) also control the beliefs and values of a society.

Another significant term involved in this process is **hegemony.** Hegemony is a term first described by Gramsci (1926). Cultural hegemony entails the ways society accepts, without question or resistance, being governed by those in power, even when their ideologies may not be in the best interest of the people. Hegemony comes from those in control but is not a repressive form of "mastery" over the people. According to Gramsci, there is a difference between leadership and domination, and that hegemony is not domination. Instead, hegemony is about leading the people through assimilating the intellectuals of a society and, as a result, gently leading society toward a specific group's way of thinking.

The hegemony is a means of spreading specific ideologies, primarily through the media (as discussed in Chapter 10), and these have a significant impact on who we are as people. They are also often the things that draw us to other people. Those who have similar ideologies as us are people that we want to befriend. When social injustices occur, they often focus on pushing back against ideologies that some see as repressive toward particular identity groups. Walters (2018) says, "Contemporary identity politics—in its most robust manifestations—offers up a critique of what constitutes 'mainstream,' what 'issues' get attached to what bodies, and the hierarchies that result from that attachment" (p. 477). Understanding the ways in which these ideological social movements deal with identity politics is essential to understanding how identity and intercultural communication work together. Two major social movements that have been at the center of lots of identity politics in the United States and around the world center on race and gender identity.

Critical Race Theory: Should we be calling attention to racism within our social systems?

Race refers to supposed biological differences between groups. We say "supposed" because even scientists who study people groups cannot agree on how many "races" there are, and the biological make-up of people of different racial groups is much more similar than it is different. In fact, race is as much (or more) political and social as it is biological. For example, the United States at one time determined that "one drop" (legally 1/16) of so-called Black blood made one White. The fact that the government did not define it the other way around highlights the racist assumptions of such a law.

Ethnicity is not race or culture; rather, it refers to a sense of shared history and geographical ancestry, usually along with other markers, such as culture, language, or religion (Herbst, 1997). We see that a single race can have people of many different ethnicities, but just because someone in the United States shares Native ancestry (ethnicity), they may not hold any elements of Native culture. Notably, most of these ethnicities refer to regions that only made sense after the rise of the nation state. Ethnicity is usually understood to relate to one's heritage both in terms of culture and location of ancestry, though many people think in terms of ancestry, even if they do not celebrate the culture of that ancestral group. Herbert Gans (1979) describes what he calls **symbolic ethnicity**, often held by the third and later generations of an ethnic group in a culture, where rather than engaging in ethnic cultures or organizations, people assimilate to the dominant culture but still use symbols, such as the Jewish star, to represent their identity of ancestry. In sum, ethnicity is not equal to race, nor is either equal to culture. Two people of the same race can be of totally different cultures.

As evidenced in this discussion, race and ethnicity have a long history in the United States as a point of contention in culture and in other areas of society. One area in which extensive work has been done to investigate the role that race and ethnicity play is Legal Studies. A movement has long existed in the United States and has recently moved out of the legal classrooms and research journals and into the mainstream, that aims to change the legal system to not be oppressive and unjust toward racial and ethnic minorities. This movement is called "**Critical Race Theory**" (CRT) or "Critical Legal Studies."

CRT is essentially an analysis tool for looking at legal practices to ensure that they are treating all people fairly. It was first discussed in the 1960s and 1970s as part of the larger American Civil Rights movement. One of the early scholars of this movement, Richard Delgado (1995) said,

> It does not matter where one enters this universe; one comes to the same result: an inner circle of about a dozen white, male writers who comment on, take polite issue with, extol, criticize, and expand on each other's ideas. It is something like an elaborate minuet. (p. 47)

When he says "this universe," he is referring to scholarship on the Civil Rights movement. His point is white men are writing about and creating laws for minority peoples that they are not a part of and that these men go in circles around each other, never letting any other voices in.

Matsuda (1995) suggests that these voices are essential to understanding what people genuinely need. She says, "Those who have experienced discrimination speak with a special voice to which we should listen" (p. 63). She compares listening to these voices to speaking in "hypothetical[s]" where the writer/speaker puts themselves in the shoes of someone "Black and poor" (p. 63). Just because someone looks, sounds, or acts different than you, why should they be treated any differently? And why should they not be heard?

In the last few years, Critical Race Theory has become a target in American conservative media because its opponents see it as tarnishing the reputation of American History by suggesting that the country was built on the foundations of racism. In fact, Critical Race Theory is simply working to make sure that we don't forget that history and that we are constantly working to ensure that such racism does not persist in our future. Because racism is often not overt or something we do consciously, there are little things that have been taught to us since we were children that we may not even realize are built off a tradition of racism. Those things can be gradually erased from our society, but only with diligent work and acknowledgment that they are racist.

POP CULTURE

In 2015, a musical opened on New York City's Broadway that changed the way that people understood both Broadway Musicals and American History. Lin Manuel Miranda's *Hamilton* tells the story of Alexander Hamilton, one of America's Founding Fathers, but does so through a hip-hop score, focused on immigrants, with BIPOC (Black, Indigenous, People of Color) in all the primary roles (See Figure 5.2). And *Hamilton* blew up the Broadway box office. In 2018, it became the first Broadway musical to make more than $4 million *in a single week* (Janiak, 2019). Throughout *Hamilton* there are musical shout outs to both the history of musicals and the history of hip-hop. The show is specifically intended to be a celebration of both things at once and is also a perfect encapsulation of intersectionality. To add on top of the music, the cast is also diverse and rich in talent. Miranda and McCarter (2016) discuss the importance of this, saying "American history can be told and retold, claimed and reclaimed, even by people who don't look like George Washington and Betsy Ross" (p. 95). The show caused a significant amount of controversy (ex. Monteiro, 2016), but significantly more praise.

Figure 5.2 Lin-Manuel Miranda and other actors from the Broadway hit musical, *Hamilton*. What role can or should drama, music, film, or television have in addressing social injustices? What other "texts" that have sought to call attention to racial injustice in different ways? Which have been more effective and why? Source: https://www.dailymail.co.uk/video/tvshowbiz/video-2200484/Video-Disney-releases-new-trailer-Broadway-Production-Hamilton.html.

Gender and politics: How do we "structure" gender in different ways—and whom do these structures serve?

Gender is a term that we have heard nearly our entire lives, but that we often do not have a solid definition of. Part of the trouble with defining Gender is that it is often conflated with **Sex**. These are, in fact, two different concepts, that are related. Sex is the biological make up that distinguishes what kinds of sexual organs and genetic characteristics an individual is born with (Fixmer-Oraiz & Wood, 2019). Gender, on the other hand, is a socially constructed definition of how sex manifests through particular sociocultural traits. Gender is not a singular, fixed thing and many scholars have studied how gender works in our society and in the individual.

Judith Butler's *Gender Trouble* (1990) investigates the idea of gender as performative and constantly changing. She says, "Gender does not denote a substantive being, but a relative point of convergence among culturally and historically specific set of relations." In 1950s America, to be "a woman" meant primarily one specific way of presenting and performing femininity. In the 1850s, that definition would have been much different. And each gender's performance also changes depending on the cultural location of the performance. So, European and African performances of gender vary wildly. Butler's point in analyzing gender in this way is to suggest that the foundational elements of identity politics—like feminism—are not as obvious or "natural" as society might suggest. Gender, the thing that unites feminists, is not quite as binary as man vs woman.

R.W. Connell suggests the same but considers the issue from a masculine angle. Connell's work on masculinity is some of the foundational work of the field. She specifically works to analyze **hegemonic masculinity**. According to Connell and Messerschmidt (2005), hegemonic masculinity is the "normative" version of what it means to be a "man." They say,

> Hegemonic masculinity was not assumed to be normal in the statistical sense; only a minority of men might enact it. But it was certainly normative. It embodied the currently most honored way of being a man, it required all other men to position themselves in relation to it, and it ideologically legitimated the global subordination of women to men. (p. 832)

In other words, hegemonic masculinity is not what men are actually like, but how men are "supposed to act." The best way to conceptualize this is to think about "manly" men from the movies like John Wayne, Arnold Schwarzenegger, or Sylvester Stallone (Figure 5.3). These men have long been held up as epitomizing what a man should be like. When men do not act like this, they are belittled or degraded for being "feminine." Both Connell and Butler would say that this is nonsense. But, by treating men in this way, we situate men as "better" than women. A long history of hegemonic masculinity has pervaded Western societies, situating them as patriarchal and oppressing anyone who does not fit into the hegemonic mold of what gender should look like. Out of this society, Feminism was born.

Feminism is a movement that has gone through many transformations over the years but that has always had one ultimate goal: to ensure that women are treated equally to men. The original feminists were the suffragettes around the world who, at the end of the 19th and beginning part of the 20th centuries, fought to give women the right to vote. Modern feminists today continue to fight for women's rights but have turned their attention to women's autonomy over their bodies and equal pay rates for everyone. In the 1940s, Simone De Beauvoir's seminal text *The Second Sex* (1949) outlined the ways in which Western women are situated as lesser than men. Her observations are strikingly familiar in the 2020s. She looks at how women's anatomy is

perceived to be "weaker" than a man's and, thus, they are less capable of performing lots of tasks. Such claims continue to be made today

One of the problems with modern feminism is that it often approaches "equality" from a very Euro-centric perspective. 21st-century American or European feminists assume that the problems they face and the solutions they have found are universal problems when they are not. This began to first be noticed as a problem in the late 20th century. Hartsock (1983) suggests that feminism needs to consider its arguments based on the "standpoints" of individual women, saying "women's relational self-definition and activity exposes the world men have constructed" (p. 365). Patricia Hill Collins (2009) also discusses this idea, but specifically by considering how Black women are situated within feminist scholarship. She says, "Whites and Blacks, male, and females … are fundamentally different entities related only through their definitions as opposites" (p. 77). What applies to one group, or one person may not apply to another person or group. Thus, we should consider feminist arguments from the standpoint of those directly involved in the lived experiences. This is called **Feminist Standpoint Theory** and has been used to help women around the world.

Figure 5.4 Women in the Kashmir region of India protest in 2019 in response to severe security restrictions.
Source: REUTERS/Alamy Stock Photo.

Women Living Under Muslim Laws (WLUML) is an organization that was formed in the 1980s to help women who are suffering under oppressive Muslim governments around the world (Shaheed, 1994). The organization "gathers, builds and mobilizes knowledge, and furthers channels of communication and exchange toward the realization of gender justice, equality and human rights" (MISSION & VISION, n.d.). Increasingly, Muslim women (and men) in different countries are questioning the interpretations of Sharia law that have been used to justify gender inequality and violence, while still seeking to uphold the tenets of their faith (Massoud,2021). And women (and others) have protested in other countries for things from violence against women to restrictive immigration laws (Figure 5.4). Ardill (2013) considers how First Peoples in Australia have been left out of conversations regarding their own sovereignty and how standpoint theory could bring that conversation back to those to whom it matters most. Enloe (2014) considers the ways in which we can use standpoint theory to make sense of "international politics" by "follow[ing] diverse women to places that are usually dismissed by conventional foreign affairs experts as merely 'private,' 'domestic,' 'local,' or 'trivial'" (p. 3). These are just three examples of the numerous ways in which scholars have used standpoint theory to assist in feminist activities.

This is identity politics. Both Critical Race Theory and Feminist Theory are the scholarly adaptations of real-world identity politics. Legal scholars and academics are working toward creating a more race-neutral and generally equitable American judicial system. Feminists around the world are endeavoring to ensure that all women are treated equally to the men they exist side-by-side with. For example, politicians and political groups take up these causes to solicit votes; they become advocates for the "voiceless" at any given moment to ensure that they will win their elections.

What happened to the voices in the first place?

But a discussion of identity politics leads to a discussion of voices and the silencing of huge swaths of our society, especially cultural voices from around the world inside western countries. That is, people who are not from somewhere like the United States are often and historically marginalized and not allowed to be heard in many mainstream Western societies. We should now talk about why that has happened and what it has to do with intercultural identity.

Much of the previous discussion concerning identity groups focuses on people who are like us. We call these groups "ingroups" but now we need to consider "outgroups." Identities involve categorization, a mental process of grouping things, attributes, behaviors, and people into like clusters. Specifically, we group people into ingroups, those groups to which we see ourselves belonging, and outgroups, groups with which we do not associate or cooperate (Gudykunst & Kim, 2003). A lot of research has been done that concerns communication between and amongst groups. According to Greenaway et al. (2015), "*ingroup members*—those with whom one shares social identity—are more trusted, respected, and influential than *outgroup* members—those with whom one does not share identity" (p. 172). Turner et al. (1979), refer to this as "ingroup favoritism" (p. 187) and suggest it emerges from a motivation to "achieve a positive self-image" that is "enhanced" through the similarities found within the group (p. 190).

Another major researcher in this field, sort of, is Edward Said (2016). Said identified and examined a phenomenon that he called "**Orientalism**." He identifies this as "a western style for dominating, restructuring, and having authority over" Middle Eastern cultures (p. 113). Essentially, it is based on a racist ideology that systematically stripped Eastern cultures of any autonomy or voice in western societies. He argues that hegemonic forces have distorted others' representations specifically to situate them as "other" to further subjugate them. Another term for this phenomenon is **Cultural Imperialism**. That is the ways that historically domineering societies have entered countries they deem to be "less than" their usually western way of life and impose their culture and ideologies upon the new culture. Even a phrase as seemingly harmless as "Christopher Columbus discovered America in 1492" is the product of cultural imperialism. How could Columbus have discovered a place where people already lived? A better way of putting it would be "Christopher Columbus was the first European to land in America and did so in 1492." (Although, of course, that would be Leif Erikson's erasure, and that's no good.)

Both orientalism and cultural imperialism are working toward imposing one single version of identity on everyone. And that is typically born out of outgroup fears. As previously discussed, to have out-group fears, you must have a good sense of your ingroup. Cultural imperialism often originates from a sense that the nation you are a part of is the superior nation and that all other people would want to be a part of your nation. Benedict Anderson (2006) argues that this basic idea comes out of an "imagined community." While we don't know everybody who lives in the nation that we live in, we have a sense of camaraderie with them because we are all from the same place and have the same basic culture. That's not necessarily true but the imagined community leads us to believe that it is. Akinci (2020) studied how second-generation non-Gulf migrants in the United Arab Emirates see themselves as part of the imagined community of the UAE. These individuals balance several different, often contradictory identity categories. As a result, they often redefine what "Arabness" means, while still embodying the boundaries between citizens and migrants. The imagined community of the UAE is different in practice than in theory, but a broader "Arabness" brings people together in a different way.

What do you think? Because of the ways that many societies work, we often feel like we are a part of numerous groups and communities. How many of these that you are a part of are "imagined" and how many are real? What is the impact of an imagined community? How does believing yourself to belong to such a group influence your perception of other groups?

As we can see, the way that we *see* things such as race, gender, nationality, or other identities—including the way that we think about our own identity and those of members of outgroups, is directly related to different forms of intolerance (see Chapter 6). An important part of this process of subjugating outgroup members is the extensive creation and use of stereotypes. Stereotypes themselves are not inherently bad things. They are sort of a shorthand way of making sense of society. A **stereotype** is an oversimplified, often unvarying attribute assigned to a group, or to a person because that person is a member of a group (We will say more about stereotypes in Chapter 6). Stereotypes become a problem when we rely too heavily on them and assume that people are only the stereotype and have no other depth to them. As previously mentioned, "primacy effect" means that we often remember the first information we receive about someone better than any subsequent information. This can be especially harmful when taken in conjunction with stereotypes. If you meet someone and *assume* something about them based on the stereotypes you have about them, you might be more likely to only think of them as that stereotype. Van de Wetering (2020) looks at how the *banlieues* of Paris, the outskirts, are often stereotyped as being the homes of "the poor-, the problematic-, the migrant-, the criminal-, the unemployed-, the dangerous-, the different banlieuesards" (p. 303). Consequently, these people are thought of as "abnormal" because they do not conform to what some see as "normal" republican French values. Stereotyping here leads to stigmatization, which leads to subjugation. The role that stereotyping plays in our society and, more specifically, in the media is further investigated in Chapter 10 of this book.

All of this is a form of intercultural communication. When people outside of an individual's community try to enter, it two basic things happen. First, the individual may not know how to treat them and so look to leaders or representations in the media to understand what they are like. This results in the hegemonic representations that are filtered through western ideologies and rely heavily on stereotyping and orientalism. The second thing that happens, that is interrelated with the first, is that people in power are threatened by the new visitors and do what they can to try to secure their own power rather than be usurped. This leads to cultural imperialism, orientalism, and stereotyping.

What do we do about all this and what do we do with this information? The answer to that is not easy because we are trying to fight against centuries of cultural imperialism. Hegemonic representations in the media and the general commitment to some basic stereotypes mean that new images of outgroup members are often met with resistance. That doesn't mean you can't change things.

Call to action—What can we do as allies?

The answer to the question "what can I do" is actually found in a huge amount of the research surrounding identity politics and it's in fact very straightforward. What can you do: Talk and listen to people who aren't like you. Dalton (1995) directly says, "Talk *to* us. Listen to us—we have lots to say, out of the depths of our own experiences" (p. 81). By "us," he is referring to people of color and minorities. His point is not simply that minority voices get heard, but that those voices be an integral part of society and are a part of the decision-making process.

Later in his essay, Dalton (1995) quotes bell hooks saying, "We can use information from the margin to transform how we think about the whole" (p. 82). Chandra Mohanty (2003) also suggests that "rewriting and remembering" history through lenses that aren't necessarily constructed by the dominant hegemony can lead "to the formation of politicized consciousness and self-identity" (p. 78). Read and write and interact with people from other cultures and people with diverse identities; doing so will help you with your own identity.

But other things that you can also do include making sure that you do not get stuck in the cycles associated with cultural imperialism; don't let yourself get caught up in stereotyping; don't assume things about people based only on media representations made by other people. Expand your horizons: meet people from other cultures, consume their media, and just talk to them. It really is that simple.

Conclusion

In this chapter, we have defined what identity is and where it comes from. We also went over the ways in which identity influences society and politics. Then we analyzed how hegemony influences identity and our understanding of other people's identities. In doing so, we learned that we must push harder against our expectations about what other people are like. We must ask questions about why we make the assumptions that we make, as well as where the images we have about other people's identities are coming from. Are they coming from the individuals themselves? Or have they been filtered through ideologies that may not align with the culture being represented?

Identity is a personal experience, but it is based on society and culture. Every day we make choices about our own identities but also other people's. When you consider other people's identities, keep an open mind. That's all it takes.

KEY TERMS

Identity, 92
social identity, 93
Social Identity Theory, 93
social construction, 94
intersectionality, 95
identity politics, 96
Ideology, 96
Hegemony, 96
Race, 97
Ethnicity, 97

symbolic ethnicity, 97
Critical Race Theory, 97
Gender, 99
Sex, 99
hegemonic masculinity, 99
Feminism, 99
Feminist Standpoint Theory, 100
Orientalism, 102
Cultural Imperialism, 102
Stereotype, 103

Discussion Questions

1 List all the identity groups that you feel you belong to. Are there any that sometimes seem to contradict each other? Do you sometimes have to "code switch" within them? How do you do that?

2 What majority identity groups do you belong to? What are the advantages? Do you belong to any minority identity groups? What is it like being in that group? If you feel comfortable: what is something that happened to you as a direct result of being a minority?

3   Identity groups are often the point of resistance in 21st-century life. Identify 3–5 social movements that are linked to identity and outline what their primary arguments are.

4   How has your identity changed over the years? Do you think it will continue to change? What factors could contribute to future changes?

Action Points

1   Identities are socially constructed. Talk to your friends or family members and think about the ways that they have contributed to your identity. What things do you know they do or say that you also do or say? How are you similar? How are you different?

2   Watch your favorite television show. Then, look into the demographic breakdown of your community. Do the demographics on the show mirror the demographics of your community? What does this say about you? What does it say about the makers of the show?

3   There are always atrocities being committed around the world in which minority groups are being subjugated because of an identity category. Research one of these and write a letter to your government representative that outlines ways the government could help.

4   Are there organizations in your community that help disadvantaged people? Find one of these groups and figure out what the best way for you to help them is. Do that thing.

For more information

Billing, S. R. (2021). Indios, Sambos, Mestizos, and the social construction of racial identity in colonial Central America. *Ethnohistory, 68* (2), 269–290. https://doi.org/10.1215/00141801-8801876

Bordo, S. (2003). *Unbearable weight: Feminism, western culture, and the body* (10th anniversary). University of California Press.

Carastathis, A. (2016). *Intersectionality*. University of Nebraska Press; JSTOR. https://doi.org/10.2307/j.ctt1fzhfz8

Goffman, E. (1959). The presentation of self in everyday life. Anchor Books.

Greenland, K., & Taulke-Johnson, R. (2017). Gay men's identity work and the social construction of discrimination. *Psychology & Sexuality, 8* (1–2), 81–95. https://doi.org/10.1080/19419899.2017.1311934

Scheifele, C., Ehrke, F., Viladot, M. A., Van Laar, C., & Steffens, M. C. (2021). Testing the basic socio-structural assumptions of social identity theory in the gender context: Evidence from correlational studies on women's leadership. *European Journal of Social Psychology, 51* (1). https://doi.org/10.1002/ejsp.2678

Stoler, A. L. (2010). *Carnal knowledge and imperial power: Race and the intimate in colonial rule*. University of California Press.

Tajfel, H., & Turner, J. C. (2004). The social identity theory of intergroup behavior. In J. T. Jost & J. Sidanius (Eds.), *Political psychology* (pp. 276–293). *Psychology Press*. https://doi.org/10.4324/9780203505984-16

Wiegman, R. (2012). *Object lessons*. Duke University Press.

References

Akinci, I. (2020). Culture in the 'politics of identity': Conceptions of national identity and citizenship among second-generation non-Gulf Arab migrants in Dubai. *Journal of Ethnic and Migration Studies, 46* (11), 2309–2325. https://doi.org/10.1080/13691 83X.2019.1583095

Anderson, B. R. O. (2006). *Imagined communities: Reflections on the origin and spread of nationalism* (Rev. ed.). Verso.

APA. (2022). *APA Dictionary of psychology*. American Psychological Association Dictionary of Psychology. Accessed December 8, 2022, at https://dictionary.apa.org

Ardill, A. (2013). Australian sovereignty, Indigenous standpoint theory and feminist standpoint theory: First peoples' sovereignties matter. *Griffith Law Review, 22* (2), 315–343. https://doi.org/10.1080/10383 441.2013.10854778

Barker, C. (2004a). Identity. In C. Barker (Ed.), *The Sage dictionary of cultural studies. [E-reader version].* (pp. 93-94). Sage.

Barker, C. (2004b). Ideology. In C. Barker (Ed.), *The Sage dictionary of cultural studies. [E-reader version]* (pp. 97-99). Sage.

Butler, J. (1990). *Gender trouble: Feminism and the subversion of identity* (Kindle). Routledge.

Collins, P.H. (2009). *Black feminist thought: Knowledge, consciousness, and the politics of empowerment* (2nd ed.). Routledge.

Collins, P. H. (2015). Intersectionality's definitional dilemmas. *Annual Review of Sociology, 41* (1), 1–20. https://doi.org/10.1146/annurev-soc-073014-112142

Connell, R. W., & Messerschmidt, J. W. (2005). Hegemonic masculinity: Rethinking the concept. *Gender & Society, 19* (6), 829–859. https://doi.org/10.1177/0891243205278639

Crenshaw, K. (1989). Demarginalizing the intersection of race and sex: A black feminist critique of antidiscrimination doctrine, Feminist theory and antiracist politics. *University of Chicago Legal Forum, 1989* (1), 31. https://chicagounbound.uchicago.edu/uclf/vol1989/iss1/8

Cross, W.E. (1995). Shades of black: Diversity in African Ameican identity. Philadelphia: Temple University Press.

Dalton, H. L. (1995). The clouded prism: Minority critique of the critical legal studies movement. In K. Crenshaw, N. Gotanda, G. Peller, & K. Thomas (Eds.), *Critical race theory: The key writings that formed the movement* (pp. 80–83). New Press.

De Beauvoir, S. (1949). *The second sex* (C. Borde & S. Malovany-Chevallier, Trans.). Vintage Books.

Delgado, R. (1995). The imperial scholar: Reflections on a review of civil rights literature. In K. Crenshaw, N. Gotanda, G. Peller, & K. Thomas (Eds.), *Critical race theory: The key writings that formed the movement* (pp. 46–57). New Press.

Durham, M. G., & Kellner, D. (2006). Adventures in media and cultural studies: Introducing the keyworks. In M. G. Durham & D. Kellner (Eds.), *Media and cultural studies: Keyworks* (Rev. ed., pp. ix–xxxviii). Blackwell.

Enloe, C. H. (2014). *Bananas, beaches and bases: Making feminist sense of international politics* (2nd ed., Completely Revised and Updated). University of California Press.

Fixmer-Oraiz, N., & Wood, J. T. (2019). *Gendered lives: Communication, gender, and culture*. Cengage.

Gans, H. J. (1979). Symbolic ethnicity: The future of ethnic groups and cultures in America. *Ethnic and Racial Studies, 2* (1), 1–20. https://doi.org/10.1080/014 19870.1979.9993248

Gramsci, A. (1926). *Prison notebooks* (J. A. Buttigieg, Ed., Vol. 1). Columbia University Press.

Greenaway, K. H., Wright, R. G., Willingham, J., Reynolds, K. J., & Haslam, S. A. (2015). Shared identity is key to effective communication. *Personality and Social Psychology Bulletin, 41* (2), 171–182. https://doi.org/10.1177/0146167214559709

Gudykunst, W. B., & Kim, Y. Y. (2003). *Communicating with strangers: An approach to intercultural communication* (3rd ed.). McGraw Hill.

Hartsock, N. C. M. (1983). The feminist standpoint: Toward a specifically feminist historical materialism. In C. R. McCann & S.-K. Kim (Eds.), *Feminist theory reader: Local and global perspectives* (3rd ed., pp. 354–369). Routledge.

Harwood, J., & Giles, H. (Eds.). (2005). Intergroup communication: Multiple perspectives. Peter Lang.

Hecht, M. L., Warren, J. R., Jung, E., & Krieger, J. (2005). The communication theory of identity: Development, theoretical perspective, and future directions. In W. B. Gudykunst (Ed.), *Theorizing intercultural communication* (pp. 257–278). Sage.

Herbst, P. (1997). *The color of words: An encyclopedia of ethnic bias in the United States*. Intercultural Press.

Helms, J.E. (1995). An update of Helms's white and people of color racial identity models. In J.G. Ponterotto, J.M. Casas, L.A. Suzuki, & C.M.

Alexander (Eds.), *Handbook of multicultural counselling* (pp. 181–198). Thousand Oaks, CA: Sage.

Janiak, L. (2019, January). 'Hamilton' by the numbers. *SF Chronicle Datebook.* https://datebook.sfchronicle.com/theater/hamilton-by-the-numbers

Larson, D. W., & Shevchenko, A. (2019). Lost in misconceptions about social identity theory. *International Studies Quarterly, 63* (4), 1189–1191. https://doi.org/10.1093/isq/sqz071

Massoud, M. F. (2021, May 18). Muslim women are using Sharia to push for gender equality. *The Conversation.* Accessed April 26, 2023, at https://theconversation.com/muslim-women-are-using-sharia-to-push-for-gender-equality-158371

Matsuda, M. (1995). Looking to the bottom: Critical legal studies and reparations. In K. Crenshaw, N. Gotanda, G. Peller, & K. Thomas (Eds.), *Critical race theory: The key writings that formed the movement* (pp. 63–79). New Press.

Miranda, L.-M., & McCarter, J. (2016). Hamilton: The revolution: Being the complete libretto of the Broadway musical, with a true account of its creation, and concise remarks on hip-hop, the power of stories, and the new America (1st ed.). Grand Central Publishing: Melcher Media.

MISSION & VISION. (n.d.). WLUML: Women Living under Muslim Laws. Accessed April 26, 2023, at https://www.wluml.org/mission-vision/

Mohanty, C. T. (2003). *Feminism without borders: Decolonizing theory, practicing solidarity.* Duke University Press.

Molinsky, A. (2007). Cross-cultural code-switching: The psychological challenges of adapting behavior in foreign cultural interactions. *Academy of Management Review, 32* (2), 622–640. https://doi.org/10.5465/amr.2007.24351878

Monteiro, L. D. (2016). Race-conscious casting and the erasure of the black past in Lin-Manuel Miranda's Hamilton. *The Public Historian, 38* (1), 10. https://doi.org/10.1525/tph.2016.38.1.89

Moran, M. (2018). Identity and identity politics: A cultural-materialist history. *Historical Materialism, 26* (2), 21–45. https://doi.org/10.1163/1569206X-00001630

Nance, T.A., & Foeman, A.K. (2002). On being biracial in the United States. In J.N. Martin, T.K. Nakayama, & L.A. Flores (Eds.), *Readings in intercultural communication: Experiences and contexts* (2nd, ed., pp. 35–44). Boston: McGraw-Hill.

Ng., S.H., Candlin, C.N., & Chiu, C.Y. (Eds.). (2004). Language Matters: Communication, culture, and identity. Hong Kong: City University of Hong Kong Press.

Rouse, E. (1993). Understanding fashion. Blackwell.

Said, E. (2016). Introduction to orientalism. In P. K. Nayar (Ed.), *Postcolonial studies* (pp. 33–52). John Wiley & Sons, Ltd. https://doi.org/10.1002/9781119118589.ch2

Shaheed, F. (1994). Controlled or autonomous: Identity and the experience of the network, women living under Muslim laws. In E. Disch (Ed.), *Reconstructing gender: A multicultural anthology* (4th ed., pp. 76–81). McGraw-Hill.

Sue. D.W. & Sue, D. (2008). Counseling the culturally diverse: Theory and practice (5th ed). Hoboken, NJ: Wiley.

Terhune, C. P. (2006). Biculturalism, code-switching, and shifting. *International Journal of Diversity in Organizations, Communities, and Nations, 5* (6), 9–16. https://doi.org/10.18848/1447-9532/CGP/v05i06/38800

The Who. (1978). *Who are you?* Polydor Records.

Turner, J. C., Brown, R. J., & Tajfel, H. (1979). Social comparison and group interest in ingroup favouritism. *European Journal of Social Psychology, 9* (2), 187–204. https://doi.org/10.1002/ejsp.2420090207

van de Wetering, S. A. L. (2020). Stigmatization and the social construction of a normal identity in the Parisian banlieues. *Geoforum, 116,* 303–312. https://doi.org/10.1016/j.geoforum.2017.05.009

Walters, S. D. (2018). In defense of identity politics. *Signs: Journal of Women in Culture and Society, 43* (2), 16. https://doi.org/10.1086/693557

Wilson, E. (1987). *Adorned in dreams: Fashion and modernity.* University of California Press.

Chapter 6

Intolerance–acceptance–appreciation–equity–inclusion: How can we make the world a more tolerant and inclusive place?

Chapter objectives

After this chapter, you should be able to:

→ Define key terms relating to prejudice and intolerance

→ Distinguish between different aspects of perception as they relate to intolerance

→ Compare and contrast what may or may not be intolerance, based on several tensions from literature and popular discussion

→ Outline causes of intolerance at individual, societal, and other levels

→ Develop a platform of solutions for a particular intolerance that recognizes the complexity and cultural specificity of the problem

Intercultural Communication for Everyday Life, Second Edition. John R. Baldwin, Alberto González, Nettie Brock, Ming Xie, and Chin-Chung Chao.
© 2024 John Wiley & Sons Ltd. Published 2024 by John Wiley & Sons Ltd.
Companion Website: http://www.wiley.com/go/baldwin2e

Malala Yousafzai was a young Pakistani girl with great promise—the daughter of a teacher who ran a girl's school and wanted to provide for his daughter every benefit a boy would have. In 2008, when she was 11, the Taliban took over and closed the school, saying, among other things, that girls could no longer go to school. By the age of 15, Yousafzai was speaking out on behalf of girls' rights (Figure 6.1), when a masked gunman boarded her school bus, asked for her specifically, and shot her in the head. After months of surgery and rehabilitation, she moved to join her family who had fled to the United Kingdom. This was a turning point for her. She states, "It was then I knew I had a choice: I could live a quiet life, or I could make the most of this new life I had been given. I determined to continue in my fight until every girl could go to school" (Malala's Story, n.d.).

Yousafzai, with the help of her father, began a fund to help girls around the world have a better future. At the age of 17, she became the youngest person ever to win the Nobel Peace Prize. She has now graduated from Oxford University and continues to travel around the world to address issues facing girls—forced child marriage, poverty, war, and denial of education. Her story and legacy join well with the focus of this chapter—intolerance—and an underlying theme of this book—civic engagement and activism. Her example illustrates how intolerance links internal thoughts and ideas—often about identity (see Chapter 5)—with action, in this case, a hate crime. It shows how hate crimes may not be based just on race or sexual orientation, but may be based on ideologies, or might even relate to overlapping, "intersectional" identities (here, religious identity and sex). And it demonstrates how any intolerance might have manifestations across the world though also their own unique social and historical context.

At the same time, an analysis of such a horrific hate crime requires some disclaimers. First, only a small percentage of people commit hate crimes—although meanings shared through jokes, social media posts, speeches, media, and interpersonal conversations prepare a field fertile for hate crimes to grow. Second, limiting discussion of intergroup violence only to physical violence may hide from our view the small acts of verbal or policy mistreatment, often unintentional, that occur every day.

Intolerance is key to intercultural communication. As we saw in our model of communication (see Chapter 3), all communication involves not only real cultural differences but also the perception of self and others in terms of groups. Because of group-based perception and

Figure 6.1 Malala Yousafzai, as a teenager, begins to speak out about girls' rights in Pakistan.
Source: https://malala.org/malalas-story

reatment, intolerance or appreciation of other groups is a central part of intercultural communication. But what types of intolerance exist? Where do these begin and what contributes to
them? And how can we seek to reduce intolerance? These are the topics of the current chapter.

Break It Down

Recent Internet news gives reports of statistics and stories on hate crimes from Chile to
Canada, from Russia to Rwanda, from Germany to Ghana. These hate crimes might be against
people of a particular ethnic or racial group, religion, sexual orientation, gender expression, or
some other basis of difference. Locate information on hate crimes in your own area. Think
about some of the possible reasons such hate crimes occur. What is it about the culture, the
economic or political environment, the media and entertainment systems, or the perpetrator
themself, that may frame a context for such violence?

Framing the problem: Where can we recognize intolerance?

In this chapter, we explain a variety of forms of intolerance in a world that seems not to be growing any more tolerant with the passage of time. In 1992, there were 4558 hate crimes in the
United States and 2000 in Germany (Tempe Daily News Tribune, 1993). In 2021, the Federal
Bureau of Investigation in the United States recorded the highest level of hate crimes in a decade,
at 7,759, mostly related to race, ethnicity, or ancestry (Buchholz, 2021). The Office for Democratic
Institutions and Human Rights (ODIHR), which collects data for several European countries,
reports 2239 hate crimes in 2020 (with an additional 10,000+ reports of hate speech), centered
mostly on racism and xenophobia, with anti-Semitic attacks second in number (Germany,
2020). We see ongoing strife that includes both attitudes and social policy in Ireland, Israel,
Cyprus, and Columbia. At the same time, we see progress, such as laws against untouchability in
India and the rise of intercultural and interracial marriages in many countries. Our eventual
purpose in this chapter is to propose some solutions for intolerance; however, an effective solution to any problem requires thoughtful consideration of the nature of the problem.

In this section, we outline some of the potential forms of intolerance, and then end with some
debates about the "location" of intolerance, with **racism** as an example. But before we begin, we
need to define some terms. **Intolerance** refers to any thought, behavior, policy, or social structure that treats people unequally based on group terms. By contrast, **tolerance** is "the application
of the same moral principles and rules, caring and empathy, and feeling of connection to human
beings of other perceived groups" (Hecht & Baldwin, 1998, pp. 66–67). We might think that tolerance is the opposite of intolerance, and that tolerance should be our goal. But scholars and activists have lamented the half-hearted feeling associated with tolerance. To "tolerate" someone
implies merely putting up with them. So, many authors suggest an even greater acceptance than

tolerance: appreciation. **Appreciation** refers to the attitude and action not only of accepting a group's behaviors but also seeing the good in and adopting the behaviors, and actively including the individuals of a group. Appreciation involves such things as "respect, sensitivity, engagement, recognition, and solidarity" (Hecht & Baldwin, 1998, p. 67). However, "appreciation" itself is an insufficient goal, as it focuses only on individuals' attitudes and personal behavior.

Certainly, acceptance of diversity is greater than "tolerating" it—but one limitation of these concepts is they still treat intolerance at a strictly personal level. Increasingly, scholars and policymakers are looking at "tolerance" at the policy level. Thus, **equity** moves beyond feeling good about someone to provide—at the institutional or societal level—social justice and fairness, with fair treatment and equality of opportunity, accounting for the specific contexts of disadvantage experienced by people of traditionally disadvantaged groups. And **inclusion** involves creating a climate, through words, actions, and policy, where people of diverse groups feel welcome and feel that they can participate fully.

Terms: What are some different types of intolerance?

As we seek solutions to prejudice, there are several interconnected things to consider. These include different ways or "locations" that intolerance might exist, which is connected to, but different, from things that might influence intolerance. It is sometimes difficult to know if something is a *form* of intolerance (e.g., prejudiced thinking) or a factor that *leads* to intolerance (e.g., selective perception), so we will treat these together here. In other places, we have outlined in more detail many of the aspects that might contribute to intolerance (Baldwin, 1998, 2017; Baldwin & Hecht, 2003), and in some ways, these echo the "locations" where intolerance can exist.

Intolerance or inclusion can exist at many different levels that all inform one another. They exist in our thoughts and attitudes, relationships, rituals, and social and organizational policies. And they are inherently communicative, as we create, spread, and resist intolerance through face-to-face and mediated communication. In this section, we consider several types of intolerance.

Biological impulses Some authors (e.g., sociobiologists) have argued that there are biological or hereditary components to intolerance. For example, it is a natural instinct to fear the "stranger," and some argue that there is an innate drive to preserve our gene pool, which makes us prefer that our "people" not mate with outsiders. Others have suggested that such thinking has led individuals and states to support racist and xenophobic policies. However, even if we fear the stranger, we still use messages (communication) to "create" who that stranger is and the socially acceptable ways to treat them.

Thought processes and prejudice Gordon Allport, a famous social psychologist who wrote on prejudice (1979/1954), divides his discussion of thought and prejudice into two main areas—psychodynamics and cognition. First, Allport describes several psychological needs or states that might impact how we think about people from other groups. Psychologically, this might stem from a person's feeling of individual or group-based inferiority, a need to shift guilt from one's own group to the other ("displacement"), a liking of authority structures (authoritarianism), and so on.

Cognitive biases In terms of thought processes, most individual-level approaches to intolerance is the notion of group perception. Henri Tajfel and John Turner (1979) describe, in their social identity theory, how we think of ourselves and others in terms of groups—in-groups and outgroups (see Chapter 5). **Categorization**, the mental process of grouping things, attributes, behaviors, and people into like clusters, is necessary; without it, we would have to make sense of each new object, action, and person anew. According to social identity theory, when we see others, we automatically put them into groups (student/teacher, man/woman, my group/not my group), and then evaluate them. While the putting of people and things into categories may be an essential and natural part of thinking (and might not, in itself, be negative), the thoughts about and evaluation of the groups we put people into can be prejudiced.

Our minds and senses, like a computer, are constantly gathering data from what goes on around us. It is impossible to notice everything, so we make choices in what we see or hear. **Selective attention** is the idea that we only pay attention to certain things, impacted by what we hold to be important and our negative or positive expectations. If we expect male athletes to perform more poorly in a classroom, we might not notice the rugby player or online gamer who participates in class frequently or see the intellectual strength in their essays. Once we see something, **selective perception** shapes how we interpret it. In the current example, if we have negative expectations of the male athlete, then when Bedo, a rugby player, writes an essay, we might perceive his arguments to be weak. Finally, as we go to retrieve the "data" from the computer-that-is-our-brain, we only remember certain things (**selective recall**). If we are trying to remember what Bedo said or did in class, we only remember the things that confirm our pre-existing ideas (Baldwin & Hunt, 2002). Gordon Allport (1979/1954) gives an example of how people from two groups might act in a similar way—saving money. We perceive members of one group positively, as "thrifty," but members of the other group as negative, "stingy."

Psychological research introduces the notion of **attribution**, a process by which we give meaning to our own behavior and the behavior of others. Attributions are important in all communication because when we interact with others, we do not respond to what they do or why they do it, but to why we think they did it. We make a variety of mistakes when we give meaning to behavior because we often do not see our own motivations (or those of others) objectively. In the **fundamental attribution error**, we overestimate the role of personal characteristics in someone's behavior and do not place as much weight on context. In personal relationships, if an acquaintance shows up late, we think it is because they are careless, lazy, or do not value the relationship, rather than that it might be because of a difficult bus schedule (Ross, 1977). The **self-serving (or egocentric) attribution bias** leads us to give attributions that frame our behavior as normal and appropriate and give meanings to others' behavior that make us look better—at least in our own minds (Kelley, 1967). The **ultimate attribution error** combines the last two errors: If people we do not like have success, we attribute it to the context (they were lucky, the coaches were on their side), but if they fail, we blame personal characteristics (they are incompetent; Pettigrew, 1979). But we blame our own failures, and those of people or groups we like, on context, and attribute success to character (Figure 6.2).

Figure 6.2 We give meaning differently to our own behaviors and those of our group than we do to that of others or other groups, especially if they are groups that we do not like.

	Something good happens	*Something bad happens*
Out-group member	**External**: Attribute it to context: She got the job because the boss plays favorites	**Internal** (personal characteristics): He lost the business deal because he's lazy and a sloppy worker
In-group member	**Internal**: Attribute it to personal characteristics: She got the job because she's a hard worker	**External** (context): He lost the business deal because he wasn't given enough time to prepare

Research on attribution and bias is ongoing and mixed, both within nations and for cross-national groups. Research finds that between Muslim and Hindu South Asians (specifically, India and Pakistan), both groups assign more positive traits to their own group than the other in a variety of scenarios but did not find that negative outgroup behaviors were assigned to personality traits rather than context (Khan & Liu, 2008). And a study of mock White and Black jurors in the United States found that there was no difference in suggested verdicts within and across races, but that White jurors felt Black defendants had more control over their crimes and were more likely to commit another crime (Yamamoto & Maeder, 2017).

Break It Down

Do some Internet research on global attitudes toward your country (try search words "perceptions of X" or "stereotypes of X"). For example, "perceptions of United States" leads to articles that suggest that Muslims elsewhere in the world feel that the United States acts "unilaterally," or without considering the needs and interests of others (even allies) on the world stage (Kohut, 2005). What are the perceptions others have of your country? What historical or social backgrounds might be behind the perceptions? How do you feel about them?

Stereotypes One of the primary cognitions that researchers have considered is **stereotypes** (see Chapter 5)—oversimplified attitudes we have toward others because we assume they hold the characteristics of a certain group, or "a generalization about what people are like; an exaggerated image of their characteristics, without regard to individual attributes" (Herbst, 1997, p. 212). Research suggests that:

1 Stereotypes function to help people make sense of the world. They are related to the categories we have but are the thoughts or attributes we associate with groups of people.

2 People have stereotypes of other groups and of their own group. A study of the stereotypes Aboriginal and Anglo Australian high school students had of their own and the other group showed that Anglo Australians' stereotypes of Aboriginals were fairly negative, intense, and consistent, while the stereotype of their own group was quite favorable. In one study, Aboriginals felt positively toward Anglo Australians, and only moderately positively toward their own group (Marjoribanks & Jordan, 1986).

3 Stereotypes are often based on a "kernel of truth" (Allport, 1979/1954). For example, North Americans often stereotype Latin Americans as having a "lax" view of

time—"*mañana* time," in which people are always late. There is a truth that in some Latin American co-cultures, the present relationship one is in might be more important than the time on the clock; however, Latino punctuality may depend on the type of appointment (e.g., a business meeting versus a party), co-cultural differences based on social class, urban versus rural cultures, and individual preferences in time orientation.

4   All people have the tendency to rely on stereotypes. Patricia Devine has led a line of research that demonstrates that when people are able to focus on it, they can use their emotional energy to override their stereotypes and to **individuate** or personalize the other—to see the person as an individual, rather than as a group member. But when we are busy thinking about something else, we tend to resort to the stereotypes we learn in our culture about other groups; that is, while we can control stereotypes, they are, in part, automatic (Devine & Sharp, 2009).

5   We may stereotype people differently depending on the group in which we mentally place them. If we have stereotypes toward people who are blind but also toward people who smoke, if we see a blind person smoking a cigarette, it will likely trigger stereotypes about smokers; but if they are using a cane, it will more likely trigger stereotypes about blind people.

Prejudice   Perhaps the main distinction between an intolerant and tolerant cognitive process is the affect, or emotion, that accompanies it. Allport (1979/1954) defines **prejudice** as "an attitude in which we are hostile towards or avoid another person because of the group to which that person belongs" (p. 7). It is important to recognize prejudice as an attitude or feeling, because if we focus only on reducing stereotypes or changing other thoughts, but do not change feelings, the prejudiced person may just find another reason to dislike the members of the target group. Realistically, however, changing attitudes will impact feelings, and altering feelings will lead to more appreciative expectations, perceptions, and attributions.

A specific type of prejudice is ethnocentrism. William Sumner (1940) describes **ethnocentrism** as a perception in which "one's own group is the center of everything, and all others are scaled with reference to it" (p. 13). Some distinguish between ethnocentrism as a belief in the goodness of one's own group, a feeling that may actually serve some positive functions for group survival and the efficacy of a group (Rosenblatt, 1964), and a more negative ethnocentrism, in which one sees other groups negatively. It may be that ethnocentrism is "a belief in the inferiority of other groups" (Herbst, 1997, p. 80), or we might even inadvertently judge others (that is, make attributions of behavior) based on our own culture's standards. As we see, ethnocentrism involves both a perception, for example, of the right or natural way to do things, and an attitude of evaluation, in which we see our way as better. As noted in Chapter 3, ethnocentrism may be one of the few traits that may be universal to all cultures (Herbst, 1997), as seen even in how we think of the world, such as the way we draw maps (see Figure 6.3).

Ethnocentrism is relevant to intercultural communication. In one study (Neuliep et al., 2005), Americans higher in ethnocentrism, when watching a video of an Asian manager reprimanding an American employee, rated the manager as less attractive and competent than those lower in ethnocentrism; they also reported they would be less likely to hire such a manager.

Figure 6.3 Compare the Mercator standard map (Ríos, n.d.), used for centuries in the Western world, in which Greenland (0.8 million square miles) takes up about the same amount of space as Africa (11.6 million square miles), with the Peters projection.

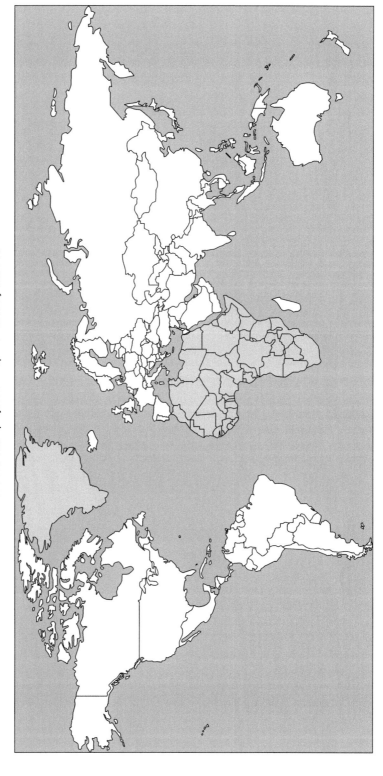

World mercator projection map with country outlines

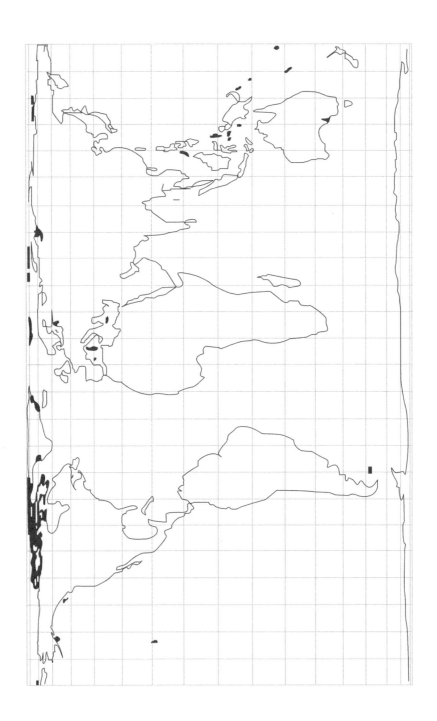

What do you think? Often, we hear calls for **nationalism**, a sense of pride in and loyalty to our nation. This pride can serve many functions, such as allowing us to protect our families and way of life. Some people call us to be economically loyal to our country (e.g., "Buy American"). What are the strengths and limitations of such loyalty? Some suggest that nationalism is linked to ethnocentrism. What do you think? Can one be loyal to one's nation without placing it above or as superior to others? Why or why not?

Related to but distinct from ethnocentrism, **xenophobia** is the fear of people of a group that one perceives to be different from their own. It means, literally, a fear of foreigners. Fear of people who are different might be a natural human response, though our societies tell us whom we should fear and why. For example, politicians in Britain and other countries have hidden racism behind the supposedly natural desire to protect national culture. Sometimes, "xenophobia" hides other forms of intolerance. Paul Gilroy (1987), in a well-known book called *There Ain't no Black in the Union Jack*, describes how British racism is wrapped up in defining its national identity as something that is White and Christian. Teun van Dijk (1993) argues that in Central European countries such as Holland, Germany, and Austria, "racism" is often associated in the collective mind with the Holocaust. Instead, people do not like to think in terms of racism, but rather in terms of *Ausländerfeindlichkeit*—fear of foreigners (xenophobia). He contends that this fear is not directed at all foreigners, but only those perceived to be racially different, and thus is really racism, disguised as ethnocentrism. Ruth Mandel (2008) frames the intolerance as religion-based, noting that Turkish descendants are not integrated into Germany, in part due to Turkish immigrants' desire to maintain their own religion while living in what she calls the "Christian Club" of Europe (p. 11). Likely, the intolerance blends racism and religious intolerance with ethnocentrism and xenophobia.

Behavior   Intolerant behaviors include a wide variety of behaviors, from very subtle to very overt. Behaviors that reflect, promote, or resist intolerance exist in a wide range, from the sort of hate crime that started this chapter to subtle behaviors, to the behavior of saying or doing nothing. At the most extreme end of a possible "continuum" of behavior are slavery and **ethnic cleansing** (the attempt to remove a population by murder or forced deportation from a country or area of a country; Herbst, 1997), such as the Holocaust or the genocides of Rwanda, Darfur, or Bosnia. Individual physical acts against others based on group belonging are often called **hate crimes.** These may include open **discrimination** (the treatment of someone differently because of the group to which they belong), vandalism, physical or sexual abuse, or other harmful behavior (including "flaming" behaviors on Internet video and news sites). Agencies like the Federal Bureau of Investigation (FBI, n.d.) or the Southern Poverty Law Center (n.d.) in the United States, the Organization for Security and Cooperation in Europe (OSCE, n.d.), or the Office of the High Commissioner of Human Rights (OHCHR, "What are human rights," n.d.)— a branch of the United Nations–track hate crimes and hate groups.

Cross-cultural psychologist Richard Brislin (1991) outlines several types of interpersonally expressed intolerance. **Redneck racism** is the blatant intolerance of speaking openly and negatively about other groups. This includes racist, sexist, anti-gay (etc.), anti-disability ("ableist") jokes or other statements with an intent to hurt or put down members of the other group as well as names for those groups (**ethnophaulisms)** such as racial slurs.

We might simply avoid people from certain groups. Brislin (1991) discusses what he calls **arms-length racism**, in which one might even be openly friendly toward people of another group but prefer to keep them at "arm's length" (p. 368). We often allow people from other groups varying degrees of social closeness. A particular South African White might be comfortable working side by side with a Black but may not want the Black to move into the neighborhood. Or they might be okay with the Black living in the neighborhood but would not consider being close friends. Or they might even be friends, but not want to have the Black person marry their sibling, even while preferring or allowing a different level of relationship with one of the Indian-descended South Africans. Emory Bogardus called the different levels of intimacy we prefer with outgroup members **social distance** (Bogardus, 1925; Wark & Galliher, 2007).

What do you think? Is it a compliment or is it sexist? In many Latin American countries, men engage in the practice of *piropos*—compliments (usually) to a pretty woman, who is a stranger walking by. The *piropo* can be poetic, romantic, or crude. Elizabeth Kissling and Cheris Kramarae (1991) argue that such compliments build a hostile and threatening environment for women or, at a minimum, maintain sexual hierarchies, though in some cultures, they are very common. Do you feel such street comments are sexist and promote inequality, or are they compliments to be appreciated? What would happen if women said them to men, or men to other men?

Political correctness, the avoiding of words, images, or actions that marginalize or put down other groups or people that belong to those groups, was one possible solution—to create a social atmosphere where it was not socially acceptable to (openly) express intolerance. But this notion has come under attack from different sectors. In recent politics in the United States, for example, some have argued against political correctness, saying that it stifles open expression. Advocates of saying what they want about whoever they want perhaps fertilized the American mental soil for the more aggressive forms of intolerance we noted above.

At the same time, advocates against intolerance also hail the failure of political correctness as merely changing open expression but doing little to address underlying thoughts and feelings of prejudice. Instead, writers and change advocates have argued, forms of prejudice such as racism and sexism have gone "underground," often hidden in public to avoid public criticism. Even a generation ago, John McConahay (1986) discussed **symbolic racism**, a combined feeling of anti-Black sentiment and political attitudes (minority members are demanding too many rights;

discrimination is no longer an issue). Such attitudes might be that racial intolerance no longer exists, that minority members are getting more than they deserve and are pushing too hard for change, and that failure to advance economically is due strictly to group members' own lack of motivation (Sears & Henry, 2003). In The Netherlands, Teun van Dijk (1987) describes **subtle racism**, expressions that hide racism inside other symbolic behaviors (e.g., talking about gangs, welfare, immigration, and other social issues in disguised racial terms), and Philomena Essed (1991) described the everyday subtle "othering" received by non-Whites in White societies as **everyday racism**, arguing that racism is neither just psychological nor maintained in social structures, but is "routinely created and reinforced through everyday practices" (p. 2). As we will see below, these expressions are often unintentional, though some speakers or writers use them intentionally to "call out" to others—a sort of "dog whistle" to other prejudiced individuals of similar thought.

More recently, these more subtle forms of intolerance have received academic and scholarly attention under the title of microaggressions. **Microaggressions** are communicative acts that express "a harmful, stereotypical, and dehumanizing message against a marginalized individual and/or community" (Campbell, 2021). These can include things such as words or phrases—using "us/them" language in relation to other groups or words or phrases such as saying "that's so gay" or calling someone a "retard" or "spazz" for doing something silly. It can also include subtle nonverbal behaviors, such as a cashier putting change on the counter for people of one group, but in the hand of people of another group. They can be against any marginalized group. For example, Jaymie Campbell (2021) outlines different types of microaggressions (microassaults, microinsults, microinvalidations, with the last two being largely unintentional and even beyond the awareness of the perpetrator) and their effect on trans individuals (See Figure 6.4). Of course, any of these behavioral forms of intolerance, from overt to subtle, may appear in social media, rhetoric (speeches), or media productions (songs, videogames, television series), something we address more in Chapters 10 and 11.

Derald Wing Sue (2017), a leading psychologist in the area of intolerance notes that he is a traditionally "quantitative" researcher; However, Sue says that statistics alone do not tell the full story: "Microaggressions are about experiential reality and about listening to the stories of those most oppressed, ignored, and silenced" as they tell about the "hurts, humiliations, lost opportunities" and "need for change" that they often face in dominant cultures" (p. 171). As "Lourdes," a Latinx woman in the United States reflects, in a qualitative study that gathered the *testimonios* (stories) of Latinx women, she was treated by more advanced teachers like she didn't belong in the best classes and found herself internalizing the low expectations cast upon her by the dominant-culture students (Pérez Huber & Cueva, 2012). Still, social scientific research shows that, while subtly expressed, microaggressions add to the depression of individuals of marginalized groups above and beyond the other traumas of more explicit prejudiced treatment (Auguste et al., 2021).

Finally, in terms of behavior, some have argued that **silence**, itself, can be a form of intolerance. Ibram Kendi (2019) makes this argument a book regarding "antiracism." Kendi argues, essentially, that if one is not deliberately fighting against racism (and sexism, and Queer oppression), one is complicit with it, passing it on. Such a stance is controversial, though it does receive support from the "humanness" or "peace" ethic described in Chapter 2—that to see suffering and not address it is, in a sense, unethical.

Figure 6.4 Microaggressions: Do some research online (videos, websites) and make a list of different specific microaggressions, including verbal or nonverbal microaggressions in face-to-face or media communication. What types of microaggressions might be related to different identity groups? Have you experienced these sorts of messages as a sender or receiver of communication messages? Source: Krakenimages.com/ Adobe Stock

It might be useful to think of the expression of racism as a continuum, in that we can measure the degree to which individuals express or experience different sorts of intolerance, or, to follow Sue's (2017) suggestion above, listen to people's stories and learn more about the *experience* of these forms of intolerance. A danger of such a continuum is that it might lead us to think of prejudice only in the more extreme forms of hate crimes and "redneck" prejudice and ignore the ways that others (or we ourselves) engage in little behaviors that reproduce intolerance (or use nonaction to condone it). Another consideration is that the experience of multiple "everyday" acts of subtle othering is still powerful in the lives of the targets of such prejudice and can have strong negative impacts.

Social context, policy, and social structure   Finally, some people look at intolerance woven into and impacted by social structures. Allport (1979/1954) outlines a variety of group-level factors that might influence prejudice that scholars today continue to investigate in different disciplines, including things such as periods of economic crisis or related competition for scarce resources—which people often perceive in terms of *group*-based competition, immigration, and settlement patterns (e.g., culturally "ethnic" neighborhoods versus "integrated neighborhoods," and so on).

Policies and social structures can also *reflect* or *reproduce* prejudice. Debates rage about the existence of social policies such as unequal punishments for crimes more frequently committed by Blacks or Whites in a given society, funding structures for public education that propagate class and racial inequalities (Kozol, 1991), organizational and legal policies that "blame the victim" in cases of rape or sexual harassment, national language policies that work against the pride and identity of certain language groups, and so on. For example, **redlining** is a practice in which U.S. banks avoid giving mortgages to people wanting to purchase in certain neighborhoods or to people of different ethnic or racial groups. Real estate agents may choose not to show families of color homes in predominantly White affluent neighborhoods, because they do not want to lose the business of White owners in the neighborhood. The Immigration Service might be more likely to stop and ask for identification from someone who supposedly looks like a foreigner (different color skin); airport security might "profile" to search people who appear to have certain ethnic or national backgrounds, and the shopping mall security might be more likely to follow and observe people of certain ethnic groups. Unequal policing, housing, education, medical treatment, and life expectancies reflect intolerance that is built into the very social structure of society. Sometimes organizational policies are informal, such as a "good old boys' network," in which one gains opportunities for advancement based on whom one knows—with such positions often going to those who look, act, or believe like those already in power.

One of the lightning-rod issues in the United States at the writing of this chapter is **Critical Race Theory (CRT)**, which we introduce in Chapter 5. Critical theory, along with Whiteness studies, are central to many discussions of prejudice in modern societies. Many have critiqued CRT, stating that proponents of CRT (including anti-racists) are seeking to indoctrinate students and citizens and forcing teachers and other employees to undergo or promote racial training that touts racial division as the main American problem, with all Whites as being inherently racist. In its origin, CRT, begun by lawyer Derrick Bell, law professor Kimberlé Crenshaw, and others, is simply a movement to analyze "the relationship among race, racism, and power" in legal, social, political, educational, and other systems (Delgado & Stefancic, 2012, p. 3). It focuses on how "contemporary economic and political arrangements, as well as the historical distribution of public and private resources" favor Whites over People of Color (Torres, 2013). CRT advocates and anti-racists claim that opponents often are seeking to avoid responsibility for social inequalities. Others note that critics often point to extreme voices in the CRT movement, while other antiracists, such as Ibram X. Kendi (2019), advocate against assuming someone is racist just because they are White.

At the heart of the issue here is whether there are, in fact, structural inequalities that disadvantage people of a color, **systemic prejudice**—in law, education, business, health, media ownership, religion, or other contexts—and how those impact the ultimate sending and receiving of mediated and interpersonal messages. This prejudice might include White, male, heterosexual, able-bodied, or other systemic benefits. To the degree that such systemic privilege exists, it will interact with, support, or make worse the day-to-day experiences of intolerance received by people who do not have such power. The existence of such forms of power is fiercely debated today, often opposed the most by those who would benefit from having such power recognized.

Combining the influences The various influences of intolerance are interconnected. For example, the thoughts we have about a group may be influenced in part by our interpersonal experiences but are largely shaped by the rhetoric we hear (see Chapter 9) and the media imagery to which we are exposed (Chapter 10). There may be real differences in groups, for example, in crime rates; but these are often shaped by other social forces, such as differences in educational spending and job opportunity. Laws and policies sometimes hold intolerance in place, but this is at least in part because people with intolerant ideas penned the laws, or because people who are unaware of the effects of exclusion sit by and say nothing about them. For example, if we treat it as an overarching system of inequality, sexism includes unequal treatment of women (often built into policies and opportunities)—but those inequalities are based on stereotypes of women, which are reproduced through jokes and media imagery. The stereotypes and beliefs play out in denying women equal opportunities or assaults against women.

Debates: Where does racism lie, and who can be racist?

With a better understanding of the thoughts, feelings, behaviors, and policies that can reflect or promote intolerance or inclusion, we can turn to difficult questions that often come up in discussions with others.

Break it down

Think about your own community and the types of intolerance that are present.

- What are the groups in your community that are more frequently targets of intolerance, and what forms do the intolerance take?
- Why do some people act on their stereotypes and intolerance, and others not?
- Are there any social structures, laws, educational policies, and so on that work against or for the targets of intolerance.
- What are concrete things we can do to reduce the expression of intolerance? Can we impact the thoughts and feelings that lead to that expression?

Is racism (or sexism, etc.,) an attitude or a behavior? As we've seen earlier, intolerance exists within the minds of individuals, in behavior—including communication behavior—and in policies and social structures. Some feel that an attitude, for example, that one racial group is superior to another, is "racist," whereas others feel that racism must include behavior or even social policy (as we shall see below). Each of us likely has prejudices, and these are likely beyond our awareness, a notion called **implicit bias.** But this can come out in behaviors we are not aware of, such as teachers watching students of Color more than White students for problems in the classroom.

How overt does it have to be to be "racist" (sexist, etc.)? A second question that arises as we think about intolerance is how visible (or "overt") something must be to be considered intolerant. Does one have to *express* racism for it to be racist? Is a joke "sexist" if "no harm" or ethnic humor acceptable if told by members of the group the joke is about? It is possible that people define what is racist (sexist etc.) in ways that exclude where they themselves are—if they use racial slurs, then they reserve "racism" for those who use physical violence (Baldwin, 1994).

Should racism (etc.) be determined by intent or result? One way to consider whether something is intolerant is to talk to those who are targets of intolerance to determine the harm the actions inflict, despite their level of overtness. In many cultures, organizations or individuals engage in practices for what seem to be economic reasons—policies noted earlier, such as redlining or racial profiling. The reason people state (and may believe) for the behavior might be financial—the banker (real estate agent, immigration agent, mall security) might not perceive any personal prejudice. In the same way, media makers may simply want to sell a product. People defend such actions based on intent: "I'm not trying to hurt Blacks..." (women, Queer individuals, Turks, Haoles, *gaijin*, Gentiles, Palestinians, Greek Cypriots, Roma, etc.); "I'm just protecting my business" (or culture, or homeland, etc.).

However, recent authors have redefined racism not in terms of what one intends to do, but by "exclusionary practices"—practices that treat people differently because of supposed racial differences. These practices refer "to both intentional actions and unintended consequences which create patterns of inequality" (Miles, 1989, p. 78). We pass on sets of ideas that oppress others not because we want to, but simply because these are the ideas with which we were brought up.

Is racism (etc.) individual, institutional, or societal? Core to the question of who can be racist (sexist, etc.) is whether racism is strictly based on individual thought or behavior. In much general thought today, racism is personal avoidance, dislike, or mistreatment of a group coupled with societal power. **Sexism** is defined as a system of ideas, images, laws, beliefs, and practices that work against women in the favor of **patriarchy** (a system of male-based power), and **heterosexism** as a system of images, policies, and collective thought that privileges heterosexual relationships and marginalizes or disenfranchises those in homosexual relationships. (This last concept is quite different from **homophobia**, an irrational fear of someone who is lesbian or gay, as homophobia really describes a problem in the individual mind, while heterosexism describes organizational policy.) In each of these cases—racism, sexism, and heterosexism—societal power combines with group-based negative attitude. By this logic, in Western Europe, for example, Blacks cannot be racist, and women cannot be sexist. The Black person might have "racial prejudice," but it would not be called racism. Others feel that each of these words should be able to refer to an individual's thought or action regardless of her or his group belonging. To return to Miles' (1989) definition earlier, if a Black person engages in a behavior that excludes or treats Whites differently based on race, it would be racist. We must consider, however, that if both a White and a Black person—in a society where Whites hold privilege—experience a hate crime or epithet based on race, the White will experience it differently, as a violation of expected (privileged) treatment, but the Black person will experience in the context of a long history of similar group- and personal-based attacks based on identity.

POP CULTURE

Intolerance is held in place by those in power—not always deliberately—but also by systems of laws, ideas, and images. People in the empowered group are often unaware that their practices support those systems, and those disadvantaged by the systems also unintentionally consent to the control. A recent fictional book series, *The Hunger Games*, by Suzanne Collins (http://www.scholastic.com/thehungergames) tells the story of oppression by one group, the Capitol, over all of the other districts. For many years, the districts have consented to the oppression, through media manipulation and threat of violence and death. But Katniss Everdeen, the heroine, begins accidentally to bring the oppression to people's awareness. Readers are left wondering at each stage if the districts will continue to yield to the Capitol or stand up to the oppression. The first book was the source for a popular movie in 2012.

Looking to a better future: What are some solutions for intolerance?

As we consider possible responses to intolerance, it is easy to think of education as a solution. Many organizations, universities, and community programs make education about differences a primary part of their platform for change. This solution ignores that intolerance exists beyond the individual. We see an example of this limitation in the debate among educational authors between "multicultural education" and "anti-racist" education. The first takes a well-intentioned and honest attempt to reduce intolerance by letting students know more about different groups. But those who support anti-racist education feel that the multiculturalists focus social change at the level of the individual student's mind: if the student has tolerant ideas, that should reduce intolerantacts. This ignores intolerance built into laws, organizational policies, and media systems (Rattansi, 1992). Simply put, if social system factors impact intolerance, solutions must also include those factors. Education by itself may be too simple a solution for a complicated problem—we might miss the chance for more effective change. A true platform of change should address solutions at the levels of the individual, interpersonal communication, mediated communication, social structure, and law and policy.

Individual-focused initiatives

It is easy to find exercises—or whole books of exercises—on the Internet for changing the way people think. Many use education, especially in the workplace. Strategies for education or training include education to make people more aware of differences (such as a "diversity bingo" icebreaker) interactive games such as Barnga or BaFa BaFa, role plays, and group problem-solving games (see Fowler & Blohm, 2004, for an analysis of the strengths and limitations of various methods). Many organizations have time periods (days or months), publications, and events dedicated to learning more about the major cultures that make up the organization or community. Schools might have a month to focus on "women's history," or the contributions of various groups. We feel that these solutions provide a fair start, but such events usually leave many groups out, and they do much less good than adopting diversity as a mindset that rides throughout the curriculum, throughout the organization, and throughout the calendar year, rather than limiting focus to a month or day.

Aside from efforts to change *others*, we as individuals can be responsible for knowing ourselves, becoming aware of our own biases, such as by taking online personal bias tests or attending programs and doing reading to educate ourselves. Notably, asking a person from a minority group is often *not* the best solution, because people from some groups feel tired of bearing an additional burden of educating people of dominant groups about their experience. Peggy McIntosh, in a famous essay entitled *White Privilege: Unpacking the Invisible Knapsack* (1988) discusses the many privileges she has every day as a White person in the United States, mostly beyond her awareness. And, of course, we can engage responsibly and with respect—assuming others have good motives for the opinions they hold, but still engaging in discussion over important issues—in our interpersonal relationships. Authors such as Mark Orbe and Tina Harris (2015) or Joseph Zompetti (2018) provide useful lists of recommendations for civil discussion over difficult topics such as identity politics (see Chapter 12) and issues that can apply in the classroom or on social media.

Break It Down

Go to Harvard University's website on implicit bias and choose one or more of the implicit bias tests, such as on weight, age, ability, sexuality, skin tone, or some other bias ((https://implicit.harvard.edu/implicit/aboutus.html) and). Think or journal about your findings. If the findings lead you to seek to change, what are some concrete steps you could use to change your own level of personal bias?

Contact theory One theoretical approach, from a social scientific perspective, that has received much research support is called the **contact theory**, an approach that suggests that contact between people from groups that have a history of dislike between them can, under the right conditions, reduce intolerance between groups. Contact works best if members in the contact event (a) have equal status, (b) work together on a task rather than competing against each other, (c) have a shared goal, (c) have communication with each other, (d) have the opportunity to develop ongoing friendships, and (e) have the support of an overseeing group, such as a school administration (Dovidio et al., 2003). Such events can work to change both thought (cognition) and feeling (affect). They allow us to see others not simply as group members, but as individuals.

We see a good example of contact at work in the 2000 movie, *Remember the Titans*, based on a real story, in which U.S. high school football coach Herman Boone (played by Denzel Washington) works through Black–White prejudices to create an integrated and successful American football team in 1971. Of course, contact situations only work if members apply their liking for members of the event to others in the group after they leave the event, and research is still trying to determine if such events have long-lasting effects.

Before leaving individual-level solutions, we should note that **color blindness** (and, by extension other types of blindness, such as gender blindness), attempting to ignore "race" or ethnicity in social interaction, is not a goal that most trainers or researchers promote. Although some people of different races may prefer this, many do not. If I am African American, I may value that identity, and someone trying (or just claiming) to be blind to it denies that important part of who I am. Since all policies and values reflect some cultural orientation, an approach that claims to be culturally blind will probably reflect and benefit the dominant culture, erasing or silencing minority cultural voices. Further, in each culture, there are aspects of difference that we simply cannot ignore. For example, some writers have argued that the United States is divided to its very core by both race and sex. Even if we are trying to be blind, some argue, we cannot think in terms of race and sex differences.

Communicative solutions   Communicative solutions focus on interpersonal or mediated communication. We can be more aware of the words we use, the jokes we tell, the things we say. Directly and verbally addressing intolerance is a useful solution, though it may be best to focus on why behaviors or policies exclude groups, rather than calling them "racist," or "sexist," as these words often make people focus more on defending themselves against a charge than addressing the impacts of their behavior. But sometimes, it is important to call out a behavior or policy for what it is—racist, etc. In such cases, it will still be more helpful for discussions to call the *action, message* or *policy* racist, rather than the person.

As with color blindness, **political correctness** is not the goal here. This attempt at changing everyday communication through terminology and references (e.g., "letter carrier" instead of "mailman") may have some benefit, but it often becomes the target of jokes, and, as noted above, it sometimes slows down deeper, more meaningful change (Morris, 2005). We should be aware of using language that includes others (gender-neutral language), as this creates a way of thinking that allows for more possibilities. But we can also use less patronizing speech when talking to older (or younger) people, be more inclusive in our nonverbal behaviors, and so on. Becoming aware of issues in this chapter, such as subtle intolerance and invisible centers of privilege, like Whiteness, may help us be more responsible communicators. We can also create rhetoric—for example, public messages, letters to the editor, and so on—based on more egalitarian assumptions. Even if we do not create mass media, we may make blogs or websites or actively challenge media makers by writing letters to them or staging protests, advocating for more inclusive and positive images of different groups.

Structural and policy solutions

Social-structural solutions are more of a challenge. These typically call for some sort of social movement, such as group-based protest. As much communication research, especially intercultural research, has focused on the individual, we are not often good at visualizing this sort of change. To return to our introduction, while some responses to intolerance may help individual "tolerance" or even "appreciation," such responses are limited, as they do not create climates or policies of "inclusion." Solutions might range from changing the seating structure in classrooms or changing assignment structures to solutions that aim at creating jobs, reducing urban flight, equalizing opportunities, and so on. Often, such decisions, such as regional and national political decisions, are strongly influenced by lawmakers, who respond to letters. We might write letters just by ourselves, but some of us are more outgoing, have more contacts, and may successfully launch a petition campaign. In some countries, where such campaigns are not legal, citizens may need to find other solutions that work within the framework of the culture, while at the same time stretching that framework to make it more inclusive and tolerant. And, in many cultures... we can vote.

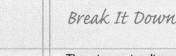

Break It Down

There is ongoing discussion and research on what it means for a dominant group member to be an "ally" for groups that have less privilege or access in society. Alone or in groups, look up the notion of "allyship" (e.g., of dominant culture members towards ethnic minorities). What are some types of behaviors an "ally" can engage in? What are some things that "allies" should avoid?

Summary

We considered in this chapter the basic notion of intolerance and noted how it is central to intercultural communication. Intolerance has many manifestations, such as hate crimes and genocide. But, even if these are not present, there are more subtle forms of intolerance, which some say are worse than overt name-calling or discrimination, because people's true feelings are masked by smiles and polite behavior. We have looked at mental processes that go along with intolerance, such as categorization and in-group/out-group perception, which may not be intolerant, but easily give way to stereotypes, ethnocentrism, or xenophobia. The expression of intolerance is changing, as is the way academic writers talk about it, so that there are many debates now about where an intolerance like sexism or racism lies, whether it is explicit or hidden, whether it must be deliberate or can be determined based on the result of behavior, whether certain intolerances are strictly individual or only held in place with societal power, and so on. One thing is certain, though—all manifestations of intolerance, from social structural inequalities to psychological prejudices, are created, maintained, and resisted through symbolic activity, making the study and treatment of intolerance inherently communicative.

Many possible factors and processes feed intolerance. Some of these are internal to the mind of the prejudiced person, such as thoughts and psychological needs that intolerance might fulfill. But others are social factors—historical relations, group-based differences, movements of groups—and with these, rhetorical and media representations of the other, which feed the stereotypes and feelings of superiority and inferiority that are internal. Laws and organizational policies can also either challenge or support inequality and inclusion. Each intolerance is different, and in some cases multiple oppressions compound. Patricia Hill Collins (1990) argues that oppression of Black women in the United States, for example, is a triple oppression, based on social class, race, and sex (see "intersectionality" in Chapter 5). In the same way, any given intolerance may seem to be about religion but is likely also often about class, competition for jobs, and the personal and social insecurities of the prejudiced parties. Because of the complexity of intolerance, we have argued that in most cases, education on differences and similarities, while important, is only part of a larger, more complex solution. Real change will be nearer when we work together addressing individual, communicative, social, and legal sites of intolerance. Perhaps then, we will see a world that is not only more "tolerant," but also more inclusive of others and appreciative of their differences.

KEY TERMS

racism, 110
intolerance, 110
tolerance, 110
appreciation, 111
equity, 111
inclusion, 111
categorization, 111
selective attention, 112
selective perception, 112
selective recall, 112
attribution, 112
fundamental attribution error, 112
self-serving (or egocentric)
attribution bias, 112
ultimate attribution error, 112
stereotype, 113
individuation, 114
prejudice, 114
ethnocentrism, 114
nationalism, 117
xenophobia, 117
ethnic cleansing, 117

hate crimes, 117
discrimination, 117
redneck racism, 118
ethnophaulism, 118
arms-length racism, 118
social distance, 118
political correctness, 118
symbolic racism, 118
subtle/everyday racism, 119
microaggressions, 119
silence, 119
redlining, 121
Critical Race Theory, 121
systemic prejudice, 121
implicit bias, 122
sexism, 123
patriarchy, 123
heterosexism, 123
homophobia, 123
contact theory, 125
color blindness, 125

Discussion questions

1 The notion of **sexism** is strongly influenced by feminist authors in the West. To what degree does it extend to other cultures? If beliefs and norms in a culture support men's "protection" of women, and so on, is it still sexist? Why or why not?

2 Who can be racist (etc.)? As we were writing this chapter, we posted a news note on our Facebook page about a woman pilot in Brazil who ejected a male passenger who was making sexist comments about woman pilots, and one of our friends complained about the inability to discuss how women can be sexist toward men. What do you think? Can women be sexist, people of color racist, and so on? Why or why not? How do our beliefs about this inform the response we take to intolerance?

3 Read Peggy McIntosh's (1988) essay about the Invisible Knapsack or visit the Microaggressions Project website (http://www.microaggressions.com). Extend the examples in these texts to your own culture. What are some examples of how invisible privileges might be experienced by those with privilege? Which aspects of privilege have changed?

4 Locate a website that tracks group-based intolerance in your country. What types of solutions could individuals or groups enact to address hate crimes or more subtle intolerance in your country or area?

Action points

1 Conduct an analysis of media in terms of the representation of a group (such as women in sports magazines, people with disabilities in prime-time television, for example). The analysis might be quantitative (a content analysis that counts how often certain types of representation occur) or interpretive (looking at the ideas behind the images). Share your findings with the public through blogs, newspaper articles, and so on, and send your findings to the people who made the media.

2 Plan a contact event that brings together members of different groups that may not always get along. Work to include some of the factors from contact theory research that lead to successful contacts, such as the possibility for dialogue and ongoing interaction after the event.

3 If your community has festivals to celebrate identity or marches that address intolerance or oppression, learn more about them and share the information with your class. If your investigation leads you to believe that this is an organization or cause you can support, join the march!

For more information

Allyne, M. D. (Ed.). (2011). *Anti-racism & multiculturalism: Studies in international communication.* Transaction.

Austin, J., Orbe, M. P., & Sims, J. D. (Eds.). (2023). *Communication theory: Racially diverse and inclusive perspectives.* Cognella.

Baird, R. M., & Rosenbaum, S. E. (Eds.). (1999). *Hatred, bigotry, and prejudice: Definitions, causes, and solutions.* Prometheus Books.

Ruscher, J. B. (2001). *Prejudiced communication: A social psychological perspective.* Guilford.

Stroh, D. P. (2015). *Systems thinking for social change: A practical guide to solving complex problems, avoiding unintended consequences, and achieving lasting results.* Chelsea Green.

Tan, A. (Ed.). (2021). *Communication and prejudice: Theories, effects, and interventions* (3rd ed.). Cognella.

References

Allport, G. W. (1979). *The nature of prejudice* (originally published 1954). Addison-Wesley.

Auguste, E. E., Cruise, K. R., & Jimenez, M. C. (2021). The effects of microaggressions on depression in young adults of color: Investigating the impact of traumatic event exposures and trauma reactions. *Journal of Traumatic Stress, 34*(5), 985–994. DOI: 10.1002/jts.22675

Baldwin, J. R. (1994). *European Americans' perceptions of "race" and "racist" communication: An interpretive (and critical) study. Unpublished dissertation.* Arizona State University.

Baldwin, J. R. (1998). Tolerance/intolerance: A multidisciplinary view of prejudice. In M. L. Hecht (Ed.), *Communicating prejudice* (pp. 24–56). Sage.

Baldwin, J. R. (2017). Culture, prejudice, racism, and discrimination. In J. Nussbaum (Ed.), *Oxford research encyclopedia of communication*. Oxford University Press. http://communication.oxfordre.com/view/10.1093/acrefore/9780190228613.001.0001/acrefore-9780190228613-e-164

Baldwin, J. R., & Hecht, M. L. (2003). Unpacking groupbased hatred: A holographic look at identity and intolerance. In L. A. Samovar & R. E. Porter (Eds.), *Intercultural communication: A reader* (10th ed., pp. 354–364). Wadsworth.

Baldwin, J. R., & Hunt, S. K. (2002). Information seeking behavior in intercultural and intergroup communication. *Human Communication Research*, *28*(2), 272–286. DOI: 10.1111/j.1468-2958.2002.tb00808.x

Bogardus, E. S. (1925). Social distance and its origins. *Journal of Applied Sociology*, *9*, 216–226. Accessed August 24, 2022, https://brocku.ca/MeadProject/Bogardus/Bogardus_1925b.html

Brislin, R. W. (1991). Prejudice in intercultural communication. In L. A. Samovar & R. E. Porter (Eds.), *Intercultural communication: A reader* (6th ed., pp.366–370). Wadsworth.

Buchholz, K. (2021, August 31). U.S. hate crimes at new decade high. *Statista*. Accessed August 18, 2022, at https://www.statista.com/chart/16100/total-number-of-hate-crime-incidents-recorded-by-the-fbi

Campbell, J. (2021). Microaggressions. In A. E. Goldberg & G. Beemyn (Eds.), *The Sage encyclopedia of trans studies* (pp. 529-532) Sage. https://doi.org/10.4135/9781544393858

Collins, P. H. (1990). *Black feminist thought*. Routledge.

Delgado, R., & Stefancic, J. (2012). *Critical race theory: An introduction*. University Press.

Devine, P. G., & Sharp, L. B. (2009). Automaticity and control in stereotyping and prejudice. In D. Nelson (Ed.), *Handbook of prejudice, stereotyping, and discrimination* (pp. 61–87). Psychology Press.

Dovidio, J. F., Gaertner, S. L., & Kawakami, K. (2003). Intergroup contact: The past, present, and future. *Group Processes & Intergroup Relations*, *6*(1), 5–21. DOI: 10.1177/1368430203006001009

Essed, P. (1991). *Understanding everyday racism: An interdisciplinary theory*. Sage.

Federal Bureau of Investigations. (n.d.). Hate crime statistics. *FBI*. Accessed August 24, 2022, at https://www.fbi.gov/services/cjis/ucr/hate-crime

Fowler, S. M., & Blohm, J. M. (2004). An analysis of methods for intercultural training. In D. Landis, J. M.

Bennett, & M. J. Bennett (Eds.), *Handbook of intercultural training* (3rd ed., pp. 37–84). Sage.

Germany. (2020). *OSCE: ODIHR: Hate Crime Reporting*. Accessed August 18, 2022, at https://hatecrime.osce.org/germany

Gilroy, P. (1987). *There ain't no black in the Union Jack: The cultural politics of race and nation*. Routledge.

Hecht, M. L., & Baldwin, J. R. (1998). Layers and holograms: A new look at prejudice. In M. L. Hecht (Ed.), *Communicating prejudice* (pp. 57–84). Sage.

Herbst, P. H. (1997). *The color of words: An encyclopædic dictionary of ethnic bias in the United States*. Intercultural Press.

Kelley, H. (1967). Attribution theory in social psychology. *Nebraska Symposium on Motivation*, *15*(11), 192–238.

Kendi, I. X. (2019). *How to be an antiracist*. One World/Random House.

Khan, S. S., & Liu, J. H. (2008). Intergroup attributions and ethnocentrism in the Indian subcontinent: The ultimate attribution error revisited. *Journal of Cross-Cultural Psychology*, *39*, 16–36. https://doi.org/10.1177/0022022107311843

Kissling, E. A., & Kramarae, C. (1991). Stranger compliments: The interpretation of street remarks. *Women's Studies in Communication*, *14*(1), 75–93. https://doi.org/10.1080/07491409.1991.11089751

Kohut, A. (2005). Arab and Muslim perceptions of the United States. *Pew Research Center Publications*. Accessed August 12, 2012, at http://pewresearch.org/pubs/6/arab-and-muslim-perceptions-of-the-united-states

Kozol, J. (1991). *Savage inequalities: Children in America's schools*. Harper Perennial.

Malala's story. (n.d.).MalalaFund. Accessed September 9, 2022, at https://malala.org/malalas-story

Mandel, R. (2008). *Cosmopolitan anxieties: Turkish challenges to citizenship and belonging in Germany*. Duke University Press.

Marjoribanks, K., & Jordan, D. F. (1986). Stereotyping among Aboriginal and Anglo Australians: The uniformity, intensity, direction, and quality of auto- and heterostereotypes. *Journal of Cross-Cultural Psychology*, *17*, 17–28. https://doi.org/10.1177/0022002186017001002

McConahay, J. B. (1986). Modern racism, ambivalence, and the modern racism scale. In J. S. Dovidio & S. L. Gaertner (Eds.), *Prejudice, discrimination, and racism* (pp. 99–125). Academic Press.

McIntosh, P. (1988). *White privilege: Unpacking the invisible knapsack. Excerpted from P. McIntosh, White privilege and male privilege: A personal account of coming to see correspondences through work in women's studies.* Working paper 189. Wellesley, MA: Wellesley College Center for Research on Women. Accessed August 20, 2013, at https://nationalseedproject.org/Key-SEED-Texts/white-privilege-unpacking-the-invisible-knapsack

Miles, R. (1989). *Racism*. Routledge.

Morris, M. (2005). Political correctness. In T. Bennett, L. Grossberg, & M. Morris (Eds.), *New keywords: A revised vocabulary of culture and society* (pp. 260–262). Blackwell.

Neuliep, J. W., Hintz, S. M., & McCroskey, J. C. (2005). The influence of ethnocentrism in organizational contexts: Perceptions of interviewee and managerial attractiveness, credibility, and effectiveness. *Communication Quarterly*, *53*(1), 41–56. DOI: 10.1080/01463370500055954

Orbe, M. P., & Harris, T. M. (2015). *Interracial communication: Theory into practice* (3rd ed.). Sage.

OSCE: Who we are. (n.d.). *OSCE*. Accessed August 24, 2022, at https://www.osce.org/whatistheosce

Pérez Huber, L., & Cueva, B. M. (2012). Chicana/Latina *testimonios* on effects and responses to microaggressions. *Equity & Excellence in Education*, *45*, 392–410. https://doi.org/10.1080/10665684.2012.698193

Pettigrew, T. (1979). The ultimate attribution error. *Personality and Social Psychology Bulletin*, *5*, 461–476. DOI: 10.1177/014616727900500407

Rattansi, A. (1992). Changing the subject? Racism, culture, and education. In J. Donald & A. Rattansi (Eds.), *'Race,' culture, and difference* (pp. 11–48). The Open University.

Ríos, A. (n.d.). *Mercator map of the world*. Accessed April 10, 2012, at http://www.public.asu.edu/~aarios/resourcebank/maps/page10.html

Rosenblatt, P. C. (1964). Origins and effects of group ethnocentrism and nationalism. *Journal of Conflict Resolutions*, *8*(2), 131–146. DOI: 10.1177/002200276400800204

Ross, L. D. (1977). The intuitive psychologist and his shortcomings: Distortions in the attribution process. In L. Berkowitz (Ed.), *Advances in experimental psychology* (Vol. *10*, pp. 173–220). Academic Press.

Sears, D. O., & Henry, P. J. (2003). The origins of symbolic racism. *Journal of Personality and Social Psychology*, *85*, 259–275. https://doi.org/10.1037/0022-3514.85.2.259

Southern Poverty Law Center. (n.d.). Hate & extremism. *SPLC: Southern Poverty Law Center*. Accessed August 24, 2022, at https://www.splcenter.org/issues/hate-and-extremism

Sue, D. W. (2017). Microaggressions and "evidence": Empirical or experiential reality. *Perspectives on Psychological Science*, *12*(1), 170–172. https://doi.org/10.1177/1745691616664437

Sumner, W. G. (1940). *Folkways*. Ginn.

Tajfel, H., & Turner, J.C. (1979). An integrative theory of inter-group conflict. In W. G. Austin & S. Worchel (Eds.), *The social psychology of inter-group relations* (pp.33–47). Brooks/Cole.

Tempe Daily News Tribune. (1993, January 5). *FBI: Racism cause of most hate crime*. p. A3

Torres, G. (2013). Critical race theory. In P. L. Mason (Ed.), *Encyclopedia of race and racism* (2nd ed., Vol. *1*. pp. 462–465). Macmillan Reference USA. Accessed August 26, 2022, at link.gale.com/apps/doc/CX4190600130/GVRL?u=ilstu_milner&sid=bookmark-GVRL&xid=2c25ff75

van Dijk, T. A. (1987). *Communicating racism: Ethnic prejudice in thought and talk*. Sage.

van Dijk, T. A. (1993). *Elite discourse and racism*. Sage.

Wark, C., & Galliher, J. F. (2007). Emory Bogardus and the origins of the social distance scale. *The American Sociologist*, *38*, 383–395. https://www.jstor.org/stable/27700519

What are human rights. (n.d.) *United Nations Human Rights Office of the High Commissioner*. Accessed August 24, 2022, at https://www.ohchr.org/en/what-are-human-rights.

Yamamoto, S., & Maeder, E. M. (2017). Defendant and juror race in a necessity case: An ultimate attribution error. *Journal of Ethnicity in Criminal Justice*, *15*, 270–284. https://doi.org/10.1080/15377938.2017.1347542

Zompetti, J. P. (2018). *Divisive discourse: The extreme rhetoric of contemporary American politics* (2nd ed.). Cognella.

Messages

Part three

With a deeper understanding of the foundations and key elements that undergird our communication, especially communication with people from different cultures or groups, we are now ready to consider the production and consumption of messages. Messages can be sent through many different channels. While some authors suggest that all communication is in some form an extension of verbal communication (e.g., Carroll, 1999), in this unit, we will consider face-to-face communication (verbal and nonverbal), rhetoric (a specific form of spoken or mediated communication with the purpose of persuading), and mediated communication. The latter will include traditional media forms such as news and entertainment television (e.g., film, TV) as well as social media.

Chapter 7 deals with verbal communication and language as these relate to culture. We talk about the nature of meaning within language and some specific ideas about how language might create meaning in different cultures and how language, in turn, is impacted by social situations. We provide examples of specific ways cultural communication can differ, such as in persuasion or compliments, and discuss these in terms of some dimensions of language difference (e.g., level of formality). We close the chapter with a discussion of groups of sentences working together in the creation of cultural discourses such as myths, conversational episodes, social dramas, and cultural metaphors.

Chapter 8 introduces nonverbal communication. Since some readers may not have a background in nonverbal communication, we begin with an introduction of the basic channels of nonverbal communication, such as touch, distance, and eye contact, giving examples of cultural differences as we go. We present the functions nonverbal communication can serve, and then turn to key issues regarding nonverbal communication that have received a lot of attention from communication scholars. One issue is whether we express or recognize emotions across cul-

Intercultural Communication for Everyday Life, Second Edition. John R. Baldwin, Alberto González, Nettie Brock, Ming Xie, and Chin-Chung Chao.
© 2024 John Wiley & Sons Ltd. Published 2024 by John Wiley & Sons Ltd.
Companion Website: http://www.wiley.com/go/baldwin2e

tures; another is whether there are such things as "high contact" cultures, with more eye contact and touch, and less distance. We close by covering some cultural differences in how we see time and silence.

In Chapter 9, the discussion of rhetoric brings together verbal and nonverbal communication to introduce communication with a specific purpose—to influence the thoughts and behaviors of others. We relate rhetoric to culture and provide steps for understanding the rhetoric of someone of your own or a different culture. For a better understanding of rhetoric, we consider several specific traditions: African American, Chinese, Latina/o, Native U.S. American, and the Western U.S. tradition, along with the limitations of discussing such traditions. We introduce vernacular rhetoric—rhetoric used in everyday speech situations—to compare this to the public rhetoric discussed in the first part of the chapter, again with specific ethnic and regional examples.

Chapter 10 presents a discussion of mediated messages. Mediated messages present language and nonverbal symbols via sound text, font, and photographs. Since media scholars sometimes use different models or approaches to communication from face-to-face researchers, we begin by discussing approaches that see media as a transmission of messages versus part of a ritual of everyday life. We discuss issues surrounding media and culture, such as how media frames our understanding of people from different groups and how cultures differ in terms of the role of media in the public sphere.

Finally, in Chapter 11, we consider the role of culture as it relates to new media, specifically social media. After introducing the ways social media connect us across cultural lines (again, not meant to be "national" lines!), we consider how the various "affordances" of social media help us achieve different tasks, such as maintaining cultural identity, adjusting to a new culture, or addressing conflict. We close the chapter by considering different types and uses of social media platforms across different cultures.

References

Carroll, D. W. (1999). *Psychology of language* (3rd ed.). Brooks/Grove.

Chapter 7

Verbal communication: How can I reduce cultural misunderstandings in my verbal communication?

Chapter objectives

After this chapter, you should be able to:

→ Apply notions of face theory and speech acts theory to understand cultural differences in specific types of verbal communication (e.g., attempts to persuade)

→ Describe and apply various dimensions of difference in verbal communication

→ Understand and explain cultural discourses

→ Explain and give examples of cultural myths, conversational episodes, and social dramas

→ Implement general ideas of communication accommodation to understand a speech episode

Intercultural Communication for Everyday Life, Second Edition. John R. Baldwin, Alberto González, Nettie Brock, Ming Xie, and Chin-Chung Chao.
© 2024 John Wiley & Sons Ltd. Published 2024 by John Wiley & Sons Ltd.
Companion Website: http://www.wiley.com/go/baldwin2e

Websites from Engrish.com to *Better Marketing* (Jurberg, 2020) give humorous translations of signs from around the world into English, such as the Coors beer ad saying "turn it loose" translated to an ad in Spain that reads "suffer from diarrhea," the Kentucky Fried ad encouraging Chinese to "eat your fingers off," or the Clairol hair product "Mist Stick" *not* translated in a German ad, where "Mist" means "manure" (not to mention several other examples that would be vulgar in many cultures). Verbal mistranslations abound! (See Figure 7.1).

Of course, language difficulties in intercultural communication are based on much more than translation errors. In this chapter, we discuss how different aspects of language reflect culture and can lead to cultural misunderstanding. We will touch on theories that explain how cultures differ in terms of verbal communication, as well as what happens when people of different groups and cultures talk with each other. We will end with some brief suggestions for more successful interaction.

Systems of language and culture: Why is talking across cultures so difficult?

Language refers to a system of verbal, nonverbal, and visual symbols that a group pieces together to share meaning. There are often forceful politics surrounding language, because making one language a "national language" gives those who speak that language prestige and power over others who do not speak the language well, or even who speak it with a different dialect or pronunciation than has become dominant. For example, in Québec, Canada, language politics between French and English have been longstanding. One policy there requires that all advertising, including in Chinese businesses and restaurants, post French as the largest language on signs and advertising (Croucher, 2006).

Figure 7.1 Cultural mistakes abound as people try to translate signs into other cultures. What kind of mistakes have you made while trying to speak or write in a second or third language?
Source: Andrew Woodley/age fotostock/SuperStock.

What do you think? In the United States, there are currently movements in some places to make English an official language. Richard Jackson (2005) analyzes politics of word usage in the United States regarding the war on Terrorism, and scholars have published research on language politics in Ukraine, Denmark, the Baltic States, Spain, China, Pakistan, and others. What language politics or debates exist in your region or culture?

Any language community contains multiple ways of speaking (speech codes)—but people in different situations have different "communicative resources" (Philipsen et al., 2005). For example, local—even classroom—cultures dictate how or if students might ask questions, challenge an instructor, or even tell a joke in class. Language structures the interaction, so that certain people have the right to do some things and others to do other things. These rights are accepted and consented to by people in the situation but are sometimes challenged. In sum, language is not something we simply participate in as individuals—it is structured by history, social situations, social relations, and hierarchies.

Systems of meaning

Languages are composed of several parts, from the smallest to the largest. The spoken sound of the language—such as Xhosa clicks, Thai tones, or the sounds of consonants and vowels in any language—are **phonemes**. These are put together in different ways (**phonology**). For example, many British English speakers put an /r/ sound between open vowels that end one word and begin another word ("saw(r) and conquered," called the "intrusive /r/" (John, 2015). These sounds are put into chunks to create root words, with other sounds joined together to create prefixes, suffixes, or enfixes (/un/ + /believe/+ /able/ + /ly/ = /unbelievably/). These smallest units of sounds that have meaning are called **morphemes**. These form parts of speech (nouns, verbs, adjectives, adverbs, and so on) that are put into a grammatical order that works for any specific language, with different orders for different languages. The ordering of words that makes sense in any language is the **syntax**. These first elements are most often the realm of research of linguists, with communication scholars more interested in the next elements of language, semantics, and pragmatics.

Semantics is the area of language study that considers what words, phrases, or sentences mean. Words have **denotation**—the relatively objective dictionary-type of definition of a word, and **connotation**—the feelings (personal or social) that individuals associate with a word. Meaning comes in part from the personal experiences we have with a word. When we are little, we see a dog on the street, and someone says either "puppy!" or *"viralata!"* (Brazilian Portuguese meaning "tin can-turner", or mongrel, used for "street" dogs). We associate the sound or image with something we see ("reality")—either face-to-face or in a mediated text—and we get a sense of how we should feel about it. "Puppies" are cuddly and cute and want to be petted; *"viralatas"* should be avoided and left alone.

Through interaction, then, we create meanings (Berger & Luckmann, 1966), and these meanings differ from culture to culture. For example, the English word "friend" translates into "amigo," "přítel," or "arkadaş" in Portuguese, Czech, and Turkish—but people who speak these as first languages often have different expectations and meanings for what a friend is and does than those who speak U.S. American English. In the mobile American culture, a friend may be someone one sees after a long absence and feels as if the relationship continues right where it left off. But in other cultures, friendship implies a deep sense of obligation and continued communication. At the same time, social ideologies also frame language, through the reproduction of mediated messages, politics (e.g., legal definitions of what it means to be Black or White in a given country), and so on.

Some argue that meanings of words are not simply neutral but are loaded with power implications. Groups struggle to define certain words, illustrating the notion of **discourse**. Discourse, in this sense, refers to the sets of ideas surrounding a concept. Michel Foucault (1978) talks about the history (what he calls the archeology) of words, noting how cultures and societies create notions such as mental illness, sexuality, and crime in a way that keeps certain sets of ideas in power. (For example, is same-sex sexual activity a "mental illness" or "crime" in your culture?) These meanings change over time, such as the notion of "race" in U.S. American culture (Banton, 1977), but they change through group striving, as people with different ideologies fight to make their meanings central. But as we shall see below, discourse can also refer to a unit of language larger than one sentence (like a story told in interaction, "interview" discourse, gossip, or chit-chat).

What you say is what you get: the Sapir-Whorf hypothesis   We have seen that cultures may differ in the way they think of language. Some writers go further to suggest that the language of a culture dictates how people within that culture can think. The **Sapir-Whorf hypothesis** posits that language creates social reality through language structure, such as the fact that different languages make different verb tenses, word order, or words available to describe certain things (see Figure 7.2). Harry Hoijer (1991) cites examples from Navajo, Hopi, and other languages in which people from different cultures have wider or narrower sets of names for color spectrum. Thomas Steinfatt (1989) concludes, however, that language may not create a "reality" for people but rather leads people in a culture to tend to think about certain things rather than others.

Figure 7.2 The Sapir-Whorf hypothesis notes that different languages classify the world differently. This may lead people who speak these languages to think of the world in different ways or focus on different aspects of reality.
Source: Whorf 2012, Figure 15.2. © 2012 Massachusetts Institute of Technology. Reproduced by permission of The MIT Press.

HOPI - ONE WORD (MASA'YTAKA)
ENGLISH - THREE WORDS

ENGLISH - ONE WORD (SNOW)
ESKIMO - THREE WORDS

HOPI - PÁHE   HOPI - KÉYI
ENGLISH - ONE WORD (WATER); HOPI - TWO WORDS

Speech acts and cultural communication

Another important area for intercultural communication is what actions we seek to accomplish with utterances—the **pragmatic** aspect of language. For example, someone tells you, "You look great." The words contain a second-person singular pronoun, "you," a linking verb suggesting how something appears, "look," and an adjective with a positive feeling behind it, "great." In one situation, this could be a compliment, but, if you have just spent all night studying and have not cleaned up before class, it could be sarcasm. It could be flattery, to your boss's wife, or a lie, to avoid hurting someone's feelings.

This example shows us that there are many things we can do with a phrase, just as there are many ways to accomplish the same sort of act. **Speech acts theory** outlines the types of actions we perform with utterances (Austin, 1962). We follow basic rules when we communicate, as long as we are trying to cooperate with others in conversation. Cooperation here implies a desire to share meaning; we can "cooperate" to understand each other even if we are arguing. If we are competent, we will stay on topic, give sufficient detail but not more than is necessary, speak things we believe to be true, and speak in a way that is relatively clear (Grice, 1957; Stanford Encyclopedia of Philosophy, 2007). We can do different types of action with words—we can make statements (observations), express our feelings or opinions (compliment, curse, greet), try to influence others (hint, question, command), commit to a future act (promise, threat, vow), or change the state of things with our words (fire someone, decree something—acts that can usually only be done by people in authority). Each of these follows a set of hidden rules about what constitutes an act (an apology must be about a negative event over which a person has control and feels sincerely sorry) or who can do it (only someone with authority can make a "pronouncement") (Nofsinger, 1991; Searle, 1969). We probably follow all of these rules without thinking about them.

Speech acts theory helps us understand cultural language difficulties. What counts as enough detail in one culture may not be the same in another culture. In one culture, people may tend to request using indirect language, which would violate unstated expectations for clarity in another culture; and the intended purpose of a message is often not what is received. We experience this in our daily lives. Deborah Tannen (1991) outlines sex-based differences in the workplace: a woman might give an order that looks and sounds like a suggestion ("you might try..."), and men might misunderstand it only as a suggestion, with the result that women's requests are often not fulfilled by men (this explanation, neglects the possibility that men undervalue women's leadership in organizations). Shoshana Blum-Kulka (1997) illustrates such forms of indirectness in requests by analyzing a scene at an Israeli dinner table, where the father is hungry and seeks permission to make himself some food, but the mother perceives it as a complaint about what is offered, so explains her choice of rice for dinner.

In intercultural communication, people often mistake the force of a statement for what it actually looks like. Many newcomers to the United States get frustrated when people ask, "How's it going?" when they do not really want to know. While "How's it going?" can be a heartfelt request for information in the United States, it often serves simply as a greeting, and the speaker does not expect a detailed response. In cultures that prefer indirectness, a statement in a negotiation session like "We'll think about it" sounds like a promise for future consideration but may be a polite way to say "no."

Getting things done with language

We can see culture's impact on how we accomplish many different communication acts. These include things like making and responding to apologies, making requests, showing camaraderie, giving criticism, and gaining agreement on a project. Each area has produced rich research in cross-cultural and intercultural communication, but we will consider just four areas.

Directives **Directives** (attempts to influence the behavior of or persuade another) can range from subtle hints to overt commands. For example, one study (Du-Babcock & Feng, 2018) found similarities and differences between the way Taiwanese and Japanese university students make requests, providing evidence for eight different types of "moves" the students made in writing their requests (e.g., establishing credentials, attracting the reader's attention). Among differences, the Japanese students were more likely to introduce the request before making the actual request and "most of the Hong Kong students adopted an explicit yet compromised approach when making the request" (p. 184). And another study (Aikhenvald, 2016) analyzes the way the Manambu speakers of Papua New Guinea word wishes, requests, invitations, and desires in a variety of subtle ways depending on the nature of the relationship between the individuals.

Insults Cultures certainly vary in the way people are appropriately able to criticize each other, especially through insults. Research has demonstrated that even terms of abuse ("swear" words) that we might call someone are informed by cultural values and traditions, as found in one study comparing 11 different cultures (the USA and 10 in Europe, Van Oudenhoven et al., 2008). Research on Egyptian (Rosenbaum, 2019) and Maghrebi dialects of Arabic (D'Anna, 2019) describe the insults deemed most aggressive in these cultures, such as attacks on one's family or one's religion. However, Sahana Udupa (2018) notes how online media in India allow for the emergence of "interlocking practices of insult, comedy, shame, and abuse," with which online communicators can develop the "skills to hurl, dodge, or otherwise criticize abuses" (p. 1509) in online spaces in a way that has the potential to promote political reform.

Apologies In response to an embarrassing situation, should someone make a joke, give an explanation or defense, or make an apology of some sort? Todd Imahori and William Cupach (1994) had student participants describe an embarrassing predicament of their choice. Japanese students were more likely to describe something that had happened with someone from their in-group, and the U.S. Americans, someone from an out-group. The Japanese were more likely to feel a sense of **shame**, in the sense of negative reflection upon their group for the embarrassing situation, but the U.S. Americans, **guilt**, or a sense of personal responsibility. While people in both cultures preferred to avoid mentioning the wrong and an "apology" as the primary responses, in some situations, Americans were much more likely to use humor to lighten the situation, whereas Japanese were more likely to use **remediation**—that is, to do something concrete to make up to the injured party for the embarrassment.

Compliments Farhad Sharifian (2008) describes how Persian speakers, even when they are speaking English as a second language, give and receive compliments. The Persian notion of *adah*, a form of politeness in which one seeks to give compliments, suggests one should give many, but sincere, compliments on various aspects of the other person's life. While one may give lots of compliments, however, a contrasting notion of *shekastehnafsi*—modesty—leads one to downplay one's own accomplishments. In response to a prompt that one had done a great job, one participant responded with, "I owe this achievement to your efforts. If it hadn't been for your help, I would never have achieved this" (p. 62). Another study classifies the various types of compliments given in Pidgin English in Cameroon (Nkwain, 2011), such as direct appraisals ("What a beautiful blouse you have!", p. 67), or interrogative appraisals ("Where do you do your hair?", p. 68). The author suggests that the compliments, shared between people of different ethnic or tribal groups but shared in a common trade language of Pidgin, serve to build solidarity between speakers, as long as they are perceived as genuine.

Explaining the details: Seeking ways to explain differences across cultures

As we have seen, people use different ways to make an argument, negotiate, joke, request, compliment, promise (or threat), show respect, or give instructions. Even with fluency in the grammar and vocabulary of a language, if we do not master the pragmatics of the local culture, we will lack competence. Researchers have proposed several frameworks to try to make sense of a wide variety of communication behavior (verbal and nonverbal). Some seek explanations that apply across cultures. Here we provide some of these frameworks.

Relational orientations   Many scholars define relational orientations in two primary dimensions of interaction: power and solidarity (e.g., Brown & Levinson, 1987; Tannen, 1994). **Power** refers to the level of control over another's thoughts, feelings, or behavior. This includes communication in which one person imposes upon or yields to another. In any culture, people in different situations or relationships communicate more of a hierarchical difference. We talk differently with our friends than with our employer, and differently with our employer than we might if we met the Queen or the Prime Minister. Another dimension of interaction is **solidarity (relational distance)**, the degree of familiarity and/or intimacy we have with another person. We tend to react differently—more formally or less rudely—to someone who is a stranger than to an acquaintance, a friend, or a close friend.

The two dimensions interact. In some cases, we might have a closer level of intimacy with a supervisor, even though they are also hierarchically above us in the organizational structure; but we might act more cordially to a stranger who is our age than one with a higher status. Tannen (1994) notes that some cultures, like the United States, associate power with asymmetry, hierarchy, and distance, and see it as the opposite of solidarity: it is difficult to be in a close relationship with a boss or status superior. Other cultures, such as one might find in Indonesia or Japan, imagine relationships that bind people together hierarchically, but also with a strong sense of solidarity. These dimensions exist in all cultures, though individual, cultural, and structural influences shape them in actual communication.

What do you think? Make a list of large or small favors or requests you could ask of someone. Now, list the ways you might ask or tell someone to do the favor. What are some ways your persuasion attempts can vary? What are some factors that influence how you shape your attempt to influence the other person? Brown and Levinson (1987) suggest hierarchy, relational closeness, and size of the imposition as three factors. How do these play out in your culture (for example, how would your request differ between a stranger and a close friend)? What other factors might influence how you shape your communication?

Face theory   Many authors use notions of face and politeness theory. In fact, the notion of "face" may be one of the most frequently occurring concepts found in explaining cultural differences. Irving Goffman (1959) argues that we are often concerned about what he calls **face**—the image we seek to have of ourselves in interaction. We are like actors on a stage, with props, lines, and performances; but sometimes, we let others "backstage" to see more of what we are really like. Goffman (1967) argues that in interaction, we work together with others to protect and repair loss of face, because face-loss can interrupt the flow of interaction. Once face has been damaged, conversation often stops while someone makes a joke, an apology, a threat, or some other remedy, and that remedy is accepted by others—unless the most face-saving move is to say nothing, such as we do when people pass audible gas publicly in cultures where this is disapproved of (Cupach & Metts, 2006).

Penelope Brown and Stephen Levinson (1987) find evidence that in all cultures, people seek to preserve the idea that they are free and autonomous (**negative face**) as well as the idea that they are competent and qualified for some task; people also like to feel included or liked by others (the last two notions are aspects of **positive face**). Researchers have often grouped cultures together in terms of face dimensions, a notion we will return to in Chapter 13, though some studies complicate general claims about how people in a single culture might reflect positive or negative faces.

Cultural scripts   Other researchers, rather than try to predict behaviors, use observation and talk to people to learn the communication **scripts** used in a culture. These are cultural rules regarding expected behavior that include expectations of who does what (actors, roles), and any expected sequence of actions in a communication routine. Cliff Goddard and Anna Wierzbicka (1997), using a scripted approach, describe what they call a "natural semantic metalanguage" (p. 235) that uses simple words, like *people, something, say, think, know, good,* and *bad,* to describe a behavior in a particular culture. They use this approach to describe what they call *halus* speech—a speech form in Malaysia in which people talk carefully with people outside of their immediate family. The cultural logic is that:

When people hear someone saying something

Sometimes they think something like this:

"This person knows how to say things well to other people; this is good."

Sometimes they think something like this:

"This person doesn't know how to say things well to other people; this is bad." (p. 242)

In a similar way, Donal Carbaugh (2005) unpacks a negative live-audience reaction to Phil Donahue, as he tried to goad Russian youth into talking about the "problem" of premarital sex in Russia. Carbaugh concludes that, while "public talk" and turning issues into problems is a mainstay of American talkshow television, with sex being treated very rationally, the Russians in his study at that time perceived sex to be a deeply emotional topic and did not perceive public television as the correct place to air public problems.

Dimensions of difference   Instead of theories and frameworks, many authors summarize types of differences one might expect between cultures. These provide a simple way to think of how cultures can differ, as long as we realize that (a) most cultures will sit between the "extremes" on any set of terms and contain elements of both aspects of a dimension; (b) there will be differences within each culture based on age, social class, urban versus rural residence, task at hand, and so on; and (c) cultures balance change and tradition in the face of globalization.

Break it down

To learn more about cultures around you, join a cultural interest group or make frequent visits to a cultural location different from your own (e.g., a different type of worshiping community, different festivals). Interact with people enough to understand how communication in that group might differ from or be similar to your own. How does your increased understanding of the communication work together to inform—and be informed by—your understanding of the background, immigration conditions, and so on, of that group? What does your experience teach you about yourself?

→ *Direct versus indirect*: As we have already seen, people in some cultures—depending on the relationship between individuals, the urgency of the topic, and other factors—can be very direct, even "in your face." People in other cultures can be indirect. For example, Egyptians in many cases use *musayara* speech, marked by deference, commonality, and avoidance of conflict (Zaidman et al., 2008). At the same time, contradicting traditional notions of high-context cultures being more face-saving, Stephen Croucher (2013) found that Thailand participants in a largely non-university sample were more verbally aggressive than U.S. American participants.

→ *Formal versus informal*: All cultures have situations that are more or less formal, though in some cultures, there are *more* occasions for formality than others. In midwestern U.S. American classrooms, students are more informal, some even calling professors by first name (though this might differ by region, among different ethnic cultures, or for those who have served in the armed services). In other cultures, communication in business or education situations or with status superiors demands formality.

→ **Differentiated and undifferentiated codes**: Language is differentiated when there are different **registers**, or forms and levels of formality of speech for people in different societal groups, such as based on social status. Romance languages are more differentiated than English, with both formal and informal forms for singular "you" (Spanish: *tú, Usted*)—though the specific rules for going from *tú* to *Usted* vary from culture to culture, even within a single Spanish-speaking country. Korean, on the other hand, has multiple levels of formality in language, and even "honorific verbs" to describe things such as eating or sleeping for those very high in status. A reporter for *Seoulbeats* demonstrates how these levels of formality apply even in K-pop, a contemporary form of popular music from South Korea (Dana, 2012).

→ **Instrumental and affective styles**: People in some cultures may be more goal-oriented, preferring efficient linguistic forms, which relates to directness, discussed above, while other cultures may have a preference for more emotional and expressive communication. This combines elements we discuss in Chapter 4, such as being versus doing. We see this in the way that offers are made in some U.S. American and Chinese cultures. In many U.S. circles, the correct sequence is offer → request/decline ("Would you like some iced tea?" "No, thanks." "Okay." But "no" is usually not preferred, so we give a reason for "no" but not for "yes") But in some Chinese cultures, one should offer food or hospitality even if one is not willing or able to give it at that time, just to be polite; and the other person, even if hungry or tired, should decline the request, just to be polite. The function of such offers in these cultures, is to make someone feel welcome. The correct sequence for a large offer might be offer→decline →insist→resist→double insist→accept/decline. And yet, while we say this pattern characterizes some Chinese and other "face-saving" cultures, we can certainly see similar patterns occurring, based on the size of the offer, in many cultures.

→ *Exaggerated, exacting, succinct styles*: An **exaggerated style** uses language more to embellish reality than to describe it, as a major function of communication is to reveal the speaker's ability to use language creatively. For example, many U.S. African American males might employ boasting, rapping (romantic come-ons), and verbal games like "the dozens" (Johnson, 2000), all of which allow one to demonstrate one's skill with words. An **exacting style** emphasizes saying what one means, giving the detail necessary—with a focus on efficiency similar to the instrumental style noted earlier. The **succinct style** reflects a cultural or personal preference for fewer words, perhaps even understatement. The instrumental/exacting communication is speaker-focused, with the speaker providing the detail they feel the other needs, whereas a succinct style is listener-focused, leaving the listener to fill in the gaps (Lustig & Koester, 2010), such as in the traditional notion of British understatement or some Asian forms that include more silence and subtlety in communication.

Discursive elements of cultures: What happens when we join the elements of language?

We often interact with friends and relatives for easily identifiable reasons. We engage in conversation to exchange information and express our feelings and judgments. However, there are times when our interactions with others have meaning beyond the immediate context and are explained by broader patterns of communication. For example, when sports fans arise for their national anthem before a game, they participate in a public ritual. The song is an expression of national pride and is a deliberate reminder of national greatness and national ideals. When fans stand, sing, remove their hats and show other signs of respect, they publicly confirm their loyalty to the state. The anthem along with other verbal (for example, a formal pledge of allegiance) and nonverbal (standing) symbols, compose a set of meanings—or a discourse—that guides understanding and action.

These broader patterns of communication are **discursive elements of language**. Cultural myths, conversational episodes, social dramas, and metaphors are examples of discursive elements of cultures that are examined in this section. Being prepared for successful civic action requires having an understanding of the discursive elements that guide communities.

Cultural myth

Cultural myth is a narrative that is popularly told to teach preferred ways of behaving, such as a familiar story that recommends particular values and responses to situations. An example might be the U.S. American myth of the "American Dream," traditionally a view that anyone can work hard to achieve a better life (expressed in terms of monetary wealth/ security and material goods). Myths may have origins in historical events or may be anchored in values that have evolved over time. A myth is told that Buddha called all the animals to him as he ended his earthly stay. Only 12 animals answered the call, so Buddha rewarded the rat, ox, tiger, rabbit, dragon, snake, horse, sheep, monkey, rooster, dog, and bear by giving each animal its own year (Fong, 2012). People born during the year of a particular animal have the characteristics of that animal, thus giving honor to each animal. As a cultural myth, the story allows parents to recommend to their children socially valued behaviors. Though the 12 animals are assigned different traits, all have traits that point toward passion, focus, and hard work.

Myths are conveyed through a variety of methods, including popular culture. For example, the U.S. song *The Ballad of Davy Crockett*, found on a popular children's CD titled *For Our Children* (Stern & Kleiner, 1999), tells the story of Davy, who was "born on a mountaintop in Tennessee" and who was so skilled in the woods that he "kilt him a bar [killed him a bear] when he was only three." In addition to conquering the land, he fought different Native tribes and got elected to the U.S. Congress. He "saw his duty clear" and went off to fight with the Texas Revolution at the Alamo, where he met his demise in 1836. The actual Davy Crockett dropped out of school, ran away from home and angrily left Tennessee after losing an election. So why is Crockett commemorated in this song? The song emphasizes (and exaggerates) aspects of a U.S. American character that are deeply rooted in American folklore. Crockett, as the "King of the wild frontier," reinforces the goodness of turning natural resources to human use—by force if necessary. He reinforces the goodness of individualism and single-minded determination, and he legitimizes the superiority of Euro-American Protestantism over other beliefs. Additional stories of characters such as Paul Bunyan and Babe the Blue Ox serve much the same purpose.

In contrast, the late environmentalist and Nobel Laureate Wangari Maathai (2010) tells a story about the hummingbird. In the story, the forest is on fire and all the animals flee and turn to watch the fire burn their habitat. The hummingbird decides to try to put out the fire one drop at a time. The animals ridicule the hummingbird and the hopeless effort. The hummingbird turns to the animals and says, "I'm doing the best that I can." Indeed, "I will be a hummingbird" became the slogan for the Green Belt Movement that fought deforestation in Central Africa. In telling the story of the hummingbird, Maathai utilizes "the African storytelling tradition [to provide] a counter discourse that discourages inaction and promotes action" (Yartey, 2018, p. 53). The story builds from the common idea that in times of overwhelming odds the least among us are often the most important. *The Parable of the Hummingbird* and *The Ballad of Davy Crockett* express different cultural values and recommend different approaches to acting in the world.

Conversational episodes

A **conversational episode (CE)** or **communication ritual** is a routine portion of conversation that has an expected beginning and end, like ordering a meal at a restaurant, exchanging details with a friend about what they did last night, or buying petrol (gas) at the pump (Figure 7.3). Though usually brief, exchanges are important and guided by tradition. As language philosopher

Figure 7.3 If a person goes to the payment window to buy gas for their vehicle and says, "I'll put $30 on 4," what they are really saying is, "I'll pay $30 using pump #4." The window teller might ask, "Card?" They are asking for a discount card and might say, "That's ten cents," meaning a ten-cent discount per gallon of gas. Many conversational episodes are quick and ritualistic. What communication rituals do you engage in within your own culture? What functions do they serve? Source: kimberrywood/Adobe Stock

Judith Butler (1997) wrote, the episode "exceeds itself in past and future directions" (p. 3). In this sense, CEs are performances of cultural knowledge. When a Spanish-speaking individual is introduced to another, the common reply is "*mucho gusto*" or "nice to meet you." In Morocco, it is nearly impossible to greet someone without invoking Allah. In a CE, something specific gets accomplished: a joke is told, a bet is made, and a greeting is given, much as in speech acts earlier though the CE involves more than one turn, as opposed to a hint or a threat. So, "*mucho gusto*" would be a speech act, but it would occur within an episode, typically upon first meeting someone, and would be followed with an expected follow-up, like, "*el gusto es mio*" ("the pleasure is mine"). In a different example, during the first three days of the Chinese New Year, people commonly use the expression "*gung hay fat choy*" (may you have a happy and prosperous new year) and avoid negative topics. If a speaker makes a disparaging remark and invites bad luck, the hearer replies, "*Tou heu soey dzoi geng gwa*" (spit out your saliva and speak once more) (Fong, 2012, p. 157). Some writers speak of different discourses as expectations and patterns of speech that occur in different situations, such as courtroom discourse, television interview discourse, or informal conversation. Who shares what in each situation is shaped by social roles, norms, and hierarchies, like other aspects of language.

Social dramas

A **social drama** is a conflict that arises in a community after a social norm is violated. The violation becomes a social drama when discussion about it calls into question that social norm, and the resolution of the conflict validates, strengthens, or weakens the norm for members of the community (Turner, 1982). Social dramas can occur on an international scale, on a national scale, or at local levels.

Social dramas can spark national dialogues. In October 2022, performing artist Kanye West, also known as Ye, voiced antisemitic opinions on news programs and on social media (Rector, 2022). He repeated common themes that Jewish people control the U.S. economy and exert too much influence on the entertainment industry. Subsequently, he was banned from his Twitter and Instagram accounts for violating community standards. Yet others spoke in support of Ye and demonstrators in Los Angeles marched with a banner that read: "Kanye is right about Jews" (Rector). Yet Ye's sponsors began to end their contracts with him culminating in the loss of an Adidas contract worth $1.5 billion (Voytko, 2022).

Turner identified four stages of a social drama.

→ Breach of the code—this is violation of an accepted rule or law.

→ Crisis—this is the talk or discussion in response to the breach.

→ Redress—this is the method for resolving the breach. Redress can be formal (a trial) or informal (public opinion). Redress can result in reintegration or dissensus.

→ Reintegration or dissensus—reintegration is forgiveness and inclusion back into the community. Dissensus means there is ongoing disagreement about the breach and its implications for the community.

In the case of Ye, he breached several norms—he repeated debunked conspiracy theories about Jews, he stereotyped Jews in a way that many felt would incite antisemitic violence, and he claimed that sponsors could not drop him because he was a superstar, which many took to be arrogant. The crisis stage contained responses to Ye's comments by prominent anti-hate organizations and politicians. Discussion also turned to the nature of creative "genius" and the extent to which a genius is allowed to violate social norms. Redress occurred when Adidas (as well as numerous other companies and labels) severed their partnerships with Ye. There remains dissensus. While most agree that Ye's comments are harmful toward Jews in the United States, others excuse his behavior by pointing to his great success and artistry (Lindquist, 2016). It remains to be seen whether audiences will reflect dissensus or reintegration as Ye continues to produce more music.

Our verbal communication often is about community or national and international controversies. Our opinions become part of a larger dialogue on acceptable or reprehensible conduct. As we discuss topics with others and give our judgment on our own actions or the actions performed on our behalf (and perhaps change our judgment), we examine and prioritize our individual and cultural values. Thus, not only do social dramas shape our individual cultures, but as they arise in discussion, they become part of our intercultural dialogue.

Cultural metaphor

A **metaphor** is an association of two items. A characteristic of the more familiar item is associated with the less known item. If we talk about "saving time," we are treating time in terms of something tangible that can be saved, like money. Metaphors can have many different origins. For example, "*zubda*" is an Arabic word for "the best butter or cream." *Zubda* refers to the best of what has been mixed or churned. So imagine a music CD called *The Zubda of Shakira*, which would mean "the best of Shakira" or "the essential Shakira."

Metaphors and metaphorical expressions in talk and literature have fascinated critics since Aristotle. George Lakoff and Mark Johnson (2003), a linguist and a philosopher, go so far as to say that we "live by" metaphors—they structure the very way that we think. For example, we will treat immigrants differently if we think of them as a "scaffolding for our construction economy" as opposed to a "drain on society resources." An especially helpful notion is the **metaphorical archetype**—a comparison of items that has many expressions (a "family" of metaphors, metaphorically speaking) and is deeply ingrained in a culture (Osborn, 1967). The metaphorical archetype is instantly recognized when it is used, and so assumed that it is rarely questioned. The archetypal metaphor found in President Barack Obama's 2008 campaign speeches was the metaphor of the "journey" (Darsey, 2009). Expressions such as "the journey that led me here," "path of upward mobility," and "the road to change" allow Obama to connect to the larger narrative of America's forward motion.

Metaphors of travel and motion are not hard to come across in ordinary North American speech. Expressions such as "I see where you're going with that," and "just follow me for a second" connect motion with argument and reasoning. Other metaphors such as "being concrete," "getting to the bottom line," "getting to the point," and "the weight of evidence" all suggest a linear ("now it's time to connect the dots") orientation. The dominant U.S. cultural preference for linearity (time's arrow) contrasts with Native American metaphors of circularity and *looking backward*.

Intercultural communication scholar Victoria Chen explores the metaphor of "home" as it pertains to refugees and immigrants. For Chen, home is both a "geographical construction" as well as "a web of complex relationships" that people create to gain a sense of belonging (Chen, 2010, p. 484). Chen's idea of the "portable homeland" explains how refugees from Vietnam and Cambodia recreate a sense of their original home within their new environments of Australia and France.

What do you think? Imagine a way of thinking that was premised on recurring growth (birth-to-death-to-birth) rather than travel or journey. The struggle to adopt policies that ensure a sustainable use of natural resources can be seen as a struggle over metaphors. Which metaphor families will prevail: metaphors of linear development or metaphors of growth?

As critical observers and participants in cultures, we are reminded that discursive elements of cultures serve a variety of purposes. The words and expressions that existed before us may have become popular to further marginalize a specific population or region or to privilege a particular cultural value or view of something, like success, beauty, or human nature. We should not automatically accept the verbal options given to us. We should always reflect upon who is served or under-served by a particular narrative, metaphor, or conversational episode. Typically, we view the breach of a code as negative. But we should ask: did that code need to be violated to advance social justice? Is dissensus *the* right outcome to achieve social justice?

Theories of conversation and culture: What happens when we talk to each other?

We have looked at what happens within each culture, either in terms of forms of languages (apologies, compliments) or in terms of larger levels of discourse and meaning (metaphors, rituals). But what happens when people from different cultures communicate? To the extent that differences in expectations for different behaviors are beyond our awareness, when someone else requests, criticizes, compliments, or greets us in a way we do not expect, we will give meaning to their behavior based on our own cultural norms (**attribution**, see Chapter 6). In many cases, this can lead to a negative evaluation or simply to misunderstanding. Here we introduce one theory that has gained much attention, and then address issues of dominance and power in intergroup communication.

Communication accommodation theory

Often people with different speaking styles communicate with each other, even from within the same nation. Basil Bernstein (1966) stated that the social situation, including communicative context (for example, a job interview versus a party) and social relationships (for example, peers versus status unequals), dictates the forms of speaking used in a particular situation. Bernstein suggested that in all cultures, there are different types of codes. A **restricted code** is a code used by people who know each other well, such as jargon or argot. **Jargon** refers to a vocabulary used by people within a specific profession or area (such as rugby players or mine workers), while **argot** refers to language used by those in a particular underclass, often to differentiate themselves from a dominant culture (e.g., prostitutes, prisoners). However, as people get to know each other better, even good friends can develop this sort of linguistic shorthand, speaking in terms or references that others do not understand. In an **elaborated code**, people spell out the details of meaning in the words in a way that those outside of the group can understand them. This switching back and forth between codes is called **code-switching**. Effective communicators should be able to speak in restricted codes appropriate to their context, but also know how to switch to elaborated code (for example, to include outsiders)—to change their vocabulary, level of formality, and so on, to match the audience and social occasion.

Based on the notions of different codes within a community, as well as code-switching and other theoretical ideas, Howard Giles and his colleagues introduced **communication accommodation theory** (Gallois et al., 2005; Giles & Noels, 2002). This theory predicts how people adjust their communication in certain situations, the factors that lead to such changes, and the outcomes of different types of changes.

In the U.S. television series, *Lost*, through a series of flashbacks and present communication, we observe the speech of Jin Kwon (Daniel Dae Kim), a Korean man, the son of a fisherman, but hired by a wealthy restaurant owner. In some cases, his communication is respectful, indirect,

Break it down

Tell about a time that you moved back and forth between an elaborated and a restricted code. This might have happened at a workplace, if your work has a specific jargon, or even as you move between slang your friends use and the talk you use with parents or teachers. What are some ways that "code-switching" can be effective or ineffective in communication? How can we use an awareness of others around us (such as international students) to use code-switching appropriately to make their communication adjustment easier and to make them feel more accepted?

deferential; in others, it is direct, friendly or aggressive, and nonverbally more expressive. In some cases, he might change his behavior to be more like that of the person with whom he is speaking (**convergence**), and in others, he might make no changes in his behavior (**maintenance**) or even highlight his own style to mark it as different from that of the other group (**divergence**). Jin can change his behavior in terms of nonverbal behavior (distance, posture, touch, etc.), paralinguistic behavior (tone of voice, rate of speech, volume, etc.), and verbal behavior (word choice, complexity of grammar, topic of conversation, turn-taking, etc.). Many things influence shifts in his speech, such as the status and power of the other communicator, the situation, who is present, communication goals (for example, to seem friendly, or to show status or threat), the strength of his own language in the community, and his communication abilities.

Communication and sites of dominance

Convergence can often go wrong. Giles and Noels (2002) explain that, although converging is usually well received, we can **overaccommodate**, or converge too much or in ineffective ways, by adjusting in ways we might think are appropriate, but are based on stereotypes of the other. People often speak louder and more slowly to a foreigner, thinking that they will thus be more understandable. Overaccommodation also works in situations of dominance. For example, younger people often inappropriately adjust their communication when talking with elderly people. Often called **secondary baby talk**, this includes a higher pitch in voice, simpler vocabulary, and use of plural first-person ("we"—"Would we like to put our coat on? It's very cold outside"). While some older people find this type of communication comforting, especially if done by health workers, some feel it speaks down to them and treats them as no longer competent. A similar feeling might be experienced by Blacks in the United States when Whites use **hyperexplanation**. This inappropriate form of adjustment also includes use of simpler grammar, repetition, and clearer enunciation. But Harry Waters (1992) suggests that it is a behavior some Whites engage in while talking with Blacks (or other minority members)—perhaps based on real communication differences or perhaps based on stereotypes, but certainly leaving hurt feelings or resentment on the part of the Black listeners. A similar notion is **mansplaining**, which occurs when men "talk down" to women (Figure 7.4). This can occur through providing details that the women do not need as if the man is "teaching" them, but it also takes into account

Figure 7.4 Hyperexplanation: Often people in dominant groups in culture (e.g., men to women, Whites to racial minorities in the USA) overexplain— using repetition, simpler vocabulary, giving unneeded information, maybe a "teaching" tone of voice. "Mansplaining" is one example of hyperexplanation. Mansplaining can be emotionally harmful to women as well as for trans individuals.
Source: Sloane Kazim/The Ithacan/

such things as men interrupting women (more than they might men), talking over them, or using nonverbal (such as posture) and paralinguistic (such as tone of voice) behaviors, in essence, speaking in a way that is condescending or patronizing.

Writers have outlined the ways in which word choice, turn-taking, and length, or topic selection may also serve to exclude others, often without us even being aware of it (Fairclough, 2001; Tannen, 1994). Don Zimmerman and Candace West (1975) found that while women "overlapped" speech turns in talking to men, often with "continuers" ("mm hmm," "yes") that continued the turn of the male, men were more often likely to interrupt women, often taking the turn away from them. And when women did interrupt men, the men did not yield the turn to women, while women did yield the turn to men. Jennifer Coates (2003), observing storytelling, found that men and boys often framed themselves as heroes, as being rebels or rule-breakers. In analysis of family communication, she found that there is "systematic" work done by all family members in many families to frame the father as either the primary storyteller or the one to whom children tell their stories. Coates concludes, "Family talk can be seen to construct and maintain political order within families… . to conform roles and power structures within families" (p. 158), giving men more power in most mixed-gender storytelling over women. We can see that each aspect of verbal communication could be used in ways to impose power over others, often based on group identity, cultural difference, maintenance of group power, or, simply put, prejudice.

Summary

Our focus in this chapter has been on various aspects of verbal communication as these relate to culture and intercultural communication. We considered elements that make up the language system—from the smallest parts of sound (phonemes) to language woven into myth, ritual, and practice. We considered perspectives of language and culture, such as whether linguistic relativity is a valid concept, that is, whether the language that a culture speaks creates the reality that the speakers of that language inhabit. We gave special attention to the use of language in building myths, communication episodes, and social dramas.

Beyond lists of dimensions of language variation (e.g., formal to informal), we provided some overarching ideas to explain how these might vary across cultures, such as speech acts and face theory. We considered explanations of what happens when people of different groups or cultures speak to each other, through the notion of communication accommodation. Finally, we suggested ways that people use verbal language, perhaps without intention, to reinforce power structures and social discourses, such as discourses of traditional gender roles or ideas of group stereotypes.

An understanding of the elements of language and how they can differ among cultures is useful as we engage ourselves in a multicultural world. Realizing how adjusting our language to others can often be helpful may help us to be aware of our own communication behavior when interacting with others. And, while our focus has been on how language might oppress others with or without intention, we can use this knowledge to speak more respectfully with others. Indeed, many scholars today are using this knowledge to give those who are in marginalized groups new ways of speaking that provide more equality of power among communicators.

KEY TERMS

Discussion questions

1   What mythic stories were you told as a child that influenced your values and decisions?

2   What metaphors do you commonly use in your talk? How do these work to create shared meaning with the people you are speaking with? What cultural assumptions and values do these reflect?

3   Visit a website that includes different mistranslations from one language to another. If English is not your first language, find examples in your language of English-speakers' efforts to speak your language. See if you can describe how meaning is violated in the mistranslation (sounds, grammar, word meanings, pragmatic level).

4   Give an example of a time when you adjusted your behavior toward another person, especially of another age, ethnicity, class, physical ability, or some other group. Include how you adjusted, various factors that may have influenced your adjustment, and outcomes—your feelings/perceptions or relational outcomes. What are some advantages or

disadvantages of adjusting your behavior toward someone? Are there times not to do so, or to adjust your communication away from someone?

5 What are the advantages and disadvantages of a country having a single national language? Think broadly both about economic advantages and about aspects of prestige for various groups. Do some investigation: does your country or state have an official language?

Action points

1 See what opportunities there are in your area to serve as a language instructor or tutor. Often there are volunteer agencies to teach people the local language (e.g., in the United States), or to teach visitors the local customs, immigration information, and so on.

2 Review recent events at your school or within your city. What social dramas can you identify? Were existing values reaffirmed or weakened?

3 Identify metaphorical expressions from five different cultures. How do these metaphors reflect distinctive ways of understanding the world?

4 Analyze jokes that are popular in your culture (either among comedians or among you and your friends). What are some ways the jokes build or support lines of power (e.g., putting some groups over others)? Discuss in class or with friends appropriate ways to address jokes that cast people as "Other," when you hear them.

For more information

Austin, J.T., Orbe, M.P., & Sims, J.D. (Eds.). (2023). *Communication theory: Racially diverse and inclusive perspectives*. Cognella.

Fairclough, N. (2001). *Language and power* (2nd ed.). Pearson.

Jackson, J. (Ed.). (2012). *The Routledge handbook of language and intercultural communication*. Routledge.

Johnson, F. (2000). *Speaking culturally: Language diversity in the United States*. Sage.

Ng, S.H., Candlin, C.N., & Chiu, C.Y. (Eds.). *Language matters: Communication, culture, and identity*. City University of Hong Kong.

Spencer-Oatey, H. (Ed.). (2008). *Culturally speaking: Culture, communication, and politeness theory*. Continuum.

References

Aikhenvald, A. Y. (2016). Imperatives in Manambu. *Oceanic Linguistics, 55*, 634–668. https://muse.jhu.edu/article/640602

Austin, J. L. (1962). *How to do things with words*. Harvard University Press.

Banton, M. (1977). *The idea of race*. Tavistock.

Berger, P., & Luckmann, T. (1966). *The Social construction of reality: A treatise in the sociology of knowledge*. Doubleday.

Bernstein, B. (1966). Elaborated and restricted codes. In A. Smith (Ed.), *Culture and communication* (pp. 427–441). Holt, Rineholt, & Winston.

Blum-Kulka, S. (1997). Discourse pragmatics. In T. A. van Dijk (Ed.), *Discourse as social interaction* (pp. 38–63). Sage.

Brown, P., & Levinson, S. (1987). *Politeness: Some universals in language use.* Cambridge University Press.

Butler, J. (1997). *Excitable speech: A politics of the performative.* Routledge.

Carbaugh, D. (2005). Cultures in conversation. Lawrence Erlbaum Associates.

Chen, V. (2010). Authenticity and identity in the portable homeland. In R. T. Halualani & T. K. Nakayama (Eds.), *Blackwell handbook of critical intercultural studies* (pp. 483–494). Blackwell.

Coates, J. (2003). Men talk. Oxford.

Croucher, S. M. (2006). The impact of external pressures on an ethnic community: The case of Montreal's *Quartier Chinois* and Muslim-French immigrants. *Journal of Intercultural Communication Research, 35*(3), 235–252. DOI: 10.1080/17475750601027014

Croucher, S. M. (2013). The difference in verbal aggressiveness between the United States and Thailand. *Communication Research Reports, 30*(3), 264–269. DOI: 10.1080/08824096.2013.806255

Cupach, W. R., & Metts, S. M. (2006). Face management in interpersonal communication. In K. M. Galvin, & P. J. Cooper (Eds.), *Making connections: Readings in relational communication* (2nd ed., pp. 164–171). Roxbury.

D'Anna, L. (2019). Curses, insults, and the power of words: Verbal strategies in Maghrebi dialects. *Romano-Arabica, 19,* 71–82.

Dana. (2012). Korean through K-Pop 101: Navigating speech formality. *Seoulbeats.* Accessed March 15, 2013, at http://seoulbeats.com/2012/08/korean-through-k-pop-101-navigating-speech-formality

Darsey, J. (2009). Barack Obama and America's journey. *Southern Communication Journal, 74*(1), 88–103. DOI: 10.1080/10417940802571151

Du-Babcock, B., & Feng, H. (2018). Culture and identity on intercultural business requests: A genre-based comparative study. *Iberica, 35,* 171–200.

Fairclough, N. (2001). *Language and power* (2nd ed.). Longman.

Fong, M. (2012). Communicating good luck during the Chinese New Year. In A. González, M. Houston, & V. Chen (Eds.), *Our voices: Essays in culture, ethnicity, and communication* (5th ed., pp. 154–157). Oxford University Press.

Foucault, M. (1978). *The History of sexuality: An introduction* (Vol. *1,* R. Hurley, Trans.). Vintage.

Gallois, C., Ogay, T., & Giles, H. (2005). Communication accommodation theory. In W. B. Gudykunst (Ed.), *Theorizing about intercultural communication* (pp. 121–148). Sage.

Giles, H., & Noels, K. (2002). Communication accommodation in intercultural encounters. In J. N. Martin, T. K. Nakayama, & L. A. Flores (Eds.), *Readings in cultural contexts* (2nd ed., pp. 117–126). Mayfield.

Goddard, C., & Wierzbicka, A. (1997). Discourse and culture. In T. A. van Dijk (Ed.), *Discourse as social interaction* (pp. 231–257). Sage.

Goffman, E. (1959). *The presentation of self in everyday life.* Doubleday.

Goffman, E. (1967). *Interaction ritual: Essays on face-to-face behavior.* Pantheon.

Grice, H. P. (1957). Meaning. *The Philosophical Review, 66*(3), 377–388. DOI: 10.2307/2182440

Hoijer, H. (1991). The Sapir-Whorf hypothesis. In L. A. Samovar & R. E. Porter (Eds.), *Intercultural communication: A reader* (6th ed., pp. 244–251). Wadsworth.

Imahori, T. T., & Cupach, W. R. (1994). A cross-cultural comparison of the interpretation and management of face: U.S. American and Japanese responses to embarrassing predicaments. *International Journal of Intercultural Relations, 18*(2), 193–219. DOI: 10.1016/0147-1767(94)90028-0

Jackson, R. (2005). *Writing the war on terrorism: Language, politics, and counter-terrorism.* Manchester University Press. https://doi.org/10.7765/9781526130921

Johnson, F. (2000). Speaking culturally: Language diversity in the United States. Sage.

John, K. (Jan 20, 2015). Intrusive /r/. Pronunciation Studio. Accessed March 5, 2023 at https://pronunciationstudio.com/intrusive-r/

Jurberg, A. (2020, June 24). *14 hilarious marketing translation fails.* Bettermarketing.pub. Accessed September 23, 2022, at https://bettermarketing.pub/14-hilarious-marketing-translation-fails-5b9c6ef6daa9

Lakoff, G., & Johnson, M. (2003). *Metaphors we live by.* University of Chicago Press.

Lindquist, D. (2016). In defense of Kanye. *Indystar/USA Today.* Accessed November 27, 2022, at https://www.usatoday.com/videos/embed/89262422/?placement=mobileweb-amp&cst=entertainment%2Fmusic&ssts=entertainment%2Fmusic&series=&keywords=Kanye+West

Lustig, M. W., & Koester, J. (2010). Intercultural competence: *Interpersonal communication across cultures* (6th ed.). Allyn and Bacon.

Maathai, W. (2010). I will be a hummingbird. Accessed November 27, 2022, at https://www.youtube.com/watch?v=IGMW6YWjMxw

Nkwain, J. (2011). Complimenting and face: A pragmastylistic analysis of appraisal speech acts in Cameroon Pidgin English. *Acta Linguistica Hafniensia: International Journal of Linguistics*, *43*, 60–79. https://doi.org/10.1080/03740463.2011.589992

Nofsinger, R. E. (1991). *Everyday conversation*. Waveland.

Osborn, M. (1967). Archetypal metaphor: The light-dark family. *The Quarterly Journal of Speech*, *53*(2), 115–126. DOI: 10.1080/00335636709382823

Philipsen, G., Couto, L. M., & Covarrubias, P. (2005). Speech codes theory: Restatement, revisions, and response to criticisms. In W. B. Gudykunst (Ed.), *Theorizing about intercultural communication* (pp. 55–68). Sage.

Rector, K. (2022). More antisemitic hate seen in L.A. after Kanye West's hateful rants. La Times. Accessed October 25, 2022, at https://www.latimes.com/california/story/2022-10-23/kanye-is-right-about-the-jews-more-antisemitic-hate-seen-in-l-a-after-rappers-remarks

Rosenbaum, G. M. (2019). Curses, insults, and taboo words in Egyptian Arabic: In daily speech and in written literature. *Romano-Arabica*, *19*, 155–191.

Searle, J. R. (1969). *Speech acts: An essay in the philosophy of language*. Cambridge University Press.

Sharifian, F. (2008). Complimenting and face: A pragma-stylistic analysis of appraisal speech acts in Cameroon Pidgin English. *International Journal of Linguistics*, *43*, 60–79. https://doi.org/10.1080/03740463.2011.589992

Stanford Encyclopedia of Philosophy. (2007). Speech acts. Accessed July 14, 2021, at http://plato.stanford.edu/entries/speech-acts

Steinfatt, T. (1989). Linguistic relativity: Toward a broader view. In S. Ting-Toomey & F. Korzenny (Eds.), *Language, communication, and culture* (pp. 35–75). Sage.

Stern, S., & Kleiner, H. J. (1999). *For our children*. Elizabeth Glaser Pediatric AIDS Foundation.

Tannen, D. (May, 1991). How to close the communication gap between men and women. *McCall's*, *118*(8), 99–102, 140.

Tannen, D. (1994). *Gender and discourse*. Oxford University Press.

Turner, V. (1982). From ritual to theatre: The human seriousness of play. PAJ Publications.

Udupa, S. (2018). *Gaali* cultures: The politics of abusive exchange on social media. *New Media & Society*, *20*, 1506–1522. https://doi.org/10.1177/1461444817698776

Van Oudenhoven, J. P., de Raad, B., & Woods, S. (2008). Terms of abuse as expression and reinforcement of cultures. *International Journal of Intercultural Relations*, *32*, 174–185. https://doi.org/10.1016/j.ijintrel.2008.02.001

Voytko, L. Billionaire no more: Kanye West's antisemitism obliterates his net worth as Adidas cuts ties. Forbes. Accessed October 25, 2022, at https://www.forbes.com/sites/lisettevoytko/2022/10/25/billionaire-no-more-kanye-wests-anti-semitism-obliterates-his-net-worth-as-adidas-cuts-ties/?sh=351b221717e7

Waters, H., Jr. (1992). Race, culture, and interpersonal conflict. *International Journal of Intercultural Relations*, *16*(4), 437–454. DOI: 10.1016/0147-1767(92)90032-P

Whorf, B. L. (2012). *Language, thought, and reality: Selected writings of Benjamin Lee Whorf* (J. B. Carroll, S. C. Levinson, & P. Lee, Eds., 2nd ed.). MIT Press.

Yartey, F. N. A. (2018). The rhetorical potency of storytelling: The narrative role of the hummingbird in the Green Belt Movement. In E. M. Mutua, A. González, & A. Wolbert (Eds.), *The rhetorical legacy of Wangari Maathai: Planting the future* (pp. 47–63). Lexington Books.

Zaidman, N., Te'eni, D., & Schwartz, D. G. (2008). Discourse-based technology support for intercultural communication in multinationals. *Journal of Communication Management*, *12*(3), 263–272. DOI: 10.1108/13632540810899434

Zimmerman, D. H., & West, C. (1975). Sex roles, interruptions, and silences in conversation. In B. Thorne & N. Henley (Eds.), *Language and sex: Difference and dominance* (pp. 105–129). Newbury House.

Chapter 8

Nonverbal communication: Can I make nonverbal blunders and not even know it?

Chapter objectives

After this chapter, you should be able to:

→ Differentiate functions of nonverbal communication as it relates to verbal communication

→ Describe different cultural views of silence

→ Summarize perspectives on the universal expression of emotion

→ Explain and evaluate the notion of the contact cultures as an explanation of cross-cultural differences in nonverbal communication

→ List and define three different ways of thinking about cultural differences in time orientation

Intercultural Communication for Everyday Life, Second Edition. John R. Baldwin, Alberto González, Nettie Brock, Ming Xie, and Chin-Chung Chao.
© 2024 John Wiley & Sons Ltd. Published 2024 by John Wiley & Sons Ltd.
Companion Website: http://www.wiley.com/go/baldwin2e

U.S. President Barack Obama was famous—or in some circles infamous—for his deferential bows to different people. Abby Ohlheiser (2014), in an article in *The Atlantic*, describes Obama's bows to the Japanese emperor, the Queen of England, the Chinese president, a group of children in Mumbai, and…a robot. One of the most controversial of his bows was to Saudi King Abdullah at a G-20 meeting in 2009 (Figure 8.1). Many news sources and political pundits said Obama was paying "deference" to these world leaders and other people. Conspiracy theorists argued he was showing "allegiance" to Islam or to an Islamic leader. A White House aide gave what seems to be a flimsy explanation: "It wasn't a bow. He grasped his hand with two hands, and he's taller than King Abdullah." But is a bow always and only a placing of one's self under the authority of another? Are there different reasons to bow—respect, solemn thought, or even bowing unintentionally, as in hearty laughter?

The gesture and the following storm of opposing interpretations illustrate several points about nonverbal communication. First, nonverbal behavior can sometimes have clear meaning; but it is frequently ambiguous. If someone looks too long at you, it might be a gesture of personal or sexual interest, a sign of aggression, or a hint that you have something hanging out of your nose. A pat on the shoulder can show affection or it can indicate that the other person sees you with pity and as someone of lower social status. If someone stands closer than you expect, it might mean he cannot hear you very well or that they like your cologne.

This event also shows that the meaning of nonverbal behavior, like verbal and mediated behavior, is negotiated. Someone's intention with a behavior—if in fact the person has any intention in mind—is often not the intention others take from the behavior. People make decisions about us—to continue a relationship, to avoid future contact, to give us a job, and so on—not based on what *we* mean by a behavior, but by the meanings *they* give to it.

This leads to our third point: People give meaning to nonverbal behavior within a variety of contexts. If we interpret Obama's bow as giving loyalty or "fealty" to someone, we will

Figure 8.1 President Obama's gesture, often interpreted as a "bow," to King Abdullah of Saudi Arabia must be understood in terms of other contexts, such as how he interacts in other situations.
Source: PA Images/Alamy Stock Photo.

understand it in terms of placing his status under that of other world leaders (and robots). A different relational context would suggest that Obama was seeking to gain favor from the people that he bowed to. A second context is previous behavior and experiences of the individuals. On what occasions and to what people does Obama bow? It is a sign of respect for someone's work, suffering, or leadership, rather than a gesture of submission to someone's authority? Or does Obama, himself, perceive it simply as a nod, not intending it to be a bow? A third context would be situation. What are the details of each unique situation in which Obama appears to bow? We can see how commentators have used the situation to draw their conclusions of the behavior. In the same way, how we greet, commend, or show respect to someone else varies from culture to culture. In the end, each of these contexts sheds light on how we interpret nonverbal behavior.

An important context of nonverbal communication is the "speech episode"—what is going on in the situation: a touch on the shoulder may mean one thing in a moment of tenderness or comforting, but in an "argument" episode, the same sort of touch may not be welcome (Cronen et al., 1988). This relates to one of the most important contexts of nonverbal communication, and that is the context of verbal communication. Finally, nonverbal behaviors are understood in the context of culture. Often people in one culture use nonverbal behaviors—distance, eye contact, gestures, and so on—that are misunderstood by people in other cultures. Thus, our cultures form a large part of how we negotiate and understand nonverbal behaviors. These last two contexts are central to this chapter. We will introduce these together, covering basic forms and functions of nonverbal communication, and then turn to four main questions that culture raises for understanding specific types of nonverbal behavior.

Forms and functions: How should we act nonverbally when in another culture?

The history of the academic study of nonverbal communication is intertwined with that of intercultural communication. The U.S. government brought together a group of scholars in the Foreign Service Institute in the 1940s to 1950s to better understand cultures around the world (Leeds-Hurwitz, 1990). Using language as a framework, these scholars saw nonverbal communication and culture as patterned, regular, and predictable. Researchers from linguistics, anthropology, and other disciplines, like E.T. Hall, George Trager, and Ray Birdwhistell, began a systematic study of the "silent language" (Hall, 1966). This silent language of communication can occur through various nonverbal channels.

Channels (forms) of nonverbal communication

Nonverbal communication has been classified into a variety of channels. **Kinesics** deals with body movement, including gestures, stance, gait (how one walks), posture, and facial expressions of emotion. For example, Cynthia Ntuli (2012) provides detailed case studies of differences from Zulu culture, in South Africa, both from a South African raised in the United States and returning to South Africa and between Zulu culture and Afrikaner culture—two cultures from within South Africa. These differences center around handshaking versus embracing, sitting versus standing, and even use of space (can someone park their car in front of your house during a funeral?)

Haptics refers to the study of touch. Edwin McDaniel and Peter Andersen (1998), observing touching behavior at an international airport with follow-up questions to passengers, found that people from northern Asian cultures were less likely to touch than those of southern Asian, Caribbean, Latin American, U.S., or northern European cultures (with no differences in the last five groups). Closeness of relationship (e.g., lovers versus friends) may determine touch behavior (e.g., Williams & Hughes', 2005 naturalistic study of touch in Italy), and nonverbal researchers note that touch relates also to topic of conversation, furnishings/physical environment, and other factors.

Proxemics pertains to a culture's use of space. Edward T. Hall (1966) wrote a book describing space as a "hidden dimension" of culture. Hall suggests that there are different dimensions of communication that is intimate (between lovers or spouses), personal (between friends), social (between acquaintances, say, in public settings, restaurants, and so on), and public (between people talking across a distance). These, along with topic, posture (sitting/standing), and relationship may influence how close people choose to be. People from different cultures may prefer different amounts of distance at each level, a point we will return to below. Interestingly, such differences may even apply to online communication.

Another aspect of distance is **territoriality**, how a person or group perceives of and marks territory. For example, where many U.S. Americans might give a guest a "tour of the house" (perhaps to show off the "goods" they have accumulated), in another country, you might be friends with someone for years but never get beyond the front room of the house. In terms of public place, in some national cultures, it is common, if someone is sitting alone at a café table, for someone else to join them, seeing only that person's side of the table as the current table occupant's territory. In another country, people consider the whole table to be that person's temporary territory.

Oculesics pertains to a culture's use of eye behavior, particularly gaze. For example, people from different cultures (as well as people of different sexes) differ in how much they maintain eye contact while speaking versus listening. Differences in this behavior are subtle and may not be noticed but might impact whether one sees the other person as distant, invasive, threatening, or interested in future conversation (probably interacting with stereotypes one already has of the other group; See Chapter 6).

Paralinguistics (or **paralanguage**) is a term that some use to describe voice patterns—the characteristics of voice and vocalization that are not verbal, but not strictly nonverbal either. This includes rate of speech, volume, intonation, pronunciation, tone of voice, and other vocalizations such as sighs, laughter, and grunts. People in some cultures speak in regular conversation more loudly than those in other cultures. Indeed, loudness is a stereotype that those in many national cultures have of Americans, but also a stereotype White and Black Americans have of each other (Leonard & Locke, 1993). Paralinguistics include the notion of verbal pauses or backchanneling. **Backchanneling**, the subtle verbal, nonverbal, and paralanguage cues we use to indicate we're listening may also be cultural, both as to when we give them and as to the content of the channeling. Harry Waters (1992) suggests that Black and White Americans give backchannel cues at different times and for different reasons, and Laura Sicola (2005) relates her own experience of returning from Japan, using only "*mm mm*" as a backchannel devise, rather than the socially accepted variety of "yeah", "okay", and "right."

What do you think? Cultural training books such as *Gestures: The DOs and TABOOs of Body Language Around the World* (Axtell, 1998) or *Kiss, Bow, or Shake Hands* (Morrison et al., 1994) list etiquette tips for visiting countries around the world. Note the observations about the following cultures from *Kiss, Bow, or Shake Hands*. Which of the channels mentioned in this section do they exemplify?

→ Bolivia: Keep your hands on the table, not in your lap, while dining.

→ Egypt: Speakers stand much closer than in some countries, such as America. Don't back away if the other speaker stands closer than you expect.

→ Hungary: Use a handshake both when greeting and saying goodbye. Men follow a sequence: handshake, embrace, cheek-to-cheek contact (similar to fake "kiss")—left cheek then right.

→ Malaysia: Don't express anger in public, or you will be seen as someone who lacks self-control, and you will lose face.

→ Philippines: Speak in "quiet, gentle tones" to show respect and discretion and promote harmony. Loud talk is only for when you are "boisterously happy" (p. 292).

→ Romania: Bring your shorts! But only expect to wear them to the beach or in the country, not in the city.

→ Russia: As a business visitor, be punctual; but for Russians, "patience, not punctuality, is considered a virtue" (p. 317). Russians may be one to two hours late for an appointment.

→ Sweden: Toasts are formal—and allow people older than you to toast first. If your host seats you next to the hostess, you might be expected to make a speech.

If you know someone from these cultures, ask if these generalizations are true for their countries. Are there exceptions or conditions to these rules? Do they apply to all groups or regions within the national culture? How do rules from these countries compare to rules in your own culture? What might be some historical, social, or cultural reasons the rules are in place?

Each of these channels is important, but usually, we use and interpret behavior from several channels at the same time, depending on the function of the behavior. For example, an interview study of Chinese and Malaysian college students found that the students determined whether another person had a "good" character based on facial expression, posture, clothing choice, and paralinguistic cues (Hashmi & Waheed, 2020).

Functions of nonverbal communication and relations to verbal communication

Nonverbal behavior, together with verbal, can accomplish several tasks (Burgoon et al., 1996; Knapp et al., 2014). These include showing emotion (affect display), showing attitudes and our relationship to others, revealing our moods and personality, marking our identities, managing turn-taking, and releasing emotional or nervous tension. Culture can differ on several of these dimensions. For example, John Gumperz (1982), through discourse analysis, describes an ineffective interaction between an Indian studying in Britain and a British financial aid agent. Many of the difficulties were due to **prosody**, or the vocalic shaping of utterances, including pitch, volume, tempo, and rhythm. Due to different intonation patterns between Subcontinental Asian and British English, the British university employee thought the student was continuing to ask for confirmation, when in fact the student was not.

Nonverbal behaviors also work together with verbal communication. Nonverbal behaviors can clarify or accent what the verbal behaviors say, or they can contradict each other—as happens in sarcasm. They work together in turn-taking. Head nods, eye contact, intonation, and shifts in body posture all work in subtle ways for us to hand the turn to each other. And these can differ from culture to culture. For example, in a qualitative study of organizational negotiation settings in Ethiopia, Tanzania, Hong Kong, and China, Phyllis Ngai (2000) found sometimes subtle differences even between supposedly similar or nearby "country" cultures (Ethiopia versus Tanzania, Hong Kong PRC versus mainland PRC) in terms of things such as seating arrangements, comfort with or use of silence, pace of negotiation, and eye contact.

Finally, some gestures have an explicit verbal translation that is known among most members of a group (that is, it is an **emblem**; Richmond et al., 2008). These are used intentionally to convey verbal meanings, such as "okay," "he's cheap," "go away," "check please," "money," or "she's crazy," or, as found in one study, "goodbye," "Namaste," and "I have to pee" (Matsumoto & Hwang, 2013, p. 5). With emblems, a nonverbal behavior can substitute a verbal behavior or repeat the same message as the verbal behavior.

Because emblems have a specific verbal meaning, they often lead to trouble in intercultural communication. Holding out your hand to say "enough" is an illustrative behavior in the United States, meaningless by itself. But in Greece, it means, "Eat feces"—or something similar (Cameron, 2008). Sometimes an emblem in one culture is also one in another, but with an entirely different meaning. The circled thumb and finger with fingers outspread means "okay" in the United States, "money" in Japan, "homosexual" in Türkiye, and "screw you" in several Latin American cultures (Siljerud, 2008). And holding the middle fingers down with one's thumb, palm facing another person, with pinky and forefinger extended (Figure 8.2) can mean—depending on how it is used—a symbol of the occult (the Devil's horns); rock n' roll; warding off bad luck; or a sign of solidarity with a Texas college football team (Hook 'em Horns!). And two fingers behind someone's head can be cute "bunny ears" to harmlessly mess up a photo, or an indication that a man's girlfriend or wife is cheating on him.

Figure 8.2 Gestures in different cultures often have different meanings—and some of these might be quite offensive.
Source: Damien Baldino/Alamy Stock Photo.

What do you think? The subject of gestures around the world is a popular topic for bloggers, journalists, and business and academic writers. Look on the Internet for "gestures around the world" or similar search words (e.g., http://www.youtube.com/watch?v=BM9Iu4OQXAw). Locate a list of gestures and what they mean in different cultures. Much of the sites are "popular"—that is, not supported by systematic evidence. Now look online for research that includes the terms *gestures* and *culture*. What sorts of investigation have researchers done? How might this research be useful?

Issues in nonverbal communication: What are some possible nonverbal difficulties researchers are looking at?

As we have noted above, many writers have provided lists of behaviors, and it is easy to find "how-to" lists about what (not) to do in this culture or that. Some researchers have looked beyond individual cultures to provide frameworks or discuss issues that cut across cultures. In this section, we will summarize four specific issues that have received attention in intercultural literature.

Issue number 1: Why are you looking at me like that? Cultural meanings and expressions of emotion

Many researchers suggest that emotional expression is culturally learned (Matsumoto, 1991). This is something that ethnographers of communication have supported. At the same time, others argue that expression of emotion is universal. Countless studies over the years by many authors have looked at the ability of people in different cultures to recognize the same emotions. Researchers have established firmly that six emotions are recognized around the world: sadness, happiness, anger, disgust, surprise, and fear. Using a carefully developed measure known as the Facial Action Coding Scheme, Paul Ekman, Walt Friesen, and other researchers (1987) found that participants in 10 different countries around the world recognized these emotions with a high degree of accuracy—over 90% in most cases. Agreement was lower for countries with less exposure to White or Western cultures (e.g., Sumatra). A study in Ethiopia (Ducci et al., 1982) found that people in rural areas agreed less on the meanings of the emotions than those in the city, perhaps due to the higher television exposure of those in the city. Supporting this, Ekman et al.'s (1987) study above did find that people from Western cultures rated the emotions (in the photos of Whites) more intensely than those from Asian cultures.

So, is emotional expression universal? Ekman and Friesen (1969), the same scholars who provided support for the universal recognition of emotion, above, had Japanese and American participants watch films, some mild and some containing graphic violence. They found that when participants were alone in the viewing room, those from both cultures showed the same emotion, but when they were aware of a researcher sitting in the room observing, the Japanese tended to shield or mute their emotional displays. This study demonstrates that people in all cultures may also *show* emotions the same way, but that there are cultural expectations about when, how much, and with whom to show emotions—what the authors call **display rules**. A comparison of advertisements in South Korea and the United States found display rules to be at work in media as well as face-to-face communication. South Korean models used fewer hand gestures, showed less skin, and touched less than American models. Regarding facial expression specifically, they smiled less and were overall less expressive (Kim, 1992), though a similar study done today might find different results.

As noted in Chapter 2, intercultural researchers have taken different approaches to understanding this tension. From a critical perspective, for example, researchers have noted that expressions of emotion may reinforce traditional social structures. We saw in Chapter 7 how power could come to play in verbal communication. Although some research shows minimal difference in U.S. American men and women's nonverbal behavior, other research suggests that both women and men might, even without knowing it, reinforce and consent to male power in group or organizational settings and in other face-to-face or mediated communication, such as through silence, tone of voice, volume, touch, eye contact, facial display, and use of distance. From an interpretive perspective, Donal Carbaugh (1994), a scholar who does primarily observational research (ethnography of communication), suggests that facial expression is specific to cultures and can best be understood by an approach that looks at the rules of each culture in its own context.

Break it down

This week, think carefully about your own nonverbal display toward people of different groups. Do you treat them equally? Do you show tolerance or acceptance in your nonverbal behavior, or arrogance, offishness, or disrespect? How could you use nonverbal gestures, from facial display to posture to "paralinguistics" to include others? How aware are you usually of these behaviors? If they are beyond your awareness, is it possible that you could be condescending or confirming towards others without being aware of it?

Issue number 2: Why are you standing so close to me? Space and other aspects of contact

A second issue in intercultural research surrounds E.T. Hall's (1966) notion of **contact cultures**. In high-contact cultures, people tend to seek more sensory input during face-to-face interaction. This involves several channels of nonverbal communication—increased eye contact and touch between communicators, decreased distance, and a tighter body angle. People talking who are members of a high-contact culture, according to Hall, are more likely to look at each other more, touch more, stand closer together, and stand more face-to-face (rather than at a wider angle). As with most cultural dimensions and frameworks (e.g., individualism/collectivism, Chapter 4), it might be better for us not to think of cultures in terms of a dichotomy of "high-" and "low-contact," though this is the way that many writers and organizational trainers frame them. Rather, we might think of cultures as *higher* or *lower* in contact behaviors than other cultures.

Today, many researchers consider Hall's research, on which understandings of contact are based, to be based on personal stories, but without systematic research behind it. Still, many studies support the idea of contact cultures. Researchers had students from Japan, the United States, and Venezuela talk with people from their own countries (Sussman & Rosenfeld, 1982). When speaking their own language, Venezuelans sat closer than U.S. Americans, who sat closer than Japanese, when speaking the language of their countries; however, when speaking English, the Venezuelans sat further apart. Female participants from all three nations sat closer together than did males from their country., A more recent study finds that Asian partners in mediated communication use more distance between their avatars than Europeans do—but they adjust to closer distances when interacting with Europeans (Hasler & Friedman, 2012).

At the same time, some research raises questions about a blanket application of the idea of contact cultures. Robert Shuter did two studies using photographs of people in public places. First (1976), he found differences in contact, eye contact, and distance between Costa Rica, Panama, and Colombia—three geographically close nations in Latin America. This challenges the idea of clustering all Latin Americans as high-contact in all aspects of the construct. In a 1997 study of people communicating in Italy, Germany, and the United States, Shuter found unexpected differences, with different cultures (supposedly "high" or "low" context) having higher "contact" behaviors based on specific variables, such as whether one is in a same-sex dyad or a cross-sex dyad, related. A similar study of naturally occurring behavior in several major European cities both supported and contradicted Hall's notion of contact cultures. Sometimes people from neighboring nations used contact differently: For example, Irish and Scottish participants used more touch with each other than the English (Remland et al., 1995). Likely, if people assume someone to be from a nation that they assume to be culturally similar, they might draw mistaken conclusions about the other person's intentions, feelings, or character, because the other touches, looks, or uses distance differently. Even in so-called low-contact cultures, young people might hug and touch their friends, laugh, and use louder volume in some contexts (e.g., close South Korean friends after an evening of karaoke and drinks). Contact in this case might relate to the fact that the people involved are close friends and are younger.

In sum, the idea of contact cultures may be useful in some ways as a general framework. If we go to Mexico, people may, indeed, stand closer. If we go to India, Pakistan, or China ("low-contact" cultures), people *may* stand further away or use less eye contact. We must keep in mind that even if people stand closer, this does not mean that all contact behaviors will coincide with distance—especially in terms of male-female behavior. In addition, how close people stand—as well as how much they touch, how much they look at each other, and so on may be dictated by cultural rules that are best learned in the culture itself and that will be impacted by things such as the topic of the conversation, the environment, and aspects of the communicators such as age, status, co-cultural group, personal disposition toward contact, and relationship (Figure 8.3).

Issue number 3: Does anybody really know what time it is? Culture and time

Nonverbal scholars often refer to a culture's beliefs and behaviors regarding time as **chronemics**. Time is an important concept that guides social behavior, and it is complicated as authors have proposed different frameworks to explain cultural differences in time orientations: past/present/future time; monochronic versus polychronic time; and formal versus informal time.

Figure 8.3 People in different cultures have different expectations for use of interpersonal space, eye contact, and touch, though these are always influenced by situation, relationship, and other factors. Here, people in Udaipur, India share a bus ride. Source: Jochen Tack/ Alamy Stock Photo.

As we saw in Chapter 4, Kluckhohn and Strodtbeck (1973) discuss among their value orientations the notion of past, present, or future time orientations. People in cultures that orient toward the past likely resist change and will value tradition. Those in cultures that are future-oriented are more to likely value change, including progress as determined by some measurable definition. People who live in cultures that focus on the present may focus on the present enjoyment of life. Certain groups even within a national culture focused on the future, for example, may be more present-focused. A present focus might derive from concern about where the next meal comes or from a focus on self-gratification at the moment. At the same time, a national culture *in general* may value one orientation over the other. Mainstream (White, middle-class) United States culture has traditionally been future-oriented, where people save and look to the future—often buying different kinds of insurance for protection from future disasters (health, life, disability, flood, pets). Some Latin American cultures have tended to include norms that suggest a present focus. The somewhat stereotypical notion of a *mañana* culture, where one shows up late for many appointments, may reflect a focus on present relationships; but this may not apply across all classes, groups, cities, or regions of Latin America.

A time dimension well-known among interculturalists is E.T. Hall's (1983) notion of polychronic and monochronic time. People in **monochronic cultures** (or M-time cultures) tend to do tasks one at a time (e.g., the North European system), and those in **polychronic cultures** might do several things at once (what Hall calls the "Mediterranean model"). In monochronic cultures, people speak of saving, spending, and wasting time, and time is seen more linearly, with a value of task accomplishment. In polychronic cultures, on the other hand, people treat time more flexibly. We might see this in how one treats time for appointment, for example focusing on the present relationship or activity rather than the time on a clock or a business person meeting with different people at the same time. Hall notes that we might see this orientation even in professions, such as in academia. In M-time cultures, a student might work on one project at a time, bringing it to completion before beginning another; the P-time student might jump back and forth between projects at the same time.

Hall contends that "P-time stresses involvement of people and completion of current transactions" (1983, p. 46), such that the conversation one is currently in often has precedence over a marked schedule. M-time people often compartmentalize appointments and engagements and might even stop a conversation in order to arrive at some location at a designated time on the clock. Fern Johnson (2000) notes such a difference between mainstream U.S. White Americans, who live "on time" and some African American cultures, where people live "in time."

As with other dimensions, people who prefer one or other types of time exist in all cultures—and they often frustrate each other. If you are a P-time person on a group project with an M-time person, you might feel the M-time person is inflexible and too task-focused. You might prefer working on different parts of the project at one time or prefer "multi-tasking." But if you are an M-time person working with a P-time partner, you may feel your partner is not task-focused and may find they have difficulty with task completion.

Finally, some have discussed the distinction between formal and informal time. **Formal time** pertains to a specific time on the clock. This holds true especially in the digital age. Now, when we ask our friend what time she woke up, she might say, "10:13." **Informal time** includes the host of expressions that we use in our cultures to refer to more vague expressions of time, such as "after a while," "later," and so on. Informal time expressions are more likely to create cultural dilemmas than formal ones. On one hand, someone from one culture might use an expression like, "See ya later," meaning another day, while the other communicator may think "later" implies sometime during the same day. "Don't take too long…"—but how long is too long? Beyond the verbal expressions, we see that people from each culture have different temporal orientations for all activities, including the pace of work, the expected length of courtship, or how long the spaces between speech turns should be.

Issue number 4: Why are you being so quiet? Cultural understandings of silence

Writers have tried to understand silence from the point of view of specific cultures. For example, Satoshi Ishii and Tom Bruneau (1994) suggest that there are different "silences." People from Japan and other cultures might use silence for any number of reasons. It might be to show disagreement, as a response to something someone else has done that might be embarrassing, or simply to show respect and that one is thinking about an idea the other has proposed. Indeed, often, the best response to a beautiful sunset or one's deepest sentiment of love for another is silence, and not the words that so permeate the United States and other Western cultures.

Using ethnography, Keith Basso (1970) investigated uses of silence by people in the Apache nation in North America. After much observation, he noted that people used silence in particular situations, such as when placed with a new worker on a job, when one was first married, or when someone raised her or his voice in a public setting, like a bar. Looking for what held these instances together, Basso concluded that people may use silence in situations of uncertainty, a proposition later called **Basso's hypothesis**. He illustrated how each of these situations was a situation of uncertainty. You wouldn't know the new worker for a few days; husbands and wives had no contact prior to their wedding and had not been raised around people of the other sex; and the person who raises their voice must be crazy, so it is safest to respond with silence. Charles Braithwaite (1990) extended Basso's hypothesis by looking at research accounts of the use of silence in many different cultures. He added to our understanding of silence the notion that people in all cultures may use silence as a marker of status, either to respect someone of higher status or disdain someone of lower status, if they are aware of status differences.

Theory, culture, and nonverbal behavior: What does your nonverbal behavior mean?

One of the benefits of the attempts by Hall and his colleagues to gain a new understanding of intercultural communication (Chapter 1; Leeds-Hurwitz, 1990) is that they directed the focus of those wanting to learn about other cultures away from culture as a broad, complex phenomenon. Instead, they focused on cultural specifics, dimensions that we have seen in several chapters, especially in regard to nonverbal communication (high/low contact; monochronic/polychronic time). One of the disadvantages of such frameworks is that they oversimplify cultures since, despite general cultural preferences, people holding *different* orientations exist in all cultures. There might be differences between how people use time, space, or facial display of emotions, according to their occupations, the region of the country in which they live (e.g., rural versus urban), or their age and sex. The alternative to simplistic frameworks is to learn the specifics of each culture from the sorts of guides we introduced in the "What do you think?" textbox on cultural training books earlier in this chapter. These can be very useful in that one can learn the specific verbal and nonverbal behaviors that will be more or less effective, generally, in a given culture. But the result of this sort of learning is that one must learn long lists of behaviors. We are left wondering if there are no ways of simplifying the long lists of behavioral preferences with some sort of theory, as theories can provide us with a nice shorthand of understanding.

As interesting as nonverbal behavior is, it has less theory than many areas of intercultural communication. One area of theorization, though it may not rise to the level of a theory, is Hall's notion of high- and low-contact cultures, mentioned above. Others have used Hofstede's dimensions (Chapter 4) to understand nonverbal behaviors in general (Hecht et al., 1989) or specific aspects of behavior. For example, David Matsumoto (1991) predicts that high power-distance cultures will have a greater difference in display rules between those with status difference than low power-distance cultures. So, in Malaysia, one might be much less likely to show anger or extreme happiness to a boss but would use more discretion in showing emotion, than in Australia.

Other researchers are investigating the idea of communicative immediacy across cultures. **Immediacy** refers to verbal and nonverbal behaviors that show warmth, liking, and affiliation. These include things such as forward body lean, smiling, tone of voice, use of other's name, and so on. We might assume that students in high power-distance cultures prefer less immediate instructors. Instructors might use fewer smiles, not use students' names, and stand behind the podium to deliver a lecture, instead of using an interactive (more immediate) style. However, different studies show that in several cultures studied, including Australia, Finland, Puerto Rico, France, South Korea, and the USA, immediacy—especially nonverbal immediacy—is linked to better learning outcomes (McCroskey et al., 1996; Roach et al., 2005).

Culture and the expectancy violations model

Judee Burgoon proposed one of the more commonly mentioned communication theories relating to non-verbal communication. In 1978, she (with Hale, 1988) proposed her expectancy violations model in response to other explanations of what happens when someone stands too close. Previous theories suggested that, for different reasons, someone violating our special expectations would lead to negative responses and, if they had moved too close, we would move away. Burgoon noted that this is often not the case, such as when we perceive the other communicator as rewarding or attractive in some way. Her expectancy violations model suggests that we have **expectancies**—expectations for communication behavior based on our culture, our personal preferences, and our knowledge of the other communicator. When someone violates these behaviors, it draws our attention and we (almost instantly) evaluate the behavior (**behavior valence)** and the communicator (**communicator reward valence**). If both are positive, we may respond positively to the violation. In fact, a violation of expectations may be more helpful than going along with behavioral norms, because it might remind the other communicator that they like us as communicator, so their liking, as well as our message, may work to persuade them of our communication goals. If both are negative, then the response to the violation will be negative. But if the behavior is ambiguous, such as a glance longer than one would expect or a pat on the shoulder, we will interpret it based on whether we see the communicator as rewarding.

Burgoon (Burgoon & Hubbard, 2005) has outlined the usefulness of the approach in areas of intercultural communication. She has noted, for example, that often whether someone violating expectations in a new culture is perceived as "cute" and endearing, or as "weird" and unacceptable will depend on whether the people in the culture see the communicator as possibly rewarding. Burgoon also uses Hofstede's dimensions, noting, for example, that in a high uncertainty avoidance culture, people will likely be less accepting of violations of communication expectations and may define these expectations more narrowly. Countries with lower power distance (her example is the United States, though Hofstede places the United States toward the middle of power-distance cultures) may have fewer rules about certain verbal and nonverbal behaviors. Burgoon suggests that we must think about aspects of the communicator (for example, status, sex, age), the relationship between communicators, and the context to understand what violations are important, how they are perceived, and how people respond to them.

Burgoon's theory has potential for intercultural communication researchers and those who travel to other cultures. It lets us know that we must be aware of cultural specifics, influenced by cultural values, in terms of nonverbal expectations. Knowing the underlying values may help us anticipate nonverbal expectations, even if we don't know the specifics. Her theory suggests that if we are positive, well-intentioned communicators, those in other cultures may be more lenient in overlooking our more subtle cultural mistakes. What we do not yet know is if people in other cultures expect us to act like people in their culture or people from our own culture. Future research still needs to investigate the degree to which violating others' *stereotypes* of behavior of people from our own nation will work for or against us in intercultural communication.

What do you think? Think about a time that someone violated what you expected, especially in terms of nonverbal communication. Did they violate your cultural expectations, your expectations of the individual, or what you would have wanted to happen personally? Did the violation have a clear meaning, or was it open for interpretation? What did you think about the person who violated your expectation (pretty? rude? smelly?)? Finally, how did you respond? In what way does your experience support or contradict the expectancy violation theory?

Culture and meaning: Semiotics

The main approaches we have introduced above are all "social scientific" in focus (see Chapter 2), seeking to make predictions about outcomes with variables. Not all nonverbal intercultural research follows this model. As noted above, some in ethnography of communication have sought culturally unique patterns of behavior, such as how a group uses silence or expression of emotion. Another humanistic approach that often has a critical edge is semiotics. **Semiotics**, a cross-disciplinary approach that looks at how meaning is conveyed through "signs," is a very large field, with some of its own journals (e.g., *Semiotica*), and a full explanation of it would take more than this chapter—or book. Just a few concepts can help us see their usefulness in understanding nonverbal communication.

Semiotics focuses on the symbolic nature of communication, noting that when we communicate, including making a sentence, posting a selfie, getting dressed, or playing music, we assemble sounds or images to represent ideas. Several writers began looking at semiotics (e.g., Peirce, 1991). One of the key writers, French linguist, Ferdinand de Saussure (1983) describes the nature of signs and language, noting the nature of linguistic signs. Specifically, he noted how we use a word, like "arbor"—either visually or orally (a "sound pattern")—to represent a reality, like a real tree ("concept," p. 67). Over time, meaning might shift, so that the same sound pattern might now refer to something different (e.g., a "family tree"). The Italian author, Umberto Eco (1976), in addition to writing famous books-turned-into-movies, also philosophized on semiotics, noting that semiotics is "the discipline studying everything that can be used in order to lie" (p. 7). Already, we see the nonverbal aspect of signs: someone can use make-up, a wig, false eyelashes, platform shoes, and so on to "represent" some image or identity that may or may not be the truth (Berger, 2005)! Since words and nonverbal signals can also be used to lie, they can also have "sign" value.

A good nonverbal example of a sign is a wink. The wink "represents," or, in semiotic language, "signifies" something. It might mean that you like someone or that you and the other person have a hidden meaning, like an inside joke or arrangement. The object or idea it represents is the **signified**, and the sound or image that represents it is the **signifier** (Fiske, 1990). The **sign** is the combination of the signified and the signifier and the relationship between them (Barthes, 1968).

We represent ideas with several images, gestures, and sounds, borrowed from our culture from a set of related sounds/images that represent the idea (a **code**). Whether we are posting a selfie or getting dressed in the morning, and we want to put together an image of "cool," or "sexy," or "professional," we put together a set of signifiers. "Cool" (an ever-changing code!) might be represented—at a particular time and among a particular age group in U.S. American culture—by making sure one's tattoo or body piercing is seen, wearing certain clothes, and even walking or holding oneself a certain way (not to mention "coolly" appropriate verbal behaviors). The code can be the set of various symbols we use to illustrate "cool," but it is also the culturally agreed-upon ideas linked to "cool" in society at the time. When we put signs from the "cool" code together (nonverbally, or in media, or in a spoken message) with signs from other codes, we now have **sign systems**. For example, someone applying for a job might blend signifiers (scents, behaviors, words) of professionalism, but also of physical beauty, and, depending on the job, either conformity or forward-thinking.

The assembling of signs to create ideas—through our dress, gait, scent, posture, gesture, and so on, is a rich field of semiotic meaning. Even if different cultures have similar values (e.g., respect for the status of the other communicator), they might have a different relationship between signifier and signified. In one culture, one might show respect by looking down, but in the other, by looking the other communicator in the eye. Some researchers (e.g., Leeds-Hurwitz, 1993) suggest semiotics as a tool not only for understanding nonverbal behavior, but also all aspects of culture myth, artifact, and behavior.

Finally, semiotics can have implications for power in communication. We always encode personal power differences in verbal and nonverbal communication: We use posture, tone of voice, volume, and so on to establish power over others or consent to their person's power over us. Some researchers in this area consider how in media imagery, we use sign systems to battle over correct ideas (or better said, **ideologies**, see Chapter 5). We frame a certain idea or image as democratic—or beautiful or successful or respectful—by placing it with other ideas, and no set of ideas is politically neutral. In the same way, one could argue that if we buy into a culture's notion of how to act and dress in a particular code of "beauty"—one that is probably crafted and promoted by advertisers and product-makers who benefit by us having that particular view of beauty—we are buying into a set of ideas that (1) excludes the appearance of some by promoting a narrow set of standards, and (2) gains control over our own expression, as we buy into it often without thinking. People often battle over beauty standards, either within themselves or against a dominant culture.

What do you think? Do research on how people in your culture or a different culture alter their body through tattoos (or piercings or other modifications), especially as these modifications relate to resistance of dominant ideas (e.g., tattoos of Amazigh women in Morocco that resist colonialism); ex White supremacists erasing racist tattoos in the United States; people using tattoos for protest or resistance in Iran and Myanmar (Figure 8.4). Think of others who tattoo for different reasons (sports fans, "punk rockers," etc.). How might aspects of physical appearance work together with other aspects (way of walking, bodybuilding to change physical appearance, posture, use of gesture) to serve as a "code" for a particular identity? How can they be used for social activism? How do you represent your identities through nonverbal communication?

Figure 8.4 Social action and nonverbal behaviors: Look up protest tattoos in Myanmar to understand this image. In what ways does the tattoo (content, placement) reproduce, borrow, or even challenge social "codes" of meanings?
Source: Reuters Staff/Reuters.

Summary

Peter Andersen and his colleagues (2002) claim, "Cultural differences are not random events; they occur because cultures develop with different geographies, climates, economies, religions and histories, each exerting unique influence" (p. 90). Indeed, one of the authors of this book, who travels frequently and considers themself to be fairly culturally competent was recognized as a U.S. American in Brazil just by the way they walked, and in Austria, by the coat and shoes that they wore into a restaurant. Culture shapes every aspect of nonverbal communication. But, just as we have noted in other chapters, we should not only think of such differences as *national*, but as differences between any two groups of people who share different "speech codes."

In this chapter, we considered issues related to nonverbal communication and culture. We first described basic aspects of nonverbal communication—the functions and channels of nonverbal and paralinguistic behavior, and its relationship to verbal communication. We investigated four specific areas of nonverbal communication research and practice as these related to culture—issues of "contact cultures," universally recognized facial expression of emotion, use of time, and use of silence. Finally, we explored some theories that seek to understand why or how people use nonverbal and verbal communication (we really cannot separate these). Some seek to predict how people might respond to violations of our nonverbal expectations or how someone might use nonverbal behaviors based on cultural values.

Other researchers explore nonverbal communication in ways that show culturally specific rules for behavior, or even how we might use nonverbal communication in ways that support or challenge power structures. It is here, perhaps, that nonverbal behavior meets civic engagement. We can use appropriate nonverbal behavior—dressing and acting for the part—as part of our own engagement efforts—showing respect and interest nonverbally when we are working in part of a civic project or taking part in community action to promote change or deliberately violate the codes to protest traditional structures of meaning and power. We can also be aware in our daily interactions how we often draw conclusions and might even have our prejudices triggered by the nonverbal behavior of others, especially from other groups or nations.

Regardless of how we think about culture and cultural difference (as prediction, as in-depth explanation, or as passing on and resisting power), a clearer understanding of nonverbal differences and the subtle—and not-so-subtle—meanings of nonverbal behaviors can make us better intercultural communicators and help us to recognize how our own nonverbal behaviors may hurt or help the dignity of others.

KEY TERMS

faux pas, 158
kinesics, 159
haptics, 159
proxemics, 159
territoriality, 159
oculesics, 159
paralinguistics/paralanguage, 159
backchanneling, 160

prosody, 161
emblem, 161
display rules, 163
contact culture, 164
chronemics, 165
monochronic culture, 166
polychronic culture, 166
formal time, 167

Discussion questions

1 Think about different co-cultural groups in your own culture. Do you think that there are nonverbal differences between the groups (for example, between men and women; older or younger; different ethnic groups within your country)? Explain possible differences in terms of the specific channels that we mention in this chapter. If possible, ask a member of the groups in question to verify if your understandings are correct.

2 What are some specific display rules for your own cultural group? For example, when might you exaggerate or mute an emotional expression? Or, to think of it differently, how might you show great joy or displeasure to a boss? How should you respond when you receive a gift you do not like? Are there different display rules for men and women? What possible positive or negative outcomes might come from these expectations?

3 Many intercultural authors focus on how cultures represent a fairly *consistent* set of behaviors (e.g., how they use touch, contact, facial expressions the same way). But very often, groups surprise us! We think that Koreans will show subdued emotions, then we see young friends showing great happiness and laughing loudly. Choose a specific channel of behavior (e.g., touch). Instead of focusing on similarities, describe the *differences* among people of your cultural group. What are some things that might influence how the channel is used?

4 In this chapter, we do not talk about interpersonal power—that is, who might have more power in a situation (this may not be *formal* power!). Beyond the chapter, what are some nonverbal and paralinguistic ways one communicator might show—or try to establish— power over another communicator?

5 Do you think that more meaning lies in nonverbal or verbal communication? Justify your answer.

Action points

1 Talk to someone who belongs to a group different from you, such as an immigrant or international traveler to your culture, a person in a wheelchair (if you are not), someone with a different sexual orientation, or of a different racial group. Ask about how people of your group might use nonverbal and paralinguistic communication in a way that shows disrespect to them. Share the ideas with your class. What are some behaviors *you* might need to change, if any?

2   Many people use nonverbal markers (tattoos, clothing, jewelry, etc.) to mark identities. But we can also use these to support important causes or raise awareness for issues. Think about an issue or cause or belief that is important to you. Find a nonverbal marker that represents this identity and wear it to class and talk about it.

3   Consider the way you might act around people of different groups. If you know someone who will be honest, and you are ready for a frank discussion of your behavior, ask a friend in another group to give you feedback on behaviors of people from your own group, and of your own nonverbal behavior.

For more information

DeVito, J. A., & Hecht, M. (Eds.). (1990). *The nonverbal communication reader*. Waveland.

Hall, E. T. (1973). *The silent language*. Anchor.

Leeds-Hurwitz, W. (1993). *Semiotics and communication: Signs, codes, cultures*. Lawrence Erlbaum Associates.

Manusov, V., & Patterson, M. L. (Eds.). (2006). *The SAGE handbook of nonverbal behavior*. Sage.

Matsumoto, D., Frank, M. G., & Hwang, M. S. (Eds.). (2013). *Nonverbal communication: Science and applications*. Sage.

Molinár, P., & Segerstråle, U. C. O. (1997). *Nonverbal communication: Where nature meets culture*. Lawrence Erlbaum Associates.

References

Andersen, P. A., Hecht, M. L., Hoobler, G. D., & Smallwood, M. (2002). Nonverbal communication across cultures. In W. B. Gudykunst & B. Mody (Eds.), *Handbook of international and intercultural communication* (pp. 89–106). Sage.

Axtell, R. E. (1998). *Gestures: The DO's and TABOOS of body language around the world* (Rev. & expanded ed.). Wiley.

Barthes, R. (1968). *Elements of semiology* (A. Lavers & C. Smith, Trans.). Hill & Wang.

Basso, K. (1970). To give up on words: Silence in the Western Apache culture. *Southwestern Journal of Anthropology, 26*(3), 213–230. DOI: 10.1086/soutjanth.26.3.3629378

Berger, A. A. (2005). *Media analysis techniques* (3rd ed.). Sage.

Booth-Butterfield, M., & Jordan, F. (1989). Communication adaptation among racially homogeneous and heterogeneous groups. *Southern Communication Journal, 54*(3), 253–272. https://doi.org/10.1080/10417948909372760

Braithwaite, C. A. (1990). Communicative silence: A cross-cultural study of Basso's hypothesis. In D. Carbaugh (Ed.), *Cultural communication and intercultural contact* (pp. 321–327). Lawrence Erlbaum Associates.

Burgoon, J. K., Buller, D. B., & Woodall, W. G. (1996). *Nonverbal communication: The unspoken dialogue* (2nd ed.). McGraw-Hill.

Burgoon, J. K., & Hale, J. L. (1988). Nonverbal expectancy violations: Model elaboration and application to immediacy behaviors. *Communication Monographs, 55*(1), 58–79. https://doi.org/10.1080/03637758809376158

Burgoon, J. K., & Hubbard, A. S. E. (2005). Cross-cultural and intercultural applications of expectancy violations theory and interaction adaptation theory. In W. B. Gudykunst (Ed.), *Theorizing about intercultural communication* (pp. 149–171). Sage.

Cameron, T. (2008). 7 innocent gestures that can get you killed overseas. Cracked.com. Accessed September 9, 2011, at http://www.cracked.com/article_16335_7-innocent-gestures-that-can-get-you-killed-overseas.html

Carbaugh, D. (1994). Toward a perspective on cultural communication and intercultural contact. In L. A. Samovar & R. E. Porter (Eds.), *Intercultural communication: A reader* (pp. 45–59). Wadsworth.

Cronen, V. E., Chen, V., & Pearce, W. B. (1988). Coordinated management of meaning: A critical theory. In Y. Y. Kim & W. B. Gudykunst (Eds.), *Theories in intercultural communication* (pp. 66–98). Sage.

de Saussure, F. (1983). *Course in general linguistics* (C. Bally & A. Sechehaye, Eds., R. Harris, Trans.). Open Court.

Ducci, L., Arcuri, L., Georgis, T., & Sineshaw, D. (1982). Emotion recognition in Ethiopia: The effect of familiarity with Western culture on accuracy of recognition. *Journal of Cross-Cultural Psychology*, *13*(3), 340–351. https://doi.org/10.1177/0022002182013003005

Eco, H. (1976). *A theory of semiotics.* Indiana University Press.

Ekman, P., & Friesen, W. V. (1969). The repertoire of nonverbal behavior: Categories, origins, usage, and coding. *Semiotica*, *1*, 49–98. https://doi.org/10.1515/semi.1969.1.1.49

Ekman, P., Friesen, W. V., O'Sullivan, M., Chan, A., Diacoyanni-Tarlatzis, I., Heider, K., Krause, R., LeCompte, W.A., Pitcairn, T., Ricci-Bitti, P.E., Scherer, K., Tomita, M., & Tzavaras, A. (1987). Universals and cultural differences in the judgments of facial expressions of emotion. *Journal of Personality and Social Psychology*, *53*(4), 712–717. DOI: 10.1037//0022-3514.53.4.712

Fiske, J. (1990). *Introduction to communication studies* (2nd ed.). Routledge.

Gumperz, J. J. (1982). *Discourse strategies.* Cambridge University Press.

Halberstadt, A. (1985). Race, socioeconomic status, and nonverbal behavior. In A. W. Siegman & S. Feldstein (Eds.), *Multichannel integrations of nonverbal behavior* (pp. 227–266). Lawrence Erlbaum Associates.

Hall, E. T. (1966). *The hidden dimension.* Doubleday.

Hall, E. T. (1983). *The dance of life: The other dimension of time.* Anchor.

Hashmi, M., & Waheed, M. (2020). Discerning goodness via nonverbal cues: Perspectives from high-context cultures. *Journal of Intercultural Communication*, *54*, 74-88.

Hasler, B. S., & Friedman, D. A. (2012). Sociocultural conventions in avatar-mediated nonverbal communication: A cross-cultural analysis of virtual proxemics. *Journal of Intercultural Communication Research*, *41*(3), 238–259. http://doi.org/10.1080/17475759.2012.728764

Hecht, M. L., Andersen, P. A., & Ribeau, S. A. (1989). The cultural dimensions of nonverbal communication. In M. K. Asante & W. B. Gudykunst (Eds.), *Handbook of intercultural communication* (pp. 163–185). Sage.

Ishii, S., & Bruneau, T. (1994). Silence and silences in cross-cultural perspective: Japan and the United States. In L. A. Samovar & R. E. Porter (Eds.), *Intercultural communication: A reader* (7th ed., pp 246-251). Wadsworth.

Johnson, F. (2000). *Speaking culturally: Language diversity in the United States.* Sage.

Kim, M.-S. (1992). A comparative analysis of nonverbal expressions as portrayed by Korean and American print-media advertising. *Howard Journal of Communications*, *3*(3-4), 317–339. https://doi.org/10.1080/10646179209359758

Kluckhohn, F. R., & Strodtbeck, F. L. (1973). *Variations in value orientations* (2nd ed.). Greenwood.

Knapp, M. L., Hall, J. A., & Horgan, T. G. (2014). *Nonverbal communication in human interaction* (8th ed.). Wadsworth.

Leeds-Hurwitz, W. (1990). Notes in the history of intercultural communication: The Foreign Service Institute and the mandate for intercultural training. *Quarterly Journal of Speech*, *76*(3), 262–281. https://doi.org/10.1080/00335639009383919

Leeds-Hurwitz, W. (1993). *Semiotics and communication: Signs, codes, cultures.* Lawrence Erlbaum Associates.

Leonard, R., & Locke, D. C. (1993). Communication stereotypes: Is interracial communication possible? *Journal of Black Studies*, *23*(3), 332–343. https://doi.org/10.1177/002193479302300303

Matsumoto, D. (1991). Cultural influences on facial expressions of emotion. *Southern Communication Journal*, *56*(2), 128–137. DOI: 10.1080/10417949109372824

Matsumoto, D., & Hwang, H.C. (2013). Cultual similarities and differences in emblematic gestures. *Journal of Nonverbal Behavior*, *37*(1). DOI: 10.1007/s10919-012-0143-8

McCroskey, J. C., Fayer, J. M., Richmond, V. P., Sallinen, A., & Barraclough, R. A. (1996). A multi-cultural examination of the relationship between nonverbal immediacy and affective learning. *Communication Quarterly*, *44*(3), 297–307. 10.1080/01463379609370019

McDaniel, E., & Andersen, P. A. (1998). International patterns of interpersonal tactile communication: A field study. *Journal of Nonverbal Behavior*, *22* (1), 59–75. DOI: 10.1023/A:1022952509743

Morrison, T., Conaway, W. A., & Borden, G. A. (1994). *Kiss, bow, or shake hands: How to do business in sixty countries.* Adams Media Corporation.

Ngai, P. B.-Y. (2000). Nonverbal communicative behavior in intercultural negotiations: Insights and applications based on findings from Ethiopia, Tanzania, Hong Kong, and the China mainland. *World Communication*, *29*(4), 5–35.

Ntuli, C. D. (2012). Intercultural misunderstanding in South Africa: An analysis of nonverbal communication behaviour in contexts. *Intercultural Communication Studies*, *21*(2), 20–31.

Ohlheiser, A. (2014, April 24). A not-so-brief list of all the things President Obama has bowed to. The Atlantic. Accessed July 7, 2022, at https://www. theatlantic.com/politics/archive/2014/04/a-not-so-brief-list-of-all-the-things-president-obama-has-bowed-to/361160

Peirce, C. S. (1991). *Peirce on signs* (J. Hoopes, Ed.). University of North Carolina Press.

Remland, M. S., Jones, T. S., & Brinkman, H. (1995). Interpersonal distance, body orientation, and touch: Effects of culture, gender, and age. *The Journal of Social Psychology*, *135*(3), 281–297. DOI: 10.1080/00224545.1995.9713958

Richmond, V. P., McCroskey, J. C., & Hickson, M. L., III. (2008). *Nonverbal communication in interpersonal relations* (6th ed.). Pearson.

Roach, K. D., Cornett-Devito, M., & DeVito, R. (2005). A cross-cultural examination of instructor communication in American and French classrooms. *Communication Quarterly*, *53*(1), 87–107. DOI:10.1080/01463370500056127

Shuter, R. (1976). Proxemics and tactility in Latin America. *Journal of Communication*, *26*(3), 46–52. https://doi.org/10.1111/j.1460-2466.1976.tb01902.x

Shuter, R. (1977). A field study of nonverbal communication in Germany, Italy, and the United States. *Communication Monographs*, *44*(4), 298–305. DOI: 10.1080/03637757709390141

Sicola, L. (2005). "Communicative lingerings": Exploring awareness of L2 influence on L1 in American expatriates after re-entry. *Language Awareness*, *14*(2-3), 153–169. https://doi.org/10.1080/09658410508668831

Siljerud, P. (2008). The meaning of the OK hand gesture around the world—Learn the meaning of hand gestures. *Ezine@rticles*. Accessed September 9, 2011, at http://ezinearticles.com/?The-Meaning-of-the-OK-Hand-Gesture-Around-the-World—Learn-the-meaning-of-Hand-Gestures&id=1640238

Sussman, N. M., & Rosenfeld, H. M. (1982). Influence of culture, language and sex on conversational distance. *Journal of Personality and Social Psychology*, *42*(1), 66–74. https://doi.org/10.1037/0022-3514.42.1.66

Waters, H., Jr. (1992). Race, culture, and interpersonal conflict. *International Journal of Intercultural Relations*, *16*(4), 437–454. https://doi.org/10.1016/0147-1767(92)90032-P

Williams, D. E., & Hughes, P. C. (2005). Nonverbal communication in Italy: An analysis of interpersonal touch, body position, eye contact, and seating behaviors. *North Dakota Journal of Speech & Theatre*, *18*, 17–24.

Chapter 9

Rhetoric and culture: How does my culture relate to persuasive writing and speaking?

Chapter objectives

After this chapter, you should be able to:

→ Understand rhetoric as a unique aspect of communication

→ Explain how rhetoric and culture are interrelated

→ Identify examples of rhetorical traditions

→ Understand and explain vernacular rhetoric

→ Reflect a greater understanding and appreciation for the complexities of trying to persuade multicultural audiences

Rhetorical communication: How does culture inform persuasion? 178

Vernacular rhetoric: How does everyday communication seek to persuade? 189

Intercultural rhetoric: What are the implications for civic engagement? 193

Intercultural Communication for Everyday Life, Second Edition. John R. Baldwin, Alberto González, Nettie Brock, Ming Xie, and Chin-Chung Chao.
© 2024 John Wiley & Sons Ltd. Published 2024 by John Wiley & Sons Ltd.
Companion Website: http://www.wiley.com/go/baldwin2e

The process of learning about cultures is important and complex. Sometimes this process is comically shown in Pop entertainment. The 2021 film, *Namaste Wahala* (produced and directed by Hamisha Daryani Ahuja), depicts a very fundamental rhetorical strategy: building commonality between speaker and audience. *Namaste Wahala* (meaning "greetings trouble," and is a combination of Hindi and Nigerian Pidgin) is a romantic comedy in which Indian-born Raj meets Nigerian-born Didi in the Nigerian city of Lagos. They fall in love, but both sets of parents object to their relationship, preferring a union with someone from their native countries. Constant bickering ensues, as the parents try to separate Raj and Didi. Finally, Leila, who is Didi's friend and also Raj's cousin, explains to Raj's mother that Indian women and Nigerian women have many of the same values and face many of the same challenges in society. This proves to be the winning strategy for having the parents accept the new intercultural romance.

Why? Literary critic Kenneth Burke famously wrote that we persuade others by speaking their language and knowing their ways. For Burke, persuasion hinges on our ability to create commonality or **identification** with others because "identification is compensatory to division" (Burke, 1969, p. 22). **Division** consists of the differences in beliefs and ways of interacting that might create conflict. Not only do people live differently, they express themselves differently. In this case, Leila persuades Raj's mother that Indian women and Nigerian women share a common ground of both oppression and empowerment.

Namaste Wahala helps us to understand the relationship between rhetoric and culture. In order for Raj's and Didi's parents to identify with the other culture they needed to become aware of common cultural values and see them in action. This chapter explains rhetorical communication as a cultural activity and describes implications for rhetorical action and civic engagement in an uncertain world.

Rhetorical communication: How does culture inform persuasion?

Following Burke, we define **rhetoric** and **rhetorical action** as the use of symbols to "induce cooperation" (Burke, 1969, p. 43). Within and across communities, there is an ongoing tension between identification and division, and rhetoric mediates this tension. In the U.S. Cold War with the former Soviet Union, political and cultural differences were emphasized in order to establish one side as superior to the other. In the 1970s, both engaged in a rhetoric of détente that instead emphasized mutual interests. **Rhetorical communication** is a message that is planned and adapted to an audience (or audiences) (Herrick, 2009, pp. 8–9). When President Biden signed a series of Executive Orders on his first day as U.S. President, he wanted to reassure the nation that he was fulfilling campaign promises. Verbally, the president described the government's efforts to create healthcare equity in the United States and he stated that the United States was rejoining an international climate protection treaty. There was a visual strategy also: President Biden signed the Executive Orders from the White House, specifically from the Oval Office—the president's primary office—which conveyed to domestic and international audiences that the importance of these actions was understood at the highest level of government (Biden signs executive orders, 2021).

Rhetorical communication occurs not only publicly but also in interpersonal situations. With observation, we can discover that seemingly small pieces of talk can display the planned and identification-seeking quality of rhetorical interactions. At a U.S. university, a graduate student from Xi'an, China, records her voicemail message to end with "See 'ya." A bank teller from the Catalan region of Spain, who is working in a town in the midwestern United States, closes each conversation with the expression, "Have a good one!" In each instance, the goal is to create a sense of shared identity by incorporating local expressions. While the Spanish bank teller might occasionally end a conversation by saying "*Ciao*," her hope is that she has still adapted her way of talking to the U.S. listener.

So how do we know what persuades people? How do we know what kinds of arguments and information will lead people into positive relationships and mutual action? In order to be persuasive, speakers need to employ more than knowledge of a particular topic; they must also draw upon cultural knowledge. Rhetorical action does not take place in a vacuum. It is created within, and reflects, a cultural context. As language scholar Fern Johnson observes, "Rhetoric arises from cultural contexts rather than being universal, and rhetorical communication is perceived and evaluated through cultural frames" (2000, p. 37). In the next section, we explore the concepts that critics of rhetorical communication have developed for understanding the connections between rhetoric and culture.

What do you think? Think of an ad that you have seen online or on TV that had a celebrity spokesperson. How did the speaker advocate a particular view of the world or a particular action? How did the advocate seek to create identification with you? What shared values did they associate with their cause? What common images did they associate with their cause? How do you decide whether to accept or ignore what a spokesperson recommends?

Rhetorical traditions: How do people in different cultures try to persuade?

The concept of the **rhetorical tradition** has greatly added to analysis of rhetoric and cultures. The notion is simple and intuitive: we should try to understand rhetorical communication in terms of the historical and social influences and ethnic practices of the speakers (Garrett, 2000; Garrett & Xiao, 1994).

The work of interpretive scholar Gerry Philipsen provides a clear example of analysis that places a speech within a rhetorical tradition. Philipsen (1992) examined a speech given by Richard J. Daley, the long-term mayor of Chicago, Illinois, USA. Mayor Daley had been criticized by a member of city council for making appointments to city jobs on the basis of family connections and favoritism rather than expertise and qualifications. Daley lashed out at his accuser by associating him with "hypocrites and fakers" (p. 46) who only wanted to criticize the city. Daley's speech praised one appointee's mother for having raised such a fine son—a son worthy of working for the City of Chicago. Philipsen placed Daley's speech and style of governing within the expectations of the working-class neighborhoods of South Chicago. There, people watched out for one another, defended their families, and rewarded loyalty according to a hierarchy that was commonly understood. Philipsen traced the neighborhood norms and Daley's response to criticism to a centuries-old Irish "code of honor" that requires immediate and harsh defense in the face of disrespect. Outside of this tradition, Daley's speech was described as incoherent and egotistical, but within that tradition he was seen as being true to the code of honor.

When two differing cultural perspectives come together in public or interpersonal persuasion, we have an instance of **intercultural rhetoric**. Mayor Daley was speaking from one cultural perspective (working-class Irish American) and the mainstream media were assessing the speech from their cultural perspective (conventional Western journalism and Western deliberative politics). Making sense of intercultural rhetoric requires that we adopt a provisional attitude, "check the impulse to condemn," and work to understand a speech "on its own terms" (Philipsen, p. 48).

Rhetoric scholars have identified steps for the analysis and assessment of intercultural rhetoric. These steps are useful guides for gaining a cultural understanding of public discourse and persuasion. As listeners and observers, we should:

1 Delineate historical relations between the speaker's culture and that of the audience.

2 Identify those elements of a speaker's culture that normally determine the speaker's style of presentation.

3 Specify any preconceptions the audience may have of the speaker.

4 Identify public expectations regarding the address.

5 Describe expectations from an understanding of cultural presuppositions as well as the rhetorical legacy of the form of communication.

6 Examine the significance of the specific rhetorical medium (speech, poem, proclamation, etc.) in the speaker's culture.

7 Examine the speaker's style of discourse broadly to include the various structures, images, content, strategies, and appeals of a rhetorical piece.

(Adapted from Hammerback & Jensen, 1994; Starosta & Coleman, 1986)

With these guides in mind, we can turn to examples of political activism and deliberation and their rhetorical traditions. These public discourses are selected because they co-exist with the dominant Euro-American tradition that emphasizes objectivity and individuality.

What do you think? How would you describe the typical methods of persuasion in your country or culture? Why are these methods effective? Search online to find the roots or traditions that guide the rhetoric in your culture (e.g., Arabic rhetoric, Western rhetoric, Chinese rhetoric, Indian rhetoric). How much are we taught about approaches to persuasion that come from different roots or traditions?

African American tradition: Rooted in resistance

African American voices have delivered powerful critiques and affirmations of U.S. social and cultural structures. In the 20th century, Angela Davis and Malcolm X provided alternative histories and social theories to counter the prevailing Puritan myth. In literature, James Baldwin, Maya Angelou, and August Wilson dramatized the lasting effects of marginalization as well as irrepressible hope in the lives of their characters. From the pulpit, the Reverends Dr. Martin Luther King, Jr., Jesse Jackson, and Al Sharpton mobilized audiences to advance civil rights. In each case, they reminded the United States that its collective memory included the creation of a labor pool obtained by force and currency. The African American rhetorical tradition begins with Africa, but it is a unique blend of African and Western cultural influences.

African American rhetoric locates an origin—Africa—that taps "a core African value system" that creates similarities in the social lives of Blacks of African descent wherever they are found (Collins, 1989, p. 755). The rhetorical qualities of the African tradition focus on the "almost universal African regard for the power of the spoken word" (Smith, 1970, p. 265). The primary African legacy was a belief in "the transforming power of vocal expression" (Smith, 1970, p. 265). Through words, slaves of various ethnicities from different regions of West and Central Africa could create a common identity as well as transcend (if only temporarily) the horrors of their captivity and servitude through song and lamentation. In this tradition, language and **paralanguage** (tone, volume, speech rate, etc.) are creative tools for expressing the whole range of human emotions and feelings. Language use is characterized by improvisation and inventiveness, as seen in original rap music or verbal dueling games like "the dozens" (Johnson, 2000).

This core belief in the power of language together with remnants of African religious traditions combined with Western denominations of Christianity produced in post-slavery a form of worship and expression that centered on freedom. The formation of the African Methodist Episcopal (A.M.E.) church in 1816 created a space for Christian worship free from the judgments and constraints of mainstream Christianity (Weaver, 1991). The church service became a counterpoint to mainstream exclusion and invisibility. The free involvement of the worshippers was a metaphor for the inclusion that mainstream society often denied African Americans. In the Black Church, "worshippers experience a catharsis through the freedom in which they are allowed to express themselves" (Hamlet, 2011, p. 113). Freedom in the church service is expressed by singing, calling out to the preacher during the sermon, standing, and moving and clapping with the music.

The preacher is the focal point of the church service. The preacher "has an individualized style which is drawn from the larger paradigm of performance" that displays improvisation and inventiveness (Weaver, 1991, p. 59). The successful preacher performs the Biblical text dynamically, using repetition, analogy, and rhyme, and sometimes singing the sermon with stomping, hollering, and dramatic pause. The spirituals, as well as other musical forms such as jazz and blues, "represent a continuous linkage with the rituals and arrangements of West Africa" (Asante, 1980, p. 75). It is out of this tradition that the most influential African American speakers emerged.

When most people think of an African American presidential candidate, they often think of Barack Obama, the Senator from Illinois. It is natural to reference Senator Obama because he was elected U.S. President in 2008. Fewer will remember that 20 years earlier, another African American, Jesse Jackson, ran for U.S. President (and that, in 1972, an African American female, Shirley Chisholm, sought the Democratic nomination—and faced three assassination attempts). The Reverend Jesse Jackson, also from Illinois, inherited the mantle of social justice spokesperson after the Civil Rights Movement. Jackson headed the Chicago-based Operation PUSH that championed policies that empowered the working class and those in poverty.

On July 20, 1988, the Reverend Jackson addressed the Democratic National Convention, in Atlanta Georgia, as a presidential candidate. Jackson delivered the speech, "Common Ground and Common Sense" (Sullivan, 1993) amid speculation over whether he would be named to the Democratic ticket as vice-presidential candidate or throw his support behind another candidate.

Rosa Parks and Aaron Henry were in attendance. Jackson recognized these icons of activism and also noted that the tomb of Martin Luther King, Jr. lay only a few miles from the convention site. Jackson began his speech by noting that the country was at a crossroads: "Shall we expand, be inclusive, find unity and power? Or suffer division and impotence?" Jackson used Biblical references and imagery, naming Jerusalem as the intersection where different people, different cultures, and different civilizations "could meet and find common ground" (Sullivan, 1993, p. 8).

He urged "common sense" that would inform U.S. domestic and foreign policy. "I just want to take common sense to high places," he declared, by saving family farms, reducing tax loopholes for the wealthy, increasing health care and education, and supporting human rights internationally. The rhythmic quality of the speech, together with its religious imagery and personal stories "are vital for the Black speaker who represents an oral tradition" (Sullivan, 1993, p. 5). Jackson attempts to reframe or transform the aims of political action. The "real world" requires the support of various "basic principles" that will compose a new moral authority. Parts of Jackson's speech illustrate the transformative potential of words:

> This generation must offer leadership to the real world. We're losing ground in Latin America, the Middle East, and South Africa, because we're not focusing on the real world.
> That real world.
> We must use basic principles, support international law. We stand to gain the most from it.
> Support human rights; we believe in that.
> Support self-determination; we'll build on that.
> Support economic development; you know it's right.
> Be consistent and gain our moral authority in the world!
>
> (Jackson, 1988, p. 652)

Like Mayor Daley, who spoke guided by his Irish American rhetorical tradition, Jesse Jackson spoke from within an African American rhetorical tradition. Sensing the cultural difference, some did not believe that "Common Ground and Common Sense" met the expectations of mainstream political discourse. However, the vast majority concluded that Jackson reached across cultural communities to create an inspiring national vision (Sullivan, 1993).

Chinese tradition: Rooted in social reflection

The Chinese rhetorical tradition draws from spirituality and philosophy, folklore and the arts, and contains the culturally distinctive values of "*tao* (Way), *sheng* (life-giving, production), *ren* (love) and *tian* (Heaven)" (Xiao, 1995, p. 87). The Chinese speaker can "anchor" arguments to these values and create identification with an audience (Garrett & Xiao, 1994). Perhaps the best-known example of the merging of rhetoric and Chinese tradition is found in the rule of Mao Zedong, one of China's most famous leaders.

Mao Zedong (Figure 9.1) ruled China for over 33 years until his death in 1976. As Chairman of the Communist Party of China, he devised a socialist "Cultural Revolution." Mao sought to eliminate private wealth and the affluent class was persecuted and largely eliminated. Millions died, either executed for harboring Western sentiments or due to starvation as the country's infrastructure declined. Still, Mao was worshipped as a god (Huang, 1997). Masses of young people joined the Red Guards and they passionately enforced Mao's socialist dictates. How was he able to create such devotion and loyalty? One part of the answer involves Chinese ancient

紧跟伟大领袖毛主席奋勇前进！

Figure 9.1 In order to gain the people's support, Mao Zedong blended his Communist ideology with traditional Chinese rituals.
Source: Robertvt/Adobe Stock.

traditions and their modern rhetorical application. Sharong Huang (1997) studied the cultural elements in Cultural Revolution rhetoric. He found that:

> Traditionally, the Chinese are religious people. Some believe in Buddhism, some in Taoism, and some in other religions such as Islam and Christianity. During the [Cultural Revolution Movement], all kinds of religions were abolished. Many Buddhist and Taoist temples were burned down by the Red Guards. However, the Chinese people were used to worshipping. If they were not allowed to worship the old gods, they looked for a new one to worship. Naturally, Mao became the only god for them. (p. 130)

Mao understood the persuasive power of tradition as he crafted his strategies to closely match existing social understandings (Cai & González, 1997). Mao's strategy was to adapt centuries-old customs and beliefs to his Cultural Revolution ideology. For example, the people had followed the teachings of Confucius for over 2000 years. Mao adopted the Confucian model of family authority and hierarchy to his leadership. As "father" of the Chinese people, Mao's moral authority was absolute (Teiwes, 2010). This was an assertion people could accept. Additionally, the ritual study and repetition of Mao's sayings mirrored the learning of Confucian thought. The hyperbole used to describe Mao and his actions borrowed from classical Chinese poetry and forms of address in the Chinese dynasties. Finally, the daily political gatherings where people shouted slogans and moved together in a "loyalty dance" mirrored the collectivism of Chinese society (Huang, 1997, p. 134).

Another example of a powerful term is found in contemporary China. Chinese President Xi Jinping has expressed a vision of the "China Dream." In the China Dream, the Chinese people are prosperous, and China plays a major and determining role in international affairs (Jiang & González, 2021). The term contains deep cultural meaning as it invokes the endurance of a civilization that has spanned millennia. Politically, the term "created a rhetorical space both to continue the prevailing ideology of the [Chinese Communist Party] and to continue to facilitate the most current economic and social transition in China" (Jiang & González, p. 6).

From the standpoint of rhetoric and culture, it is important to observe that neither Mao nor Xi created a new rhetorical strategy to gain and maintain power. They did not borrow from the outside—the West—to legitimize their rule and vision. They utilized the values and rituals of the people they sought to dominate. At the same time, China serves as an excellent case study in the way that rhetoric changes. Mei Zhong's (2003) outline of major historical points that impacted Chinese language may also have relevance to the study of rhetoric. She notes five distinct eras of Chinese language, starting from the New Culture era, in which writing moved from an "ancient literature" style to a "new and fresh style that is coherent with spoken language" (p. 207), making writing more accessible for the average person. She discusses the impact of Mao Zedong, as we have noted earlier, but then highlights the anti-intellectualism of the Cultural Revolution era. She notes that modern rhetoric is being influenced by an "All Around Open and Western Influence Era" (p. 213). Her observations are specifically about language, such as the turn in the 1990s from addressing people as "Comrade" to "Mr." and "Ms." But they have implications for rhetoric in showing us that, while strongly influenced by its Communist past, Chinese rhetoric continues to evolve with new historical and philosophical influences.

Latino/a tradition: Rooted in revolution

Mexican social essayist and critic, Octavio Paz, attempted in his writings to capture the essences of Mexican culture. Recipient of the 1990 Nobel Prize in Literature, he described a national character that largely avoids public discourse except in the cause of revolution (Paz, 1961, 1972). For Paz, the Mexican—who has withstood the traumas of multiple invasions, natural disasters, and political instability—finds safety in ambiguity and withdrawal from public expression. This tendency to withdraw is shattered in the case of fiesta and revolution. The rhetorical challenge faced by Mexican Americans (U.S. citizens of Mexican descent) was to balance the tension between silence and advocacy. This challenge was successfully met by activist Cesar Chavez (Figure 9.2).

Figure 9.2 Farm labor activist Cesar Chavez drew upon traditional Mexican oratory. Source: Bettmann/Corbis.

Born in Arizona in 1927, Chavez experienced firsthand the poor treatment given to migrant farmworkers by growers, the state and federal government, and those who would exploit the low status of the workers. With Dolores Huerta—who in 2012 received the Presidential Medal of Freedom—Chavez co-founded the United Farm Workers. Their goal was to unionize the California farmworkers so that they could for the first time enter into legally binding agreements with the growers. This would assure humane treatment and better wages. Perhaps Chavez is best known for leading a national boycott of California grapes and their products. Any aficionado of merlot or pinot noir wine will understand the significance of the California grape crop. But to be successful, Chavez first had to gain credibility as a public advocate among a people who tended to reject public advocacy.

A recent biography of the life and activism of Cesar Chavez, *The Fight in the Fields: Cesar Chavez and the Farmworkers Movement*, lists major influences upon Chavez as Saint Francis of Assisi, the writings of Saint Paul, and biographies of U.S. labor leaders John L. Lewis and Eugene Debs, Machiavelli, Alexis de Tocqueville, and Mahatma Gandhi (Ferriss & Sandoval, 1997, p. 47). While these were no doubt important influences, this list must be considered partial for a man who coined the slogan, "*sí se puede*" [yes, it can be done] and who called his activism "*el movimiento*" [the movement]. To gain recognition and establish identification, Chavez countered the "ideology of silence" (González, 1989) and drew upon the revolutionary rhetoric of Mexican leaders who fought to maintain a close connection between the people and the land that they toiled.

To best understand Chavez and his tactics, we need to place them "within the context of their own rhetorical tradition, a tradition anchored in Mexican history and developed from the Mexican American's culture and experiences" (Hammerback & Jensen, 1994, p. 54). The issuance of guiding principles and proclamations for persuasive movements—called "plans"—is patterned after the political plans issued during Mexico's revolutionary era in the 1800s. A plan was typically named for the city in which it was written and it could list grievances, provide a rationale for action, and announce proposed actions to redress injustice or specific problems. The Plan of Tomé and the Plan of Ayala (which dealt with agriculture and land rights) are among Mexico's most famous plans (Hammerback & Jensen, 1994).

Additionally, Chavez and his associates were influenced by Emiliano Zapata, a military leader of the Mexican Revolution of 1910, who championed land reform. They were also fond of quoting much-celebrated Mexican President Benito Juarez's most famous saying: "*el respeto al derecho ajeno es la paz*" (to respect the rights of others is peace). Chavez named his movement newsletter *El Malcriado*, after a Revolutionary-era newspaper. Cartoons satirized California landowners and politicians in *El Malcriado* in much the same way as the Mexican ruling elite was satirized in Mexican newspapers.

The Plan of Delano, written in 1966, was intended to generate public support for farmworkers who were striking in nearby vineyards and to reinforce the resolve of farmworkers who were paid low wages and forced to live in shacks by the fields. Though written in the 1960s, the Plan of Delano was modeled after Zapata's Plan of Ayala of 1911. The early inspiration for the movement came from the Mexican Revolution. The plan was an important persuasive tool since it could be read in both Spanish and English and could be copied and delivered to many workers and politicians. The plan stated that the workers were entitled to fundamental human rights, that the workers' belief in God would ensure their endurance, and that they were united in their cause (Hammerback & Jensen, 1994).

Without doubt, Cesar Chavez was influenced by the early labor leaders, and peace activists such as Gandhi and Martin Luther King, Jr. However, including the rhetorical tradition of Mexico lends a fuller explanation of how Chavez achieved identification with the farmworkers whose trust he needed.

Break it Down

Watch several episodes of the series *Gentefied*. The show focuses on the Morales family and how family members unite to oppose gentrification of their Las Angeles neighborhood. Sometimes using food, art, and public protest, what strategies do the main characters use to build identification with community members? How do they *disidentify* with the threatening corporate interests?

Native American tradition: Rooted in nature

An important cultural value among many Native American communities is a "circular and flexible" notion of time (Shutiva, 2012, p. 134). When enacted, this approach to time would observe the connectedness of the present to the past. This approach also would observe approximate times for the beginning and ending of events. The people and the event itself—rather than time—are the controlling factors. This approach is in contrast to the dominant Western notion of linear and exact time. Whenever we expect punctuality or when we say that we've "moved beyond" or "gotten over" something, we are enacting the linear notion of time (see Chapter 9).

In public advocacy, these differing values are apparent. In Arizona, a dispute arose over a proposed astronomical observatory on Mount Graham (Carbaugh & Wolf, 2000). The four tribes of the Western Apache Nation regarded the mountain as a sacred space, a place of worship for generations that connected modern Apaches to their past. The tribes argued that it must be protected; and one way to protect the space against outside interference and show reverence was not to speak about it. The belief was that the time-tested sacredness of the space was self-evident and beyond argument.

The astronomers and the scientific community, on the other hand, regarded the site as ideal for astronomical research: the sky was clear most of the time, it was elevated, it was away from light pollution, and it was near a major university. Yet, when the scientific community tried to engage the Apache leaders, they were met with silence. While the Apache leaders enacted silence to revere and protect, the scientists interpreted their behavior as indicating a lack of knowledge and a disregard for progress. This is an example of a problem of **mutual intelligibility** (Carbaugh & Wolf, 2000, p. 21). Mutual intelligibility refers to the common meanings and interests people share in order to understand each other. Mutual intelligibility is necessary for identification. This case illustrates the importance of notions of time in framing the significance of places and determining uses for places. When rhetoric is practiced from traditions that are very different from one another, mediating disputes is difficult.

While several telescopes have been operating on Mount Graham (*Dzil Nchaa Si An*, in Apache) since the 1990s, and a new Large Binocular Telescope (LBT) was dedicated in 2004, Native American and environmental groups continue to seek limitations on the use of the site (Saunders, 2010).

A second example reveals how rhetorical traditions influence advocacy. Competing notions of time are captured by the metaphors "time's arrow" and "time's cycle" (Lake, 1991). The arrow represents linear time and the mainstream Euro-American values that are associated with it: social progress, improvement, development, and innovation. The cycle represents circular time and several prevalent Native American values: the natural world and its rhythms, the knowledge of myths and rituals handed down from the past, and the interdependence of all things (often symbolized by the hoop). Notably, this circular view of time of Native Americans in the United States is very similar to a cyclical and natural view of time held by Aboriginals in Australia (Silverman, 1997).

These distinct metaphors converged as the U.S. government and Native American protesters clashed in 1973 at Wounded Knee, South Dakota. Members of the American Indian Movement (AIM) occupied Wounded Knee for 71 days to protest the terrible living condition on the Pine Ridge Reservation. AIM members protested the leadership of Richard A. Wilson, tribal chair of the reservation, whom they accused of nepotism in steering the few jobs available on the reservation to family and friends. The U.S. government deployed troops, weapons, and vehicles to Wounded Knee to force out the protesters. The troops killed two protesters, and one U.S. Marshall was wounded by a gunshot.

Our interest in rhetorical communication focuses our attention on the ways in which participants frame their purposes and actions. The mainstream Euro-American perspective portrays Native American activism as "hopelessly out-of-date," since society has moved on (Lake, 1991, p. 129). From the perspective of time's arrow, history cannot be changed and what matters is what is done today, rather than dwelling on the past. Rhetorically, this allowed the government to dismiss the grievances of the protestors and make their unlawfulness the main factor for consideration and response.

From the perspective of time's cycle, the material conditions at Pine Ridge warranted action, but equally important was the need to restore tribal identity; that is, to reconnect tribal ways to the past. As imposed by the larger society, the poverty on the reservation interrupted the observance of ritual, breaking the circle of tradition. Protest rhetoric was concerned with transcendent meanings—meanings that encompassed past, present, and future—in ways the government and the general public could not understand. In seeking to restore time's endless cycle, the protesters at Wounded Knee enacted "a group-tribalistic approach to life, [where] time is meaningless" (Lake, 1991, p. 135).

POP CULTURE

Watch episodes of the series *Reservation Dogs*. The series follows four Indigenous teens and their lives on a reservation in Oklahoma. How are the past and future represented? How are nature and spirit forces represented? What do you think of this representation of Native Americans?

Western tradition: Rooted in argument

The Greek philosopher Aristotle has had an enduring and immense influence on Western politics, ethics, and communication. In *The Rhetoric* (Cooper, 1960), he made a distinction that would be reflected in public speaking for more than two millennia. For Aristotle, **dialectic** was the formal objective method of reasoning and arriving at truthful claims, and "rhetoric" was the "counterpart of dialectic," that is, rhetoric was the discovery of the means for persuading an audience that would include "common knowledge and accepted opinions" (Cooper, 1960, p. 6). This distinction between dialectic and rhetoric made the latter a practical art. The skilled persuader was a person who understood audience values and preferences and who could establish credibility and goodwill with an audience. In seeking agreement with one's position, the speaker implicitly attacked all other positions. The adversarial model for public deliberation was launched as Aristotle advised: "You have to upset the opposite hypothesis and frame your discourse against that as if it were your opponent" (p. 141).

Today, this practical, competitive, and objective approach to public speaking remains. This Western speech tradition is sometimes referred to as the Euro-American or dominant culture speech tradition. Several contemporary qualities of speech consistent with this tradition are self-assertive and goal-oriented statements, the desire to be right, a preference for objective information, and a future-oriented perspective. Public speaking classes today cover audience analysis, building credibility, anticipating and addressing counter arguments, use of evidence, and other topics that originate with the Greek formulations of effective persuasion.

So foundational is the analytical nature of the Western rhetoric that intercultural scholars occasionally warn of its limitations. For example, Hall (1976/1989) remarked that "we Westerners … find ourselves deeply preoccupied with specifics … to the exclusion of everything else" (p. 123). Hall's point is that because scientific or logical demonstration involves precise and controlled conditions, it is almost impossible to think and argue in a way that integrates conclusions from various ways of knowing. *An Inconvenient Truth*, the 2006 Academy Award-winning documentary film with former U.S. Vice President Al Gore, was impressive not because it presented different bodies of knowledge that holistically converged on a conclusion of global warming, but for the overwhelming amount of scientific data on global changes. The documentary also was impressive in the way it presented a seemingly inescapable future vision of a depleted planet. The persuasiveness of the argument was anchored in three very powerful Western cultural values: science, the future, and casual delivery.

If we return to the contrast between time's arrow and time's cycle, we see that the Western tradition of linear time privileges the future and treats the Native American past as savage and outdated (Lake, 1991). The competitive model of argument does not seek accommodation. It seeks a winner, locking the U.S. government and indigenous concerns in an either/or conflict: each side is either right or wrong. Similarly, the conflict at Mount Graham reveals that the scientists and the broader community in Tucson required a "precise explanation" from the Apaches of the mountain's significance (Carbaugh & Wolf, 2000, p. 22) making a historical or spiritual account unacceptable. In other words, the community in power sought an argument it could recognize rather than an argument the Apaches could deliver.

In the United States, the examination of the invisible and assumed centrality of Western power is known as Whiteness Studies. This work attempts to reveal the ways in which Whiteness—as a social position—exerts privilege (Nakayama & Krizek, 1995). For example, when NBA Commissioner David Stern imposed a dress code in 2005 that mandated suits and ties and prohibited hip-hop-style clothing, he claimed race had nothing to do with his decision. In the face of opposition from African American players, Stern was able to mask any accusation of racism by claiming that it was appropriate for management to expect that players have a "traditional" business appearance. Yet he reinforced racist stereotypes about African Americans when he claimed that the European American (White) business look would improve the NBA's reputation and the urban look would hurt the NBA's reputation (Griffin & Calafell, 2011, p. 127). Similarly, the television sitcom *Friends* has been interpreted to represent the inherent goodness of Whiteness, as the characters lead largely superficial and privileged lives while maintaining a non-diverse circle of friends (Chidester, 2008). This criticism can also be directed toward a more recent television show, *Girls*.

The Western speech tradition and performances of Whiteness are powerful in their prescriptive force and in their ubiquitous quality. When high school officials in suburban Washington, D.C. refused to award Thomas Benya his diploma because the bolo tie he wore to commencement was not considered a "traditional" tie (Manning, 2005), the officials uncritically reinforced the management/worker divide created during the Industrial Revolution, which made the knotted tie the sign of authority and success. The competitive speech model, the preference for objective data as evidence, and the future orientation of speeches emerge from particular cultural values that have been made universal. As practitioners of intercultural communication, we always must be aware of the dominant culture practices and what these practices imply for our interactions with those who speak from speech traditions of their own.

Limitations when considering rhetorical traditions

The concept of the rhetorical tradition is very useful when considering the relationships among rhetoric, culture, and intercultural communication. As with all explanatory tools, there are some precautions. Rhetorical traditions, especially those that span centuries (like Chinese, Arabic, and European traditions) change over time. Traditions—their meaning and significance—are themselves subject to perspective and interpretation. For example, Garrett reminds us that "the Chinese tradition" had different emphases in different dynasties; sometimes Confucianism guided discourse and at other times Buddhism guided discourse (Garrett, 2000, p. 60). Contemporary Chinese discourse is guided by a blend of previous emphases.

Furthermore, Garrett observes that the discourse we would examine to construct the Chinese rhetorical tradition was written by the elite for the elite. The historical record emerges from the concerns and interests of the "well-off, educated, male elite" (p. 60). In other words, it only partially reflects Chinese thought and practice.

Finally, in approaching contemporary Chinese rhetoric, how do we distinguish what is genuinely Chinese from Western influence? This question applies to African rhetoric as well. The "I am African" speech delivered by Thabo Mbeki in 1996 was inspired as much by the "Camelot vision" of the Kennedy presidency as by traditional South African influences (Sheckels, 2010). The lesson here is that any "tradition" is never as straightforward as we might suspect. A tradition cannot be used to predict how a particular speaker will state their case but it can be helpful to explain some features of their argument. As students of culture and inclusion, we are obligated to interrogate and acknowledge the selective quality of traditions.

Vernacular rhetoric: How does everyday communication seek to persuade?

While an understanding of rhetorical traditions is important in placing a speech or text in a cultural context, another exciting concept is also available. **Vernacular discourse** refers to locally produced meanings; that is, speech that has been adapted to audiences to elicit persuasion or cooperation by taking the form of the everyday communication of the community in which the speech occurs. Critical focus is on marginalized communities because vernacular discourse "makes visible power relations among subjects" (Calafell & Delgado, 2004, p. 6). Since local meanings often function persuasively to mediate relationships between marginalized and dominant communities, we also use the term **vernacular rhetoric**.

Vernacular rhetoric online

The rise of online communities has necessitated a reformulation of vernacular communication that considers online environments as well as physical localities, or neighborhoods. Rhetorical critics have turned attention to online advocacy that creates a sense of close community, that is, construction of a virtual vernacular spaces. Guo and Lee (2013) describe the YouTube vlogs of two Asian celebrities, Ryan Hyga and Kevin Wu. They note that a sense of locality by recording in their bedrooms and kitchens, appearing in their pajamas, Wu bickers with his father in their kitchen, and both present themselves as relatable "ordinary" young Asian males. At the same time, Hyga and Wu offer commentary on social contradictions of race in the United States and the complexities of Asian identity in a humorous and casual way. The authors argue that the vloggers draw from familiar cultural references (both mainstream and ethnic) to build "a new YouTubed Asian community" (p. 404).

In online environments, communities can gather around other aspects of identity. Sarah Parsloe (2015) examined the "aspie" community, people who either had or knew someone with Asperger's syndrome (AS). The online comments of members attempted to recenter AS from neurological disorder to cultural identity. In other words, Aspie Central wanted to counter an oppressive disability discourse with a discourse that "reclaimed normalcy," redefined the symptoms of AS in positive terms, and expanded members' sense of agency (pp. 344–348). Aspie Central became a vernacular online community. Since the members of Aspie Central defined themselves as a cultural group, interactions with non-aspies are intercultural. With the proliferation of online communities, intercultural communication skills are vital online as well as offline.

Vernacular rhetoric in Africa

In the early 2000s, the Feminist International Radio Endeavor (FIRE) expanded its South American operations to Sub-Saharan Africa. The goal of FIRE was to facilitate community radio broadcasting that centered on women's voices and women's issues (Gatua et al., 2010). Through a variety of means, including audiotapes, or recorded content, and the Internet, FIRE created programming for tens of thousands of women and their families.

The programs created by FIRE contained many vernacular elements. In countries such as Kenya, Nigeria, Uganda, Burundi, and Congo, FIRE used community radio to promote local issues in locally understood ways. Radio in Africa remains an affordable, accessible, and versatile communication medium. First, FIRE sponsored workshops to train women journalists. Many African countries have no independent media, only state-owned media. The FIRE-trained journalists are aware of community issues and know how to create independent content for local media. Second, the program content reflects community issues. Circumstances vary across the continent. At times, information about food, employment, and health may be most important. At other times, illiteracy and general education may be most important. Community radio can quickly address topics that are immediately relevant to the community. Third, programs were recorded and broadcast in local dialects. UNESCO estimates that there are more than 2000 languages and 4000 dialects spoken on the continent. FIRE recorded programs in the dialect of the community as opposed to a "standard" dialect. This ensured that a maximum number of listeners would be able to understand the information delivered (Gatua et al., 2010).

A second example of vernacular rhetoric in Africa is the Knowledge Center project in Ihiala, Nigeria (Ha et al., 2008). This project provided free Internet service to the people of Ihiala. A special website was established that allowed farmers to share information with each other. The farmers found the website to be informative and enjoyable since the local knowledge of the community was the basis of its content. The farmers were able to socialize via the website using references to places, people, and events that were well understood.

FIRE and the Knowledge Center engaged in vernacular rhetoric as they empowered communities to respond to self-identified priorities. Furthermore, the community members engaged radio and the website to persuade the community to avoid infection, read more, or grow better crops, in their own dialect and with well-understood community meanings. These practices often resist larger government structures that centralize the needs of capital cities and urban areas to neglect smaller and remote villages.

With its Creole imagery, King Cakes and Krewes, Mardi Gras is a ritual that is truly identified with New Orleans (Figure 9.3). Mardi Gras is an example of a vernacular celebration. What vernacular celebrations surround you?

Figure 9.3 Mardi Gras is a local celebration on the eve of the Christian Lenten period. Source: Atlantide Phototravel/Getty Images.

A third example of vernacular rhetoric also comes from the Sub-Saharan region of Africa. In this example, the main rhetorical medium is clothing. *Pagne* refers to the cloth worn by women in Western Africa (Figure 9.4). Women in the African nation of Côte d'Ivoire communicate their perspectives on a variety of local issues through pagne designs (Hagan, 2010).

Each pagne is given a name in the local marketplace. The women who sell them suggest names for each pagne to the customers. After several tries, a name is agreed upon by the woman

buying the pagne and the purchase is completed. Pagne names can be associated with well-known proverbs, political positions, and even specific political personalities. By wearing a pagne, the woman may visually express her support for equity and fairness when her verbal support may be prohibited. Pagne can indicate the status of the wearer, since pagne elements (imported or local, fancy or plain, etc.) convey information about the social class of the wearer (Hagan, 2010, p. 150).

The pagne works rhetorically to mediate relations between men and women. In many postcolonial nations, traditional African kinship structures in which women's roles were valued were replaced by European structures that privileged male participation. The woman signifies her support for traditional communal structures through the pagne she wears. As vernacular rhetoric, pagne is a way for women in a community to critique and resist patriarchy and the slowness of government reform.

Vernacular rhetoric in South Toledo, Ohio, USA

The Old South End of Toledo, Ohio, is generally known as a lower working-class neighborhood. Its residents are mostly Latino and African American. The neighborhood sits south of the downtown area and it is bordered on the south by the Maumee River. A traveler driving south on Broadway enters the South End by passing through the I-75 freeway underpass. The underpass serves as an informal gateway into the neighborhood and it serves for most Toledoans as a symbolic reminder of the marginalized status of the community. Additionally, 28 grain silos create an eyesore that invites locals to look past this area.

In 2010, local artists and art students from a nearby university painted a mural on one of the pylons underneath I-75 along Broadway Avenue. Soon additional murals were painted, and Broadway came to life with color and culture. In 2020, funds were raised to paint a mural—the largest in the United States—across the 28 silos (Figure 9.5). Completed in 2022 the design features sunflowers and the images of members of three Ohio indigenous peoples: the Shawnee, the Miami, and the Dakota. These native communities are credited with being the "first farmers" of Northwest Ohio (Zenner, 2022). Now, local residents point to the mural with pride and a new

Figure 9.5 This mural behind the Old South End of Toledo, along the Maumee River. Source: CBS Interactive Inc. https://www.cbsnews.com/news/glass-city-river-wall-mural-toledo-ohio/ /last accessed January 10, 2023.

awareness of the Indigenous history of the Great Black Swamp in Ohio. Furthermore, residents of the Old South End can claim ownership of a major city landmark.

Obviously, we are receptive to persuasive communication that does not have us specifically in mind. Many political messages and advertisements are created far away from us and are directed to general publics. Still, in response to these messages, we might make a campaign contribution, volunteer for a charitable cause, or buy a product. Television or web messages can be so common that we might not notice persuasion that has nearby origins. Furthermore, we might not notice the special power of vernacular discourse. A recent study of the community impact of murals in Philadelphia, Pennsylvania, identified the special influence of locally created art:

1 Murals that closely matched the input of the nearby residents were most favorably received.

2 Affirming or positive images in the murals tended to smooth over conflicts among diverse identities.

3 Murals encouraged a sense of neighborhood pride and delight.

4 Murals encouraged a sense of empowerment and resistance to negative forces outside the neighborhood.

(Adapted from Moss, 2010)

Vernacular rhetorics are important in the study of intercultural communication, because they lead us to the distinctive and highly detailed meanings of cultures. Those images, slogans, or other appeals that are invented locally have much to offer the outsider. Recognizing those appeals and asking residents about their significance will allow us to better understand communities that are new to us.

Intercultural rhetoric: What are the implications for civic engagement?

In February 2022, Russian military forces invaded Ukraine. While Russian forces made initial gains, Ukrainian forces were able to retake territory lost early in the war. An estimated 5.2 million Ukrainians have fled the country and are in Western Europe and the United Kingdom (BBC) (Figure 9.6). Thousands of residents in neighboring Moldova, Poland, Germany, and

Figure 9.6 Ukrainian Refugees.
Source: Associated Press/Sergei
Grits).

other countries opened their homes to the refugees. They responded to the appeals from Ukraine president Volodymyr Zelenski for humanitarian, economic, and military assistance. President Zelenski spoke by Zoom before the UN and to many governing bodies appealing for solidarity and calling for harsh sanctions against Russian businesses. He even made a video appearance at the 2022 Grammy Awards and noted that "our musicians wear body armor instead of tuxedos. They sing to the wounded in hospitals" (Ukraine's president Zelenski delivers speech at Grammys, 2022). In his speeches, he reached across cultures to establish common ground with his audiences and to close division.

If we scan our environment, we will observe that people from cultures and nations other than our own are attempting to persuade us. People are attempting to build relationships with us and they invite us to consider new ways to understand the world through arguments, testimonies, and powerful images. These communicative actions are intercultural rhetoric. In the case of President Zelensky, we see that he was attempting to build identification with U.S. viewers through a familiar and admirable narrative: standing up to tyranny for the cause of freedom. In effectively reaching across significant cultural differences, he was able to build support for U.S. and NATO military equipment and expertise.

Communication scholars have reflected upon the possibilities for civic engagement in the communities where they conduct their research. While typically working in situations less severe than in Ukraine, activist-scholars have an opportunity to take "action that attempts to make a positive difference in situations where people's lives are affected by oppression … conflict, and other forms of cultural struggle" (Broome et al., 2005, p. 146). Many of us who have studied rhetorical communication (perhaps as undergraduate or graduate students) are in a position to assist local nonprofit organizations or neighborhood community centers. As volunteers, we might assist residents by holding public speaking workshops, evaluating arguments in petitions or other documents, writing announcements for the local media, teaching interviewing techniques, or conducting an audience analysis in advance of a public forum. As in the case of a war seemingly so far away, these activities often require us to reach effectively across cultural divides.

To work productively as an intercultural advocate involves several key considerations. The primary orientation is an ethic of **speaking with** members of a community in one's efforts to advance issues important to them (Alcoff, 1991), rather than speaking to them (see Chapter 2).

"Speaking with" means that the advocate understands and accepts the common knowledge of a community through extensive contact with its members. The advocate is allied with the interests—the "real issues"—of the community, and works with its members on issues the members have identified as important (Broome et al., 2005, p. 169). The ethic of speaking includes the following guides:

1   Begin, proceed, and end honestly and respectfully.

2   Enter into active dialogue and participation with community residents.

3   Seek to understand the broader social structures that silence the community or suppress its interests.

4   Be prepared to challenge those structures at public meetings or in public forums.

5   Assist and facilitate the expression of those who do not have access to communication media.

6   Be willing to reciprocate; that is, share your academic knowledge when appropriate, but never consider it "better than" local knowledge.

(Adapted from Broome et al., 2005)

Maybe someday we will have the chance to reach across cultural lines as global citizens. We may be faced with empowering Latin American and African women to use radio programming to help their communities or maybe we will be faced with asking residents in an urban neighborhood about the kinds of images they would like to see painted on the sides of buildings and homes. Maybe we will be asked to help refugees who are fleeing a conflict that we must learn more about. In the same vein, maybe someone in another culture will need to reach across lines *to help us in some way*, either in terms of material goods or to understanding things about our own culture that we cannot see from our perspective. Successfully meeting these goals interculturally—learning to *speak with*—requires us to learn about new sources of influence and new ways to create identification.

Summary

In this chapter, we have learned that rhetoric and culture are closely bound concepts. Rhetorical communication is designed to persuade people to accept an action or belief. Rhetorical communication can also be designed to mediate relationships and contrasting beliefs. Identification is a key rhetorical strategy. Identification means promoting a common identity that then allows cooperation and harmony. Identification is the remedy to division.

There is no single standard for persuasion and mediation. Cultures produce distinctive rhetorical traditions. What counts as believable and influential varies from culture to culture. Intercultural rhetoric refers to situations where at least two rhetorical traditions meet. When Dr. Martin Luther King, Jr. gave the "I Have A Dream" speech in Washington, D.C. in 1964, the vernacular rhetoric of southern African American preachers met Euro-American expectations. This speech continues to be an example of successful intercultural rhetoric because listeners from various cultural backgrounds understand, accept, and are inspired by King's imagery and delivery.

For successful civic engagement, we should have an awareness of the rhetorical traditions that influence how community members seek to persuade others. Practicing an ethic of speaking with community members means that our interests are aligned with those of community members. Speaking with others also obligates us to understand and challenge inequities that disadvantage the community.

KEY TERMS

identification, 181
division, 181
rhetoric, 181
rhetorical action, 181
rhetorical communication, 181
rhetorical tradition, 182
intercultural rhetoric, 183

paralanguage, 184
mutual intelligibility, 190
dialectic, 191
vernacular discourse, 193
vernacular rhetoric, 193
speaking with, 198

Discussion questions

1   How do you attempt to create identification with others? In social settings? At work? At school? Do you think about how others are attempting to create identification with you?

2   Make a list of three public figures you admire. What rhetorical tradition (or traditions) helps to explain how these individuals relate to audiences? What rhetorical tradition guides what these individuals say and do?

3   What vernacular terms and meanings are found in your community? Make a list of terms that "only insiders" know how to define.

4   Have you ever *spoken with* members of a community on a particular issue? How did you build the relationship? What was the outcome?

Action points

1   In 2010, members of the Iroquois lacrosse team were denied travel to England to compete in the lacrosse world championships. To respect the sovereignty of their native nation—the Iroquois Confederacy—team members would not obtain U.S. passports. Yet due to new rules by Homeland Security, the United States and England required that team members have U.S.-issued identification. Research this case. How did this situation end?

2   Conduct a Google search for Mount Graham. Why is this a unique location for Native Americans, scientists, and environmentalists? What current actions are underway to resist development of this area?

3   Select a local store or business. How does it promote itself online? How does it draw upon local knowledge?

For more information

Hagan, M. A. (2006). Culture, communication, and identity in the Cote d'Ivoire: *Le pagne parle*. In M. P. Orbe, B. J. Allen, & L. A. Flores (Eds.), *The same and different: Acknowledging the diversity between and within cultural groups* (pp. 193–125). National Communication Association.

Joseph, W. A., Wong, C., & Zweig, D. (Eds.). (1991). *New perspectives on the cultural revolution.* Harvard University Press.

Meisner, M. (2007). *Mao Zedong: A political and intellectual portrait.* Polity.

Rogers, R. A. (2009). "Your guess is as good as any": Indeterminacy, dialogue, and dissemination in interpretations of Native American rock art. *Journal of International and Intercultural Communication, 2*(1), 44–65. doi.org/10.1080/17513050802567056

Shi, Y. (2008). Chinese immigrant women workers: Everyday forms of resistance and "coagulate politics." *Communication and Critical/Cultural Studies, 5*(4), 363–382.

Sorrells, K., & Nakagawa, G. (2008). Intercultural communication *praxis* and the struggle for social responsibility and social justice. In O. Swartz (Ed.), *Transformative communication studies: Culture, hierarchy and the human condition* (pp. 17–43). Troubador Press.

References

Alcoff, L. (1991). The problem of speaking for others. *Cultural Critique, 20*(1), 5–33.

Asante, M. K. (1980). *Afrocentricity: The theory of social change.* Amulefi Publishing.

BBC News. (2022, July 4). How many Ukrainian refugees are there and where have they gone? Accessed August 4, 2022, at https://www.bbc.com/news/world-60555472.

Biden signs executive orders on climate, COVID-19 on first day in office. (2021). *PBS NewsHour.* Accessed November 25, 2022, at https://www.youtube.com/watch?v=085Y08jKqew

Broome, B., Carey, C., De la Garza, S. A., Martin, J. M., & Morris, R. (2005). "In the thick of things": A dialogue about the activist turn in intercultural communication. In W. J. Starosta & G. Chen (Eds.), *Taking stock in intercultural communication: Where to now?* (pp. 145–175). National Communication Association.

Burke, K. (1969). *A rhetoric of motives.* University of California Press.

Cai, B., & González, A. (1997). The Three Gorges Project: Technological discourse and the resolution of competing interests. *Journal of Intercultural Communication, 7*(1), 101–111.

Calafell, B. M., & Delgado, F. P. (2004). Reading Latina/o images: Interrogating *Americanos. Critical Studies in Media Communication, 21*(1), 1–21. DOI: 10.1080/0739318042000184370.

Carbaugh, D., & Wolf, K. (2000). Situating rhetoric in cultural discourses. In A. González & D. V. Tanno (Eds.), *Rhetoric in intercultural contexts* (pp. 19–30). Sage.

Chidester, P. (2008). May the circle stay unbroken: *Friends*, the presence of absence, and the rhetorical reinforcement of whiteness. *Critical Studies in Media Communication, 25*(2), 157–174. DOI: 10.1080/15295030802031772.

Collins, P. H. (1989). The social construction of Black feminist thought. *Signs: Journal of Women in Culture and Society, 14*(4), 745–773.

Cooper, L. (Trans.). (1960). *The rhetoric of Aristotle.* Prentice-Hall.

Ferriss, S., & Sandoval, R. (1997). *The fight in the fields: Cesar Chavez and the farmworkers movement.* Harcourt Brace.

Garrett, M. M. (2000). Some elementary methodological reflections on the study of the Chinese rhetorical tradition. In A. González & D. V. Tanno (Eds.), *Rhetoric in intercultural contexts* (pp. 53–63). Sage.

Garrett, M. M., & Xiao, X. (1994). The rhetorical situation revisited. *Rhetoric and Society Quarterly, 23*(2), 30–40.

Gatua, M. W., Patton, T. O., & Brown, M. R. (2010). Giving voice to invisible women: "FIRE" as model of a successful women's community radio in Africa. *The Howard Journal of Communications, 21* (2), 164–181. DOI: 10.1080/10646171003727441

González, A. (1989). "Participation" at WMEX-FM: Interventional rhetoric of Ohio Mexican Americans. *Western Journal of Communication, 53* (4), 398–410. DOI: 10.1080/10570318909374317

Griffin, R. A., & Calafell, B. M. (2011). Control, discipline, and punish: Black masculinity and (in)visible whiteness in the NBA. In M. G. Lacy & K. A. Ono (Eds.), *Critical rhetorics of race* (pp. 117–136). NYU Press.

Guo, L. & Lee, L. (2013). The critique of YouTube-based vernacular discourse: A case study of YouTube's Asian community. *Critical Studies in Media Communication, 30*(5), 391–406. DOI: 10.1080/15295036.2012.755048

Ha, L., Okigbo, R. N., & Igboaka, P. (2008). Knowledge creation and dissemination in sub-Saharan Africa. *Management Decision, 46*(3), 392–405. DOI: 10.1108/00251740810863852

Hagan, M. A. (2010). Speaking out: Women, *pagne*, and politics in the Cote d'Ivoire. *The Howard Journal of Communication, 21*(2), 141–163. DOI: 10.1080/10646171003727433

Hall, E. T. (1976/1989). *Beyond culture*. Anchor Books.

Hamlet, J. (2011). The reason why we sing: Understanding traditional African American worship. In A. González, M. Houston, & V. Chen (Eds.), *Our voices: Essays in culture, ethnicity, and communication* (5th ed., pp. 112–117). Oxford University Press.

Hammerback, J. C., & Jensen, R. J. (1994). Ethnic heritage as rhetorical legacy: The Plan of Delano. *Quarterly Journal of Speech, 80*(1), 53–70. DOI: 10.1080/00335639409384055

Herrick, J. A. (2009). *The history and theory of rhetoric: An introduction* (4th ed.). Allyn & Bacon.

Huang, S. (1997). Ritual, culture, and communication: Deification of Mao Zedong in China's cultural revolution movement. In A. González & D. V. Tanno (Eds.), *Politics, communication, and culture* (pp. 122–140). Sage.

Jackson, J. (1988). Common ground and common sense. *Vital Speeches of the Day, 54*, 649–653.

Jiang, X., & González, A. (2021). China dream and root-seeking: The rhetoric of nationalism in *The Voice of China. Journal of Contemporary China, 30*(132). https://doi.org/10.1080/10670564.2021.1893553

Johnson, F. L. (2000). *Speaking culturally: Language diversity in the United States*. Sage.

Lake, R. A. (1991). Between myth and history: Enacting time in Native American protest rhetoric. *Quarterly Journal of Speech, 77*(2), 123–151. DOI: 10.1080/00335639109383949

Manning, S. (2005). Bolo tie creates bind for graduating senior. *The Seattle Times*. Accessed March 25, 2013, at http://seattletimes.com/html/education/2002329323_tie11.html

Moss, K. L. (2010). Cultural representation in Philadelphia murals: Images of resistance and sites of identity negotiation. *Western Journal of Communication, 74*(4), 372–395. DOI: 10.1080/10570314.2010.492819

Nakayama, T. K., & Krizek, R. (1995). Whiteness: A strategic rhetoric. *Quarterly Journal of Speech, 81*(3), 291–309. DOI: 10.1080/00335639509384117

Parsloe, S. (2015). Discourses of disability, narratives of community: Reclaiming an autistic identity online. *Journal of Applied Communication Research, 43* (3), 336–356. DOI: 10.1080/00909882.2015.1052829

Paz, O. (1961). *The Labyrinth of Solitude: Life and thought in Mexico* (L. Kemp, Trans.). Grove Press.

Paz, O. (1972). *The other Mexico: Critique of the pyramid* (L. Kemp, Trans.). Grove Press.

Philipsen, G. (1992). *Speaking culturally: Explorations in social communication*. SUNY Press.

Saunders, D. (2010, September 29). Apache opposes telescope permit renewal. Mount Graham Coalition, September 29. Accessed March 27, 2011, at http://www.mountgraham.org

Sheckels, T. F. (2010). The rhetorical success of Thabo Mbeki's 1996 "I Am an African" address. *Communication Quarterly, 57*(3), 319–333. DOI: 10.1080/01463370903107345

Shutiva, C. (2012). Native American culture and communication through humor. In A. González, M. Houston, & V. Chen (Eds.), *Our voices: Essays in culture, ethnicity and communication* (5th ed., pp. 134–138). Oxford University Press.

Silverman, E. K. (1997). Politics, gender, and time in Melanesia and Aboriginal Australia. *Ethnology, 36* (2), 101–122. DOI: 10.2307/3774078

Smith, A. (1970). Socio-historical perspectives of Black oratory. *Quarterly Journal of Speech, 56*(3), 264–269. DOI: 10.1080/00335637009383010

Starosta, W. J., & Coleman, L. (1986). Jesse Jackson's "Hymietown" apology: A case study of interethnic rhetorical analysis. In Y. Y. Kim (Ed.), *Interethnic communication* (pp. 117–135). Sage.

Sullivan, P. A. (1993). Signification and African-American rhetoric: A case study of Jesse Jackson's "Common Ground and Common Sense" speech. *Communication Quarterly, 41*(1), 1–15. DOI: 10.1080/01463379309369863

Teiwes, F. C. (2010). Mao and his followers. In T. Cheek (Ed.), *A critical introduction to Mao* (pp. 129–157). Cambridge University Press.

Ukraine's president Zelenski delivers speech at Grammys. (2022, April). *The Independent*. Accessed August 15, 2022, at https://www.youtube.com/watch?v=4985U0PQ97Y

Weaver, M. S. (1991). Makers and redeemers: The theatricality of the Black Church. *Black American Literature Forum, 25*(1), 53–62. DOI: 10.2307/3041771

Xiao, X. (1995). China encounters Darwinism: A case of intercultural rhetoric. *Quarterly Journal of Speech, 81*(1), 83–99. DOI: 10.1080/00335639509384098

Zenner, S. (2022). Glass City River Wall dedicated Saturday. *The Toledo Blade*. Accessed October 16, 2022, at https://www.toledoblade.com/local/city/2022/10/15/glass-city-river-wall-mural/stories/20221015114

Zhong, M. (2003). Contemporary social and political movements and their imprints on the Chinese language. In L. A. Samovar & R. E. Porter (Eds.), *Intercultural communication: A reader* (10th ed., pp. 206–223). Wadsworth.

Chapter 10

Media and intercultural communication: How do media shape our views of others?

Chapter objectives

After this chapter, you should be able to:

→ Understand the role that the media play in your life,

→ Describe the different ways that the media can be interpreted

→ Recognize the influences upon media content and how your experiences alter your media viewing

→ Define framing and how stereotyping contributes to the media

Intercultural Communication for Everyday Life, Second Edition. John R. Baldwin, Alberto González, Nettie Brock, Ming Xie, and Chin-Chung Chao.
© 2024 John Wiley & Sons Ltd. Published 2024 by John Wiley & Sons Ltd.
Companion Website: http://www.wiley.com/go/baldwin2e

n a television broadcast from 1960, renowned media theorist Marshall McLuhan talks about his idea that the world is becoming like a "global village" and that when something happens in one location, people around the world know about it. He says, "These new media of ours … have made our world into a single unit … where everybody gets the message all the time." The examples that McLuhan uses include "a princess gets married in England … an earthquake in North Africa … a Hollywood star gets drunk" ("The World is a Global Village," 1960). McLuhan was discussing this idea of the entire world getting news at the same time in 1960, a solid *thirty* years before the invention of the World Wide Web and the widespread utilization of the internet. Imagine how he would react to social media apps like Snapchat and TikTok!

Consider the events of recent years. We still have global audiences for British weddings; an estimated 2 billion people worldwide watched Prince Harry marry Meghan Markle in 2018 (Kelly, 2018). In March 2021, the entire world watched with bated breath as the cargo ship Ever Given blocked traffic in the Suez Canal for nearly a week, preventing global shipping and costing the global trade industry an approximate $9.6 billion (Russon, 2021). Since 2017, the #MeToo movement has been exposing sexual harassment around the world (See: "#MeToo is at a crossroads," 2020). All these events have had a larger reach and more attention because of the ubiquity of the media. While it is likely that we would have known many of these things were happening, even with only newspapers and television at our disposal, the collective way in which these events were consumed could only really occur in the 21st century with the latest media technologies.

This chapter examines the ways that the media impacts our understanding of others, as well as how the media itself works to bring people together in ways that Marshall McLuhan could only dream to be possible. Imagine trying to explain to McLuhan that, in 2021, as a global pandemic had become a state of normalcy, that nearly the entire world would unite to watch nine episodes of a South Korean drama that critiques capitalism through deadly versions of children's games (Figure 10.1). Nearly 130 million people watched Netflix's *Squid Game* globally in September and October 2021 (Shaw, 2021). Media are bringing people together like never before—how does that unity influence people's intercultural communication?

Figure 10.1 Squid game: Many have seen in the highly successful Netflix series from South Korea, *Squid Game*, a dystopian critique of the extremes of capitalism. Which media texts that you watch do you feel might be critiquing (or passing on) dominant ways of thinking? Source: Everett Collection Inc/ Alamy Stock Photo.

Transmission and ritual models of communication: What role do the media play in our lives?

Lasswell's model of communication

Before we can examine the ways that media and intercultural communication intersect, we need to understand the myriad ways that the media influence the individual. To begin, let's talk about the classic model of (mediated) communication, as suggested by Harold Lasswell (1971). Lasswell says that a "convenient way" to talk about communication is to ask a single, simple question:

> Who Says
> What
> In Which Channel
> To Whom
> With What Effect?
> *(p. 216)*

Each part of the question is equally important. Just because the question is simple, does not mean it is easy to answer. Thus, each segment of the question—Who, What, Which Channel, to Whom, and With What Effect—can all be answered separately, and should be. Each segment of the question is answered by a different part of the Communication field. So, for the purposes of this section, we are primarily concerned with "in which channel." Lasswell (1971) specifies that these "channels" can include "radio, press, film" and leaves the door open for other channels—television, the internet, social media, and so on (p. 216). That being said, we cannot neglect the other four areas of the question. For instance, if we apply these questions to *Squid Game*, we could say:

> Who Says: Writer Hwang Dong-hyuk
> What: A critique of capitalism through a television series
> In Which Channel: Netflix
> To Whom: The World
> To What Effect: This part of the question could be answered in a variety of ways, depending on the research questions asked and the methodological approaches to finding those answers. The "effect" could be that people realize the harmful ways that money contributes to society; or the "effect" could be a further understanding of South Korean Culture. It would depend entirely upon the perspective undertaken by the researcher.

Communication, especially mediated communication, can only truly work as a whole. But we can investigate each individual unit.

Carey's transmission and ritual models of communication

Carey (1989) refers to Lasswell's approach as the "**transmission model**" of communication because of its focus on the sending and receiving of messages. Such a model is the most prominent in most communication research. He says that in this model, "communication is a process whereby messages are transmitted and distributed in space for the control of distance and people" (p. 15). Carey suggests that Lasswell's core model is focused not just on the relationship between a sender and a receiver, but a way of controlling others. Media can especially manipulate viewers/receivers relatively easily—mostly through the use of framing, which we will discuss later in this chapter.

However, Carey (1989) argues that there is another model of communication that also needs to be understood. This is the **"ritual model of communication."** Carey's approach opens the door to considering not only content but the roles and significance that media have in everyday life. In this model, communication functions more as a way of maintaining a shared system of beliefs. Every society has its own system of beliefs and values. Those values are created and maintained through communication.

The media makes us feel and think a certain way At the core of the way that values are maintained through communication are ideas of power and hegemony. Basically, certain ideas have become so pervasive in the different societies in which we, as communicators, live that we don't even really think about why we assume they are true. For a very long time, heterosexuality was considered "normal," and anything other than that—including everything under the LGBTQIA+ umbrella—was "wrong" and made invisible. In the 21st century, many people in different cultures are realizing that no one's sexuality is "wrong," but the long-held belief persists in some places/people/cultures. Being exposed to ideas for a very long time, especially when watching them in the media, can cause those ideas to change our perception of the world. This fact is described by Cultivation Theory.

What do you think? In 2021, China proposed measures to begin teaching "masculinity" in the classroom to encourage more "manly" figures in positions of power (Allen, 2021) Disney's *Lightyear* (2022) was banned in several Muslim countries, including the United Arab Emirates and Malaysia, for featuring a lesbian marriage and kiss (Gallagher, 2022). Hungary passed a law in 2021 banning any materials that are seen to be "promoting homosexuality and gender change" from schools (Baczynska & Campenhout, 2022). Around the world, pressure is coming down from the government to curb anything seen as "sexual deviation." What is the purpose of such legislation? Why do you think that the global community in the 2020s is so concerned with sexuality and the ways that gender norms are represented in the media?

Cultivation theory

Cultivation Theory was first posited by George Gerbner (1998) after several lengthy studies of violence on television and experiments to discover people's reactions to that violence. The results of these studies "show that television can exert an independent influence on attitudes and behaviors over time" (p. 180). In other words, watching a lot of television can change an individual's behaviors and, more importantly, beliefs. Through Gerbner's studies, he and his colleagues found that exposing people to a lot of television violence gives those people an "exaggerated perception of the number of people involved in violence" (Gerbner, 1998, p. 185). This is called "mean world syndrome."

Cultivation theory can be translated to *any* ideology found dominantly in television. And television itself is important here. Television when Gerbner was doing his studies was the most mainstream form of the media. As a result, television creators were trying to appeal to the greatest number of people and so presented images of "reality" that appealed to broad audiences and not to niche groups. BIPOC representations and alternative lifestyle choices were cast aside for majority, "normal" representations: white, heterosexual, middle class, and so on.

A study of 12 years of television leading up to 2004, by Bradley Greenberg and Tracy Worrell (2007) found that by that time, representation of African Americans in U.S. media had increased significantly, but many other groups were still relatively invisible. We need new research today to verify if such claims still hold true in the United States and other countries. Other research has looked at representation on Facebook, in video games, and other media.

Exposure to frequent media images can have negative or positive effects. For example, **heavy views**, defined in some studies as those who watched television more than fifteen hours a week (Lee et al., 2009), had stronger ethnic stereotypes and more traditional gender-role stereotypes. Older research demonstrated that heavy Latino/a viewers of mainstream U.S. television have lower self- and appearance esteem (Rivadeneyra et al., 2007), though more recent research (Tukachinksy et al., 2017) shows that effects may be different, with African and Lationa/o viewers exposed to oversexualized images of their own group have more negative in-group attitudes, but that ingroup attitudes are positive if they instead view more images of professionals from their own group. In sum, cultivation analysis tells us that watching too many negative group representations gives one a skewed sense of the world—if something is not present on television, that likely makes you think that it doesn't exist in the "real world" either.

A modern version of Cultivation Analysis is called "echo chambers." **Echo chambers** exist when people tend to only pay attention to media—including the news sources they use and the social media accounts they follow—that share the same basic ideas and spread the same information. Zhuang Liu (2022) has found that an echo chamber online in China has caused "scholars and practitioners in China [to] persistently overestimate" the public's desire for capital punishment. Liu attributes this echo chamber to a lack of democratic institutions and the fact that the judges making these claims are stuck in online misinformation echo chambers. Cornelia Sindermann et al. (2020) suggest that people often become a part of echo chambers online because it is "easy," saying, "the Internet is a high choice environment and provides the possibility of meeting many individuals from all over the world" (p. 2). They also found that certain demographics are especially prone to echo chambers. These demographics include age and gender, as well as "openness" and "right-wing authoritarianism" (p. 7). Getting stuck in an echo chamber makes you think that the world is the way that it is portrayed within the world you see; that may not be the case.

Nobody understands the media the way you do Another important theory for us to discuss has to do with how people *interpret* information they see in the media. Again, some ideas are so normalized among different groups within and across cultures that we don't even really think about why we believe them. These may be views about family, beauty, success, the importance and use of material goods, or political beliefs. And these ideas are often present in the media we watch, not for any explicitly malicious intent, but because the people creating the media don't really think about it due to their dominant cultural status. At the same time, however, audiences are not mindless, passive consumers of the media. They choose what to consume and what messages in the media they will agree with and which they disagree with. Stuart Hall (2006) explains how whenever a media text is created, the producer "encodes" the information with certain themes and values that are important to them. Again, that "encoding" process is not, necessarily, on purpose. Then, when a viewer watches the text, they "decode" the information within their important values. Some of that decoding may be in line with what our society tells us is "normal" and some of it may be resisting the status quo. The values of the producer and the viewer might be the same, but they also could be different. Every person thinks about the world differently; they also interpret the media differently.

Take, for instance, the *Frozen* movies (2013 and 2019). Many viewers of these films have seen a queer subtext filtering through Elsa's storyline (Figure 10.2). She is told to lock away her true

Figure 10.2 Elsa, from the Disney *Frozen* films. Many have seen in the representation of Elsa as positive icon for the Queer community.
Source: Sarunyu L/Shutterstock.

self, so people aren't afraid of her, and to seem as "normal" as possible when around others. After the release of the first film, viewers online advocated heavily for Elsa to be a lesbian, using #GiveElsaAGirlfriend (Megarry, 2019). After *Frozen 2* was released, the LGBTQIA+ community latched onto one of Elsa's ballads from the film—"Show Yourself." They declared that the song, which features lines such as "I've always been a fortress, cold secrets deep inside, you have secrets too, but you don't have to hide" and "I have always been so different, normal rules did not apply. Is this the day? Are you the way I finally find out why?" to be a coming out anthem (Megarry, 2019). No one from the production team has confirmed that any of these queer themes were purposefully encoded into the text. However, upon watching the films, viewers identified strongly with Elsa's journey, thereby decoding both *Frozen* and *Frozen 2* within their lived experiences to create an entirely different interpretation than those creating the text imagined.

The media are a powerful force in our society. They are a way of transmitting information and bringing people together and creating social norms. However, not everyone receives the information the same way. To return briefly to Hall (1996), he expanded upon his basic ideas of encoding/decoding to discuss the wide variety of ways that audiences can decode a media text. There are three major approaches that audiences take. First, there is the *dominant-hegemonic* position, where audiences accept the preferred meaning that the producers have encoded into the text. Second, there is a *negotiated* position, in which audiences accept some messages and reject others dependent upon their personal preferences and history. Finally, there is an *oppositional* approach, where audiences reject all the meanings within the text and either interpret their own meanings upon the texts or fight the messages entirely and refuse to accept the hegemony. Each of these different means of decoding a media text is important in their own right. With the *Frozen 2* example above, the LGBTQIA+ community appears to be *negotiating* their meaning; they do not reject the outward messages of the film, but nor are they accepting the basic meaning at its face value. They have found their own meaning within the story of Elsa.

In addition to these different ways of interpreting the media, the media also serve to teach people about society and themselves. When it comes to representations in the media, those representations can influence individuals profoundly, for the good or for the bad. So, to have a full understanding of the ways that media representations can impact our understanding of our own and other cultures, we need to consider three aspects of culture: democracy, imperialism, and capitalism.

Media, society, and the public sphere: What kinds of media influences factor into our perception of others?

Cultural approaches to the media

Every country, every culture, every person has various impediments to receiving media texts. No one receives everything freely and many people don't receive anything without some level of interference. In the United States, the public is used to the idea of "freedom of expression" as outlined in the First Amendment of their Constitution. This amendment reads:

> Congress shall make no law respecting an establishment of religion, or prohibiting the free exercise thereof; or abridging the freedom of speech, or of the press; or the right of the people peaceably to assemble, and to petition the Government for a redress of grievances. (U.S. Const. amend. I)

Almost the entirety of American society is based around this amendment and the ability it affords citizens to speak their minds in just about any given situation. This amendment also frees the media to be able to spread messages in whatever form it desires.

Break it Down

Even within the United States, the notion of freedom of speech has complications. Laws can only restrict the non-content related aspects of speech, for instance, the time, location, or volume of speech. Some examples of this can be found in Clark v. Community for Creative Non-Violence (1984) where the U.S. Supreme Court determined that the National Parks service was allowed to restrict where the public could camp inside a park. Ward v. Rock against Racism (1989) was a case about whether or not the City of New York could control the volume of concerts in Central Park—the Supreme Court determined they could. Beyond that, within the United States, there have long been efforts to limit free speech in terms of what can be read (banned books), taught (in primary and secondary schools and higher education), and broadcast (e.g., the banning of televised cigarette commercials in 1971 and control over some sexual imagery on network television). And the debate over the ability of some Americans to freely broadcast media into other cultures led to a several-year withdrawal by America from UNESCO in 1984, in part due to other countries' desire to restrict the import of U.S. American media (McPhail, 2019). What official attempts have you seen in your country or area to control what sorts of speech or representation are allowed on the media (including movies, television, billboards, textbooks, or social media)?

However, other countries have different approaches to the media. Siebert, Schramm, and Peterson (1984) discuss the different purposes that mass communication serves in different countries. They identify four: **Authoritarian, Libertarian, Social Responsibility,** and **Soviet** (Pavlik & McIntosh, 2019; Siebert et al., 1984). They specifically apply these theories to journalism around the world, but they can be applied to a great number of different forms of media as well. The Soviet theory is, obviously, no longer relevant, but all three of the others are. Authoritarian theory occurs when the government controls the media. Anything that comes from the media must be approved by the government first. Libertarian theory, in contrast, values the total reverse: no one should control anything in the media and the individual should be free to publish whatever they so choose. This freedom even extends to criticisms of the government. It is a "freedom *from* external restraint" (Siebert et al., 1984, p. 93). Similarly, and yet differently, Social Responsibility theory is a "freedom for" the individual (Siebert et al., 1984, p. 93). Social Responsibility theory is the governing principle of the U.S. journalism, when the media endeavors to act as a watchdog to the government, making sure that they are informing the public in the most unbiased way possible. However, this freedom is always balanced "against the private rights of others and against vital social interests" (Siebert et al., 1984, p. 97). Some things, specifically things that could cause harm, can be censored by the government. Putting anything and everything out into the world could be dangerous.

Media and the public sphere

These theories of mass communication can help us understand a lot about how people around the world receive messages. In the United States and most Western cultures, individual citizens expect to participate in the "**public sphere**"—any area of social life where discussion of public opinions occur (Habermas, 2021)—and for their voices to not be stifled. On the Internet, Americans often complain about their "freedom of speech" being taken away. These individuals have been told their entire lives that they have a right to say whatever they like wherever and whenever they want. Most of the world does not have such rights guaranteed to them and the Americans online do not seem to understand that the rules of their country do not govern online interactions. Additionally, a decent number of Americans do not fully understand the limits of that "freedom of speech."

Namely, the freedoms ensured by the Constitution do not always extend to private spaces. Most online spaces—such as social networking sites (SNS)—are privately owned entities. Just like when you walk into a grocery store that has a "shirt and shoes" sign posted, you are required to wear a shirt and shoes in that store, social networking sites make you agree to a "terms and conditions" before you sign up with them. That "T&C" is a contract between you and the SNS to do or not do certain things. Therefore, you basically agree to abide by their rules, which are not the same rules as those outlined in the U.S. Constitution (Phillips, 2020).

But more specifically, the First Amendment to the U.S. Constitution guarantees that anyone, *including media outlets*, is allowed to say what they would like (within reason) and is not prevented from saying those things by the government. This creates some level of difficulty when it comes to the prevalence of certain imagery and who is controlling the messages. In 2021, the Pew Research Center (Wike et al., 2021) found that 71% of people in Non-U.S. countries with "advanced economies" (ranging from Canada and Sweden to Taiwan and

Singapore) found that U.S. American entertainment is the best. Therefore, considering how American media functions as a gatekeeper for cultural representations is imperative to understand media consumption around the world. An important element of understanding how American media works as a gatekeeper involves understanding the economic aspects of American media.

Media ownership often determines media messaging

In the early days of American television and film, only a handful of people/organizations had the money and resources to make the media. As a result, there were limited options when it came to an individual's media consumption. Today, with the development of new technologies, all the media, including film and television, are significantly easier to make. The individual can curate their own media taste with ease. However, a significant amount of that individual choice is an illusion. Most of the media content of the world is owned by a handful of major companies. These companies have lots of smaller companies that they own. These are called **Media Conglomerates** and you've heard of most of them—Disney, Comcast, WarnerMedia, ViacomCBS, Meta, and so on. These conglomerates own much of the content that we find in our media (McPhail, 2019).

There are two major problems with large media conglomerates. First, media conglomeration means that a handful of companies (see Figure 10.3) are in control of what kinds of messages are disseminated through the media. And those companies are generally centered in the Western countries and perpetuate Western ideologies/representations. Thus, the media are stuck in a cycle of cultural imperialism, not having spaces for minority voices.

Figure 10.3 World's Largest Media Companies in 2022, as assessed by *Forbes*.
Source: Abigail Freeman, The World's Largest Media Companies 2022: Netflix Falls in the Ranks After Subscriber Loss, Disney Climbs to No. 2, 2022. Forbes. Retrieved from: https://www.forbes.com/sites/abigailfreeman/2022/05/12/the-worlds-largest-media-companies-2022-netflix-falls-in-the-ranks-after-subscriber-loss-disney-climbs-to-no-2/?sh=6606d0557442.

Ranking	Company	Market Value	Sales	Profits	Assets
1	Comcast Corporation Class A	205,718	116,385	14,159	275,905
2	Walt Disney Company	215,326	72,982	3,082	203,311
3	Charter Communications, Inc. Class A	97,924	51,682	4,654	143,392
4	Netflix, Inc.	95,683	30,402	5,007	45,331
5	Paramount	20,132	28,586	4,543	58,620
6	Naspers Limited Class N	40,310	7,009	13,966	70,813
7	DISH Network Corporation Class A	16,203	17,881	2,411	48,465
8	Liberty Global Plc Class A	12,591	10,543	13,427	46,917
9	Warner Bros. Discovery	49,915	12,180	1,022	34,427
10	Publicis Groupse SA	15,808	13,874	1,214	37,352

This cycle causes a homogenization of ideals to overtake the media. The media need to appeal to the largest possible marketplace, thus focusing on stories and visuals that appeal to that broad audience. Additionally, the stories that are told are those of cultural imperialism. However, American stories for American audiences (that just happen to be disseminated in other countries) and stories that do not fit in the Western mold of filmmaking are simply ignored.

Take, for example, Nigeria, which produces the second highest number of films each year—after India and one above America. It has the third highest-grossing film industry in the world, at nearly $1 billion (Akinwotu, 2021), compared to $4.5 billion domestically in the United States in 2021 (McClintock, 2022) and $2.83 billion in India (Santoreneos, 2019). But few people outside of Africa have heard of this film industry; for example, most of you, unless you keep up with African media or live in Africa, have not heard of the blockbuster, *King of Thieves*, the highest-grossing film in Nigeria in 2022 (Figure 10.4). Even Indian film, which is the highest-producing and

Figure 10.4 *King of Thieves* (2022) was the highest-grossing Nigerian film from 2022.
Source: usheru / https://www. filmoneng.com/home / last accessed January 10, 2023.

highest-grossing film in the industry, is little disseminated in the United States. Part of the problem is that these film industries do not have connections with any of the major media conglomerates. Without those connections, it is difficult for any media to transcend global boundaries.

A second problem with media conglomerates is that the media produced continues to appeal to the broadest possible audience, across the world. There are a lot of media objects that are intended to be distributed globally. The content of those films needs to appeal to all cultures and be able to transcend language boundaries. One of the most prominent examples of this happening is through *Iron Man 3*. The Walt Disney Company co-produced this film with DMG Entertainment, which is a Beijing-based production company ("*Iron Man* gets 3 Chinese partners," 2012). Disney did so specifically so they could reach a broader audience in China, and co-producing with a Chinese company is the easiest way to break into the very tight, government-controlled Chinese film market (Burkitt, 2013). However, the story also heavily featured Chinese characters, as well as having additional scenes for the Chinese version of the film (Acuna, 2013). The film ended up grossing $400 million in the United States and $800 million internationally. Disney's gamble paid off. People from other countries and cultures may not be so lucky. They watch American films, starring American people, telling American stories, and they never see themselves on screen. And American audiences never see any stories that talk about the people that live in these cultures.

Some people are shut out of the media altogether In 1978, Edward Said (see Chapter 5) discussed the idea of "**Orientalism**," saying it is "a Western style for dominating, restructuring, and having authority over the Orient" (Said, 2016, p. 113). His basic point is that most representations that people in Western countries (the United States and Europe, primarily) have of other countries are filtered through colonialism and cultural imperialism. The representations of other cultures that most people in the United States see do not come from those cultures; instead, they are American images of what they *think* those people are like. Even with the advent of **narrowcast media**—media that is created for a specific audience rather than a broad, general one (Danesi, 2009)—with online streaming services, the process of introducing a wide variety of cultural images from myriad cultural voices has been a slow one.

There are some representations of cultures that are completely absent from our screens. Consequently, those cultures are entirely invisible to anyone outside of the group itself. This is called **symbolic annihilation.** The term was first coined by George Gerbner and Larry Gross (1976) when discussing television content. According to Michelle Caswell (2014), symbolic annihilation is "what happens to members of marginalized groups when they are absent, grossly under-represented, maligned, or trivialized by mainstream television programming, news outlets, and magazine coverage" (p. 27). Representations in the media validate identities—if a person sees themself on television, they know that who they are is "valid." Imagine not ever seeing anyone who looked like you or acted like you in the media. Or if there are people like you, they are always the subject of ridicule and/or bullying.

Corinne Sugino (2019) discusses the ways that several recent films and movies have pushed against such annihilation and featured stories about and from multicultural perspectives. Her main focus is on *Crazy, Rich, Asians* (2018; see Figure 10.5) and its "departure from tired stereotypical depictions of Asians" (para. 3). She suggests that this film, and others like it—including *Black Panther, To All the Boys I've Love Before*, and TV shows such as *Master of None*—tell their multicultural stories through a lens of whiteness, thereby showing ways that minorities overcome their oppression using the tools of whiteness. In other words, the numerous diverse films and television shows that have proven to be the exception to the norm—or perhaps the future of

Figure 10.5 *Crazy Rich Asians* (2018) Directed by Jon M. Chu, From Warner Bros. Pictures. Source: Faiz Zaki/Shutterstock.

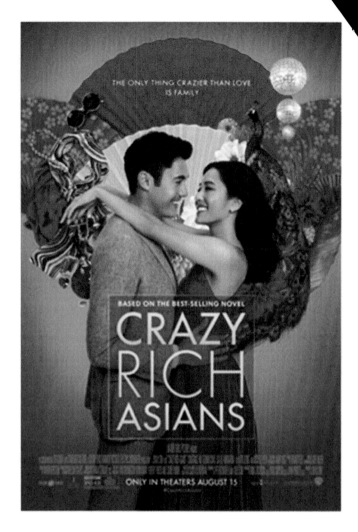

media—can only exist by being framed within the whiteness that has long been normative in those media.

The notion of symbolic annihilation also applies to other groups. For example, Gaye Tuchman (1978) observes that "from children's shows to commercials to prime-time adventures and situation comedies, television proclaims that women don't count for much" (p. 10). Women existed in American media in the 1970s—because how could they not—but they were symbolically annihilated due to the infantilization and trivialization of them and their lives. Lauren Gurieri (2021) describes, for example, how advertising marginalizes women through narrow representations of beauty, conventional portrayals of powerlessness, and representation primarily as homemakers or sex objects. Such representation is not limited to the United States. A literature search will uncover studies on the symbolic annihilation of women in media in Indonesia, Qatar, Nigeria, Morocco, Spain, and Turkey, in genres such as sports coverage, TV advertisements, news coverage, political cartoons, television shows, and film.

Another group that has been symbolically annihilated is the Mizrahim on Israeli television (Katz & Nossek, 2019). Again, there are some representations of this cultural group, but they experience a "banal flattening" as they differ from the "Ashkenazi-Secular-Jewish-Male-Heterosexual-Healthy" (p. 644) or AHUSLIM, which is considered to be the "cultural icon of the majority" (p. 635). Michelle Caswell and Samip Mallick have created the "South Asian American Digital Archive" (https://www.saada.org). They did so because they personally saw a lack of South Asian representation in the media and wanted "to counter this kind of alienation by documenting the long history of South Asians in the United States through a freely accessible digital archive" (Caswell, 2014, p. 27). They decided to fight back against the symbolic annihilation they saw occurring. Through these examples, we can see that we can symbolically annihilate a group (e.g., women, ethnic minorities, people of different political persuasions, sexual minorities) within a single culture, but we can also do so with people from different parts of the world.

POP CULTURE

The 2010s have seen American Streaming Services, such as Netflix, Hulu, and Amazon, featuring an increasing number of shows about minorities by minorities. Some of these include *Never Have I Ever* (2020), *One Day at a Time* (2017), *Reservation Dogs* (2021), and *Gentefied* (2020). Have you seen any of these shows? Why did you choose to watch (or not watch) them? What kinds of representations are present in these shows that you do not see in other media?

A lot of the representations that we see in the media, especially of particular racial and ethnic groups, are reduced to stereotypes. **Stereotypes** are oversimplified understandings of what a person or thing is like (see Chapter 6). We all make use of stereotypes in our day-to-day lives to make sense of the world. Stereotypes help individuals to "order" the complexities of the world (Dyer, 2009). Most people recognize that stereotypes are a bad thing. As Walter Lippmann (1922), who created most of the definitions that we currently have for stereotyping, said, stereotype are "highly charged with the feelings that are attached to them" (p. 146). The problem comes when an individual is reduced only to the categories their stereotypes have placed them in and others cannot see anything but the stereotype. Stereotypes are a starting point in understanding other people but cannot be the ending point. If a character in the media is only their stereotypes, then that character is flat and incapable of growing. People do grow and are not capable of being truly flat. Conflating what media characters are like with what real people are like can be harmful to an individual's understanding of other people and cultures. Harmful stereotyping and symbolic annihilation are both symptoms of the cultural imperialism that Said (2016) describes in his discussion of Orientalism. Lei Guo and Lorin Lee (2013) examined the ways that Asian/Asian-American YouTubers use rhetoric to cross borders between race and other social categories. However, in order to "prioritize entertainment," stereotyping and racism are still present, and even "reinforced during this process" (p. 404).

Another form of media that this chapter has not yet discussed in any depth is social media. The following chapter (Chapter 11) focuses more specifically on this area of the media landscape. But online forums are just as full of stereotyping as traditional forums are. For instance,

Haider and Al-Abbas (2022) found that 40% of Arabic jokes posted on Facebook and WhatsApp in Spring 2020 focused on gender stereotypes and that 90% of those jokes were focused on women and stereotypes. Ariadna Matamoros-Fernández et al. (2022) similarly found that TikTok users in 2020 made extensive use of **digital blackface** and yellow face to discuss the Coronavirus Pandemic. Digital blackface is the practice of "appropriating Black bodies, sounds, and culture by non-Black people online for humorous and playful purposes" (Matamoros-Fernández et al., 2022, p. 183).

The media have a direct influence on the ways that individuals perceive others. Whether a result of cultural imperialism or capitalism, the stories that the media tell make a difference in the world. You need to make sure that you aren't being passive consumers of the media but are opening yourself up to diverse media messages and are challenging hegemonic discourses found in your media. One of the biggest things to be aware of when challenging the media is that all of the media is filtered through Frames.

Media framing: Does the way a story is told influence the meaning of the story?

Every time you post a picture on Instagram, you are prompted to choose a lens through which to filter the picture. The lenses are designed to make your picture look a certain way—fancier or happier or darker or sillier. Lenses on pictures alter the meaning of the picture. When you hang a painting on the wall, you select a frame to put it in. The frame can be basic or fancy, elaborate or barely visible. No matter what the frame looks like, it contributes to the way the image looks. This same idea holds true for the media. Every piece of the media is filtered through the ideas/beliefs/values of the people who created it. This filtering process is called **Framing**. But framing also applies to the way that a source, such as a newscast, tells a story by focusing on a perspective or selecting certain elements, from facts to photos, "making some piece of information more noticeable to the audience" (Cowart et al., 2022, p. 681). From the news to social media posts, everything has a frame.

It is impossible to relay any piece of information without presenting a perspective on it. Think of the piece of food that you absolutely cannot stand—say, Brussels sprouts—can you make a convincing argument that Brussels sprouts are good for you without making it clear, even so slightly, that you dislike them? Or the opposite, can you inform someone of the health benefits of your favorite food—perhaps potatoes—without also expressing to them how much you love them? Those are basic examples of frames. The media are no different. However, because of the issues discussed above, the frames that are imposed upon the messages are not, necessarily, those of the person speaking. Instead, they could be the views of the conglomerate/owner, the producer, or the creator.

Sometimes, frames are relatively harmless. The news framing crime as bad is not wrong. However, frames can also be manipulative. The news framing actions of some people as criminal when they are not evil is wrong. A media frame can be as simple as stressing the importance of an issue to the public or as complicated as making it clear which side in a debate the owners of the media believe is correct. As an example of framing research, Reza Safitri and Ulwan Fakhri Noviadhista (2020) analyzed the Detik.com news coverage of the 2019 Indonesian government's internet shutdowns. They found that the news website framed the shutdowns in a positive light, suggesting purposes "such as national security, normalization of conditions in Papua, and to reduce the circulation of hoaxes" (p. 7). The website used numerous strategies to create these frames including choosing particular words, only telling parts of the stories, heavily featuring information from high-ranking government officials, and not presenting alternative perspectives.

Frames are not always obvious. Unless an individual is reading all of the media—every perspective on every news story, for instance—then they are not going to be able to reach outside of the frames to see the story for just its facts. However, that does not mean all hope is lost. Recognizing that frames exist is step one in understanding how frames could be manipulating consumers. Additionally, echo chambers, as discussed above, can contribute to the power of framing. When all the media that you surround yourself with features the same ideas/beliefs/values—the same frames—then you will never be able to hear any perspectives from outside. If you surround yourself with multiple voices, multiple ideas, multiple frames, you will be significantly more successful.

In a study of how frames are used with regard to Social Movements, Teresa Sádaba (2021) observes that Social Movement Organizations (SMOs) both are the *producers* of frames and are also at the mercy of the *frames produced by others*, while also facilitating any social action on the part of the public. As a result, frames serve three functions to SMOs: "mobilization, legitimization, and congruence" (p. 4). Sádaba uses the Black Lives Matter (BLM) movement as a case study for her examination. She says, "The movement is abandoning old Black frames and creating new ones" (p. 11). Thus, the leaders of BLM use frames, through the use of their hashtag #BlackLivesMatter, to further diversify images of the African American/Black community. In addition, the prominence of BLM in mainstream news media, as well as how celebrities and companies have tapped into the hashtag, furthers the legitimacy of this frame. However, some news outlets framed elements of BLM as dangerous. Eduard Fabregat and Timothy Beck (2019) outline some of the ways that the news coverage of the shooting that spurred BLM to action—that of Trayvon Martin. These frames include Martin as a thug, as a drug dealer, and as to blame for his own murder. BLM is intended to shift the frame of the shootings of Black Americans but is often stymied by the institutional frames found in the traditional news media.

Summary

In this chapter, we have discussed the ways in which the media can influence our perceptions of other cultures and people. We looked at the ways that the media influences us—through several theories and ideas about how mediated communication works. We considered the factors that shape the media and mediated messaging, including democracy, imperialism, and capitalism. Then, we discussed how frames work to manipulate audiences into thinking a certain way on topics.

So, what can you do to counter the effects of the media? There are two basic strategies you can use. First, be aware of what the media can do and make sure that you aren't being passive in your media consumption. As long as you are being active in your media consumption, you will not simply succumb to the media's influences. Watch a variety of types of media from around the world; don't approach the media from a singular perspective; be open minded toward other kinds of media than what you're used to.

The second way that you can counter the effects of the media is to take advantage of the good parts of the media. In the introduction to this section, we discussed how Marshal McLuhan ("The World is a Global Village," 1960) thought that the world was becoming a global village because of the ways that everyone comes together for certain events. The media have only increased our abilities to do this. Pay more attention to social media influencers from other countries/cultures. Read and watch entertainment media made in a different country. And think about the things we've discussed here about how the media influences our perceptions.

To learn about other countries, consume the media *made in that country by those people*. Two news channels that you can easily watch include Arirang, from Korea, and Al Jazeera, from the Middle East. These channels both include coverage of the world and of the United States and report in English. There are also lots of global films on most streaming services. Give some of them a try—the genres are similar to the ones you are probably used to; the narrative conventions may take some getting used to. But you never know until you try.

Finally, media can be used in both civic engagement and activism. The most obvious way to do so is, of course, to engage with social movements using social media. In Chapter 11, we will go into more depth on the ways that digital activism can function. This chapter has focused primarily on traditional forms of media—film and television—to set the stage for the discussion of social media that comes next. However, that is not to say that film and television do not provide us with the means to be active and engaged global citizens. Beyond simply watching the media, being an active participant in that media is also important. Engage with the media not simply by watching it, but also by spreading it and discussing it with others. Share the diverse things you enjoy. Make sure you do so using legitimate means, so that the economic elements that are behind the media acknowledge your engagement and that the producers of the media get the money they deserve.

Additionally, the internet and recent technological advances have made it significantly easier for each of us to create our own media. Filming and sharing injustices; letting your own voice be heard amongst the cacophony of hateful rhetoric online; becoming a voice for those less fortunate than you—these are all ways to be engaged in your community and use the media for good. But beyond all that, connect with other cultures, talk to individuals from those cultures. The media give us the opportunity to actually reach out to people far away from ourselves. Take advantage.

KEY TERMS

transmission model, 202
ritual model of communication, 203
cultivation theory, 203
heavy views, 204
echo chambers, 204
authoritarian, libertarian, social
responsibility, and Soviet, 207
public sphere, 207

media conglomerates, 208
Orientalism, 210
narrowcast media, 210
symbolic annihilation, 210
stereotypes, 212
digital blackface, 213
framing, 213

Discussion Questions

1   Choose one of the media conglomerates and trace the different properties owned by that organization. What surprises you the most? How do you think that media text is influenced by its conglomerate?

2   Have you ever seen someone who looks like you in the media? How did it feel? Can you imagine what it would feel like to never see yourself on screen?

3   Film and television are often considered to just be "entertaining" and not important to the world or the individual. How have these forms of media influenced you? How do you think the media move beyond merely entertainment and into something important?

4   Stereotypes are very easy ways of making sense of the world. What are some ways you can make sure that you aren't relying too heavily on stereotypes?

Action Points

1   Talk to an older friend or family member about stereotypes on television or in film. What are some differences between their sense of other cultures and yours? What factors might contribute to this?

2   There are lots of shows/films that originated somewhere other than the United States that have been remade into an American show or movie. See if you can find both versions. Watch and compare them. What things changed? What remained the same?

3   Find a current news event and read journalistic coverage of that event from several different countries. How is the event covered differently around the world? Does it matter what kind of event it is? What about *where* the event occurs compared to where it is *reported on*?

4   Converse with a classmate who is from a different culture than you about what media you regularly consume. Are there distinct differences? What might cause such differences? Can you share some small pieces of media from your culture—perhaps music? Do you like what they shared with you? Why not?

For more information

Bourdieu, P. (1999). *On television*. New Press.

Douglas, S. J. (2010). *The rise of enlightened sexism: How pop culture took us from girl power to girls gone wild*. St. Martin's Griffin.

Frandsen, J. A., & Mortensen, M. (2022). Media events in the age of global, digital media: Centring, scale, and participatory liveness. *Nordic Journal of Media Studies, 4* (1), 1–18. https://doi.org/10.2478/njms-2022-0001

Jenkins, H. (2008). *Convergence culture: Where old and new media collide* (Updated and with a new afterword). New York University Press.

Jin, D. Y. (2020). *Globalization and media in the digital platform age*. Routledge, Taylor & Francis Group.

Lee, M. J., Bichard, S. L., Irey, M. S., Walt, H. M., & Carlson, A. J. (2009). Television viewing and ethnic stereotypes: Do college students form stereotypical perceptions of ethnic groups as a result of heavy television consumption? *Howard Journal of Communications, 20* (1), 95–110. https://doi.org/10.1080/10646170802665281

McLuhan, M. (1994). *Understanding media: The extensions of man* (1st MIT Press ed.). MIT Press.

Newcomb, H., & Hirsch, P. M. (2000). *Television: The critical view*. Oxford University Press.

Newman, M. Z., & Levine, E. (2012). *Legitimating television: Media convergence and cultural status*. Routledge.

Shohat, E., & Stam, R. (1994). *Unthinking Eurocentrism: Multiculturalism and the media*. Routledge.

References

Acuna, K. (2013). The biggest differences in China's version of *Iron Man 3* [WWW Document]. *Business Insider*. Accessed January 31, 2022, at https://www.businessinsider.com/chinas-version-of-iron-man-3-2013-5

Akinwotu, E. (2021). Nollywood moment: African film industries 'could create 20m jobs'. The Guardian. Accessed December 2, 2022, at http://www.theguardian.com/global-development/2021/oct/05/nollywood-booming-while-african-film-industries-could-create-20m-jobs-report#

Allen, K. (2021, February 4). China promotes education drive to make boys more "manly." BBC News. Accessed December 3, 2022, at https://www.bbc.com/news/world-asia-china-55926248

Baczynska, G., & Campenhout, C. (2022, July 15). EU executive will sue Hungary over LGBT law, radio broadcaster. Reuters. Accessed December 3, 2022, at https://www.reuters.com/world/europe/eu-commission-sue-hungary-over-anti-lgbt-law-politico-2022-07-15

Burkitt, L. (2013, March 8). 'Iron Man 3' blasts away at China co-production myth. Wall Street Journal. Accessed December 2, 2022, at https://www.wsj.com/articles/BL-CJB-17373

Carey, J. W. (1989). *Communication as culture: Essays on media and society*. Unwin Hyman.

Caswell, M. (2014). Seeing yourself in history. *Public History*, 36 (4), 26–37. https://doi.org/10.1525/tph.2014.36.4.26

Cowart, H. S., Blackstone, G. E., & Riley, J. K. (2022). Framing of a movement: Media portrayals of the George Floyd protests on Twitter. *Journalism & Mass Communication Quarterly*, 99 (3), 676–695. https://doi.org/10.1177/10776990221109232

Danesi, M. (2009). *Dictionary of media and communications*. Routledge.

Dyer, R. (2009). The role of stereotypes. In S. Thornham, C. Bassett, & P. Marris (Eds.), *Media Studies: A reader* (pp. 206–212). Edinburgh University Press.

Fabregat, E., & Beck, T. J. (2019). On the erasure of race in control culture discourse: A case study of Trayvon Martin's role in the Black Lives Matter movement. *Social Identities*, 25 (6), 759–774. https://doi.org/10.1080/13504630.2019.1572502

Gallagher, T., (2022, June 22). Why has the new Pixar film been banned in so many countries? Euronews. Accessed September 20, 2022, at https://www. euronews.com/culture/2022/06/13/toy-story-spin-off-lightyear-banned-in-saudi-arabia-kuwait-and-uae-over-lgbt-storylines

Gerbner, G. (1998). Cultivation analysis: An overview. *Mass Communication and Society*, 1(3-4), 175–194. https://doi.org/10.1080/15205436.1998.9677855

Gerbner, G., & Gross, L. (1976). Living with television: The Violence Profile. *Journal of Communication*, 26(2), 172–199.

Greenberg, G. S., & Worrell, T. R. (2007). New faces on television: A 12-season replication. *The Howard Journal of Communications*, 18 (4), 277–290. https://doi.org/10.1080/10646170701653651

Guo, L., & Lee, L. (2013). The critique of YouTube-based vernacular discourse: A case study of YouTube's Asian community. *Critical Studies in Media Communication*, 30 (5), 391–406. https://doi.org/10.1080/15295036.2012.755048

Gurieri, L. (2021). Patriarchal marketing and the symbolic annihilation of women. *Journal of Marketing Management*, 37(3-4), 364–370. https://doi.org/10.1080/0267257X.2020.1826179

Habermas, J. (2021). The public sphere. In S. Thornham, C. Bassett, & P. Marris (Eds.), *Media studies: A reader* (pp. 45–51). Edinburgh University Press.

Haider, A. S., & Al-Abbas, L. S. (2022). Stereotyping Arab women in jokes circulated on social media during the coronavirus crisis. *European Journal of Humour Research*, 10(1), 168–185. https://doi.org/10.7592/EJHR2022.10.1.569

Hall, S. (1996). Cultural studies and its theoretical legacies. In K.-H. Chen & D. Morley (Eds.), *Stuart Hall: Critical dialogues in cultural studies* (pp. 262–275). Routledge.

Hall, S. (2006). Encoding/decoding. In M. G. Durham & D. Kellner (Eds.), *Media and cultural studies: Keywords* (pp. 163–173). Blackwell.

Iron Man 3 gets Chinese partners. (2012, April 16). BBC News. Accessed December 2, 2022, at https://www.bbc.com/news/entertainment-arts-17734655

Katz, N., & Nossek, H. (2019). Mizrahi perceptions of their TV portrayal in Israel. *Israel Affairs*, 25 (4), 635–659. https://doi.org/10.1080/13537121.2019.1626084

Kelly, H. (2018, May 20). Royal Wedding 2018 viewing figures: How many people watched Meghan Markle marry Harry? Express.co.uk. Accessed December 27,

2021, at https://www.express.co.uk/showbiz/tv-radio/962610/Royal-Wedding-viewing-figures-Meghan-Markle-Prince-Harry-kiss-David-Beckham

Lasswell, H. D. (1971). The structure and function of communication in society. In W. Schramm & D. F. Roberts (Eds.), *The process and effects of mass communication* (pp. 216–228). University of Illinois Press.

Lee, M. J., Bichard, S. L., Irey, M. S., Walt, H. M., & Carlson, A. J. (2009). Television viewing and ethnic stereotypes: Do college students form stereotypical perceptions of ethnic groups as a result of heavy television consumption? *Howard Journal of Communications*, 20 (1), 95–110. https://doi.org/10.1080/10646170802665281

Lippmann, W. (1922). *Public opinion*. Harcourt, Brace, and Company.

Liu, Z. (2022). The internet echo chamber and the misinformation of judges: The case of judges' perception of public support for the death penalty in China. *International Review of Law & Economics*, 69. https://doi.org/10.1016/j.irle.2021.106028.

Matamoros-Fernández, A., Rodriguez, A., & Wikström, P. (2022). Humor That harms? Examining racist audio-visual memetic media on TikTok during Covid-19. *Media and Communication*, 10 (2), 180–191. https://doi.org/10.17645/mac.v10i2.5154

McClintock, P. (2022, January 1). Box office ends year 60 percent behind 2019 with $4.5B – *The Hollywood Reporter*. Hollywood Report. Accessed December 3, 2022, at https://www.hollywoodreporter.com/business/business-news/2021-box-office-revenue-stormy-year-1235067966

McLuhan, M. (1960). *The world is a global village*. Explorations.

McPhail, T. L. (2019). *Global communication: Theories, stakeholders, and trends* (5th ed.). Wiley-Blackwell.

Megarry, D. (2019). Disney fans have decided this Frozen 2 song is a queer coming out anthem. Gay Times. Accessed December 3, 2022, at https://www.gaytimes.co.uk/culture/disney-fans-have-decided-this-frozen-2-song-is-a-queer-coming-out-anthem

#MeToo is at a crossroads in America. Around the world, it's just beginning. (2020, May 8). Washington Post. Accessed December 27, 2021, at https://www.washingtonpost.com/opinions/2020/05/08/metoo-around-the-world

Pavlik, J. V., & McIntosh, S. (2019). *Converging media: A new introduction to mass communication* (6th ed.). Oxford University Press.

Phillips, A. (2020, March 29). No, Twitter is not violating Trump's freedom of speech. Washington Post. Accessed December 3, 2022, at https://www.washingtonpost.com/politics/2020/05/29/no-twitter-did-not-violate-trumps-freedom-speech

Rivadeneyra, R., Ward, L. M., & Gordon, M. (2007). Distorted reflections: Media exposure and Latino adolescents' conceptions of self. *Media Psychology*, 9 (2), 261–290. https://doi.org/10.1080/15213260701285926

Russon, M.-A. (2021, March 29). The cost of the Suez Canal blockage. BBC News. Accessed December 3, 2022, at https://www.bbc.com/news/business-56559073

Sádaba, T. (2021). Framing as modus operandi for social movements: The case of Black Lives Matter. *Przegląd Narodowościowy / Review of Nationalities*, 11(1), 1–13. https://doi.org/10.2478/pn-2021-0001

Safitri, R., & Noviadhista, U. F. (2020). Where did Indonesian online media pioneer stand on internet shutdown issue? *Komunikator*, 12(1). https://doi.org/10.18196/jkm.121030

Said, E. (2016). Introduction to orientalism. In P. K. Nayar (Ed.), *Postcolonial studies* (pp. 32–52). John Wiley & Sons. https://doi.org/10.1002/9781119118589.ch2

Santoreneos, A. (2019, May 15). Bollywood, Hollywood or Chinese Cinema: Which film industry makes the most? Yahoo!Finance. Accessed December 3, 2022, at https://au.finance.yahoo.com/news/bollywood-hollywood-or-chinese-cinema-which-film-industry-makes-the-most-052802841.html

Shaw, L. (2021, October 16). Netflix estimates 'Squid Game' will be worth almost $900 million. Bloomberg. Accessed December 2, 2022, at https://www.bloomberg.com/news/articles/2021-10-17/squid-game-season-2-series-worth-900-million-to-netflix-so-far

Siebert, F. S., Peterson, T., & Schramm, W. (1984). *Four theories of the press*. University of Illinois Press. https://doi.org/10.5406/j.ctv1nhr0v

Sindermann, C., Elhai, J. D., Moshagen, M., & Montag, C. (2020). Age, gender, personality, ideological attitudes and individual differences in a person's news spectrum: How many and who might be prone to "filter bubbles" and "echo chambers" online? *Heliyon*, 6(1), e03214. https://doi.org/10.1016/j.heliyon.2020.e03214

Sugino, C. (2019). Multicultural redemption: "Crazy Rich Asians" and the politics of representation. *Lateral*, *8*(2). https://doi.org/10.25158/L8.2.6

Tuchman, G. (1978). Introduction: The symbolic annihilation of women by the mass media. In G. Tuchman, A. K. Daniels, & J. W. Benét (Eds.), *Hearth and home: Images of women in the mass media* (pp. 3–38). Oxford University.

Tukachinksy, R., Mastro, D., & Yarchi, M. (2017). The effect of prime time television ethnic/racial stereotypes on Latino and Black Americans: A longitudinal national study. *Journal of Broadcasting & Electronic Media*, *61*(3), 538–556. https://doi.org/10.1080/08838151.2017.1344669

Wike, R., Silver, L., Fetterolf, J., Huang, C., & Moncus, J. J. (2021, November 1). What people around the world like – And dislike – About American society and politics. Pew Research Center Global Attitudes Project. Accessed September 22, 2022, at https://www.pewresearch.org/global/2021/11/01/what-people-around-the-world-like-and-dislike-about-american-society-and-politics

Chapter 11

Information and communication technologies: How do social media impact culture?

Chapter Objectives

After this chapter, you should be able to:

→ Outline the characteristics of social media

→ Provide examples of social media's effects on local culture

→ Describe the historical and technological influences in the context of social media

→ Evaluate the impact of social media on globalization regarding notions of time and space

→ Discuss positive and negative implications for social media in terms of local cultures

→ Assess how social media affect intercultural communication and apply techniques for successful oral and written interactions across cultures

Characteristics and functionality of Social Media: How do Social Media Connect Us? 222

Social Media Affordances: How do Social Media Facilitate Aspects of Culture-Related Adjustment, Competence, or Activism? 224

Platformation of Modern Society: How Do Social Media Platforms Differ Between Cultures? 233

Intercultural Communication for Everyday Life, Second Edition. John R. Baldwin, Alberto González, Nettie Brock, Ming Xie, and Chin-Chung Chao.
© 2024 John Wiley & Sons Ltd. Published 2024 by John Wiley & Sons Ltd.
Companion Website: http://www.wiley.com/go/baldwin2e

Brittany Tomlinson, 22, who graduated from Texas A&M University and worked at a bank near Dallas, Texas, recorded her reaction when she tried Kombucha, a kind of fermented tea, and shared the 21-second video clip "Kombucha girl gives us her honest opinion" on TikTok (Figure 11.1). This video reached 11 million total engagements (likes, comments, views, and shares), launched a thousand reaction memes, and was one of the top 10 viral TikTok videos of 2019. The video reached 40 million views after she shared it on Twitter from her TikTok account. The extent of reach of this simple engagement of media with everyday life shows the importance of social media in our society.

TikTok, known as Douyin in China, is a short-form video-sharing platform primarily for lip-synching and dancing videos. The app was launched in September 2016 in China and internationally in September 2017. In 2021, TikTok had about 78.7 million users, making it one of the fastest-growing social media apps in the United States and the world's third-largest social network, following Facebook and Instagram (Ceci, 2022; Perez, 2021). Outside of China, TikTok's largest markets are the United States, Indonesia, and Brazil (Iqbal, 2022). Insider Intelligence estimated that Facebook would have 2.1 billion monthly users in 2022, followed by Instagram with 1.28 billion users and TikTok with 755 million monthly users (Perez, 2021). TikTok's growth has been accompanied by controversies. In 2019, India and Pakistan banned it for "morality issues" and rescinded the bans later. In June 2020, India banned TikTok again and upheld the ban in January 2021.

People from all over the world express their emotions and communicate with others beyond time and space distance through social media platforms such as Facebook, Instagram, and TikTok. People from different backgrounds, cultures, races, and countries are using social media, which means interactions among people are not only within the same culture but also for intercultural communication. New media not only influence the form and content of information/messages, but they also affect how people understand each other in the process of human communication, especially with those from different cultural or ethnic groups. This chapter focuses on the intersection of social media and intercultural communication and discusses (1) what kind of functionalities of social media support and encourage intercultural communication; (2) how social media refines and expands intercultural communication theories; and (3) how the advanced information technology has changed our culture at the local level and formed new forms of intercultural communication at the global level.

Figure 11.1 Kombucha Girl on TikTok.
Source: The New York Times Company.

Characteristics and functionality of social media: How do social media connect us?

Social media are channels and platforms that offer "advanced features as well as functions that support social networking such as sharing ideas, information, knowledge, and so forth over network" (Monika et al., 2019, p. 483). Information technology-based platforms and channels enable individuals to equally control messages and interact with multiple people simultaneously (G.-M. Chen, 2012). Chen (2012) summarized five distinctive characteristics of social media: digitality, convergency, interactivity, hypertextuality, and virtuality. First, **digitality** describes how all the information and content on social media are digitalized and converted into digital form, "which allows all kinds of mathematical operations" (Chen, 2012, p. 2). Second, social media "converges the forms and functions of information, media, electronic communication, and electronic computing" (Chen, 2012, p. 3), a notion called **convergency**. The combination of content, product, and service makes social media companies powerful in controlling information flow and communication. An excellent example of convergency is the constant merger of prominent social media companies in social media products and services. For example, journalist Carly Hallman (n.d.) summarizes and visualizes the 78 companies Facebook bought in the 15 years leading up to 2019, including Friendster in 2010, Instagram in 2012, and WhatsApp in 2014.

Third, **interactivity** refers to how social media's interactive function provides users with opportunities to produce and reproduce information content during interactions. Fourth, **hypertextuality** refers to the networking function of information technology that allows a large quantity of information to freely move around within a series of interconnected nodes in the network (G.-M. Chen & Zhang, 2010).Manuel Castells (2000), a leading theorist of the new information age, proposed that we now experience a "timeless time." He argues that space and time have been transformed with timeless time superseding clock time of the industrial era. New communication technologies, namely online networks, are fundamentally changing our sense of time and how it proceeds (Castells, 2000). Finally, **virtuality** refers to the phenomenon that social media form a virtual space and a virtual community that crosses all the boundaries of human society (G.-M. Chen, 2012).

What do you think? WeChat has gained attention as the super app in China. Originating as a messaging app like WhatsApp and Telegram, WeChat was designed for users to message each other and share their updates in a feed. The app provides audio and video calls, a text message function, and the ability to create group threads containing up to 500 people. Nowadays, WeChat provides financial services, daily services, travel, and transportation, as well as shopping and entertainment (Figure 11.2). Users can use WeChat to buy flight tickets, pay utilities, transfer money, order food delivery, make restaurant reservations, games, and take out a loan to buy a car. Users can do all these things and many more without having to exit the app. Big companies like Tencent, which is the host company of WeChat in China, have become gate-keepers to a wide array of things people do online.

Figure 11.2 Services provided by WeChat.
Source: Screenshot by author.

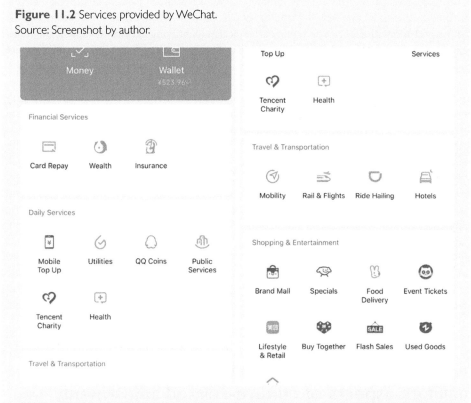

Similar to WeChat, super apps have emerged in many countries, such as KakaoTalk in Korea, Line in Japan and Taiwan, Gojek in Indonesia, and Rappi in Colombia. Andrea Diaz Baquero (2021) summarized the benefits of super apps as less cost for customer acquisition, ability to share data between mini-programs or mini-apps, unique single sign-on, variety of services, a uniformed and individual user experience, and memory storage on the user's device. On the contrary, there have also been controversies and debates regarding the emergence of super apps, especially the users' privacy, the power concentrated on social media companies, and business competition issues.

What do you think? Do you use a super app like WeChat? What functions or benefits do you get from the use? What are some limitations of these super apps for individuals or society?

Concerned with how social media shape and construct reality, José van Dijck and Thomas Poell (2015) pointed out four elements of social media strategies and mechanisms: programmability, popularity, connectivity, and datafication. **Programmability** is defined as

the ability of a social media platform to trigger and steer users' creative or communicative contributions, while users, through their interaction with these code environments, may in turn influence the flow of communication and information activated by such a platform (van Dijck & Poell, 2013, p. 5).

Many social media platforms are programmed to give a prominent place to institutionalize certain cultural norms and behaviors. **Popularity** refers to social media's strategy of increasing the renown and admiration of certain topics or people. By quantifying likes, most viewed, and number of followers, social media algorithms clearly develop ranking mechanisms and measure popularity. **Connectivity** is about the networked structure among social media users. Sociologist Barry Wellman and colleagues argued that information technology made social connections from densely knit groups to loosely bounded social networks of relations, which they defined as "network individualism" (Haythornthwaite & Wellman, 1998; Wellman, 2002). Social media provides opportunities for individual users to connect with others on a personal basis rather than the existing group bounds or locality, allowing "people to directly connect to other people with whom they are involved in specialized relationships of common interest" (van Dijck & Poell, 2013, p. 8). **Datafication** refers to the ability to quantify many social aspects into data. For example, human relationships such as friendship and sentiments can be quantified and measured through online interaction. Shyam Krishna (2021) studied India's national biometric and digital identity program, Aadhaar, which creates a digital identity verification database and system. Although this kind of large-scale identity verification program might increase the scope and efficiency of public service, there have been growing concerns regarding digital injustice among vulnerable communities and groups because of the lack of digital literacy and resources.

With these distinctive features, social media influences not only information/message's form and content but also how people understand each other, especially among people from different cultural and ethnic backgrounds.

Social media affordances: How do social media facilitate aspects of culture-related adjustment, competence, or activism?

Social media have changed the way people communicate. No matter where they are, everybody can click a button and send a message to individuals or massive people thousands of miles away immediately. That has had a significant impact on cultures across the world. With Social media platforms like Facebook, Instagram, TikTok, and Twitter, we are able to see someone's life story and culture in texts, photos, audio, and videos. For people with shared interests, it is convenient and fast to find their community and share the same issues and conflicts.

The existing research suggests that social media play a major role in intercultural encounters and expand intercultural communication theories such as acculturation/adaptation, intercultural competence, high context/low context communication, co-cultural communication, cultural identity, culture shock/stress, stereotyping, ethnocentrism, racism, intercultural awareness, intercultural conflict, and intercultural relationship development (Shuter, 2012). However, the way media play this role is through the "affordances" that they provide.

Social media affordances

The concept of affordances has been used to analyze how social media affect people's lives. Affordances are defined as "social media functions" that solicit users to take certain actions accordingly (Trepte, 2015) or as the relation between the "action possibilities" of a technology and how users adapt it to their purposes (Evans et al., 2017). Scholars have studied affordances from various perspectives, such as physical affordances, technology affordances, vernacular affordances, and cultural affordances (boyd, 2010; Sun & Suthers, 2021). *Technology affordances* are about an object's independent, inherent, and physical properties that are compatible with a user for possible action (Graves, 2007). *Social affordances* are described as properties that facilitate social interaction (Krejins, 2004), such as the ability to network with others or tag a post, connecting it to others. Related to these is the notion of *vernacular affordances* as "unfolding relationships, emergent practices and sense-making processes" (McVeigh-Schultz & Baym, 2015, p. 2). An *emotional affordance* refers to a technology's "capacities to enable, prompt, and restrict the enactment of particular emotional experiences unfolding in between the media technology and an actor's practical sense for its user" (Bareither, 2019, p. 15), such as the ability to up- or downvote or post a photo. There are also *cognitive affordances*, through which you can expand your learning (e.g., "alerts" to someone's post); *identity affordances* (how and the degree to which a medium allows you to present yourself), and *functional* affordances (your ability to save or reproduce or "repost" a message) (Moreno & D'Angelo, 2019).

The "affordances" of social media and other technologies relate directly to culture, for, as Sandra Evans and her colleagues (2017) argue, the affordance is not merely the aspect of the technology but how the users adapt it to their own use. Focusing on cultural aspects of society and social lives, Yinan Sun and Daniel Suthers (2021) introduced the concept of *cultural affordances* that arise "from the making, using, or modifying of the artifact and in doing so endowing it with the values of culture from which it arises" and "can only be recognized by a member of the culture which created it" (Turner & Turner, 2002, cited by Sun & Suthers, 2021, p. 5). According to Sun and Suthers (2021), cultural affordances can be categorized as *cultural affordances of technology*, which is "what technology, designers, or a social media platform could offer to users to either reinforce established cultural values and meanings or to destabilize them, it is contingent and contextual": and *cultural affordance of culture*. They define these as:

> what an ideology that is holistically and deeply embedded in a community and consciously or subconsciously maintained by community members could provide to affect individuals' ways of doing and thinking, including ways of designing and using technology or a social media platform [that] reveals the power dynamics of a network that involves various actors in a particular context. (p. 5)

The cultural affordances of technology examine how technology could shape users' ways of doing and thinking and embed these into a technological frame. The affordances of culture explore people's thinking and doing that has been taken for granted, revealing the unconsciousness and subconsciousness.

Affordances can influence social media users' experiences with technology and their communication in various settings. Studies have demonstrated that social media platforms play a critical role in maintaining traditional cultural values and forming new cultures. The digital red envelope on WeChat is a great example of the expansion of traditional Chinese cultural value of filial piety into the digital space. Si Chen and colleagues (2018) pointed out that the concept of face, which is "deeply rooted in Chinese culture and the daily social behavior of Chinese people" (See Chapter 13) significantly affects users' behaviors of disclosing their location on WeChat (p. 3). At the same time, WeChat also forms new cultural values such as public discussion and civic engagement. The public account platform on WeChat allows individuals, and grassroots activists to facilitate public discussion and raise public awareness on some social issues.

Cultural identity: cultural transition and maintenance

We have discussed cultural identity in Chapter 5. According to social identity theory, cultural identity is derived from relationships and communication with others. The classic work of Goffman (1955, 1959, 1976) on performance and identity management suggests that a cultural identity is a communicative act. Existing studies revealed that a **hybridized cultural identity** could emerge from a virtual community composed of diverse people (Chen, 2012; Shuter, 2012). People such as diasporas—populations of people who have spread out from their homeland to other locations—and minorities use social media to retain and reinforce their cultural identities. For example, Stephen Croucher and Daniel Cronn-Mills (2011) found that French-Muslim used social media to maintain their Muslim identities. David Oh (2012) noted that Korean Americans used transnational Korean media to support their Korean identities. Yali Chen et al. (2021) reported that Chinese female immigrants in Switzerland used WeChat to remain connected with their native culture.

In the era of social media, as we discussed earlier, people are able to interact and communicate with others in virtual spaces across the boundaries of geography, space, and time. Charu Singh (2010) argued that the advancement and innovation of information technology were the root cause of cultural change, and individuals were inducted into "**virtual cultures**." Virtual cultures can alter pre-existing cultural identities and therefore threaten traditional indigenous identifications. Similarly, Guo-Ming Chen (2012) suggested that **virtual communities**, which are not culturally neutral, challenge pre-existing cultural identities and shape the development of new cultural identities. Several empirical studies have supported these scholars' arguments. For example, Yidong Wang (2019) studied the Hong Kong localist movement on social media and found that the local identity articulated in the localist movement is a fluid and contested construct. Elif Kavakci and Camille Kraeplin (2017) studied Muslim women's online identity construction and identified the increasingly important role of social media in the socialization of young Muslims worldwide. Karen Waltorp (2015) noted that Muslim women living in Europe often used social media to follow and challenge social norms.

The ability of social media to transcend geographical space receives evidence not just from academic research, but from popular culture itself. Yasemin Kanar, who is a Miami-based hijabi blogger, has been active on Instagram, Facebook, YouTube, TikTok, and Pinterest. She has 302 thousand followers on Instagram. The video of her wedding received more than 1.3 million views on YouTube, where her list of subscribers is over 86.5 thousand (Figure 11.3). On the one hand, Yasemin asserts her hijabi identity, while on the other hand, she promotes a highly marketable image of her marriage and happy life (Kavakci & Kraeplin, 2017).

Social media platforms have social, cultural, and technical affordances that enable people in diasporas as well as sojourners (those who travel to a country for a longer, but limited period of time, such as students or workers; see Chapter 12) to exchange heterogeneous opinions and engage in cross-cultural adaptation practices (Pang, 2018). Sherry Turkle (1995) claimed that "computer-mediated communication can serve as a place for construction or reconstruction of identity" (p. 342). She also concluded that people adopt "multiple identities" as "many more people experience identity as a set of roles that can be mixed and matched, whose diverse demands need to be negotiated" (p. 180). Cyberspace can empower individuals and groups who do not have the power and opportunity to present their voices and identities. Social media prompts individuals to construct their online identities, negotiate their existing identities, and even enact multiple identities (Kasperiuniene & Zydziunaite, 2019).

Figure 11.3 Yasemin Kanar on social media.
Source: YouTube, LLC.

Hijab Tutorial #2 (Cute & YoungTwisty Head Design)

 The Real Yaz (Yasemin K.)
86.1K subscribers   Subscribe

Bridging cultural gaps and cultural adaptation

Intercultural communication is based on an understanding of each other and the awareness of communicators' own values and predispositions (Shuter, 2012). Although social media provides opportunities for all people to have dialogues and interactions, existing research suggests that social media-based intercultural dialogues and collaborations might be affected by the existing social networks and intergroup boundaries. For example, Hichang Cho and Jae-Shin Lee (2008) studied computer-mediated groups composed of students from the United States and Singapore and found that students' willingness to collaborate and share information with others was affected by the factor of whether their virtual partners were their in-group members and shared their cultural values.

Cultural gaps become significant when people enter a new culture. "The multicultural world is enhanced by the experiences of sojourners, immigrants, and others who successfully make the transition from one culture to another" (Kim, 2001, p. xi). For members of diasporas and for sojourners who have been immersed in multicultural contexts, social media has played an important role in their lives. Social media prepares immigrants, international workers, and exchange students to adapt to new cultures and lessen the **culture shock** (see Chapter 12). On the one hand, scholars have studied the impact of social media on the cultural integration of immigrants into the host society. Rebecca Sawyer and Guo-Ming Chen (2012) studied the impact of social media on **intercultural adaptation** and found that social media created a universal community that provides companionship to a worldwide population. Chun-Min Wang (2012) found that Facebook was able to build cross-cultural friendships among American and Taiwanese university students. A study on East Asian students in the United States demonstrated that using Facebook could reduce acculturative stress and result in a higher level of psychological well-being (Park et al., 2014). Another study on Latino immigrant youth found that the youth gained participatory and deliberative skills useful for civic engagement through online newsgathering and content sharing (Marchi, 2017). These studies revealed that immigrants have been able to negotiate their cultural identity and transit to the new cultural environment through online engagement.

On the other hand, other studies take a **disintegration approach** to social media, which refers to the social phenomenon that minorities and immigrants remain marginalized (Leurs, 2015). Kyong Yoon (2018) claimed that "digital media not only resonates with offline inequality, such as racial and gender divides but also reinforces national boundaries and nationalism" (p. 151). Josh Rose (2011) conducted an informal poll by asking his friends whether social media made people feel closer or further away and quoted one answer: "I'm closer to people I'm far away from, but maybe farther from the people I'm close enough to."

Low-cost or free chat and social messaging apps have proven themselves to be important in increasing the self-esteem and perceived social support of diaspora members and sojourners, and in reducing loneliness, depression, and acculturative stress (Sandel, 2014; Shaw & Gant, 2002; C. Wang, 2012). Social media provide platforms and opportunities for immigrants to explore multicultural senses of belonging and identity. The convergency of social media platforms allows users to access different platforms and contribute to an in-between identity of people within a multicultural setting (Yoon, 2018). Specifically, the use of social media from host countries, such as Facebook, has been found to be significantly and positively related to cultural adaptation (B. Kim & Kim, 2017; Li & Chen, 2014). However, the use of social media from the home country has been seen as negatively related to their cultural adaptation processes (Fox & Moreland, 2015). Kyung-Hee Kim et al. (2009) found that Asian international students maintained "a transcultural space" where they navigated the cultural norms and values between their home countries and the host countries and carried "out an uninhibited cultural navigation amid the distinct yet connected zones' on [social networking sites]" (p. 152). In addition, online communication is not sufficient for "a fully successful acculturation" without examining pre-existing boundaries and offline interactions across cultural boundaries (Odağ & Hanke, 2019, p. 175). As Dohyun Ahn and Dong-Hee Shin (2013) assert, social media communication enabled individuals to seek social connectedness but could not avoid social isolation and replace face-to-face communication.

What do you think? Social media is an important piece of the puzzle for understanding how intercultural communication happens and how problems in intercultural communication can arise. Social media forms a "third space," a space between two different cultures (Figure 11.4). The third space allows people to exchange ideas across linguacultural boundaries and shares expectations of both cultures. However, the third space can also be viewed as being free from both cultures. Imagine a person from Spain communicating with an individual from Japan on WhatsApp. Their online interaction creates a new space in which they might adopt both Spanish and Japanese styles to communicate with each other. And their online interaction might be very different from the ways they communicate with people from the same country or their in-person communication either in Spain or Japan.

What are some of the different ways that you interact with people outside of your culture online? Do you follow your cultural rules or theirs—or do you step outside of your own cultures to take "third space" perspective? What sorts of barriers have you faced? What strategies to improve communication? What benefits of the interaction have you experienced?

Figure 11.4 The third space in intercultural communication.
Source: Adapted from Sobre-Denton, 2017.

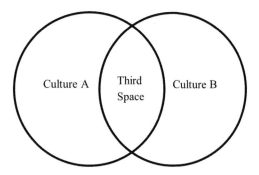

Culture is made and remade by individuals' actions and discursive practices (Kress, 2012). Empirical studies reveal that social media provides useful dimensions for intercultural teaching and learning and has been effective in improving language learners' **intercultural communication competence,** something we will say more about in Chapter 12. The internationalization and globalization of education prepare and equip students with the awareness of cultural differences and intercultural communication knowledge and skills. Studies have reported that social media had the potential to enhance language learners' intercultural skills (Álvarez Valencia & Fernández Benavides, 2019). With the involvement of social media platform WeChat, students have gained knowledge of cultural differences; increased their curiosity, openness, and willingness to learn a new language and culture; and improved their ability to interpret and relate cultural differences and interact accordingly in different situations (Zhou & Sun, 2020). However, Catherine Brooks and Margaret Pitts (2016) also found that U.S. students lacked intercultural competence and sensitivity. They pointed out that cultural competence training and preparedness were necessary for international students to engage in the online educational and communicative setting and therefore reduce the personal and community identity gaps. For educators, social media provides useful and effective tools to encourage students to explore the current digital technology and ways to link local and global experiences, as well as engage in responsible and inclusive intercultural communication.

Intercultural conflict management and social media

In terms of cultural gaps, intercultural conflict is common and salient during the intercultural communication process. Stella Ting-Toomey and Leeva Chung (2012) define intercultural conflict as "the implicit or explicit emotional struggle or frustration between persons of different cultures over perceived incompatible values, norms, face orientations, goals, scarce resources, processes, and/or outcomes in a communication situation." Conflict among cultures arises when communicators feel as if the other people are against their norms, values, or beliefs (Rios-Rodriguez, 2016). A person from a high power distance culture might feel uncomfortable calling one's superior's first name, which is common in low distance culture. Or a person from a western country might be surprised when he/she is asked for age in South Korea, which is a common social practice and the social contract in South Korea to establish the pecking order between speakers. To manage intercultural conflict, as above mentioned, individuals need to be aware of their own values and beliefs and be willing to find some kind of common ground in order to reach the level of adaptation and integration (Bennett, 2003). We say more about intercultural conflict in Chapter 13.

As social media are involved in the everyday lives of many individuals, intercultural conflicts can emerge and be managed on social media platforms. Alma Rios-Rodriguez (2016) compared conflict management through social media and face-to-face and found that social media helped communicators develop thoughtful responses and coherent answers. They break the limitations of time and space; information from different sources and various opinions spread easily and quickly among a massive amount of people. Diverse social media platforms have significantly influenced the development of civil society and the public sphere by creating "sustainable channels for public dialogue with the state and other opportunities to influence the policy in urgent areas" (Fedorenko & Sun, 2016, p. 2099). Specific examples from different countries with different political institutions and contexts have experienced success in social media campaigns, such as the Arab Spring, Egypt's Tahrir Square Protests, Iceland's Kitchenware Revolution, Tunisia's Jasmine Revolution, and online social movements #MeToo, and Stop Asian Hate. Social media also greatly facilitated broad-based political efforts such as Occupy Wallstreet and Black Lives Matter.

These events presented opportunities for researchers to study how public spheres are created on various social media platforms and thus promote critical discourse and political and social change. Mykola Makhortykh and Maryna Sydorova (2017) investigated the role of the social media platform Vkontakte, which is one of the most popular social networking sites among Russian speakers, in framing the conflict between Ukraine and Russia. On Vkontakte, both pro-Ukraine and pro-Russia communities tended to avoid the most gruesome sides of the war and emphasize the symbols (national flags and Orthodox icons) and the human consequences of the conflict. The increased connectivity makes social media the medium to bring people together to understand each other and have conversations.

Figure 11.5 Prevalence of online discrimination.
Source: Tynes, 2015/With permission of American Psychological Association.

Online Discrimination Items	Time 1	Time 2	Time 3
People have said mean or rude things about me because of my race or ethnic group	28%	34%	36%
People have shown me a racist image online	32%	46%	50%
People have cracked jokes about people of my race or ethnic group online	48%	55%	60%
People have said things that were untrue about people in my race or ethnic group	46%	56%	55%
I have witnessed people saying mean or rude things about another person's ethnic group online	55%	60%	58%
People have excluded me from a site because of my race or ethnic group online	9%	9%	13%
People have threatened me online with violence because of my race or ethnic group	10%	7%	13%

Although social media can be the medium for communicators to create a third space or to manage or mitigate conflict, the anonymity and connectivity of social media also make these platforms a breeding ground for racism, which is a radical presence of cultural and racial differences. Scholars have paid attention to racism and hate speech online. Jessie Daniels (2013) points out that social media platforms and social networking sites are spaces "where race and racism play out in interesting, sometimes disturbing, ways" (p. 702). With the prevalence and dominance of social media in our socio-political lives, racist speech has been thriving on social media. On social media platforms such as Reddit, YouTube, and Twitter, users can use fake identities to incite racist hatred (Chandrasekharan et al., 2017; Farkas et al., 2018a; Murthy & Sharma, 2019; Shepherd et al., 2015). On TikTok, researchers found that nearly a third of videos amplified White supremacy, and many TikTok videos spewed hate about Asians, LGBTQ, migrants and refugees, women, Muslims, and Jews (Guynn, 2021). A research study of 340 African-American, Latino, Asian, and biracial adolescents from sixth to 12th grades found that 42 percent of minority youth experienced at least one direct discriminatory incident in the first year, with 55 percent in the second year and 58 percent in the third year (Figure 11.5) (Tynes, 2015). Accordingly, anti-racism content has been found to be censored and removed on social media platforms such as Instagram and LinkedIn (Asare, 2021; Martin, 2020). A popular Instagram account, No White Saviors (Figure 11.6), with over 900,000 followers, described their experience thusly:

> Instagram has given our team access to a global audience that would have been hard to reach in such a short amount of time. We started our page in June 2018, so we haven't even been around for three years yet… we have dealt with many censorship issues from Instagram from the beginning. From our content taken down for 'hate speech' to shadow banning to having Instagram threaten [to] have our entire profile deleted…Instagram seems to do better to protect white supremacists and Nazi pages than those of us working to hold anti-Blackness and white supremacy accountable. (Asare, 2021, para. 4)

Figure 11.6 Instagram account of no white saviors.
Source: Meta.

Scholars have explored online racism, misinformation, and polarization and developed concepts such as **filter bubble**s (Pariser, 2011) and **echo chambers** (Bunker & Varnum, 2021). Filter bubbles and echo chambers (see also Chapter 10) describe the phenomenon that the users selectively choose attitude-consistent content on social media, and their existing attitudes are reinforced without hearing the other perspectives and different opinions (Jones-Jang & Chung, 2022). Eytan Bakshy et al. (2015) studied news sharing and consumption on Facebook and measured the extent to which users are exposed to ideologically discordant content. They identified three mechanisms of selective exposure, including individual choice, homogeneous networks, and algorithmic decisions, and found that individual choice limited exposure to attitude-challenging content on Facebook more than algorithmic rankings.

Social media contribute to reshaping "racist dynamics through their affordances, policies, algorithms and corporate decisions" (Matamoros-Fernández, 2017, p. 933). Ariadna Matamoros-Fernández and Johan Farkas (2021) reviewed the literature on racism and social media and suggested that the **Indigenous framework** and perspective might be effective in promoting diverse ways of understanding the production of meaning-making on social media. Everybody can create and share their own content. Therefore, social media are also a place for counter-speech and anti-racism. A report from Pew Research Center noted that many Black social media users consider social media important for purposes of finding others who share their views, getting involved in issues that are important to them, and expressing their political opinions (Auxier, 2020). In January 2022, amid record levels of violence targeting Asian Americans in the United States, the hashtag "Very Asian" was viral on Twitter. A Korean American and an NBC anchor Michelle Li shared traditional New Year's food on social media; a viewer complained that she was being "very Asian." The viewer said, "I kind of take offense to that. What if one of your White anchors said White people eat this on New Year's Day? I don't think it's appropriate she said that. She's being very Asian. She can keep her Korean to herself. If a White person said that, they would get fired." Many journalists, activists, and celebrities used the hashtag "VeryAsian" to criticize the viewer's racist comment and support Li (Bellamy-Walker, 2022).

The VeryAsian movement (Figure 11.7) is a great example of **digital activism**, which means "political participation, activities, and protests organized in digital networks beyond representational politics" (Karatzogianni, 2015, p. 1). Digital activism is a means for historically and socially oppressed groups to challenge and disrupt existing social structures and power relations. According to Suay Ozkula (2021), the practices of digital activism can be categorized as: "(1) advocacy and political commentary, (2) recruitment and movement-building, (3) organization and coordination, (4) online direct action, hacktivism, and civil disobedience, and (5) research and documentation" (p. 67). The different forms of digital activism provide opportunities for social media users to examine and understand social issues, raise awareness, and actively resist and challenge these issues. And, as we have seen above, such issues frequently involve aspects of culture, diversity, or identity.

Overall, social media have affected intercultural communication in several different ways. Increasingly people are using social media to facilitate content sharing, interact with others, create a sense of community, develop relationships, and share cultural interests, transcending geographical, social, psychological, linguistic, and cultural barriers. Also, social media has the power to amplify or minimize some people's voices. It is necessary for us to understand how people's online interactions impact information flows, identity framing, and knowledge production in a networked society. As Jones-Jang and Chung (2022) suggested, the "online space is a site of struggle where users negotiate competing notions of cultural norms and practices" (p. 358).

Figure 11.7 #VeryAsian on Twitter.
Source: Twitter, Inc.

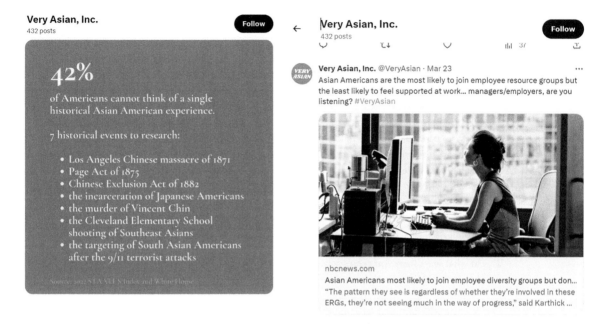

Platformation of modern society: How do social media platforms differ between cultures?

Social media have developed and evolved drastically in the world. The diversity of social media platforms also prompts new studies regarding the integration of social media platforms and socioopolitical contexts. Nowadays, people commonly utilize multiple social media platforms to meet different needs in different contexts. The concept of platform society describes the platformization of society all over the world (van Dijck & Poell, 2015). TikTok and Instagram have been the fastest-growing platforms. On the one hand, global platforms such as Facebook, Twitter, and WhatsApp have been the widely used social media platforms worldwide. On the other hand, there has been a trend of localization regarding communication. The majority of Chinese use WeChat, while LINE is popular in Japan and Taiwan, and KakaoTalk has a major following in South Korea. Also, new apps have emerged in other countries, such as Indonesia's Go-Jek, Philippine's Chikka, and Vietnam's Zalo. The platformization and localization of social media reflect the social, cultural, and political implications of intercultural communication. Moreover, the divergent social affordances of these platforms may facilitate different modes of intercultural communication.

Each social media platform has its own technical and regulatory infrastructures and policies regarding the editorial procedure, censoring sensitive and offensive content,

What do you think? Race relations in Australia have been complex, rooted in a long history of tensions between the Indigenous people, the White, and the settled people from Asian countries (Elias et al., 2021). In 2015, the Australia Football League (AFL) Indigenous star Adam Goodes sparked controversies about racism in Australia, reflecting the tensions of race relations in Australia and racism on social media. At an annual celebration of Aboriginal and Torres Strait Islander people in Australia during the 2015 AFL season, Goodes performed a war dance and mimicked the action of throwing a spear at the crowd. This gesture ignited the debate on racism in Australia because it was viewed by some people as offensive. The controversy expanded to social media. His Wikipedia page was vandalized, and his pictures were replaced with images of chimpanzees. People on Twitter, Facebook, and YouTube ridiculed and vilified him, which became a harassment campaign (Matamoros-Fernández, 2017). Memes of Goodes and the racist content were shared and liked thousands of times across these platforms. Every time Goodes played, he got booed. In September 2015, Goodes retired from the game, and then he deleted his Twitter account in June 2016. In 2019, the AFL apologized to Goodes for failing to intervene in the racial abuse he experienced.

In what ways have you seen social media used in your nation or culture to promote or resist intolerance? Do some research on racism, sexism, or other forms of intolerance in particular platforms (e.g., Reddit, WeChat, Line, Chikka). What "affordances" do you think different platforms might have that facilitate the spreading (or fighting/resisting) of group-based hatred?

which reflect their cultural values and cultural difference. As Ian Bogost and Nick Montfort (2009) suggest, technology and platforms were created by humans "in response to social and cultural effects, ideals, goals, problems or related factors" (p. 2). Therefore, social media users' experiences, the social media interface, form and function, code, and platform, are all fully embedded in the culture. Facebook has been criticized a lot for its lack of understanding of cultural differences, especially the Indigenous cultures, and its tendency to favor Western ideals of free speech (Farkas et al., 2018b; Gillespie, 2010; Matamoros-Fernández, 2017; see also Chapter 10). In fact, the idea of "electronic colonialism" suggests that as a country exports a technology (including hardware or platforms), it is also, inherently, exporting cultural values (McPhail, 2019). As an example of this, YouTube has been called the great radicalizer and far-Right propaganda machine (Rieder et al., 2020).

As discussed in the above section, social media can be tools for both mediating cultural differences and amplifying the existing social bias. Social media platforms contribute to racist discourse and activities through their algorithms, **affordances**, corporate decisions, and policies (Matamoros-Fernández, 2017). Social media platforms' algorithms generate and recommend similar content to users who watch, like, and share some content, which contributes to the amplification of controversial and extremist content. Social media platforms are managed by for-profit companies. The quest for profitability determines these platforms' design and content. In 2019, YouTube announced that it generated U.S.$15 billion from advertising (Statt, 2020).

Although most social media platforms can be accessed worldwide, their operation might differ substantially in different countries and cultures. Earlier studies of cultural differences and social media have been mainly based on Hall's (1976) dimensions (high/low context and polychromic/monochromic cultures) and Hofstede's (1984) cultural dimensions (power distance, individualism/collectivism, masculinity/femininity, uncertainty avoidance, and long term/short term orientation; see Chapter 4) (Vitkauskaitė, 2010). Xuequn Wang and Zilong Liu (2019) noted that people from high uncertainty avoidance cultures might not post political or civic information on social media because they don't feel comfortable with deviant behaviors and the associated risks. Kyung-Hee Kim and Haejin Yun (2007) studied Cyworld, which is a South Korean social network site, and found that Cyworld's design features and functions encouraged elaborate and emotional communication and, therefore, promoted users to transcend the high-context communication of Korean culture and reframed relational issues offline. Figure 11.8 shows the most popular social media platforms, including both social networking sites and instant message apps, by country. WhatsApp is the top-used social media platform with two billion monthly active users in West Europe, Russia, Latin America, India, and Africa. Facebook leads in the United States and Canada, while Facebook Messenger is popular in Australia and East Europe. In China WeChat reigns, while KakaoTalk dominates South Korea, and LINE is mostly used in Japan and Taiwan (Cosenza, 2022).

KakaoTalk is the most widely used social media app, which integrates instant messaging service, social networking, and gaming in South Korea (Lee & Lee, 2020). Users can initiate one-on-one conversations or group chats by entering phone numbers without registering or logging in. Its storytelling and gameplay features have made it popular among Korean youths and redefined the concept and practice of mobile messaging (Jin & Yoon, 2016). It is different from Facebook, KakaoTalk, and WeChat, which are based on a closed network that might form more strong ties with acquaintants. Users' friends and followers cannot see the others' followers and friends. As communal spaces, users can nurture and develop intimate relationships with friends and family through ongoing and dialogic communication (Moon, 2020). Also, Korea is a strongly community-driven society (Jin et al., 2015). For Korean youths, mobile games are not only an entertainment but also a way to maintain friendships and social ties. Those mobile games integrate social networking features. For example, the game Anipang requires users to

FIGURE 11.8 World map of social networks.
Source: Vincenzo Cosenza, 2022/ Vincenzo Cosenza.

WORLD MAP OF SOCIAL APPS
January 2023

WhatsApp   Facebook   Facebook Messenger
Line   WeChat   KakaoTalk

have hearts received from friends to play. It also has a ranking system where players can compete with their friends on KakaoTalk.

Similarly, WeChat has been found to adhere to the Chinese cultural values of favoring social connections/*guanxi*, reciprocal favors/*renqing*, face/*mianzi*, and collectivism (Vodanovich et al., 2017). For instance, the manager of a subscription account on WeChat can review their subscribers' comments before publishing those, which shows "the cultural attribute of respect for authority" (Vodanovich et al., 2017, p. 6). Gianluigi Negro et al. (2020) found that WeChat has undergone a Sinicization process to adapt to the Chinese cultural context.

Summary

In this chapter, we discussed the interplay of social media and intercultural communication and how social media have transformed intercultural communication. The advancement of information technology and the prevalence of social media in every aspect of our lives have promoted intercultural interactions and exchanges. Intercultural communication is a process of negotiating cultural and linguistic differences through communication and interaction. Social media affordances provide environments and opportunities for everybody to communicate with people from diverse cultures and stimulate people to compare cultures and reflect on their own and other cultures.

With the convenience of connectivity, social media-based communication might also result in division, fragmentation, and polarization and generate misconceptions of certain people and cultures, reinforcing stereotypes and bias. Spanish sociologist Manuel Castells (2002) warned that technology could lead to "one of the most damaging forms of exclusion in our economy and in our culture" (p. 3). Another issue we need to keep in mind is the inequality of information flow on social media and globalization. The **digital divide**, which refers to the inequalities of digital access and digital literacy, has been discussed a lot. The unequal access significantly affects people's intercultural dialogue and their ability to explore and examine social media platforms and content.

Social media promote new modes and norms of intercultural communication and create fragmentation and polarization simultaneously. The interplay of online and offline activities, the design and algorithms of social media platforms, and the institutions and cultures with which the platforms are operated and controlled—all of these factors affect users' perceptions and online behaviors.

It is hard to say whether social media impacts intercultural communication either positively or negatively. However, it is necessary for every social media user to develop critical digital literacy, understand how social media can be a tool of oppression and social transformation, and create an equitable and inclusive online space (Dooly & Darvin, 2022).

KEY TERMS

digitality, 222

convergency, 222

interactivity, 222

hypertextuality, 222

virtuality, 222

programmability, 223

popularity, 224

connectivity, 224

datafication, 224

hybridized cultural identity, 226

virtual cultures, 226

virtual communities, 226

culture shock, 227

intercultural adaptation, 227

Discussion Questions

1   In what ways do social media and online communication affect language use and communication style?

2   How does social media-based communication different from face-to-face interactions?

3   Consider where you think we are headed in this social media age. Is it toward cultural convergence or cultural divergence?

4   In what ways has technology served to facilitate intercultural communication across national borders?

5   Think about the social media reviewed in this chapter and what you are exposed to in your life. Would you consider the forces of convergence, divergence, or something else?

Action Points

1   Create a closed Facebook group for your class, where all the students and instructors can interact with each other as members. Observe the group dynamics and how your teacher and classmates consume and share information.

2   Make a 5–10 minute short video on the topic of a specific cultural perception or practice of your own culture. Share this video on YouTube with your instructor and classmates. Your classmates will review and comment on your video. Collect the comments and analyze your audience's impression and awareness of cultural differences.

3   Create a cause-oriented hashtag campaign and use your online voice to engage in digital activism. The process starts by choosing a particular cause of one social issue you are interested in. Plan your messaging and decide what hashtag to use, create social media posts, and promote your hashtag campaign. Collect information about the number of follows, likes, and comments, and analyze the impact of your hashtag.

4   In groups or pairs, with your instructor's supervision, conduct a small research project in which you either interview or survey people *within* a group (e.g., the motivations of members or the activities of the group) about whether and how many social media platforms from other countries are used. Discuss your findings with the class. What type of knowledge does your study give you? What are some types of knowledge or claims that you could *not* make from your study?

For more information

Bucher, T. (2012). Want to be on the top? Algorithmic power and the threat of invisibility on Facebook. *New Media & Society*, 14 (7), 1164–1180. https://doi.org/10.1177/1461444812440159

Daly, T., & Regan, C. (2018). *#BeyongTheClick: Exploring global digital citizenship- A toolkit. 80:20 Educating and Acting for a Better World*. Accessed December 4, 2022, at https://toolkit.8020.ie/using-this-toolkit

Jenkins, H., Ford, S., & Green, J. (2013). *Spreadable media. Creating value and meaning in a networked culture*. New York University Press.

Poell, T., & Darmoni, K. (2012). Twitter as a multilingual space: The articulation of the Tunisian revolution through #sidibouzid. *The European Journal of Media Studies*, 1 (1), 14–34 DOI: https://doi.org/10.25969/mediarep/15038

SPLC. (2017). *Learning for Justice Digital Literacy framework*. Accessed December 4, 2022, at https://www.learningforjustice.org/frameworks/digital-literacy

The New York Times. (2017). How China is changing your internet. *YouTube*. Accessed December 4, 2022, at https://www.youtube.com/watch?v=VAesMQ6VtK8

van Dijck, J. (2013). *The culture of connectivity. A critical history of social media*. Oxford University Press

References

Ahn, D., & Shin, D.-H. (2013). Is the social use of media for seeking connectedness or for avoiding social isolation? Mechanisms underlying media use and subjective well-being. *Computers in Human Behavior*, 29(6), 2453–2462. https://doi.org/10.1016/j.chb.2012.12.022

Asare, J. G. (2021, January 8). Social media continues to amplify white supremacy and suppress anti-racism. *Forbes*. Accessed December 8, 2022, at https://www.forbes.com/sites/janicegassam/2021/01/08/social-media-continues-to-amplify-white-supremacy-and-suppress-anti-racism

Auxier, B. (2020, December 11). Social media continue to be important political outlets for Black Americans. *Pew Research Center*. Accessed December 8, 2022, at https://www.pewresearch.org/fact-tank/2020/12/11/social-media-continue-to-be-important-political-outlets-for-black-americans

Bakshy, E., Messing, S., & Adamic, L. A. (2015). Exposure to ideologically diverse news and opinion on Facebook. *Science*, 348(6239), 1130–1132. DOI: 10.1126/science.aaa1160

Bareither, C. (2019). Doing emotion through digital media: An ethnographic perspective on media practices and emotional affordances. *Ethnologia Europaea*, 49(1), Article 1. https://doi.org/10.16995/ee.822

Bellamy-Walker, T. (2022, January 3). #VeryAsian hashtag goes viral after racist criticism of Korean American news anchor. *NBC News*. https://www.nbcnews.com/news/asian-america/veryasian-hashtag-goes-viral-racist-criticism-korean-american-news-anc-rcna10777

Bennett, J. M. (2003). Turning frogs into interculturalists: A student-centered development approach to teach intercultural communication. In R. Goodman, M. Phillips, & N. Boyacigiller (Eds.), *Crossing cultures: Insights from master teachers* (pp. 157–170). Routledge.

Bogost, I., & Montfort, N. (2009, December 12). *Platform studies: Frequently questioned answers. The Digitial Arts and Culture Conference*, Irvine, CA. https://escholarship.org/uc/item/01r0k9br

boyd, d. (2010). Social network sites as networked publics: Affordances, dynamics, and implications. In Z. A. Papacharissi (Ed.), *Networked self: Identity, community, and culture on social network sites* (pp. 39–58). Routledge.

Brooks, C. F., & Pitts, M. J. (2016). Communication and identity management in a globally connected classroom: An online international and intercultural learning experience. *Journal of International and Intercultural Communication*, 9(1), 52–68. https://doi.org/10.1080/17513057.2016.1120849

Bunker, C. J., & Varnum, M. E. W. (2021). How strong is the association between social media use and false consensus? *Computers in Human Behavior*, 125, 106947. https://doi.org/10.1016/j.chb.2021.106947.

Castells, M. (2000). *The rise of the network society: The information age: Economy, society and culture*. Wiley.

Castells, M. (2002). *The Internet galaxy: Reflections on the Internet, business, and society*. Oxford University Press.

Ceci, L. (2022, January 28). Number of TikTok users in the United States from 2020 to 2023. *Statista*.

Accessed December 8, 2022, at https://www.statista.com/statistics/1100836/number-of-us-tiktok-users

Chandrasekharan, E., Pavalanathan, U., Srinivasan, A., Glynn, A., Eisenstein, J., & Gilbert, E. (2017). You can't stay here: The efficacy of Reddit's 2015 ban examined through hate speech. *Proceedings of the ACM on Human-Computer Interaction*, 1 (CSCW), 31: 1–22. https://doi.org/10.1145/3134666

Chen, G.-M. (2012). The impact of new media on intercultural communication in global context. *China Media Research*, 8(2), 1–10. http://www.wwdw.chinamediaresearch.net/index.php/back-issues?id=54

Chen, G.-M., & Zhang, K. (2010). *New media and cultural identity in the global society* (pp. 795–809). IGI Global. https://doi.org/10.4018/978-1-61520-773-2.ch051

Chen, S., Shao, B., & Zhi, K. (2018). Predictors of Chinese users' location disclosure behavior: An empirical study on WeChat. *Information*, 9(9). https://doi.org/10.3390/info9090219

Chen, Y., Tian, H., & Chang, J. (2021). Chinese first, woman second: Social media and the cultural identity of female immigrants. *Asian Journal of Women's Studies*, 27(1), 22–45. https://doi.org/10.1080/12259276.2021.1873575

Cho, H., & Lee, J.-S. (2008). Collaborative information seeking in intercultural computer-mediated communication groups: Testing the influence of social context using social network analysis. *Communication Research*, 35(4), 548–573. https://doi.org/10.1177/0093650208315982

Cosenza, V. (2022, January). World map of social networks. *VincosBlog*. Accessed December 4, 2022, at https://vincos.it/world-map-of-social-networks

Croucher, S., & Cronn-Mills, D. (2011). *Religious misperceptions: The case of Muslims and Christians in France and Britain*. Hampton Press.

Daniels, J. (2013). Race and racism in Internet studies: A review and critique. *New Media & Society*, 15(5), 695–719. https://doi.org/10.1177/1461444812462849

Diaz Baquero, A. D. (2021). *Super apps: Opportunities and challenges*. Unpublished masters degree. Massachusetts Institute of Technology.

Dooly, M., & Darvin, R. (2022). Intercultural communicative competence in the digital age: Critical digital literacy and inquiry-based pedagogy. *Language and Intercultural Communication*, 22(3), 354–366. https://doi.org/10.1080/14708477.2022.2063304

Elias, A., Ben, J., Mansouri, F., & Paradies, Y. (2021). Racism and nationalism during and beyond the COVID-19 pandemic. *Ethnic and Racial Studies*, 44(5), 783–793. DOI: 10.1080/01419870.2020.1851382

Evans, S. K., Pearce, K. E., Vitak, J., & Treem, J. W. (2017). Explicating affordances: A conceptual framework for understanding affordances in communication research. *Journal of Computer Mediated Communication*, 22(1), 35–52. https://doi.org/10.1111/jcc4.12180

Farkas, J., Schou, J., & Neumayer, C. (2018a). Cloaked Facebook pages: Exploring fake Islamist propaganda in social media. *New Media & Society*, 20(5), 1850–1867. https://doi.org/10.1177/1461444817707759

Farkas, J., Schou, J., & Neumayer, C. (2018b). Platformed antagonism: Racist discourses on fake Muslim Facebook pages. *Critical Discourse Studies*, 15(5), 463–480. https://doi.org/10.1080/17405904.2018.1450276

Fedorenko, I., & Sun, Y. (2016). Microblogging-based civic participation on environment in China: A case study of the PM 2.5 campaign. *VOLUNTAS: International Journal of Voluntary and Nonprofit Organizations*, 27(5), 2077–2105. http://dx.doi.org.leo.lib.unomaha.edu/10.1007/s11266-015-9591-1

Fox, J., & Moreland, J. J. (2015). The dark side of social networking sites: An exploration of the relational and psychological stressors associated with Facebook use and affordances. *Computers in Human Behavior*, 45, 168–176. https://doi.org/10.1016/j.chb.2014.11.083.

Gillespie, T. (2010). The politics of 'platforms'. *New Media & Society*, 12(3), 347–364. https://doi.org/10.1177/1461444809342738

Goffman, E. (1955). On face-work: An analysis of ritual elements in social interaction. *Psychiatry*, 18(3), 213–231. https://doi.org/10.1080/00332747.1955.11023008

Goffman, E. (1959). *The presentation of self in everyday life*. Doubleday.

Goffman, E. (1976). *Beyond culture*. Doubleday.

Graves, L. (2007). The affordances of blogging: A case study in culture and technological effects. *Journal of Communication Inquiry*, 31(4), 331–346. https://doi.org/10.1177/0196859907305446

Guynn, J. (2021, August 24). *It's not just Facebook and Twitter. TikTok is "hatescape" for racism and white supremacy, study says*. USA TODAY. https://www.usatoday.com/story/tech/2021/08/24/tiktok-videos-hate-white-supremacy-racism-terrorism/8249286002

Hall, E. T. (1976). *Beyond culture*. Doubleday & Company.

Hallman, C. (n.d.). Everything Facebook owns: Mergers and acquisitions from the past 15 years. *Titlemax*. Accessed December 3, 2022, at https://www.titlemax.com/discovery-center/lifestyle/

everything-facebook-owns-mergers-and-acquisitions-from-the-past-15-years

Haythornthwaite, C., & Wellman, B. (1998). Work, friendship, and media use for information exchange in a networked organization. *Journal of the American Society for Information Science*, 49(12), 1101–1114. https://doi.org/10.1002/(SICI)1097-4571(1998)49:12<1101::AID-ASI6>3.0.CO;2-Z.

Hofstede, G. (1984). *Culture's consequences: International differences in work-related values* (Abridged ed). SAGE.

Iqbal, M. (2022, June 14). TikTok revenue and usage statistics (2022). *Business of Apps*. https://www.businessofapps.com/data/tik-tok-statistics

Jin, D. Y., Chee, F., & Kim, S. (2015). Transformative mobile game culture: A sociocultural analysis of Korean mobile gaming in the era of smartphones. *International Journal of Cultural Studies*, 18(4), 413–429. https://doi.org/10.1177/1367877913507473

Jin, D. Y., & Yoon, K. (2016). Reimagining smartphones in a local mediascape: A cultural analysis of young KakaoTalk users in Korea. *Convergence*, 22(5), 510–523. https://doi.org/10.1177/1354856514560316

Jones-Jang, S. M., & Chung, M. (2022). Can we blame social media for polarization? Counter-evidence against filter bubble claims during the COVID-19 pandemic. *New Media & Society*, 14614448221099592. https://doi.org/10.1177/14614448221099591

Karatzogianni, A. (2015). *Firebrand waves of digital activism 1994–2014: The rise and spread of kacktivism and cyberconflict*. Springer.

Kasperiuniene, J., & Zydziunaite, V. (2019). A systematic literature review on professional identity construction in social media. *SAGE Open*, 9(1), 2158244019828847. https://doi.org/10.1177/2158244019828847

Kavakci, E., & Kraeplin, C. R. (2017). Religious beings in fashionable bodies: The online identity construction of hijabi social media personalities. *Media, Culture & Society*, 39(6), 850–868. https://doi.org/10.1177/0163443716679031

Kim, B., & Kim, Y. (2017). College students' social media use and communication network heterogeneity: Implications for social capital and subjective well-being. *Computers in Human Behavior*, 73, 620–628. https://doi.org/10.1016/j.chb.2017.03.033.

Kim, K.-H., & Yun, H. (2007). Cying for me, cying for us: Relational dialectics in a Korean social network site. *Journal of Computer-Mediated Communication*, 13(1), 298–318. https://doi.org/10.1111/j.1083-6101.2007.00397.x

Kim, K.-H., Yun, H., & Yoon, Y. (2009). The Internet as a facilitator of cultural hybridization and interpersonal

relationship management for Asian international students in South Korea. *Asian Journal of Communication*, 19(2), 152–169. https://doi.org/10.1080/01292980902826880

Kim, Y. Y. (2001). *Becoming intercultural: An integrative theory of communication and cross-cultural adaptation*. Sage.

Krejins, K. (2004). *Socialbe CSCL environments: Social affordances, sociability, and social presence*. Open University of the Netherlands.

Kress, G. (2012). Thinking about the notion of 'cross-cultural' from a social semiotic perspective. *Language and Intercultural Communication*, 12(4), 369–385. https://doi.org/10.1080/14708477.2012.722102

Krishna, S. (2021). Digital identity, datafication and social justice: Understanding Aadhaar use among informal workers in south India. *Information Technology for Development*, 27(1), 67–90. https://doi.org/10.1080/02681102.2020.1818544

Lee, S. Y., & Lee, S. W. (2020). Social media use and job performance in the workplace: The effects of Facebook and KakaoTalk use on job performance in South Korea. *Sustainability*, 12(10), 4052. https://doi.org/10.3390/su12104052

Leurs, K. (2015). *Digital passages: Migrant youth 2.0, diaspora, gender and youth cultural intersections*. Amsterdam University Press.

Li, X., & Chen, W. (2014). Facebook or Renren? A comparative study of social networking site use and social capital among Chinese international students in the United States. *Computers in Human Behavior*, 35, 116–123. https://doi.org/10.1016/j.chb.2014.02.012.

Makhortykh, M., & Sydorova, M. (2017). Social media and visual framing of the conflict in Eastern Ukraine. *Media, War & Conflict*, 10(3), 359–381. https://doi.org/10.1177/1750635217702539

Marchi, R. (2017). News translators: Latino immigrant youth, social media, and citizenship training. *Journalism & Mass Communication Quarterly*, 94(1), 189–212. https://doi.org/10.1177/1077699016637119

Martin, A. M. (2020, October 8). Black LinkedIn is thriving. Does LinkedIn have a problem with that? *The New York Times*. Accessed December 8, 2022, at https://www.nytimes.com/2020/10/08/business/black-linkedin.html

Matamoros-Fernández, A. (2017). Platformed racism: The mediation and circulation of an Australian race-based controversy on Twitter, Facebook and YouTube. *Information, Communication & Society*, 20(6), 930–946. https://doi.org/10.1080/1369118X.2017.1293130

Matamoros-Fernández, A., & Farkas, J. (2021). Racism, hate speech, and social media: A systematic review and critique. *Television & New Media, 22*(2), 205–224. https://doi.org/10.1177/1527476420982230

McPhail, T. L. (2019). *Global communication: Theories, stakeholders, and trends* (5th ed.). Wiley-Blackwell.

McVeigh-Schultz, J., & Baym, N. K. (2015). Thinking of you: Vernacular affordance in the context of the microsocial relationship app, Couple. *Social Media + Society, 1*(2), 2056305115604649. https://doi.org/10.1177/2056305115604649

Monika, W., Nasution, A. H., & Nasution, S. (2019). The role of social media on intercultural communication competences. *Proceedings of the Second International Conference on Social, Economy, Education and Humanity,* 483–491. https://doi.org/10.5220/0010105604830491

Moon, J. Y. (2020). The digital wash place: Mobile messaging apps as new communal spaces for Korean 'smart Ajummas'. In J. V. A. Cabañes & C. S. Uy-Tioco (Eds.), *Mobile media and social intimacies in Asia: Reconfiguring local ties and enacting global relationships* (pp. 63–76). Springer Netherlands. https://doi.org/10.1007/978-94-024-1790-6_5

Moreno, M. A., & D'Angelo, J. (2019). Social media intervention design: Applying an affordances network. *Journal of Medical Internet Research, 21*(3), e11014. Accessed December 4, 2022, at https://www.ncbi.nlm.nih.gov/pmc/articles/PMC6454336

Murthy, D., & Sharma, S. (2019). Visualizing YouTube's comment space: Online hostility as a networked phenomenon. *New Media & Society, 21*(1), 191–213. https://doi.org/10.1177/1461444818792393

Negro, G., Balbi, G., & Bory, P. (2020). The path to WeChat: How Tencent's culture shaped the most popular Chinese app, 1998–2011. *Global Media and Communication, 16*(2), 208–226. https://doi.org/10.1177/1742766520923008

Odağ, Ö., & Hanke, K. (2019). Revisiting culture: A review of a neglected dimension in media psychology. *Journal of Media Psychology: Theories, Methods, and Applications, 31*(4), 171–184. https://doi.org/10.1027/1864-1105/a000244.

Oh, D. C. (2012). Mediating the boundaries: Second-generation Korean American adolescents' use of transnational Korean media as markers of social boundaries. *The International Communication Gazette, 74*(3), 258–276. https://doi.org/10.1177/1748048511432607

Ozkula, S. M. (2021). What is digital activism anyway? Social constructions of the "digital" in contemporary activism. *Journal of Digital Social Research, 3*(3), 60–84. https://doi.org/10.33621/jdsr.v3i3.44

Pang, H. (2018). Exploring the beneficial effects of social networking site use on Chinese students' perceptions of social capital and psychological well-being in Germany. *International Journal of Intercultural Relations, 67,* 1–11. https://doi.org/10.1016/j.ijintrel.2018.08.002.

Pariser, E. (2011). *The filter bubble: How the new personalized web is changing what we read and how we think.* Penguin.

Park, N., Song, H., & Lee, K. M. (2014). Social networking sites and other media use, acculturation stress, and psychological well-being among East Asian college students in the United States. *Computers in Human Behavior, 36,* 138–146. https://doi.org/10.1016/j.chb.2014.03.037.

Perez, S. (2021, December 20). TikTok to rank as the third largest social network, 2022 forecast notes. *TechCrunch.* https://social.techcrunch.com/2021/12/20/tiktok-to-rank-as-the-third-largest-social-network-2022-forecast-notes

Rieder, B., Coromina, Ò., & Matamoros-Fernández, A. (2020). Mapping YouTube: A quantitative exploration of a platformed media system. *First Monday, 25*(8), 1–31. https://doi.org/10.5210/fm.v25i8.10667

Rios-Rodriguez, A. D. (2016). *How people handle intercultural conflict via social media vs. in person.* Accessed December 8, 2022, at https://pilotscholars.up.edu/cgi/viewcontent.cgi?article=1112&context=cst_studpubs.

Rose, J. (2011, February 23). How social media is having a positive impact on our culture. *Mashable.* Accessed December 8, 2022, at https://mashable.com/archive/social-media-culture

Sandel, T. L. (2014). "Oh, I'm here!": Social media's impact on the cross-cultural adaptation of students studying abroad. *Journal of Intercultural Communication Research, 43*(1), 1–29. https://doi.org/10.1080/17475759.2013.865662

Sawyer, R., & Chen, G.-M. (2012). The impact of social media on intercultural adaptation. *Intercultural Communication Studies, 21*(2), 151–169. https://web.uri.edu/iaics/files/09RebeccaSawyerGuoMingChen.pdf

Shaw, L. H., & Gant, L. M. (2002). In defense of the internet: The relationship between Internet communication and depression, loneliness, self-esteem, and perceived social support. *Cyberpsychology & Behavior: The Impact of the Internet, Multimedia and Virtual Reality on Behavior and Society, 5*(2), 157–171. https://doi.org/10.1089/109493102753770552

Shepherd, T., Harvey, A., Jordan, T., Srauy, S., & Miltner, K. (2015). Histories of hating. *Social Media + Society, 1*(2), 2056305115603997. https://doi.org/10.1177/2056305115603997

Shuter, R. (2012). Intercultural new media studies: The next frontier in intercultural communication. *Journal of Intercultural Communication Research,*

41(3), 219–237. https://doi.org/10.1080/17475759.201
2.728761

Singh, C. L. (2010). New media and cultural identity. *China Media Research*, 6(1), 86–90. https://web.p.ebscohost.com/ehost/pdfviewer/pdfviewer?vid=1&sid=552a8769-e507-4c1d-a2b1-eb195204697f%40redis.

Sobre-Denton, M. (2017). Multicultural third culture building: A case study of a multicultural social support group. *Journal of Intercultural Communication*, 45. https://immi.se/intercultural/nr45/sobre.html.

Statt, N. (2020, February 3). YouTube is a $15 billion-a-year business, Google reveals for the first time—The Verge. *The Verge*. https://www.theverge.com/2020/2/3/21121207/youtube-google-alphabet-earnings-revenue-first-time-reveal-q4-2019

Sun, Y., & Suthers, D. (2021). *Cultural affordances and social media. Hawaii International Conference on System Sciences*. https://doi.org/10.24251/HICSS.2021.368

Ting-Toomey, S., & Chung, L. C. (2012). *Understanding intercultural communication* (2nd ed.). Oxford University Press.

Trepte, S. (2015). Social media, privacy, and self-disclosure: The turbulence caused by social media's affordances. *Social Media + Society*, 1(1), 2056305115578681. https://doi.org/10.1177/2056305115578681

Turkle, S. (1995). *Life on the screen: Identity in the age of the Internet. Simon and Schuster.* https://books.google.com/books/about/Life_on_the_Screen.html?id=qMjaAAAAMAAJ

Tynes, B. M. (2015, December). Online racial discrimination: A growing problem for adolescents. *American Psychological Association.* https://www.apa.org/science/about/psa/2015/12/online-racial-discrimination

Valencia, J. A. Á., & Benavides, A. F. (2019). Using social networking sites for language learning to develop intercultural competence in language education programs. *Journal of International and Intercultural Communication*, 12(1), 23–42. https://doi.org/10.1080/17513057.2018.1503318

Van Dijck, J., & Poell, T. (2013). Understanding social media logic. *Media and Communication*, 1(1), 2–14. doi:10.12924/mac2013.01010002

van Dijck, J., & Poell, T. (2015). Social media and the transformation of public space. *Social Media +*

Society, 1(2), 2056305115622482. https://doi.org/10.1177/2056305115622482

Vitkauskaitė, E. (2010). Overview of research on cross-cultural impact on social networking sites. *Economics and Management*, 15, 844–848. Accessed on March 6, 2023, at https://www.researchgate.net/profile/Elena-Vitkauskaite/publication/228418032_Overview_of_Research_on_Cross-Cultural_Impact_on_Social_Networking_Sites/links/0fcfd50b55632ae649000000/Overview-of-Research-on-Cross-Cultural-Impact-on-Social-Networking-Sites.pdf.

Vodanovich, S., McKenna, B., & Cai, W. (2017, June). *Cultural values inherent in the design of social media platforms: A case study of WeChat. 30TH Bled eConference: Digital Transformation – From Connecting Things to Transforming Our Lives*, June 18 – 21, 2017, Bled, Slovenia. https://doi.org/10.18690/978-961-286-043-1.43

Waltorp, K. (2015). Keeping cool, staying virtuous: Social media and the composite habitus of young Muslim women in Copenhagen. *MedieKultur: Journal of Media and Communication Research*, 31(58), 49–67. https://doi.org/10.7146/mediekultur.v31i58.19373

Wang, C. (2012). Using Facebook for cross-cultural collaboration: The experience of students from Taiwan. *Educational Media International*, 49(1), 63–76. https://doi.org/10.1080/09523987.2012.662625

Wang, X., & Liu, Z. (2019). Online engagement in social media: A cross-cultural comparison. *Computers in Human Behavior*, 97, 137–150. https://doi.org/10.1016/j.chb.2019.03.014.

Wang, Y. (2019). Local identity in a global city: Hong Kong localist movement on social media. *Critical Studies in Media Communication*, 36(5), 419–433. https://doi.org/10.1080/15295036.2019.1652837

Wellman, B. (2002). Little boxes, globalization, and networked individualism. In M. Tanabe, P. Besselaar, & T. Ishida (Eds.), *Digital cities II – Second Kyoto workshop on digital cities* (pp. 10–25). Springer Verlag.

Yoon, K. (2018). Multicultural digital media practices of 1.5-generation Korean immigrants in Canada. *Asian and Pacific Migration Journal*, 27(2), 148–165. https://doi.org/10.1177/0117196818766906.

Zhou, Y. & Sun, J. (2020). Using Social Media to Promote Intercultural Communication Between Chinese and American University Students. *Chinese Journal of Applied Linguistics*, 43(2), 169–187. https://doi.org/10.1515/CJAL-2020-0011

Contexts

The channels of messages that we discussed in part three are used in different contexts and present us with several issues. In this section, specifically, we will deal with contexts of cross-cultural adjustment, relationships and conflict, the political context, and organizational contexts.

Chapter 12 introduces the context of cultural adaptation. Many people travel abroad, so we should know the types of symptoms that accompany "culture shock." However, we note that cultural transition need not be a bad thing, as it also brings us personal growth. We present—and discount—the commonly used "U-curve" or stage model of acculturation that many universities use to guide their students, and present other ways to understand both going abroad and coming home. Much of what helps one adjust is also what makes one a competent communicator, and travel experience often makes one more interculturally competent, so we also address the idea of cultural competence in this chapter.

Another context in which we experience intercultural communication is relationships, so we address this in Chapter 13. Specifically, we compare different views of how relationships might grow between people of different cultures and what issues might be present in such relationships, as well as different cultural patterns an intercultural couple might adopt. A key element in most relationships is how partners resolve conflict. While conflict resolution occurs both in relationships and organizations, we look at cross-cultural aspects of conflict management, as it is integral to understanding family, friends, and romantic relationships. Finally, we consider how, in most cultures, certain types of relationships are stigmatized.

Chapter 14 presents a context of communication central to our focus on political and civic engagement: political communication. We introduce the notion of politics and its connection to culture. Here you will read about important parts of our political process that shape the cultures

Intercultural Communication for Everyday Life, Second Edition. John R. Baldwin, Alberto González, Nettie Brock, Ming Xie, and Chin-Chung Chao.
© 2024 John Wiley & Sons Ltd. Published 2024 by John Wiley & Sons Ltd.
Companion Website: http://www.wiley.com/go/baldwin2e

in which we live—hopefully for the better—such as social movements and political leadership. We include examples of specific social movements, such as the Green Belt movement in Africa and the immigrant rights and anti-racist movements in the United States. There are also examples of types of leaders and specific political leaders who have sought to change culture and the world in positive ways.

Finally, Chapter 15 presents the organizational context. The concepts in this chapter may apply in some ways to a variety of contexts, including religious, medical, or educational contexts, or even social organizations such as sports teams, fraternities or sororities, or clubs. After reviewing the important role of work in our lives, we explore how globalization is changing the culture of work around the world. We give some attention to different aspects of cultural variation in things such as organizational structures, values, and behavior. Finally, tying this context back to the civic and political engagement focus of this book, we describe and provide examples of corporate social responsibility.

Chapter 12

Adaptation and intercultural competence: How can I be effective in a new culture?

Chapter objectives

After this chapter, you should be able to:

→ Explain the notion of culture shock, its symptoms, and some basic causes

→ Compare the U-curve notion of adjustment with alternative views of how adjustment happens

→ List at least three reasons why coming home from another culture may be difficult

→ Differentiate between psychological adjustment, behavioral adaptation, and assimilation

→ Define intercultural communication competence, and list three main areas that influence it

Intercultural Communication for Everyday Life, Second Edition. John R. Baldwin, Alberto González, Nettie Brock, Ming Xie, and Chin-Chung Chao.
© 2024 John Wiley & Sons Ltd. Published 2024 by John Wiley & Sons Ltd.
Companion Website: http://www.wiley.com/go/baldwin2e

erhaps you have traveled to another country or region during school holidays or as an exchange student. Maybe you visited a different culture within your own country, such as on a service project. In such cases, you may have experienced difficulty. However, authors who study cross-cultural transitions suggest that difficulties we feel during short-term trips differ from those felt by **sojourners**—those who travel abroad for a longer time, say one to five years, with intent to return home (Kim, 2005), or who move to another culture permanently (**immigrants**), perhaps involuntarily (**refugees**). Janet Bennett (1977) suggests that when there is a "loss of a familiar frame of reference"—whether that is a move to another area, the loss of a loved one, or a major job shift—there are both loss and change: "Culture shock bears a remarkable resemblance to tensions and anxieties we face whenever change threatens the stability of our lives" (p. 45). Unlike some popular usage, scholars usually reserve the idea of "culture shock" for the longer-term adjustment process.

Anyone who travels to another culture, within or outside of their nation of origin, goes through some form of transition difficulty. But transition experiences are useful, as they help to make us more complex and complete individuals, helping us to be better intercultural communicators. The purpose of this chapter is to introduce notions of cultural adjustment and competence and to provide hints about how to recognize stress during transition and make the most of it.

Cross-cultural adaptation: How can I better adjust to a new culture?

People have different experiences when they travel abroad. If you are a university student, you know that the same is true of those who go through the transition of moving to a new university (Figure 12.1). But why do we have stress in such transitions, and why do some people process it differently than others? In this chapter, we summarize the notion of cultural adjustment and some models to explain it and explain some things that might impact it. This understanding, in turn, should help us find ways to deal with the stress of transition to a new culture.

Figure 12.1 After declining sharply during the COVID-19 epidemic, (Hendley, 2022), the number of international students traveling between cultures continues again on the rise. Pre-2019, according to UNESCO statistics, there were over 6 million international students worldwide (Inbound internationally mobile students, 2023).
Source: Michael Dwyer/Alamy.

Adjustment and culture shock: Defining the terms

On the surface, cross-cultural **adjustment** is a simple concept, referring to the process one goes through in adjusting to another culture (Kim, 2001). Young Yun Kim (2005) uses this term to encompass a variety of related terms, each with its own nuance—like "culture shock, acculturation, adjustment, assimilation, integration, and adaptation" (p. 376). The general idea of cross-cultural adjustment, according to Kim, is one of "unlearning" one culture and learning another. As we grow up in our native cultures, we go through a process of **enculturation**, learning our own culture. **Acculturation** is the learning and adapting of some amount of the values, behaviors, and ways of thinking of the new culture (Kim, 2001); at the same time, we "unlearn" or lose some of our own culture, a process known as **deculturation**. **Assimilation** is when one adopts the behaviors and ways of thinking of a host culture. ·

What do you think? To what degree do you think someone has to "lose" their own culture in order to be effective in a new culture? Can someone know and live in two different cultures? Why or why not? Does your answer differ for a sojourner as opposed to an immigrant or refugee? How can or should groups negotiate their cultural uniqueness with their sense of identity and unity with the larger nation or culture?

These terms lead to new questions: Do we ever learn enough of the other culture to get by, but deliberately keep parts of our own culture? Can we learn about the other culture and still feel miserable and depressed, as we feel we are not being true to ourselves? Or can we go about blissfully ignorant of the new culture, but be totally comfortable, even confident in our own arrogant belief that our own culture is better? Jeffrey Ady (1995) suggests that there are major problems in the study of cross-cultural adjustment, as researchers define and measure "adjustment" in different ways.

Whatever adjustment is, most scholars agree that we experience tension and discomfort when we lose the familiar cues we are used to in our environment (Hall, 1973). Kalvaro Oberg (1960) coined the term **culture shock** to refer to a sense of "anxiety that results from losing all of our familiar signs and symbols of social intercourse" (p. 177). People often see culture shock as an emotional response to the loss of one's own culture (Adler, 1975), often resulting in symptoms of disorientation, sadness or anger, grief, nostalgia, or even psychosomatic disorders. But how does this culture shock occur? Can we predict how we might experience it?

Models of cultural adjustment

The U-curve Based on a study of Norwegian Fulbright scholars, Sverre Lysgaard (1955) developed a well-known model of cultural adjustment, the **U-curve** of adjustment, which suggests that travelers go through stages (Lysgaard saw three, though many today speak of four, Figure 12.2). The first stage of euphoria, often called the **honeymoon stage**, is a time of happiness and excitement as one first arrives at a new culture. Everything is new, and even aspects that may not be as enjoyable are reframed in terms of the great experience of traveling to

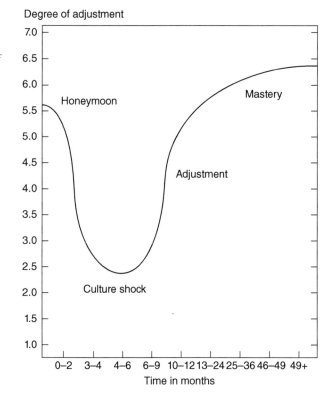

Figure 12.2 Even though the U-curve model of adjustment seems to make sense, much modern research questions its accuracy.
Source: Liu & Lee, 2008, reproduced by permission of Emerald Group Publishing Ltd.

a new culture. The second stage, often called the **crisis stage**, represents a time of difficulty as one confronts ongoing cultural differences and loss of expected cues. At this stage, travelers often go through fight or flight (Dodd, 1998). With "fight," they lash out against the culture or act out, perhaps turning to alcohol, drugs, or other escape mechanisms, or complaining about the culture and making negative comparisons to their own supposedly superior culture. Others choose "flight," running away from the culture. Travelers might spend lots of time alone, get depressed, or spend time only with people from their own culture. A third possibility is for the traveler to "go native," to totally accept the new culture while rejecting the culture of origin.

The crisis stage is said to occur often between three and six months—so it is different from stress one might have about difficulties on a short-term trip. It comes from a longer-term lack of cues and disorientation, as the cultural frameworks of the traveler melt and reform. Most travelers work through this to the third stage, the **adjustment stage** or "flex" stage (Dodd, 1998), which reflects a growing sense of understanding and ability to live and succeed in the new culture. Finally, one reaches a sense of balance, of full effectiveness. People often call this the **integration stage**, as travelers take the new culture and made it a part of themselves.

The model makes sense of the struggles many people feel during cultural transitions, and it reflects several truths about adaptation that we agree with. First, all travelers go through some sort of stress when moving to a new culture, whether around the world or from the country to the big city or one region to another. Second, adjustment is often uncomfortable, leading to feelings of loss, anger, or powerlessness in the new culture. Third, the process of adjustment takes time. One should not expect quick results, and one should expect the long-term process of adjustment to be different from the momentary setbacks or negative experiences one might have on a tourist trip. The U-curve receives tremendous support, with university travel programs, international consultants, and businesses training their travelers that these are the stages through which all travelers pass.

Unfortunately, it lacks research support, and scholars today are proposing new models to make sense of adjustment. As early as a generation ago, scholars began to debunk the U-curve. Austin Church, in 1982, reviewing 150 articles on cultural adjustment, noted that "phase" or "stage" models like the U-curve had only limited support. While most travelers experience the symptoms, they might not experience the stages in order. Some might move forward and then back. And, although the process of adjustment does take time, it is difficult to predict *when* travelers might experience shock, as travelers work through the process at different speeds. In a later study, Daniel Kealey (1989) found that out of 277 technical advisors in 20 developing nations, only about 10% experienced adjustment in what one might call a "U-curve." In addition, many scholars have discussed a wide array of factors that lead to improved cross-cultural adjustment, such as previous travel experience, knowledge of the language, willingness to travel, flexibility, age (with children adjusting quicker than adults), and so on. The growing list of variables and the inadequacy of the U-curve have led authors to propose other models for adjustment. We will consider only two approaches here.

What do You Think? Look up online travel guides or travel sites, such as StudentsAbroad. com (http://studentsabroad.com), or the Worldwide Classroom (http://www.worldwide. edu/index.html). Consider college websites for international students, including that of your university. Go to http://en.wikipedia.org/wiki/Culture_shock at Wikipedia. Do any of these teach the U-curve as if it were fact? Do they provide any word on the evidence that challenges the U-curve? What might be the implications of teaching travelers that they will all go through these phases?

Kim's theory of cross-cultural adjustment   Young Kim (2001), after years of research with many different populations, especially Korean immigrants to the United States, derived a theory of cross-cultural adjustment that builds upon our understanding of adjustment in several ways. Whereas much previous work on "culture shock" treated it largely in terms of psychological variables, Kim (2005) sees adaptation as deeply related to communication. It is through communication that the host environment pressures or encourages the traveler. And it is through communication that travelers either cling to their own cultural group or move into the new culture. Travelers need to become involved in face-to-face communication, such as spending time with host nationals and watching host-culture media (some media are better than others!). But, contrary to many writers, Kim suggests that ongoing communication with one's own group and media from one's own culture can also make adjustment easier, as long as that communication helps the traveler to build a bridge into the new culture.

Similar to previous approaches, her theory considers aspects of travelers that help them to adjust, such as flexibility to change and strength of character (for example, the ability to deal with difficult situations). A second contribution is that Kim looks beyond psychological variables that might influence adjustment to see it happening within an environment. If a host culture is hostile to a group of sojourners (for example, with prejudice or stereotypes), that may work against adjustment. This is an important consideration: Often, we assume adjustment is in the power of the traveler, but social and economic constraints, including low-paying jobs in the language of one's home culture, lack of opportunity, or prejudice from dominant culture, may get in the way of someone's adjustment. Pressure to conform could increase adjustment, if adjustment refers to one's ability to follow the rules of the culture, but it may not lead to psychological health. If one moves into a situation where there are many from the person's own group (high ethnic group strength), this, in turn, would slow down assimilation, but one might feel happier. The tension between these variables begins to suggest that there are different types of adjustment, as pressure to conform might increase assimilation but be psychologically stressful.

A third major contribution by Kim (2005) is that, unlike the notion of "culture shock," Kim sees potential in cultural transition. Adjustment is like starting a rigorous exercise program. At first, you must break down muscles in order to rebuild them. In the same way, the traveler *must* go through stress in order to break down old ways of thinking. Adaptation leads to growth, making travelers stronger than before. Disagreeing with the U-Curve, Kim sees adaptation as an ongoing process in which travelers continue to face new challenges, each bringing more growth, following what Kim calls a **stress-adaptation-growth dynamic**. Adjustment is cyclical, with increased adaptation over time, but in a two-steps-forward-one-step-back, or a "draw-back-to-leap" pattern (Kim, 2005, p. 384; see Figure 12.3). Because stress can be useful for travelers' growth, we prefer to talk about "cultural adjustment" rather than "culture shock."

Figure 12.3 Kim (2005) feels that cultural adjustment does not follow a strict U-curve, but, instead, it is cyclical, as the traveler faces new stresses.
Source: Reproduced from Kim & Ruben, 1988, p. 312, by permission of Sage Publications, Inc.

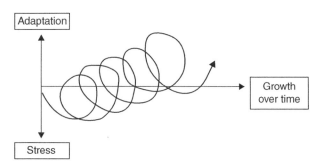

Break it down

A big part of sojourners' adjustment deals with host receptivity and the chances sojourners have to interact positively with people from the host culture. Pressure to conform may help newcomers assimilate to a new culture, but it might also make psychological adjustment more difficult.

What types of sojourners are there in your university, workplace, or community? Take a concrete step to show them your receptivity to them, to give them opportunities to interact with you, and to make their psychological adjustment easier. What can you do to be a positive part of their adjustment?

Recent research continues to support different aspects of Kim's theory. For example, Yang Soo Kim and Young Yun Kim (2022) surveyed business travelers in South Korea and Indonesia, working in each other's countries. The results showed that people with greater communication competence (see below in this chapter) and who engaged in more communication with host nationals had greater psychological health. At the same time, as the sojourners perceived host culture individuals to be more receptive to them, their interpersonal communication with those of the host culture and their psychological health both improved. One study (Han et al., 2022) has validated that certain personal dispositions were related to greater psychological health, including being open to new experiences, wanting to learn about the new culture, and having emotional stability (similar to Kim's "flexibility" and "personality strength") but also extraversion, conscientiousness, and agreeableness. Finally, a study of Bosnian refugees in St. Louis (United States) showed that increased communication with (and ties to) members of the host culture, as well as media use, helped sojourners adjust to the new culture, as did preparedness to change (Karamehic-Muratovic et al., 2016). And other research has extended Kim's recommendation of considering the role of media in cultural adjustment, noting how sojourners feel that social media can often help them to adjust, though if through that media, one is reinforcing and maintaining connections mostly to people from the home culture, social media can get in the way of cultural adjustment (Croucher & Rahmani, 2015; Sandel, 2014). Social media are so important in working for or against cultural adjustment now that some university abroad programs give tips on using social adjustment wisely for cultural adaptation (see more on social media in Chapter 11).

Different domains of adjustment   Several writers now argue that we should not think of adjustment as a single thing, but that there might be different "domains" or areas of adjustment (Black et al., 1991; Selmer & Fenner, 2009). These might be different areas of demand, such as work or school versus relationships, where someone could be performing well in school, but have poor relationships (Ady, 1995). One study found that, as international students spent more years in Japan and learned the language better, they could accomplish tasks better but had less-fulfilling relationships with the Japanese (Tanaka et al., 1994). Possibly, as language improves, Japanese hosts remove social support from travelers, who realize that they are still "outsiders" to the culture. Colleen Ward has done extensive work to outline different types of adjustment: **psychological adjustment**, "associated with psychological well-being or emotional satisfaction," and **sociocultural adjustment**, which deals with one's ability to "fit in" and get tasks done within one's environment (Ward et al., 1998, p. 279). The first dimension deals with stress and coping, and the second with learning the culture.

With this in mind, we offer more refined definitions: **Cross-cultural adjustment** deals with one's coping or psychological health when moving to a new culture (Kim, 2001; Ward, 2004). **Cross-cultural adaptation** refers to one's ability to negotiate the culture to accomplish tasks (shopping, etc.), to "fit in" by adapting some degree of aspects of the host culture (Ward, 2004, p. 186), possibly forming stable and functional relationships (Kim, 2001). Ward and her colleagues have done many studies on the two dimensions, noting that they are related to different things we encounter in a new culture. For example, a study of international aid workers in Nepal (Ward & Rana-Deuba, 1999) found that those who continued to identify with their home culture experienced less depression in Nepal, but those who identified more with the new culture had better sociocultural adaptation.

Writers continue to develop new understandings of adaptation. For example, Melissa Curtin (2010) discusses how previous literature mistakenly treats adaptation as a one-way process, with the traveler adapting to the culture; in fact, both parties adapt to each other, though in unequal power relationships. In a related way, Antonio Tomas De la Garza (2023) introduces a theory of differential adaptation to show the "messiness" of the immigration experience. The theory explores how "individuals from similar cultures might experience and react to the assimilative forces of culture in different ways" (p. 134). Other writers highlight problems in most communication theory that have implications for the theories here. In terms of Miike's (2007) critique of Western theories (see Chapter 1), these theories focus on the individual, independence, reason, and self-enhancement. Kim's theory talks about how adjustment aids individual development; and all the theories we have covered here focus on pragmatic adjustment (getting around) and psychological wellbeing of individuals. At the same time, Kim's theory considers aspects both of context (pressure to conform and the degree to which different contexts welcome specific groups of strangers) and of interconnectedness to others in the process of adaptation.

Rethinking acculturation: What happens when cultural groups live side by side?

In the Nepal study, the researchers (Ward & Rana-Deuba, 1999) relied heavily upon a conceptualization of acculturation provided by John Berry (2004). In this framework, while acculturation refers, most precisely, to one's acceptance of aspects of a culture and identification with that culture, Berry suggests that we should not think of this as straightforward adaptation. Rather, one can adopt different elements of the culture. In some cases, individuals can fully embrace and identify with both cultures (**integration,** or **biculturalism**); in other cases, they can deliberately resist the new culture and maintain elements of their original culture. Or individuals can become **marginal**, where they end up identifying with neither the host nor the original culture, often ceasing to want any interaction. Acculturation is often measured by one's acceptance of the new culture's language, use of host culture literature, friendship networks, food choice, recreational activities, and so on.

Like Kim (2005), who suggests that sojourner adjustment is impacted by the host culture's acceptance of the traveler, Richard Bourhis and his colleagues (1997) suggest that we cannot think of the minority member's acculturation as based only on an individual's adjustment. We must also consider whether the people in the majority accept or expect integration of the minority group. The dominant culture has a part in the sojourner's approach by means of their attitudes and behaviors toward strangers and minorities—to separate them intentionally or unintentionally (**segregation**), allow them to maintain both group and new/dominant culture identities (**multiculturalism**, often called **cultural pluralism**), expect them to lose their own cultural identity to become like the mainstream (**melting pot**, commonly called the assimilation model), or simply negate their existence, having no relations with them (**exclusion)** (Sam & Berry, 2010; see Figure 12.4).

In sum, recent researchers see cultural adaptation in a more complex way than the U-Curve. Many immigrants *are* acculturating, but not to dominant culture. If there is a developed co-cultural group in a country, new immigrants might adjust to that group instead of the dominant group (neither of which option is necessarily bad either for the society or for the individual's psychological health)."

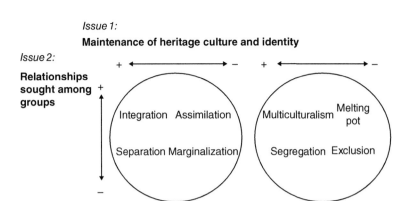

Issue 1:

Maintenance of heritage culture and identity

Issue 2:

Relationships sought among groups

Integration   Assimilation

Separation Marginalization

Multiculturalism   Melting pot

Segregation   Exclusion

Attitudes of
immigrant groups

Attitudes of
larger society

Figure 12.4 John Berry suggests that people traveling to another culture or living in a dominant culture as minority members can highlight different identities. But the dominant culture also exerts pressure on the identity of the traveler.

Source: Reproduced from Sam & Berry, 2010, p. 477, by permission of Sage Publications, Inc.

Break it down

Refugees constitute a specific type of traveler. Often, refugees move to communities with people-descended from the same culture (or with other refugee communities). The United Nations Refugee Agency (2022) reports that in 2021, over 89 million people were "forcibly displaced" around the world, including 25 million refugees and 53 million internally displaced people. As of May, 2022, the total number had increased to 100 million people, more than Germany's population. Research a refugee group (the closer to your home, the better). What are the social conditions that created the refugee problem? What social issues, conditions, barriers, and benefits face the refugees in their new home? How might this relate to their adaptation to the new culture? Share the news with your friends or your class.

This relates to the idea of cultural pluralism—the idea that members of co-cultural groups should embrace or be allowed to have their own culture. Proponents of this view may accept the notion of "unity" within a national "culture," but may feel that such unity is not based on cultural homogeneity. In some cases, members of cultural groups actively resist identification with the dominant culture or embrace what we call **selective adaptation**—the acceptance of some elements of the dominant culture but not others, adopting parts of the dominant culture such as work and school norms, but emphasizing their culture of origin in their home, social, or religious lives (Roberts, 2007), similar to de la Garza's (2023) notion of "differential adaptation."

We see such adaptation among many (but certainly not all) Asian Indian Americans. Radha Hegde (1998) interviewed Asian Indian women about the different ways the women negotiated sex, race, and cultural identities. In some cases, their choices were related to stereotypes and racism they felt from the dominant culture; in other places, such as the preservation of Indianness in the home, it was to provide a cultural haven from the dominant culture. Indians within America might maintain their religion and festivals, form cricket clubs to play in the parks on Saturdays, and continue to wear traditional Indian clothes, even while acting very "American" in the workplace.

At the same time, Asian Indians may share cultural similarities with "PIOs" (Persons of Indian Origin) throughout the world, from Toronto to Trinidad, from Uganda to the United Arab Emirates. To this end, Rona Halualani and Jolanta Drzewiecka (2008) discuss the notion of **diaspora**, when a group from a specific homeland is spread out across a wide geographic area, such as the Jewish diaspora. Among Polish identities, for example, there is a way of talking about Polish identity that links Polish-descended peoples anywhere to "romanticized notions of primordial descent" (p. 60). These ways of talking and thinking (discourses) link Polish émigrés everywhere to a certain notion of Polishness that provides a "reassuring bedrock" that sustains them through difficult times and cultural and geographic changes (p. 60). As diasporic groups rub together against local cultures, each takes from the other in cultural blends that reflect **hybridity** (Drzewiecka & Halualani, 2002). However, such blends are always negotiated, with the dominant and "immigrant" communities having different types of power. In most cases, the dominant culture picks the terms in ways that benefit its own social structure and cultural privilege.

As we see, cultural adjustment—either through travel abroad or co-cultures living together within the same geographic space—is anything but simple. In some ways, one's individual acculturation, as well as the "assimilation" of a group within a community, is predictable. In other ways, it is negotiated through communication, always shifting and changing, and rife with power relations in relation to dominant cultures. Our understanding of adaptation and acculturation can benefit from scientific, humanistic, and critical approaches we discuss in Chapter 2.

Coming home: Will it be as easy as it sounds?

At the end of the *Lord of the Rings* trilogy by J.R.R. Tolkien (1955/1965), as Frodo returns home after destroying the Ring, he has a quiet chat with Gandalf, the wizard. "There is no real going back," Frodo says. "Though I may come to the Shire, it will not be the same; for I will not be the same. I am wounded with knife, sting, and tooth, and with a long burden. Where shall I find rest?" (p. 268). Gandalf does not answer him. We would think that coming home from another culture should be easy. After all, we know our own culture, our friends, and our family—don't we?

The return home to one's culture is often so difficult, someone created the term, **return culture shock**. Just as we believe that "cultural adjustment" is a better way to think of the transition process of traveling abroad, we refer to the experience of returning home as **return cultural adjustment**. This refers to the process of adjusting to one's culture psychologically and behaviorally when returning home. Since the travelers likely know their way around, sociocultural adjustment may not be as difficult as the adjustment abroad, though people have to adapt behaviors and may, in fact, experience only partial "re-acculturation." It seems that psychological adjustment—including depression and overall wellbeing—may be the most important in returning home.

The process and nature of return cultural adjustment

John Gullahorn and Jeane Gullahorn (1963) extended the idea of the U-curve to include a new series of stages when one returns to a home culture. Just as the real stress of cultural transition (whether it happens in a "U" shape or not) occurs over a longer stay, we would expect the stages of return adjustment also to only take place, or at least be amplified, after a longer stay. Gullahorn and Gullahorn added a second "U" to the first, to make what they called the **W-curve** of return adjustment (Figure 12.5). The authors argue that returning sojourners may feel the same symptoms of "alienation, anomie, and rejection" that they may have felt traveling abroad (p. 33). The idea of the W-curve is that, as sojourners anticipate coming home, they are excited, looking forward to some of the things they missed, seeing people they love. It is like a new honeymoon stage of anticipation. After some time, the sojourner may feel a sense of loss or nostalgia for the foreign culture, sometimes even glamorizing in their mind the less enjoyable aspects of the travel abroad. Most people "adapt," coming through the process to reach a stage of functioning in the new culture.

Just as with cultural adjustment for those who live abroad, scholars have tried to understand why return adjustment is difficult. Margaret Pitts (2016), based on 24 in-depth interviews of U.S. American college students returning home from study-abroad programs. Pitts describes, using Kim's theory noted above, the emotions and stress leading up to the return home; their difficulty with former routines, feeling of difference from other Americans, and ambivalence towards the USA upon return; and the tension upon returning home between needing to share their experience abroad but finding it difficult to explain, especially in the perception of a lack of support by

Figure 12.5 The W-curve. Many international employers and schools, such as the Munich Business School, provide travelers with some adaptation of the W-curve to explain what they might expect when they return home. Source: Image used courtesy of A. Uwaje.

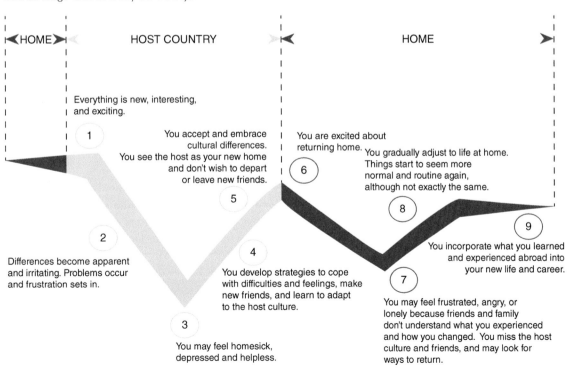

those in the home culture: "Returnees were disappointed in the level of sincere interest conveyed by their home network and 'irritated' at the kinds of questions people asked" (p. 431), including questions based on stereotypes of or lack of knowledge about cultures outside of the United States. This study sums up briefly factors others have cited for difficulties in returning home:

→ *A change in ourselves and others*: Because we have been in close contact with another culture over a period of time, we often change. Clyde Austin (1987) suggests that value change is a main reason for difficulty in return adjustment. Shelley Smith (1998) suggests that both the travel abroad and the return home should be understood in terms of identity change. A woman from a culture where women are protected by men, but with less ostensible rights, might return home and feel frustrated at her lack of liberty, just as a woman from a culture where women are ostensibly liberated might return home from the other culture feeling a lack of protection.

→ *A change in relationships*: Not only are we changing but so are the people we leave at home. Judith Martin (1986), for example, found that students who had studied abroad felt closer to their parents upon returning home than to their friends. Perhaps younger people, who are still in a time of development, are more susceptible to value change. We both remember what we were like at departure, but when we reunite, we are not the same. Our parents, however, may know us more deeply, so the relationships remain stable or even strengthen. The ease of online (e.g., video) and new (text/video messaging) communication may ease the impact of travel abroad on friendships. Research by Ming Xie and Chin-Chung "Joy" Chau (2022), for example, found that while social media helped Asian students in the United States meet material needs and develop social capital, several of the participants relied strongly on social media to gain social support from friends and family at home. This might ease the return home—but it might limit development of relationships in the host culture, something that most research has noted is a struggle for international students.

→ *Unrealistic expectations and disillusionment*: It is a common understanding that having realistic (but overall positive) expectations helps our travel abroad. But often when we come home, we find ourselves ambivalent, even critical, of our home culture. Asako Uehara (1986) found that 40% of her U.S. participants who had engaged in international student exchange "had become aware that the United States is a big, affluent, and powerful country in the world" (p. 430); 66% spoke objectively about the host culture but seemed freer to criticize the United States.

→ *Lack of appreciation*: Many who travel abroad feel that when they return, people do not really want to know about their experiences. Even some who ask about our experiences seem to tire after a few minutes of explanation. Often, employees who travel abroad grow frustrated with the narrow-mindedness (or lack of a broader cultural worldview) of their colleagues (Harris & Moran, 1996), and many times companies do not seem to want to take advantage of new knowledge and ways of thinking that employees bring back. As a result, many employees leave the company that sent them abroad within a year of returning home.

One of our students, Kyle, came back to the United States from a semester in Ireland. At one point, he got into an argument with his family, because he claimed that, based on its consumption of a large portion of the world's energy resources and slowness to adopt recycling, the United States was wasteful. His family claimed adamantly that the United States is not a wasteful culture. His father asked, "If you liked it so much in Ireland, why don't you just go back?" Kyle tried to show his pictures to his family, and a relative told him, "You don't need to bring those out. No one really wants to see them." While this might be an extreme case, in many cases, travelers have a hard time fitting back in, especially if returning from a large metropolitan area abroad to a small-town culture in their own country.

Break it down

Returning sojourners often face the problem that people really don't want to just sit and listen to them. If you know someone who has traveled and lived abroad recently, invite the person out for a cup of tea/coffee, a soda, or a meal. Ask to look at her or his pictures. Sit. Listen. Ask questions.

Making the going and coming home easier

Several authors outline success strategies for easing the transition when one travels abroad. Philip Harris and Robert Moran (1996), for example, suggest cultural preparation, learning about communication in the new culture, interacting with host nationals as much as possible, being open-minded and even adventurous, being patient, having realistic expectations, and framing the experience as a challenge. Shelley Smith (2002) adds that we should try to suspend judgment on things that are unfamiliar to us, accept the need to retreat from time to time to embrace our emotions, and be willing to talk to people in our host culture about misunderstandings. Kim's (2005) theory, which we described earlier, suggests the use of host media that familiarize us with the culture as well as using interaction and media with people from our own group to serve as a bridge. We add to these the need to consider not only the needs of the traveler, but also those of partners and children, as research has found that a spouse's expectations of a sojourn as well as the spouse's adaptation once there, are related to important aspects of the adjustment of expatriate managers (Black & Stephens, 1989).

While many companies and universities today now provide training for students and employees traveling abroad, it is much less common for them to provide training on the return home. As noted, return-home adjustment varies from person to person. While most may adjust to coming home easily enough, some may seek counseling to deal with depression or related issues. Unfortunately, returned sojourners are often reluctant to seek counseling (Gaw, 2000). Judith Martin and Teresa Harrell (2004) list things that sojourners can do prior even to leaving for another culture, while they are there, in preparation for the return home, and once they get home. One of these strategies, no doubt made much easier with Internet chat and video capabilities, is to maintain contact with the home culture so one knows what is happening with the culture and in the lives of loved ones while away. Finally, sojourners can often seek to become "mediating persons"—bridges to help those in their home cultures either understand different cultures or prepare to travel themselves (Wilson, 1985).

Again, these points echo the experience of one of our ex-students, Chérise, who upon returning to small-town midwest culture, could not cope with the local mindset. We recommended she travel to a big city and meet other former travelers and international people. She now works with children in a multi-ethnic, multinational school, travels widely, and is very satisfied negotiating both her own culture and other cultures. At first, she took what Bradford "J." Hall (2005) calls an **alienated approach** to returning abroad, missing her culture abroad, being bitter and critical about her home culture, as opposed to a **resocialized approach** taken by some who quickly shed their abroad culture and re-adopt their home culture. Now Chérise has moved to a **proactive approach** that sees the good (but is not afraid to address the bad) in both her home and former host cultures.

Intercultural communication competence: How can I get the job done… and still be liked?

Much of this book could be about being a competent communicator when traveling to or working with people from other cultures. But as we will see, intercultural communication competence has come to have some very specific meanings in the area of intercultural communication. Second, in some ways, it is closely related to adaptation, as one often gains competence through traveling to and adapting to one or more different cultures.

Understanding intercultural competence

Intercultural competence has become a major focus in mainstream academic and professional thought (Deardorff, 2009), as administrators and trainers seek to find ways to develop "intercultural sensitivity." But the exact definitions of terms like intercultural "competence," "effectiveness," or "sensitivity" has received much debate. Hiroko Abe and Richard Wiseman (1983) isolated five aspects of "effectiveness:" The ability "(1) to communicate interpersonally, (2) to adjust to different cultures, (3) to deal with different societal systems, (4) to establish interpersonal relationships, and (5) to understand others" (p. 63). In a later study, Wiseman and some colleagues (1989) measured "competence" in terms of one's culture-specific understanding, culture-general understanding, and positive feeling for the other culture, finding that things such as ethnocentrism, level of knowledge about the culture, and perceived social distance from the other culture influenced these three aspects. Brian Spitzberg (1994) lists dozens of different skills and attitudes that researchers have linked with intercultural competence and effectiveness. The list includes things such as charisma, other-centeredness, flexibility, empathy, non-ethnocentrism, personality strength, optimism, self-efficacy, and ability to facilitate communication.

Brian Spitzberg and William Cupach's (1984) book, *Interpersonal Communication Competence*, has framed much of the recent discussion of competence. First, the authors drew a clear line between effectiveness and competence. **Communication effectiveness** refers specifically to one's ability to accomplish tasks—that is, the "achievement of interaction goals" (p. 102). But **communication competence** is to be effective while also being appropriate to the rules of the situation (**communication appropriateness**), including preserving relationships, maintaining face or decorum, abiding by contextual rules, and so on. We have all known speakers who "get the job done" (effectiveness), such as persuading people to adopt some proposal, but who leave a trail of hurt feelings and anger. We also know those who follow all the rules of social communication (appropriateness) but cannot clinch a sales deal, get a date, or reach other communicative goals. To be competent, then, one must be both effective and appropriate. The second major contribution of this work was to conceptualize the vast array of aspects of competence and effectiveness into three main categories: knowledge, motivation, and skills.

Spitzberg (1994) provides a model of **intercultural communication competence** based on these notions. He sees some aspects of competence present within the knowledge, motivation, and skills of the communicator (such as valuing the communication of others—a motivation, knowledge of "how to communicate well" (p. 351) or of task-specific details, or the skills of knowing how to gain knowledge of the other culture), of the episode (for example, whether or not communicators meet one anothers' expectations), and of the relationship (for example, whether the communicators find mutual attraction or build trust with each other).

Many intercultural communication scholars, even if they do not adopt Spitzberg's model, now frame competence in terms of appropriateness and effectiveness. Guo-Ming Chen and William Starosta (2008) start with this definition of competence and then break competence down into several types, including social competence, linguistic competence, communicative competence, and relational competence. Chen and Starosta's (2008) model includes three dimensions, similar to knowledge, motivation, and skills. The affective dimension, intercultural sensitivity, focuses on emotions and feelings, including a respect for cultural differences. The cognitive/knowledge dimension, intercultural sensitivity, deals with awareness of difference; and the behavioral/skill dimension pertains to task accomplishment in intercultural situations. And Lily Arasaratnam's (2006) approach includes "empathy, motivation, attitude towards other cultures, experience, and listening (interaction involvement)" (p. 94).

Peter Adler (1977) coined a classic term that relates to intercultural competence: the "multicultural man," or, as we shall call it, the **multicultural person**. This new type of person is someone who can serve as a catalyst for dialogue between cultures. They are able to move easily between different cultures, like a surfer going between waves. In a sense, the person ceases to belong fully to any culture, but instead "lives on the boundary" (p. 26). The person is marginal, never fully belonging to one culture or the other, fitting into any culture, but outside of all of them (Bennett, 1993). This relates to a notion that Young Yun Kim and Brent Ruben (1988) introduce in their theory of intercultural transformation. They define **intercultural transformation** as a process people go through in which they learn new ways of thinking, feeling, and behaving beyond the "limits of their original culture" (p. 306). They argue that individuals who have a wide range of intercultural experiences, including travel (even adjustment to multiple cultures over time), develop a new repertoire of ways to think, act, and feel. They develop a "broadened and deepened understanding of the human condition and cultural differences that are larger than any one cultural perspective" (p. 314). The notions of the multicultural person and intercultural transformation, then, link to cultural and return adjustment, because they suggest that as we travel and return (and travel and return, and travel and return), we become more complete, broad-minded, and effective individuals even within our own cultures.

Beyond the multicultural person: Intergroup effectiveness

Of course, like notions of adjustment and acculturation, the ideas of the multicultural person and intercultural communicator competence are more complicated than they first seem, in two ways. First, many scholars who have researched the notion of intercultural competence have explained it as an idea that should apply across cultures. That is, if a manager, Rachel, has the particular sets of knowledge and skills that would make her effective in one culture, then she should be effective in any culture. Of course, researchers do not believe that any one person would be high on every single one of the many variables that relate to competence, but the more of them Rachel scores higher on, the more effective she should be, whether she goes to Trinidad, Thailand, or Turkistan. Future research, however, might consider whether certain variables are more important depending on the culture or the mission. It might be that, while some traits will help Rachel wherever she goes, if she is outgoing and energetic, she might fare well in Tegucigalpa; but if she has more of a reserved character, that might suit her in Taipei. And structural and cultural factors apart from Rachel's disposition may influence whether she is successful in Tehran or Toledo.

What do you think? Intercultural communicator competence is an important consideration for companies sending employees on international assignments, both in terms of employee selection for cross-cultural positions and in employee training. Consider some of the variables in this section. Which do you think might be trainable, and how might you go about training on these variables? Imagine you are selecting an employee for a specific location and position: will the "benchmark" standards work, or is there also something to be said for matching employee character to the position?

As we noted earlier in some cases, the environment might be particularly important to whether one is competent or can even become a "multicultural person." Lise Sparrow (2008) analyzed interviews with and essays of a variety of women who should be and wanted to be "multicultural." Contrary to the literature on the multicultural person, which suggests that one can achieve a sense of positive marginality between cultures, being accepted in any culture, Sparrow found that "women, in particular, … in spite of their commitments to intercultural communication, spoke consistently of their identities in relation to contexts of being excluded or included on the basis of their race, religion, ethnicity, and gender" (p. 250). The women, who had come to the United States from countries such as Zaire, Vietnam, and India, reported being abused or denied privileges both in their own countries and in the United States. Some confronted prejudice and barriers of status and privilege. In sum, Sparrow notes, the notion of the "multicultural person" is not as simple as it seems. Sparrow points out that, rather than marginality between cultures, women and other travelers often need to find their own sense of rootedness, a sense of relationship, and of home, to help them sustain difficulties they face in their new environments. This highlights not only the role of the environment in determining our effectiveness, but also the possibility that being "multicultural," in the sense of being fluid and without a cultural reference, might also leave us with a sense of void in our identity, which may not always be healthy.

But it also demonstrates that to be competent in intercultural communication may not equate to being competent in intergroup communication (see Chapter 3). Intergroup competence—specifically, in situations where group-based identities are involved, might also involve both "effectiveness" and "appropriateness," and some of the traits or characteristics that make one competent in an intercultural context (e.g., other-centeredness, good listening skills) may also help the person in an intergroup context.

A growing literature on intergroup communication suggests that a new set of skills—even a new approach to communication—may also be important. These include, but are not limited to, things like doing research to understand the other group's perspective, not expecting someone from the other group to "teach" one about their group's reality, being able to engage in difficult discussions without getting defensive, being able to understand the other person's side of an issue, and being able to be a "learner" of other people's view of their realities, but never an "expert" on someone else's group. Michael Hecht and his colleagues (e.g., Hecht et al., 1989; Martin et al., 2001) developed an extended research agenda trying to determine what members of co-cultural groups in the United States found to be "effective" in their own and dominant group members' communication. Strategies found in these studies, some relating to what the dominant group members should do and some, to the minority group members, included being able to assert expressions of disagreement, avoiding certain topics, engaging in active listening and turn-taking, and involving each other in the communication.

Summary

In this chapter, we summarized issues relating to adjustment, both going abroad and returning home. We considered the U- and W-curves, which suggest that when people travel to another culture for a longer period of time, they go through stages of psychological stress and adjustment. We also considered newer approaches to adjustment, which suggest that perhaps adjustment is cyclical, or that one might be adjusted in one area of life, but not in another, and that these may increase or decrease. We have argued that the stress of adjustment, including the stress of coming home, is not necessarily a bad thing. It can lead to a great sense of personal growth, as we take a broader view of the world and of the human condition, and as we learn new ways of doing things. Adjustment to other cultures is related in some ways to the notion of intercultural communication competence, in which one is able to accomplish tasks in another culture while also acting in appropriate ways. Some feel that, as we gain more and more intercultural experiences, we might become adept at surfing between cultures seamlessly, feeling tied to none, and adapting to the culture in which we find ourselves.

Traveling to other cultures shows us new ways to think, feel, and act, and this helps to uncover how much of what we do in our everyday lives is a choice. Once we have adjusted to another culture, we now have more choices, and we can adapt our own cultural views of success, beauty, friendship, and so on, or we can create new models based on the cultures to which we have traveled. At the same time, as hopeful, as we are about the benefits of travel abroad, we realize that our effectiveness and adaptation to other culture exist in the context of how that culture treats us. Racism, xenophobia, stereotypes, unequal opportunities (see Chapter 6) may keep us from becoming truly effective. Unfortunately, often when cultural situations work against the success of the stranger, the people in the culture blame the stranger for not succeeding, rather than recognizing the culture's own role in the difficulty.

KEY TERMS

sojourner, 246
immigrant, 246
refugee, 246
adjustment, 247
enculturation, 247
acculturation, 247
deculturation, 247
assimilation, 247
culture shock, 247
U-curve, 247
honeymoon stage, 247
crisis stage, 248
adjustment stage, 248
integration stage, 248
stress-adaptation-growth dynamic, 250
psychological adjustment, 251
sociocultural adjustment/cross-cultural
adaptation, 251
integration/biculturalism, 252
marginality, 252

segregation, 252
multiculturalism/cultural pluralism, 252
melting pot, 252
exclusion, 252
selective adaptation, 253
diaspora, 254
hybridity, 254
return culture shock/return cultural
adjustment, 254
W-curve, 255
alienated approach, 258
resocialized approach, 258
proactive approach, 258
communication effectiveness, 259
communication competence, 259
communication appropriateness, 259
intercultural communication
competence, 259
multicultural person, 259
intercultural transformation, 259

Discussion questions

1 Discuss with other students your own experiences moving in and out of cultures, even if that is from your home culture to the culture of your university. In what ways are domestic moves (within a country) and foreign moves similar and different?

2 If you have traveled to another culture, what are some things that made you more or less effective or helped you to adapt or not adapt? These might be aspects of yourself or the situation. What skills would you like to work on in yourself to make you a more effective intercultural communicator?

3 If you are in a class, break up into groups. Imagine a job cultural assignment to a specific culture: which of you would you send and why? Base your answer on notions of aspects of *effectiveness* and *appropriateness*. For example, what particular motivations (affect), knowledge or understandings (cognition), or competencies (behaviors) does each person in the group have that would be an advantage?

4 Do you think that the same things would make one effective in a cross-cultural situation (like moving from France to South Africa), as in an intergroup situation (say, interracial communication)? Why or why not? What skills, attitudes, or emotions might become more important in one situation or another?

5 Do some research on a major refugee group in your country. What are the social and economic conditions of the group? How might those impact the group's adjustment?

Action points

1   Your school might have an international student program or a program to teach students the language of your country. Contact these programs to see if there is an "international friend" aspect to them. Make a commitment to start spending a bit of time each week with a student, to get to know them and learn about their culture.

2   As we have seen in this chapter, part of one's adjustment to a new culture is based on the acceptance and support the new culture provides the traveler. See if your community has a second-language or citizenship program to provide assistance to immigrants in your community. Get involved in giving language or citizenship lessons, or academic tutoring to immigrants in your community.

3   If there is an immigrant group in your community, find out about local festivals or holiday seasons (such as Chinese New Year, Ramadan, or Diwali). Attend a festival, or even several, from the same group. See what you can learn about that cultural group that would add to your own understanding and experience of the world. (Note: a single experience will not make you an expert or multi-cultural person! But it will start you on the process of cultural learning.)

For more information

Arasaratnam-Smith, L. A., & Deardorff, D. K. (2022). *Developing intercultural competence in higher education: International students' stories and self-reflection.* Routledge.

Deardorff, D. K., & Arasaratnam-Smith, L. (Eds.). (2017). *Intercultural competence in higher education: International approaches, assessment, and application.* Routledge.

Paige, R. M. (Ed.). (1994). Education for the intercultural experience (2nd ed.). Intercultural Press.

Sam, D. L., & Berry, J. W. (Eds.). (2006). *The Cambridge handbook of acculturation psychology.* Cambridge University Press.

Storti, C. (2001). *The art of coming home.* Intercultural Press.

References

Abe, H., & Wiseman, R. L. (1983). A cross-cultural confirmation of the dimensions of intercultural effectiveness. *International Journal of Intercultural Communication, 7*(1), 53–67. DOI: 10.1016/0147-1767(83)90005-6

Adler, P. S. (1975). The transitional experience: An alternative view of culture shock. *Journal of Humanistic Psychology, 15* (4), 13–23. DOI: 10.1177/002216787501500403

Adler, P. S. (1977). Beyond cultural identity: Reflections on cultural and multicultural man. In R. W. Brislin (Ed.), *Culture learning: Concepts, application, and research* (pp. 24–41). University of Hawaii Press.

Ady, J. C. (1995). Toward a differential demand model of sojourner adjustment. In R. Wiseman (Ed.), *Intercultural communication theory* (pp. 92–114). Sage.

Arasaratnam, L. A. (2006). Further testing of a new model of intercultural communication competence. *Communication Research Reports, 23*(2), 93–99. DOI: 10.1080/08824090600668923

Austin, C. (Ed.). (1987). *Readings in cross-cultural re-entry.* ACU Press.

Bennett, J. (1977). Transition shock: Putting culture shock in perspective. In N. Jain (Ed.), *International and intercultural communication annual 4* (pp. 45-52). Sage.

Bennett, M.J. (1993). Towards ethnorelativism: A developmental model of intercultural sensitivity. In R. M. Paige (Ed.), *Education for the intercultural experience*(pp. 21-71). Intercultural Press.

Berry, J. W. (2004). Fundamental psychological processes in intercultural relations. In D. Landis, J. M. Bennett, & M. J. Bennett (Eds.), *Handbook of intercultural training* (3rd ed., pp. 166–184). Sage.

Black, J. S., Mendenhall, M., & Oddou, G. (1991). Toward a comprehensive model of international adjustment. An integration of multiple theoretical perspectives. *Academy of Management Review*, 16(2), 291–317. DOI: 10.2307/258863

Black, J. S., & Stephens, G. K. (1989). The influence of the spouse on American expatriate adjustment and intent to stay in Pacific Rim overseas assignments. *Journal of Management, 15(4)*, 529–544. https://doi.org/10.1177/014920638901500403

Bourhis, R., Moïse, L. C., Perreault, S., & Senécal, S. (1997). Towards an interactive acculturation model: A social psychological approach. *International Journal of Psychology*, 32(6), 369–386. DOI: 10.1080/002075997400629

Chen, G.-M., & Starosta, W. J. (2008). Intercultural communication competence: A synthesis. In M. K. Asante, Y. Miike, & J. Yin (Eds.), *The global intercultural communication reader* (pp. 215–237). Routledge.

Church, A. (1982). Sojourner adjustment. *Psychological Bulletin*, 91(3), 540–575. DOI: 10.1037/0033-2909.91.3.540

Croucher, S. M., & Rahmani, D. (2015). A longitudinal test of the effects of Facebook on cultural adaptation. *Journal of International and Intercultural Communication, 8(4)*, 330–345. https://doi.org/10.1080/17513057.2015.1087093

Curtin, M. (2010). Coculturation: Toward a critical theoretical framework of cultural adjustment. In T. K. Nakayama & R. T. Halualani (Eds.), *The handbook of critical intercultural communication* (pp. 270–285). Wiley-Blackwell.

Deardorff, D. K. (Ed.). (2009). *The Sage handbook of intercultural competence*. Sage.

De La Garza, A. T. (2023). Theory of differential adaptation. In J. T. Austin, M.P. Orbe, & J.D. Sims (Eds.), Communication theory: Racially diverse and inclusive perspectives (pp. 131–138). Cognella

Dodd, C. H. (1998) *Dynamics of intercultural communication* (5th ed.). McGraw-Hill.

Drzewiecka, J. A., & Halualani, R. T. (2002). The structural-cultural dialectic of diasporic politics. *Communication Theory*, 12(3), 340–366. https://doi.org/10.1111/j.1468-2885.2002.tb00273.x

Gaw, K. F. (2000). Reverse culture shock in students returning from overseas. *International Journal of Intercultural Relations*, 24(1), 83–104. https://doi.org/10.1016/S0147-1767(99)00024-3

Gullahorn, J.T., & Gullahorn,J.E. (1963). An extension of the U-curve hypothesis. *Journal of Social Issues*, 19(3). https://doi.org/10.1111/j.1540-4560.1963.tb00447.x

Hall, B. J. (2005). *Among cultures: The challenge of communication*. Wadsworth.

Hall, E. T. (1973). *The silent language*. Anchor.

Halualani, R. T., & Drzewiecka, J. A. (2008). Deploying "descent": The politics of diasporic belonging and intercultural communication. In L. A. Flores, M. P. Orbe, & B. J. Allen (Eds.), *Intercultural communication in a transnational world* (pp. 59–90). Sage.

Han, Y., Sears, G. J., Darr, W. A., & Wang, Y. (2022). Facilitating cross-cultural adaptation: A meta-analytics review of dispositional predictors of expatriate adjustment. *Journal of Cross-Cultural Psychology*, 53(9), 1054–1096.https://doi.org/10.1177/00220221221109559

Harris, P. R., & Moran, R. T. (1996). *Managing cultural differences: Leadership strategies for a new world of business* (4th ed.). Gulf.

Hecht, M. L., Ribeau, S., & Alberts, J. K. (1989). An Afro-American perspective on interaction. *Communication Monographs*, 56(4), 385–410. https://doi.org/10.1080/03637758909390271

Hegde, R. S. (1998). Swinging the trapeze: The negotiation of identity among Asian Indian immigrant women in the United States. In D. V. Tanno & A. González (Eds.), *Communication and identity across cultures* (pp. 34–55). Sage.

Hendley, E.. (Jan 12, 2022). Trendspotting 2022: What's next for international education? Eleven leaders in the field offer their perspectives on what's in store for international education in 2022. NAFSA. Accessed October 28, 2022, at https://www.nafsa.org/ie-magazine/2022/1/12/trendspotting-2022-whats-next-international-education.

Inbound internationally mobile students by continent of origin. (2023) *Sustainable Development Goals*. Accessed March 5, 2023, at http://data.uis.unesco.org/index.aspx?queryid=3804

Karamehic-Muratovic, A., Cheah, W. H., & Matsuo, H. (2016). Changing oneself: Communication factors and psychological responses in the cross-cultural adaptation of Bosnian Refugees. *Journal of the Communication, Speech, & Theatre Association of North Dakota*, 29, 14–27.

Kealey, D. J. (1989). A study of cross-cultural effectiveness: Theoretical issues, practical applications. *International Journal of Intercultural Relations*, 13(3), 387–428. https://doi.org/10.1016/0147-1767(89)90019-9

Kim, Y. S., & Kim, Y. Y. (2022). Communication patterns, host receptivity, and psychological health in the process of cross-cultural adaptation: A study of Korean and Indonesian ex-patriate workers. *Ohio Communication Journal*, 60, 91–109.

Kim, Y. Y. (2001). *Becoming Intercultural: An integrative theory of communication and cross-cultural adaptation*. Sage.

Kim, Y. Y. (2005). Adapting to a new culture: An integrative communication theory. In W. B. Gudykunst (Ed.), *Theorizing about intercultural communication* (pp. 375–400). Sage.

Kim, Y. Y., & Ruben, B. D. (1988). Intercultural transformation: A systems theory. In Y. Y. Kim & W. B. Gudykunst (Eds.), *Theories in intercultural communication* (pp. 299–321). Sage.

Liu, C.-S., & Lee, H. W. (2008). A proposed model of expatriates in multinational organizations. *Cross-Cultural Management, 15(2)*, 176–193. https://doi.org/10.1108/13527600810870615

Lysgaard, S. (1955). Adjustment in a foreign society: Norwegian Fulbright grantees visiting the United States. *International Social Sciences Bulletin, 7*, 45–58.

Martin, J. N. (1986). Patterns of communication in three types of reentry relationships. *Western Journal of Speech Communication, 50(2)*, 183–199. https://doi.org/10.1080/10570318609374224

Martin, J. N., & Harrell, T. (2004). Intercultural reentry of students and professionals: Theory and practice. In D. Landis, J. M. Bennett, & M. J. Bennett (Eds.), *Handbook of Intercultural Training* (3rd ed., pp. 309–336). Sage.

Martin, J. N., Moore, S., Hecht, M. L., & Larkey, L. K. (2001). An African American perspective on conversational improvement strategies. *The Howard Journal of Communications, 12(1)*, 1–27. https://doi.org/10.1080/10646170121222

Miike, Y. (2007). An Asiacentric reflection on Eurocentric bias in communication theory. *Communication Monographs, 74(2)*, 272–278. https://doi.org/10.1080/03637750701390093

Oberg, K. (1960). Culture shock: Adjustment to new culture environments. *Practical Anthropology, 7*, 170–179 https://doi.org/10.1177/009182966000700405

Pitts, M. J. (2016). Sojourner reentry: A grounded elaboration of the integrative theory of communication and cross-cultural adaptation. *Communication Monographs, 83(4)*, 419–445. http://dx.doi.org/10.1080/03637751.2015.1128557

Roberts, J. M. (2007). Wearing the hijab: An argument for moderate selective acculturation of newly immigrated Arab-American women. *Intercultural Communication, 13(13)*. Accessed November 21, 2022, at https://immi.se/oldwebsite/nr11/roberts.htm

Sam, D. L., & Berry, J. W. (2010). Acculturation: When individuals and groups of different cultural backgrounds meet. *Perspectives on Psychological Science, 5(4)*, 472–481. https://doi.org/10.1177/1745691610373075

Sandel, T. L. (2014). "Oh, I'm here!!" Social media's impact on the cross-cultural adaptation of students studying abroad. *Journal of Intercultural Communication Research, 43(1)*, 1–29. https://doi.org/10.1080/17513057.2015.1087093

Selmer, J., & Fenner, C. R., Jr. (2009). Spillover effects between work and non-work adjustment among public sector expatriates. *Personnel Review, 38(4)*, 366–379. https://doi.org/10.1108/00483480910956328

Smith, S. (1998). Identity and intercultural communication competence in reentry. In J. N. Martin, T. K. Nakayama, & L. A. Flores (Eds.), *Readings in cultural contexts* (pp. 304–314). Mayfield.

Smith, S. L. (2002). The cycle of cross-cultural adaptation and reentry. In J. N. Martin, T. K. Nakayama, & L. A. Flores (Eds.), *Readings in intercultural communication: Experiences and contexts* (2nd ed., pp. 246–259). McGraw-Hill.

Sparrow, L. M. (2008). Beyond multicultural man: Complexities of identity. In M. K. Asante, Y. Miike, & J. Yin (Eds.), *The global intercultural communication reader* (pp. 239–261). Routledge.

Spitzberg, B. M. (1994). A model of intercultural communication competence. In L. A. Samovar & R. E. Porter (Eds.), *Intercultural communication: A reader* (7th ed., pp. 347–359). Wadsworth.

Spitzberg, B. M., & Cupach, W. R. (1984). *Interpersonal communication competence*. Sage.

Tanaka, T., Takai, J., Kohyama, T., & Fujihara, T. (1994). Adjustment patterns of international students in Japan. *International Journal of Intercultural Relations, 18(1)*, 55–75. https://doi.org/10.1016/0147-1767(94)90004-3

Tolkien, J. R. R. (1955/1965). *The return of the king*. Houghton Mifflin.

Uehara, A. (1986). The nature of American student reentry adjustment and perception of the sojourn experience. *International Journal of Intercultural Relations, 10(4)*, 415–438. https://doi.org/10.1016/0147-1767(86)90043-X

Ward, C. (2004). Psychological theories of cultural contact and their implications for intercultural training and interventions. In D. Landis, J. M. Bennett, & M. J. Bennett (Eds.), *Handbook of intercultural training* (3rd ed., pp. 185–216). Sage.

Ward, C., Okura, Y., Kennedy, A., & Kojima, T. (1998). The U-curve on trial: A longitudinal study of psychological and sociocultural adjustment during cross-cultural transition. *International Journal of Intercultural Relations, 22(3)*, 277–291. https://doi.org/10.1016/S0147-1767(98)00008-X

Ward, C., & Rana-Deuba, A. (1999). Acculturation and adaptation revisited. *Journal of Cross-Cultural Psychology, 30(4)*, 422–442. https://doi.org/10.1177/0022022199030004003

Wilson, A.H. (1985). Returned exchange students: Becoming mediating persons. *International Journal of Intercultural Relations*, 9(3), 285–304. DOI: 10.1016/0147-1767(85)90030-6

Wiseman, R. L., Hammer, M. R., & Nishida, H. (1989). Predictors of intercultural communication competence. *International Journal of Intercultural Relations*, 13(3), 349–370. https://doi.org/10.1016/0147-1767(89)90017-5

Xie, M., & Chau, -C.-C. (2022). The interplay between social media and cultural adjustment: Analysis of the subjective well-being, social support, and social media use of Asian International Students in the U.S. *Journal of Intercultural Communication*, 22(2), 22–32. https://doi.org/10.36923/jicc.v22i2.37. Accessed December 5, 2022, at https://immi.se/intercultural/article/view/967-Ming-Xie-and-Chin-Chung-59-3/64.

Chapter 13

Relationships and conflict: How can I have better cross-cultural relationships?

Chapter objectives

After this chapter, you should be able to:

→ Describe several approaches to what makes relationships grow more intimate

→ Outline four patterns of possible integration of cultural differences in a relationship

→ Define the Romeo-Juliet effect, refencing, and stigma as they relate to intergroup relationships

→ Illustrate the behaviors associated with five different conflict styles and discuss how personal and cultural factors may lead someone to prefer one style over another

→ Discuss some of the issues someone would need to be aware of in intercultural negotiation

Culture and Communication in Relationship: How Do Intercultural Relationships Grow and Thrive? 269

Relational and Organizational Conflict: How Can I Make Intercultural Conflict More Productive? 276

Intercultural Communication for Everyday Life, Second Edition. John R. Baldwin, Alberto González, Nettie Brock, Ming Xie, and Chin-Chung Chao.
© 2024 John Wiley & Sons Ltd. Published 2024 by John Wiley & Sons Ltd.
Companion Website: http://www.wiley.com/go/baldwin2e

une 12 of every year is the Loving Day, which marks the anniversary of the 1967 Supreme Court decision in Loving *v*. Virginia case that legalized interracial marriage nationwide in the United States. Since then, public attitudes toward intermarriage have evolved. According to a Gallup poll in July 2021, 94% of Americans approve of interracial marriages, increasing from 4% in 1958 (McCarthy, 2021). In 2019, intercultural and interracial marriages accounted for 11% of all marriages and 19% of new marriages in the United States (Parker & Barroso, 2021). According to the U.S. Census Bureau, U.S. Americans who identify as two or more races have been the fastest-growing racial and ethnic group (Chappell, 2017). About 6.3 million American adults—2.5% of the whole adult population—identified themselves as being more than one race (Parker & Barroso, 2021). Among many intercultural celebrity couples (Fetterling, 2022), the most famous include Meghan Markle and Prince Harry, as well as the U.S. Vice President Kamala Harris and her husband Doug Emhoff. As the first Black person and first Asian American to hold the vice president office of the United States, Harris is the child of immigrants and interracial marriage. Her husband is White, which makes them also an intermarried couple (Figure 13.1).

Numerous reports, polls, and articles demonstrate that intercultural relationships are an area growing in interest around the world. Intercultural marriages have also increased in China. From 2010–2020, there were 40,000–50,000 international marriages in China every year (China Ministry of Civil Affairs, n.d.). In the United States, David Crary (2007), AP Reporter, states that "besides superstardom, Barack Obama, Tiger Woods and Derek Jeter have another common bond: Each is the child of an interracial marriage". **Miscegenation**—the marrying of individuals across ethnic or racial lines—is growing in number around the world. The number would be even stronger if we considered all forms of **intermarriage**, marriage between people of perceived outgroups regardless of the grounds—religious, cultural, racial, and so on, with an even greater number if we consider long-term or live-in romantic partners who are not married or even, simply, interracial romance.

As intermarriage becomes increasingly prevalent in the United States, more and more people become accepting of it. In 2017, 39% of Americans stated that more people of different races marrying each other was good for society (Livingston & Brown, 2017). The change in public opinions toward intermarriage reflects the change in social contexts such as migration, demo-

Figure 13.1 Kamala Harris is sworn in as Vice President by Supreme Court Justice Sonia Sotomayor on January 20, 2021, in Washington D.C., as Harris's Husband, Doug Emhoff, and the President Joe Biden look on. Source: BRENDAN SMIALOWSKI/Getty Images

graphic change, and the increasingly flexible social norms (Silva et al., 2012). It is true that intercultural relationships can promote a society's cultural diversity and inclusion. As Jackson Lu et al. (2017) suggest, intercultural friendships and romantic relationships improve individuals' creativity, innovation, and entrepreneurship. Stories of intercultural couples often frame intermarriage and always hide the complexity of intermarriage. As Malone (2011) describes, online news articles often frame intergroup relationships as a harmonious blending of food and fashion, perhaps after a brief period of struggle, perhaps by necessity of the online reader expectations for upbeat news. While intercultural relationships can enrich individuals' life and community culture, they also presents difficulties, challenges, and issues of cultural orracial difference, or social stigma that might lead to misunderstanding, uncertainty, frustration, and conflict. This chapter will explore culture and relationships, including conflict, and end with the extension of our understanding of conflict and negotiation to workplace relationships.

What Do You Think? Before you continue reading, think about possible differences between types of "inter" relationships. Jot down your answers or discuss with your classmates: What issues might be the same or different in an interethnic or interracial marriage as opposed to one that is interreligious or crosses social class lines? Will issues be different in a marriage or civil union relationship than in dating? How about between dating and friendship? What are some tips you might give to people in different types of relationships?

Culture and communication in relationship: How do intercultural relationships grow and thrive?

A **relationship** is a connection between two or more individuals in which they have both rights and responsibilities toward each other beyond what would be expected in interaction with strangers. It occurs when two people become interdependent (Berscheid & Ammazzalorso, 2004). Paul Mongeau and Lynn Henningsen (2008) state that interactions in close relationships are characterized by efficient, idiosyncratic, synchronized, and multichannel meaning systems. As authors describe friendships, dating relationships, and marriage, they look at different things. Sociologists look at how demographic, class, and other variables influence mate selection and the likelihood of **exogamy** (marrying outside of one's perceived group). Some consider the long-term social impact of intercultural marriage or intergroup friendship on levels of tolerance within a society. Psychologists might analyze relational and psychological processes within an intercultural relationship, such as the emotional satisfaction. Linguists might be interested in how children learn languages when the parents are from different language groups. Communication scholars have focused on various aspects, but especially on message exchange in the process of relational development and conflict management.

What partners bring with them into relationships

We mentioned interracial relationships above. It is important to note that intercultural relationship is broader than interracial relationship as culture is broadly defined (Silva et al., 2012). Intercultural relationships are formed between people from various cultural backgrounds.

Partners bring a variety of experiences and differences, many cultural, into a relationship. Relational partners will share both similarities and differences, based on individual and cultural factors (Figure 13.2). One major difference between intercultural relationships and within-culture relationships is the multi-dimensional cultural differences that affect the formation and development of relationships (Hu et al., 2021). The development of intercultural relationships includes concepts of cultural **values**, cosmopolitanism, and relational identity.

Cultural values, such as those described in the frameworks in Chapter 4, often impact relationships. A partner from a collectivist culture might feel much more responsibility in terms of time and financial support to extended family. Stella Ting-Toomey (1994) once suggested that culture influences conceptions of romantic love and one's ideal mate. She argues that in collectivist cultures such as China and Japan, less emphasis is placed on passionate and romantic love than in individualistic cultures such as that of America. A resident of Canada who is from the Philippines might feel obligation to ensure that nieces and nephews obtain a good education, something that does not make as much sense in the mainstream North American understanding of the **nuclear family** (spouses and children). Different commitments to extended family, workplace, or community

Figure 13.2 People in intercultural friendships, romances, and work relationships bring cultural and personal differences and similarities to the relationship. What are some concrete things they could do to recognize and solve such differences? Source: Kymri Wilt/Danita Delimont/Alamy Stock Photo.

might impact romantic or marriage relationships, as partners debate how much time to spend with extended networks or how much of the household income should go to these networks. Related to the notion of relationship to family is the extent of involvement of the extended family in relationships. In any romantic or marriage relationship, partners' families can try to influence the relationship in unwanted ways. Some researchers of intercultural marriage say that the impact of extended family is especially likely to be felt once a couple has children and the grandparents guide the parents in the "right" (i.e., their culturally understood) way of raising children.

Cosmopolitanism refers to "a broadly defined disposition of openness toward others, people, things, and experiences whose origin is non-local" (Skrbis & Woodward as cited by Kudo et al., 2019, p. 479). It resonates with the foundational concepts of intercultural communication, such as showing interest, sensitivity, understanding, acceptance, and respect for cultural differences (Kudo et al., 2019). We like to think that we grow more intimate with someone simply because we like them. But we might seek an intergroup friend because we want to feel more tolerant or because we deliberately want to raise our awareness about another group. Therefore, cosmopolitanism is essential to establish a common ground for relationships and communication beyond cultural differences. In intercultural relationships, perception and understanding of each other's culture is an important factor (Hu et al., 2021). For example, one study found that perceptions and practices of open-mindedness, respect, and self-disclosure affected the relationship and conflicts between Chinese and American partners (Tili & Barker, 2015). Stanley Gaines (2017) points out that intercultural relationships could be transformational because of the opportunity for partners to learn about other cultures and gain insight into one's own identity.

***

What Do You Think? Carley Dodd and John Baldwin (2002) highlight elements that mark positive family cultures, like supportive communication, cohesion, adaptable family rules, and communication receptivity, noting how these might be experienced in culturally different ways. Describe the specific values and communication rules in the family in which you grew up. These are usually not stated openly—they are the patterns people follow, sometimes healthy and sometimes not. In what ways do you see yourself repeating these rules—or deliberately going against them—in your current relationships?

Relational identity "is defined as a reality or culture that reflects the values, the rules, and the processes of the relationship" (Kudo et al., 2019, p. 480) and maintains the relationship (Lee, 2008). Relational identity emerges within a relationship and allows the members to know how to behave and interact appropriately (Lee, 2008). In an intercultural relationship, the participants can focus on the interactions and communications between them by sharing the relational identity and supporting each other's cultural identity with less tension. The development of relational identity is based on cultural and social conventions with flexibility and adaptability (Giménez Moreno, 2021).

Definitions and expectations for the relationship Of course, much of our discussion above assumes that the partners have the same definition of what the relationship should be. Especially in today's changing terrain of romantic relationships, it is important for romantic partners or potential spouses to know what the expectations of the other are in terms of the relationship itself. Does romance or marriage imply sexual fidelity? Do the two become "one flesh" in marriage, or are they expected, to a large degree, to maintain their distinctness?

Such questions also apply to friendships. Cross-cultural travelers soon realize that the rules and expectations of friendship change from culture to culture. Just because we can translate the word "friend" to some other language does not mean we know what friendship means in that culture. Scholarship among U.S. Americans shows there are different cultural expectations among groups within the same country. We must, at the same time, consider societal regulations and norms for the relationship as an important input factor to a relationship. These are important for relations marked by some aspect of diversity, either between partners or in relation to the dominant culture; and this influence is different enough from what is usually considered by psychologists and communication scholars that we will deal with it separately below under a discussion of "stigmatized relationships."

How do intercultural relationships work?

Relational development All of us meet a variety of people every day, in our classes, at our workplace, at get-togethers, and even on public transportation. We usually ignore the host of people that cross our paths. But some strangers become acquaintances and eventually close friends, lovers, or long-time partners. As we consider what draws us closer to one person than to another, we realize that these principles apply both to romantic relationships and friendships, to work and other types of relationships. Romantic relationships pose different issues because often we move toward living with another person in a long-term, even lifelong relationship. Different researchers provide different explanations as to why relationships—for people of the same or different cultures—grow closer.

One notion of what draws relational partners together is **propinquity**, or physical closeness between people. We are more likely to form relationships with those with whom we work or study or who live in the same apartment building—or, by extension, in our most frequently visited social media or Twitter feeds—rather than someone who is distant (physical or virtually). Of course, we have contact with a great many people who are physically or electronically "close," but we do not form relationships with them, so something besides living close must make the relationships grow. In the multicultural world we describe in Chapter 1, it is more and more likely that we will find ourselves in close contact with people culturally different from us either in our physical or cyber world.

Some scholars suggest that the more similar we are to people, the more we will grow to like them. This **similarity-attraction hypothesis** (Byrne, 1971) explains that people are more likely to date or marry within their own groups, though there are also other explanations such as ethnocentrism, prejudice, and family pressure (see Chapter 6). In general, intimate relationships are formed with others from similar social economic stratum, ethnic backgrounds, and equivalent worldviews (Byrne, 1969; Kerckhoft, 1974). Such "birds of a feather" behavior pattern is pervasive in romantic relationship formation. Research suggests that perceived similarity is an essential factor that affects the quality and function of close relationship, especially in intercultural relationships. (Froidevaux, 2019; Gould et al., 2018). The research of Bahns et al. (2017) confirmed that similarities significantly influenced individuals' selection of whom to interact with.

Others suggest that what drives relationships toward intimacy is **self-disclosure**, defined as revealing things about oneself to someone else, specifically things the other would not normally be known by the other and about which there is at least some risk of sharing. **Social penetration theory** explains this perspective (Altman & Taylor, 1973): The more we self-disclose, the closer we will grow. Self-disclosure varies in the intimacy of detail that we share (**depth** of self-disclosure) and the number of topic areas (**breadth** of self-disclosure). While some topics seem more superficial, such as hobbies or tastes in music, and others deeper, like political philosophy, we can share any topic with varying levels of depth. Sebastian could share superficially that he is a Christian Democrat or could discuss deeply how his self-esteem is related to his inability to play sports. The theory has implications for intercultural communication. First, culture influences what we share and how we share about different topics. Second, in most cases, people self-disclose differently with those they perceive to be in their in-groups rather than out-groups, with the latter influenced by cultural norms and levels of prejudice. Finally, intercultural communication researchers often assume that, in deeper relationships (and thus, deeper levels of self-disclosure), issues of ethnicity, age, class, and other diversity become much less important.

Uncertainty reduction theory (Berger & Calabrese, 1975) suggests that the better we can predict and explain the behaviors of another person (or reduce **uncertainty**), the more relationships will grow. The theory accounts for a variety of aspects of perception and communication related to reduced uncertainty, such as sharing communication, perceiving similarity, having nonverbal warmth, or having the same networks of friends. In the 1980s, William Gudykunst found, that in some high-context cultures (Japan), people seek different information—more about background and context—to understand others than people in low-context, individualistic cultures (the United States). He (2005) added the notion of **anxiety**—feelings of uneasiness, tension, or apprehension that occur in intercultural interactions. Gudykunst suggests that uncertainty and anxiety are both necessary for the growth of intercultural relationships, as they keep us interested in interactions; but if either is too high, we might want to exit the relationship. It is not the presence of these things in our relationships, but our ability to manage them that is important.

Relational maintenance The above approaches often predict relational growth with one central concept: self-disclosure, predictability, and so on. A different perspective suggests that different tensions, or **dialectics**, characterize relationships. These tensions are unique in that both ends of each tension are always present, both contradicting and completing each other (Baxter & Norwood, 2015). For example, in any relationship, one needs a balance of boundaries around information *and* sharing, of time with the partner (i.e., friend, romantic partner, spouse) *and* time with others, of predictability *and* novelty. Partners change from day to day and differ from each other. You might need more time together with your best friend right now, but they might be having a tough day and need a little space. And the tensions exist within individuals, between partners, and between the relationship and its surrounding relational contexts (should we spend more time with others outside the relationship or "just the two of us"?). It is not the presence of the tensions that determine outcomes in relationships, but how the partners work to resolve them. Research is only recently applying the idea of dialectics to relationships across cultures. For example, one study found that food consumption, which represents implicit tensions in a household's relational culture within intercultural couples, was sometimes resolved or not, leading to enduring tensions (Rogan et al., 2021, 2018).

Break it Down

Through your college or on your own (through a website like http://ppi.searchy.net/), find a conversation partner or an Internet pen-pal from another culture. Try to get to know the person. If it's an Internet pal, of course, keep in mind rules for safe chatting! While you might not become friends, what might be some things that would make your conversation relationship turn to "friendship"? How might such friendships impact your own view of the world—and how might your culture impact your view of friendship? What kind of impact, if any, might it have on your involvement in social action?

The notion of dialectical tensions makes good sense if we consider a set of patterns of resolving cultural differences that Wen-Shing Tseng proposed in (1977). Tseng suggested that partners from different cultures tend to use one of five strategies for resolving cultural differences. To illustrate these, let us consider the case of Lea, a Belgian woman married to Massoud, an Iranian. They might simply adopt the cultural pattern of one of the partners: Lea adopts Iranian ways and converts to Islam (one-way adjustment). Tseng (1977) suggests that in most cases, the wife adjusts to the culture of the husband. The couple might enact Belgian culture for a while, but then Iranian culture for a while, depending on the culture in which they live (alternating adjustment). A third approach would be to combine elements of both cultures (mixing), which Tseng suggests is the most common form of intercultural relational adjustment. Here, the couple might practice Islam, even if they live in Belgium, enacting more Western gender roles. Finally, the couple could adopt a "third culture"—a new set of patterns that is neither Iranian nor Belgian (creative adjustment). The dialectical approach, however, suggests that the cultures of origin will sometimes move more towards one culture or the other, but will always exist in tension.

The above example brings another relevant issue to play in intercultural relationships, and one that scholars have not given much attention to: interpersonal power. Beulah Rohrlich (1988) argues that one of the key areas to think about in intercultural romance and marriage is the issue of power. Who gets to make the decisions about which cultural standards, religion, and so on, the couple should adopt? Power is complicated by many factors—the location of residence, the influence of extended family, language used in the home, and the support of friends. Each partner would have "interpersonal" bases of power, such as who is more outgoing and dynamic. Also, there might be some other factors influencing the power relation in an intercultural relationship. A study on African-origin male marriage with Australian women found that the Australian spouses were bestowed with unforeseen power over the African male, especially during the visa application and sponsoring process (Hoogenraad, 2021).

Unique cultural relationship patterns

If we want to travel to another culture or understand relationships with people from other cultures, we also need to understand culture-specific views about relationships; in many cases, cultures have unique relational patterns. Even if your partner or friend is not from one of these cultures, you might find some commonalities to these themes as you discuss or develop relationships with that person. We cannot cover relational nuances relevant to every culture, so, to call your attention to such differences, we will introduce just one culturally specific relationship issue—the building of connections in Chinese relationships.

Writers have described how East Asian relationships are often different from Western relationships. Confucianism, itself, an Eastern philosophy based on the writings of Confucius (551–479 B.C.E.) framed relationships in terms of **propriety**—the proper behavior for the proper relationships and situational context. Confucius focused on five key relationships: ruler-subject, father-son, husband-wife, older brother-younger brother, and elders-juniors. There are clear societal expectations for how people in each role should behave in relation to the other. This leads to key notions such as the notion of **reciprocity**, in which each partner in the relationship gives, but also receives, and **selflessness**, in which each considers the needs of the other. In relationships influenced by Confucian philosophy, specifically, Korean, Chinese, and Japanese, (1) we would expect reciprocity to be uneven, with the more powerful partner giving more to the relationship, especially materially; (2) public and private relationships would overlap (Yum, 1988). At the same time, while there are similarities across these three cultures, we must keep in mind that there are differences between and within them.

To highlight the notion of reciprocity, let us consider the Chinese notion of **kuan-hsi**—a Chinese notion of connectedness to others. The person who develops more *kuan-hsi* has more societal leverage—for example, connections with people in official positions in businesses or the governments that help people find jobs or work through the bureaucracy of the system (Chang & Holt, 1991). In the system of *kuan-hsi*, someone always owes someone something—a favor, a connection, and so on. This unequal balance, according to June Ock Yum (1988), helps maintain interpersonal connections in relationships, as opposed to the Western notion of short-term and symmetrical reciprocity. In the U.S. American approach, people like to "keep the slate clean." If you buy me lunch this week, I'd better buy you lunch next week (or better yet, we will split the bill, each paying for our own). Not owing anyone anything maintains a U.S. sense of independence from each other, even in relationships. Other cultures have notions similar to *kuan-hsi* that involve development of interpersonal resources, though each is perhaps unique in how one builds and uses connection and influence, in Spanish speaking countries, it is called *palanca* (leverage); in Brazil, the *jeito brasileiro* (the "Brazilian way"). It is *blat* in Russia and *wasta* Saudi Arabia. In the United States, it is called *clout*, but may also be *nepotism*. Although it is desired and sought after in many countries, it has a negative connotation in the United States.

Societal power and intercultural and intergroup relationships

We have considered two approaches to relationship—a scientific approach that seeks to predict different aspects of relationships of people within, across, or between cultures, and an interpretive view that seeks to understand relationship practices specific to different cultures. But increasingly, scholars are also noting how societal power impinges on relationships. This may come in the form of stereotyping and attributions (see Chapter 6), in opposition to relationships, or, as noted above, in the way social power (such as privileging men in storytelling or adopting husband's culture) plays out in relationships.

Attributions and Stereotypes. For a long time, people of different nations, cultures, and races did not mingle for reasons of geographic barriers, national feuds, cultural distrust, racial segregation, or discrimination. Many people expect intergroup relationships, especially romance and marriage, to fail, which might work against these relationships as people in them fulfill the expectations of those around them. In one study, people involved in intercultural marriage in Hawaii tended to blame their marital difficulties on "external" factors, such as language difference, cultural differences, and family interference, while those in same-culture marriage assigned the problems to personal differences such as how to raise children or spend time with friends. In fact, in all relationships, both individual *and* cultural factors may influence the relationship. Blaming relational problems on parents or societal disapproval might protect our relationships. The **Romeo and Juliet Effect** (Graham et al., 1985) suggests that we may take an "us-against-the world" approach if we are in an intergroup romantic relationship—but this might also keep us from seeing problems within the aspects of the individuals in the relationship, or the relationship itself, rather than family, language, or culture.

Perhaps, as some argue (e.g., Gudykunst & Kim, 2003), ethnicity and other group identities become less important as relationships develop. But evidence suggests this is not always true. We might **refence** to let a group member from a group we do not like into our circle of relationships—that is, even though we develop a relationship with someone from another group, we consider that person to be different from the rest of their group ("You're not like other X's I know," Allport, 1979/1954). In this way, we still maintain stereotypes or prejudice even though we have a close relationship with someone from the other group. In an extensive study of 21 African American-European American couples in the United States, Paul Rosenblatt and his colleagues

(1995) found that, while race is not commonly a point of conflict in such couples, in times of stress, some partners resorted to calling partners racial epithets. This suggests that in societies divided by racial, caste, religious, or other differences, the ideas of society that are all around us can still sneak into our intimate relationships, even if we are usually appreciative of differences.

Opposition to relationships. Sometimes relationships between people of different groups are a target of **stigma** in a culture—that is, they are socially unacceptable, even to the point of being shamed or disgraced. For example, in some countries, like Brazil, miscegenation (racial/ethnic intermarriage) was encouraged, while in others, like the United States, it was taboo, even illegal in many states until 1967. Most research suggests that attitudes toward interracial romance are improving, with some severe exceptions ("50 years later," 2017); however, a poll by *the Economist* and YouGov showed an increase in the number of Americans who indicated that interracial marriage was morally wrong (Haughton, 2020). Rosenblatt et al. (1995) note that one aspect of communication in interracial couples in the United States is the minority partner "educating" the White partner about racism, something the White partner is often not yet aware of; the same thing might apply to close interracial friendships. Interracial and interclass friendships are sometimes challenged when political issues or the need to help someone from the marginalized group arises. In some cases, societal opposition is so great as to forbid the relationship. Research has consistent findings that interracial couples experience problems with their family, peers, and larger society (Baptist et al., 2019; Haughton, 2020). Such opposition might also apply to relationships of people of a particular group, especially gays and lesbians. Pachankis et al. (2014) found high tobacco and alcohol use among gay men because of the prejudicial attitudes towards sexual minorities and the lack of non-discrimination policies in American society. Homophobia and heterosexism (Chapter 6) can become important in these relationships. While partners bring unique and cultural aspects to relationships, appreciation or nonacceptance by friends, family, and the larger environment may be a more prominent issue.

What do you think? Do an Internet search to find out the types of diverse relationships that exist in your nation or state. Look up news articles, Internet blogs, and so on to see what types of acceptance they receive in your area. What types of issues might they face in terms of housing, integration into social circles, and so on? What might you do, personally, to encourage a more respectful life for such couples without, at the same time, making them just another "civic project" or something "interesting to look at"?

Relational and organizational conflict: How can I make intercultural conflict more productive?

Cross-cultural approaches to conflict resolution

One of the processes that characterizes most deep relationships at some point is conflict. The research on cross-cultural differences in conflict has looked at everything from brothers and sisters to romantic partners to workplace conflicts, often with the issues in the conflicts being the same. Managers, particularly those in human resources, spend hours resolving disputes, confrontations, and disagreements between warring colleagues. With regard to intercultural conflict,

Stella Ting-Toomey and John Oetzel (2001) explain that conflict emerges when groups of people from different cultural communities who are involved in interdependent communicative objectives experience an emotional frustration caused by the perceived incompatibility of desired goals. Ting-Toomey (2003) defines **conflict** as the "perceived and/or actual incompatibility of values, expectations, processes, or outcomes between two or more parties from different cultures over substantive and/or relational issues" (p. 373).

Conflict is a process of communication and interaction, and once dependent individuals realize that irreconcilability, inconsistency, and tension are beneficial, conflict usually erupts (Luthans et al., 2015). There are five styles of conflict: goal conflict, cognitive conflict, affective conflict, behavioral conflict, and procedural conflict. Goal conflict is conflict that occurs when the interested parties cannot reach an agreement on their goal (the expected result). Cognitive conflict is conflict that occurs when an individual or a group holds a different opinion or idea from other people or groups. Affective conflict is conflict resulting from the irreconcilable feelings or emotions (attitudes) between individuals or groups. Procedure conflict means that conflict is brought by each party who maintains different opinions on the method of solving a certain problem (Robbins & Judge, 2014).

Importantly, culture may impact the different stages of conflict. Thomas Kochman (1981), for example, describes Black and White styles of conflict in the United States, such as different interpretations of allegations. African Americans use more emotional vocal dynamics (Johnson, 2000) and may raise their voices in a discussion, leading White communicators to possibly perceive that an interaction has moved into a "conflict" while the African American sees it only as a "discussion" (Kochman, 1981). In addition, as African Americans are more likely to live "in time," using time for the means of relationship and understanding, and Whites to live "on time," adhering to a clock-schedule, a White may start to leave a conflict to make another appointment, while the African American feels that the two should continue the discussion until the conflict is resolved, regardless of other appointments.

Depending on how individuals balance the incompatibility of goals and feel the desire to serve individual needs and goals versus the needs and goals of others involved in the conflict, there are two dimensions and five conflict management orientations typically described in this literature (e.g., Rahim, 2002; Ting-Toomey, 2005) Scholars (i.e., Rahim, 2001, 2002) summarized the two dimensions based on the conflict on the satisfaction of desire: desire to satisfy the others' concerns and desire to satisfy ones' own concern. These five management styles serve as a basis for analyzing conflict events and management among intercultural relationships.

> **Avoiding** (or **withdrawing**) is used when the needs of both parties are not satisfied. It occurs when individuals prefer simply not to confront the other party, such as someone who has offended them, perhaps because of fear of consequences resulting from a direct confrontation of the issue. For example, they may postpone the deadline for solving a problem, withdraw from a threatening situation, or ignore the conflict, because they think it is not their business. The result of avoiding conflict, however, is that the conflict still exists.

> **Accommodating** (or **yielding**)—giving into the demands of the other party—often requires the sacrifice of personal goals for the resolution of conflict and maintaining a harmonious organizational relationship. It is used when one of the partners will not insist on their positions but instead accept other people's viewpoints. Such sacrifices take the form of appeasement, abandoning one's principles for the greater good of the

relationship in that context, and not minding one's own personal discomfort at the going-along-to-get-along mindset. This style can be used successfully when you find yourself in the wrong; when the issue of conflict is not as personally significant to you as it may be to the other party; to enable the building of social credit (or grace points) for you to be capitalized on at a later date; and when harmony, peaceful co-existence, and collaboration is more important than individual success.

→ **Competing** (or **dominating**) is often considered a win-lose situation because it works on the assumption that for one party to succeed, the other necessarily has to lose or fail. It is a style characterized by aggressive behaviors, overt disagreement, and extreme assertiveness to the discomfort of the other party. Generally, the partner with more power using this style will achieve their goals or maintain their own power no matter at what cost. A competing style can seriously damage relationships, put the parties into an attack-counterattack mode, and leave them angered, disrespected, and humiliated, with no intentions of seeking a cooperative solution. But if time is of the essence and a quick decision needs to be made, or when unpopular actions need to be implemented or there is a threat of competitors taking advantage of your accommodating or collaborating efforts, this style may be the best and only option to exercise.

→ A **collaborating** (or **integrating**) approach—a win-win situation—works best when both parties are committed to working together and resolving conflicts. This style encourages disgruntled parties to engage in dialog and work together to develop mutually beneficial solutions. Instead of avoiding or treating conflict as a contest, this approach accepts conflict as typical to organizational working lives. Brainstorming and developing creative solutions together gets all parted equally vested in the outcomes thereby improving the quality of collaborative efforts. However, arriving at a consensual and mutually acceptable solution is often challenging, emotionally exhausting, and time consuming.

→ **Compromising** (or **conceding**), a middle-range approach, is more aggressive than avoiding or accommodating but less involved than competing. In this approach, parties seek a solution collaboratively, usually with parties gaining some objectives but not all of them. The compromising style satisfies the needs of both parties through their sacrifice (yield), and with this style, both parties will try to find an alternative choice which can be accepted by both sides. Because a continuous conflict makes people unpleasant, the interested parties will compromise in order to achieve a goal that may not be the best but can be accepted by both sides (Gross & Guerrero, 2000; Rahim, 2001; Rahim & Magner, 1995; Rahim et al., 2000).

Conflict negotiation skills are a huge asset to an international manager, along with third-party alternatives to dispute resolution like mediation and arbitration. The trick is to know which strategies to use and when. Stella Ting-Toomey (2005) developed a theory that predicts how different people from different cultures might negotiate conflict on the five styles above. Her theory revolves around the notion of **face**, specifically, **positive** and **negative face** (see Chapter 7). There are two basic categories of face in the Chinese culture: *lian* and *mianzi*. A person's *lian* can be preserved by faithful compliance with ritual and social norms. One gains *lian* by displaying moral character, but when one loses *lian*, he/she cannot function properly in the community because respect is lost. However, *mianzi*, represents a more Western conception of face, a reputation, or respect achieved through success in life (Hu & Grove, 1991). Thus, while Americans may prefer not to embarrass themselves or others in public, they will not generally go as far as Chinese do to avoid embarrassment. There is a Chinese saying that a person needs face like a tree needs bark (*ren yao lian; shu yao pi*), which expresses that a person's self-esteem is often formed on the basis of others' remarks.

Ting-Toomey (2005) argues that people in collectivistic cultures are more likely to be concerned with positive face, and those from individualistic cultures, with negative face. Collectivists are more likely to be concerned with the face of the other person, and, thus, focused on the process of the communication, while individualists likely focus on own face and needs. Because conflict inherently challenges both negative face (as we try to persuade others) and positive face (as we challenge the competence of their ideas), Ting-Toomey predicts that in collectivist Asian cultures, obliging and avoiding are both effective and appropriate styles, because that personal success is not usually the primary concern in maintaining an interpersonal harmony. This probably holds true especially in work or public contexts and when the costs involved in the conflict are less. Individualists will be more likely than collectivists to seek dominating strategies. And, since collaboration requires both parties to address conflict squarely, this is also the approach that individualists are more likely to prefer (See Figure 13.3). Regardless of what style is used, one generally attributes their success to the right choice of style and failure to the faults of others (Harris, 2002).

Ting-Toomey and others have done many studies that support the main predictions of her theory, including working with colleagues to define other specific conflict behaviors, such as being passive aggressive, remaining calm, expressing feelings, or working through a third party (e.g., Oetzel et al., 2000), more recent researchers still often rely on the five overall approaches to conflict mentioned above to study culture. Different researchers have found that people with "interdependent" self-construal may avoid conflict out of concern to preserve social relationships, while people with an "independent" self-construal prefer dominating persuasion tactics (Kim et al., 2004), and that factors such as one's level of involvement with host nationals (Oommen, 2017), level of intimacy with the partner, status of the relationship, and emotional competence (Min & Takai, 2019) all influence one's choice of a conflict strategy across different cultures.

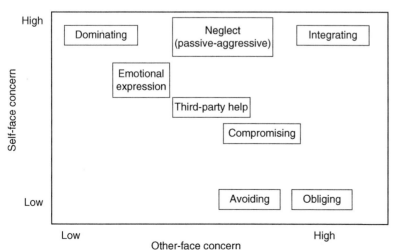

Figure 13.3 Stella Ting-Toomey (2005) predicts that collectivists will be more likely to avoid, withdraw, or compromise in conflict when possible. What influences the approach that you take? What factors besides culture may be at work?
Source: Reproduced from Ting-Toomey & Oetzel, 2002, p. 160, by permission of Sage Publications, Inc.

International negotiation

Kamal Fatehi (2008) declares that the most difficult and important task for international managers is negotiation. This process requires the careful consideration of another party's needs and goals before making a mutually agreeable decision. What makes international negotiations challenging are the sheer number of laws, regulations, business practices, standards of operations, and the cultural differences that add layers of complexity to the process. **Negotiation** is "a special form of social interaction or decision-making that (a) involves more than one party; (b) who hold potentially conflicting interests, as well as common interests or interdependence to motivate each to remain within the relationship or complete the exchange; and (c) requires a reciprocal exchange of information" (Schmidt & Conway, as cited in Schmidt et al., 2007, p. 221). Negotiation involves three aspects: the negotiation process, the parties in the negotiation, and the final outcome or agreement that emerges from the negotiation (Fatehi, 2008). In addition to these components, we need to remember aspects of negotiating such as each party's expected outcomes; the negotiating team make up and motivation; physical factors such as site, space, operational procedures, and use of time; as well as style of communicating and negotiating (Beamer & Varner, 2008).

Wallace Schmidt and his colleagues (2007) summarize a three-phase intercultural conflict negotiation model. In the **background phase**, parties undertake essential planning for the negotiation session. This includes analyzing one's own position in the process and carefully planning our one's communicating language. Each party should gather and organize pertinent information regarding the situation keeping in mind all the involved people, their varied interests, available options, and criteria such as market value, expert opinion, customs, laws, industry practices, and others (Fatehi, 2008). In addition to identifying one's own interests, priorities, goals, and strategies, one must also understand the mindset, personality attributes, perceptions, cultural values, norms, beliefs, and expectations of the other negotiating party. Even as one collects cultural information about the other party, one should also be mindful of the dangers of cultural stereotyping and cultural profiling (Schmidt et al., 2007).

In the **process phase**, the actual negotiation, collaborative engagement, or competition occurs between the parties. Parties communicate back and forth within their intercultural context and shape the reality of the ongoing negotiation with the unique characteristics they bring to the table. According to Schmidt et al. (2007), two specific negotiating styles emerge during this phase: a **distributive** or **positional negotiation,** which involves competitively pushing for one's own goals and agenda with little regard to the other party; and **integrative** or **principled negotiation** that uses collaborative strategies and considers needs and expectations of the other party to develop mutually satisfying ends. Principled negotiation (PN) advocates negotiating on merits. PN "provides parties to a negotiation with a method of focusing on basic interests and mutually advantageous solutions" (Fatehi, 2008, p. 200). PN values other members' perspectives, and negotiators, having gained trust and credibility, work to share information reciprocally and improve their mutual situations. Maki Meyer and Farida Fozdar (2020) studied intercultural families in Australia and found that these families created a multicultural cuisine through multi-directional negotiations between father and mother, parents/grandparents and children, and home and wider community. Specifically, they found that children played a significant role in the negotiation process. The last stage, the **outcome phase**, is the culmination of all events and communication that comprised the conflict negotiation process. The process itself and the outcomes are evaluated to see whether expectations were surpassed or fell short of predetermined goals. This phase determines the nature of future interactions and whether or not there is potential for more business partnerships.

Of course, an international/intercultural negotiation is never an event, it is always a process, and that process can be long and time consuming. In addition to negotiations, *mediation* and *arbitration* are two other methods used in conflict reconciliation. **Mediators** are neutral third parties that try to resolve disputes with reason and compromise instead of more aggressive measures. They have no power to impose a decision upon the disputing parties but work collaboratively with the two parties to arrive at a third-party mediated, mutually acceptable solution. Mediation by a third party is particularly helpful if the two conflicting parties have reached a stalemate or voluntarily agreed to have a third party intervene (Schmidt et al., 2007). Arbitration is yet another dispute resolution alternative that conflicting parties can opt for. **Arbitrators** are neutral, objective, third parties that can resolve a conflict based on the facts of the conflict situation presented to them. Unlike mediators, arbitrators are permitted to impose a binding decision on the parties in conflict (Schmidt et al., 2007).

Even with all the information gathered from the discussion above, if individuals do not behave in culturally intelligent and sensitive ways, no negotiation will be successful. Culture influences not only the style of negotiating but also what groups consider important within the context. Fatehi (2007) explains that collectivistic cultures have larger number of members in their negotiating teams while individualistic cultures may have just one person. A negotiating team's make-up may be based on how a culture values age and seniority of a member, a member's expertise, and members' decision-making authority and status within the organizational hierarchy or even in that society. Knowledge of the opposite negotiating team's characteristics will help the home team navigate the conflict.

When holding negotiations internationally, it is also important that we learn about nuances unique to the other culture that may differ from our own, such as how the culture uses time. Negotiators from the United States, for example, are not known for being patient and may use direct and indirect ways to push their negotiating party into a resolution, while the Japanese consider taking time to make a decision is a sign of maturity and wisdom (Beamer & Varner, 2008). Emotions are of extreme importance during the communicating and managing of conflict. People in high-context and low-context cultures may emote differently with different objectives and toward different ends. Whether to display emotions and what kinds of emotions to display are culturally motivated and interpreted. Cultural differences also exist between deal-focused (DF) and relationship-focused (RF) negotiating groups. Fatehi (2008) argues that the majority of world's cultures are RF and believes in dealing with people they trust such as their friends and family members. When doing business with strangers, they first try to develop relationships with their new negotiating or business partners to get to know them better and build trust. The DF types believe in wasting no time in seemingly pointless small talk or extended chats about what they consider irrelevant or frivolous topics. The sooner a deal gets done, the better.

In forging international relationships through successful negotiations, it is imperative that the two parties be mindful of each other's cultural norms and values. The proper way of greeting someone from a foreign culture, the acceptance of humor in professional settings, the politeness of making eye contact, perceptions of silence, expectations for personal space, appropriateness of body language and gestures, the role of religion in social and professional interaction, and so on, are all issues to consider before venturing into negotiations with a different cultural group. Individuals and groups who are culturally sensitive, flexible in communicating and negotiating styles, and considerate of differences will gain the richest of experiences from international negotiation opportunities.

Summary

We began our look at relating culturally by considering different types of relationships where culture and difference are involved. We saw people bring into relationships different motives, relational definitions, and values. Through processes such as learning about similarities, learning to predict and understand the other's behavior, self-disclosure, and resolving relational tensions, our relationships grow, as we continue to work out individual and cultural differences. Each culture also has unique aspects and nuances of relationship patterns. As we travel to other cultures and have relationships with people from other cultures within our own, we must also be aware of the role of structural power and ideologies. For example, do we only accept friends if they become like our culture expects them to be?

One type of relational pattern is conflict. Our discussion presents different types of conflict strategies and approaches, as well as issues present in negotiation as these relate to work relationships. However, the strategies also have applications to relationships with our parents, siblings, friends, and lovers.

Understanding relationships and conflict is useful in terms of civic engagement. First, we can work together within our relationships to both become and help others become socially aware within our friendship circles. Working together in socially relevant action also builds bonds of friendship, as we share "fellowship" in a task of making the world a better place. And forming friendships and romance across cultural and national lines helps to bring harmony and appreciation of other cultures to the world as a whole. Finally, in intercultural personal and work relationships, we are bound to have conflict. Understanding the ways that other groups perceive and practice conflict will keep us from imposing our own expectations on them. And, perhaps through better relationships and conflict, we can build synergy with others, rather than working on our own toward social involvement and change.

KEY TERMS

miscegenation, 268
intermarriage, 268
relationship, 269
exogamy, 269
values, 270
nuclear family, 270
cosmopolitanism, 271
relational identity, 271
propinquity, 272
similarity-attraction hypothesis, 272
self-disclosure, 272
social penetration theory, 272
depth, 272
breadth, 272
uncertainty reduction theory, 273
uncertainty, 273
anxiety, 273
dialectics/dialectical tension, 273
propriety, 274
reciprocity, 274
selflessness, 274

kuan-hsi, 275
Romeo and Juliet effect, 275
refence, 275
stigma, 276
conflict, 277
avoiding (or withdrawing), 277
accommodating (or yielding), 277
competing (or dominating), 278
collaborating (or integrating), 278
compromising (or conceding), 278
face, 278
positive face, 278
negative face, 278
negotiation, 280
background phase, 280
process phase, 280
distributive, or positional negotiation, 280
integrative, or principled negotiation, 280
outcome phase, 280
mediator, 281
arbitrator, 281

Discussion Questions

1 In groups, come up with strategies for success or coping in intercultural friendships, romance, workplace relationships, or families. The Internet has many sources that might help you come up with a list. What would you add from your own experience?

2 How do you feel that people in your culture perceive intergroup unions (romance, marriage)? Which intergroup unions do you feel are more accepted, and why? (e.g., interreligious? Inter-caste or interclass, some racial/ethnic combinations more than others?)

3 For one week, keep a journal of friends you talk to through social network sites, with for how long, how often, and how deep. After the week, compare networks with other students. How "diverse" is your network? What are some advantages of diverse relationship networks?

4 We saw in this chapter that inter*cultural* relationships (e.g., Norwegian-Belarussian) might face different issues than inter*group* relationships (e.g., Black-White). We discussed conflict between people of different national cultures. What sorts of issues might you have to consider, in addition, if you wanted to discuss interethnic, interracial, or interreligious conflict?

5 Find a cross-cultural simulation game regarding conflict or negotiation, such as The Emperor's Pot (Batchelder, 1996). In such games, people are often assigned to different cultures. After the game, discuss your feelings and aspects of negotiation you experienced during the exercise.

Action Points

1 Find another person in your church, organization, or school who is different from you. You may not become friends, but commit to meeting every one or two weeks. Try to really listen and understand about the person's life, and share yours with the other person.

2 Watch the news to find out about some of the political and social conflicts in your area. In what way is culture or group identity or politics involved in the conflict? Give a report on the conflict in class. How might information you learned in this chapter help people in the situation negotiate conflict?

3 Join a social advocacy group for a cause in which you believe. Do some deeper research on the varieties of strategies people can use to address conflict (e.g., Ting-Toomey & Oetzel, 2001). Discuss with members of your organization the usefulness of different strategies for conflict and negotiation in different settings.

For More Information

Berry, J.W. (Ed.). (2017). *Mutual intercultural relations*. Cambridge University Press.

Broome, B. (2005). *Building bridges across the Green Line: A guide to intercultural communication in Cyprus*. United Nations Office of Project Services (UNOPS).

Gudykunst, W. B., Ting-Toomey, S., & Nishida T. (Eds.). (1996). *Communication in personal relationships across cultures*. Sage.

Kriesberg, L. (2006). *Constructive conflicts: From escalation to resolution*. Rowman & Littlefield Publishers.

Romano, D. (2008). *Intercultural marriage: Promises & pitfalls* (3rd ed.). Intercultural Press.

Zakaria, N., Amelinckx, A., & Wilemon, D. (2004). Working together apart? Building a knowledge-sharing culture for global virtual teams. *Creativity and Innovation Management, 13*, 15–29.

References

50 years later, interracial couples still face hostility from strangers. (2017, June 12). *CBS News*. Accessed December 5, 2022, at https://www.cbsnews.com/news/50-years-loving-case-interracial-couples-still-face-hostility-from-strangers

Allport, G. W. (1979). *The nature of prejudice* (originally published, 1954). Addison-Wesley.

Altman, I., & Taylor, D. (1973). *Social penetration*. Holt, Rinehard, and Winston.

Bahns, A. J., Crandall, C. S., Gillath, O., & Preacher, K. J. (2017). Similarity in relationships as niche construction: Choice, stability, and influence within dyads in a free choice environment. *Journal of Personality and Social Psychology, 112*(2), 329–355. https://doi.org/10.1037/pspp0000088

Baptist, J., Craig, B., & Nicholson, B. (2019). Black-White marriages: The moderating role of openness on experience of couple discrimination and marital satisfaction. *Journal of Marital and Family Therapy, 45*(4), 635–649. https://doi.org/10.1111/jmft.12362.

Batchelder, D. (1996). The emperor's pot. In H. N. Seelye (Ed.), *Experiential activities for intercultural learning* (pp. 85–99). Intercultural Press.

Baxter, L. A., & Norwood, K. M. (2015). Relational dialectics theory. In C.R. Berger & M.E. Roloff (Eds.), *The International Encyclopedia of interpersonal communication* (pp. 1–9). John Wiley & Sons, Ltd. https://doi.org/10.1002/9781118540190.wbeic019

Beamer, L., & Varner, I. (2008). *Intercultural communication in the global workplace*. McGraw-Hill Irwin.

Berger, C. R., & Calabrese, R. (1975). Some explorations in initial interaction and beyond. *Human Communication Research, 1*(2), 99–112. https://doi.org/10.1111/j.1468-2958.1975.tb00258.x

Berscheid, E., & Ammazzalorso, H. (2004). Emotional experience in close relationships. In M. B. Brewer & M. Hewstone (Eds.), *Perspectives on social psychology: Emotion and motivation* (pp. 47–69). Blackwell Publishing.

Byrne, D. (1969). Attitudes and attraction. In L. Berknowitz (Ed.), *Advances in experimental social psychology* (pp. 35–89). Academic Press.

Byrne, D. (1971). *The attraction paradigm*. Academic Press.

Chang, H.-C., & Holt, R. (1991). More than relationship: Chinese interaction and the principle of *kuan-hsi*. *Communication Quarterly, 39*(3), 251–271. https://doi.org/10.1080/01463379109369802

Chappell, B. (2017, June 22). Census finds a more diverse America, as whites lag growth. NPR. Accessed March 6, 2023 at https://www.npr.org/sections/thetwo-way/2017/06/22/533926978/census-finds-a-more-diverse-america-as-whites-lag-growth

China Ministry of Civil Affairs. (n.d.). *Civil affairs year book*. China Statistics Press.

Crary, D. (2007, April 12). Interracial marriages surge across U.S. *USA Today*. Accessed December 9, 2022, at http://www.usatoday.com/news/health/2007-04-12-interracial-marriage_N.htm

Dodd, C. H., & Baldwin, J. R. (2002). The role of family and macrocultures in intercultural relationships. In J. N. Martin, T. K. Nakayama, & L. A. Flores (Eds.), *Readings in intercultural communication: Experiences and contexts* (pp. 279–288). McGraw Hill.

Fatehi, K. (2008). *Managing internationally: Succeeding in a culturally diverse world*. Sage.

Fetterling, J. (2022, July 11). These famous interracial celebrity couples inspire diversity. *FamilyMinded*. Accessed December 9, 2022, at www.familyminded.com/s/interracial-celebrity-couples-inspire-diversity-d8671558a3424a3d

Froidevaux, N. R. (2019). *The relevance of accommodation in understanding intercultural and intracultural relationship quality* [M.A., University of California, Irvine]. Accessed March 6, 2023, at https://www.proquest.com/docview/2394379705/abstract/D70A320BC6124470PQ/1

Gaines, S. O. (2017). *Identity and interethnic marriage in the United States*. Routledge.

Giménez Moreno, R. (2021). Lexical-semantic configuration of ordinary relational identities in multicultural groups of university students. *Language and Intercultural Communication, 21*(1), 102–117. https://doi.org/10.1080/14708477.2020.1833901

Gould, J. A., Kulik, C. T., & Sardeshmukh, S. R. (2018). Trickle-down effect: The impact of female board members on executive gender diversity. *Human Resource Management, 57*(4), 931–945. https://doi.org/10.1002/hrm.21907

Graham, M. A., Moeai, J., & Shizuru, L. S. (1985). Intercultural marriages: An interreligous perspective. *International Journal of Intercultural Relations, 9*(4), 427–434. DOI: 10.1016/0147-1767(85)90059-8

Gross, M. A., & Guerrero, L. K. (2000). Managing conflict appropriately and effectively: An application of the competence model to Rahim's organizational conflict style. *International Journal of Conflict Management, 11*(3), 200–226. https://doi.org/10.1108/eb022840

Gudykunst, W. B. (2005). An anxiety/uncertainty management (AUM) theory of effective communication. In W. B. Gudykunst (Ed.), *Theorizing about intercultural communication* (pp. 281–322). Sage.

Gudykunst, W. B., & Kim, Y. Y. (2003). *Communicating with strangers: An approach to intercultural communication* (4th ed.). McGraw Hill.

Harris, T. E. (2002). *Applied organizational communication: Principles and pragmatics for future practice* (2nd ed.). Lawrence Erlbaum Associates.

Haughton, C. N. (2020). *Resilience in interracial relationships: Relationship maintenance and communal orientation as protection against network stigma* [M.A., University of California, Santa Barbara]. Accessed March 6, 2023, at https://www.proquest.com/docview/2452891290/abstract/FE766B289D6C40BFPQ/1

Hoogenraad, H. (2021). Marriage migration as happiness projects? Africa-origin male marriage migrants' experiences with marriage migration to Australia. *Journal of Ethnic and Migration Studies, 47*(9), 2144–2160. https://doi.org/10.1080/1369183X.2020.1729106

Hu, Q., Pan, P., & Chen, X. (2021). Home-based acculturation and Chinese attitude toward intercultural marriage: A cross-generational comparison. *SAGE Open, 11*(1), 21582440211001530. https://doi.org/10.1177/21582440211001529

Hu, W., & Grove, C. L. (1991). *Encountering the Chinese: A guide for Americans*. Intercultural Press.

Johnson, F. (2000). *Speaking culturally: Language diversity in the United States*. Sage.

Kerckhoft, A. C. (1974). The social context of interpersonal attraction. In T. L. Huston (Ed.), *Foundations of interpersonal attraction* (pp. 61–78). Academic Press.

Kim, M.-S., Lee, H. R., Kim, I. D., & Hunter, J. E. (2004). A test of a cultural model of conflict styles. *Journal of Asian Pacific Communication, 14*(2), 197–222. https://doi.org/10.1075/japc.14.2.02kim

Kochman, T. (1981). *Black and White styles in conflict*. University of Chicago Press.

Kudo, K., Volet, S., & Whitsed, C. (2019). Development of intercultural relationships at university: A three-stage ecological and person-in-context conceptual framework. *Higher Education, 77*(3), 473–489. https://doi.org/10.1007/s10734-018-0283-9

Lee, P.-W. (2008). Stages and transitions of relational identity formation in intercultural friendship: Implications for identity management theory. *Journal of International and Intercultural Communication, 1*(1), 51–69. https://doi.org/10.1080/17513050701690918

Livingston, G., & Brown, A. (2017). Public views on intermarriage. *Pew Research Center*. Accessed December 9, 2022, at https://www.pewresearch.org/social-trends/2017/05/18/2-public-views-on-intermarriage

Lu, J. G., Hafenbrack, A. C., Eastwick, P. W., Wang, D. J., Maddux, W. W., & Galinsky, A. D. (2017). "Going out" of the box: Close intercultural friendships and romantic relationships spark creativity, workplace innovation, and entrepreneurship. *Journal of Applied Psychology, 102*, 1091–1108. https://doi.org/10.1037/apl0000212

Luthans, F., Luthans, B., & Luthans, K. (2015). *Organizational behavior: An evidence-based approach* (13th ed.). Information Age Publishing.

Malone, C. (2011, April 7). Celebrity intercultural relationships. *Examiner.com*. Accessed December 9, 2011, at http://www.examiner.com/intercultural-relationships-in-honolulu/celebrity-intercultural-relationships

McCarthy, J. (2021). *U.S. approval of interracial marriage at new high of 94%*. Gallup. Accessed March 6, 2023, at https://news.gallup.com/poll/354638/approval-interracial-marriage-new-high.aspx

Meyer, M., & Fozdar, F. (2020). Complex but ordinary: Intercultural negotiations among mixed families in Australia. *Journal of Family Studies, 28*(4), 1504-1526. https://doi.org/10.1080/13229400.2020.1844039

Min, M. C., & Takai, J. (2019). Emotional competence, conflict management styles, and relational factors: Cross-cultural comparison between Japan and Myanmar. *Intercultural Communication Studies, 28*(1), 109–131.

Mongeau, P. A., & Henningsen, M. L. M. (2008). Stage theories of relationship development: Charting the course of interpersonal communication. In L. A. Baxter & D. O. Braithwaite (Eds.), *Engaging theories in interpersonal communication: Multiple perspectives* (pp. 363–375). Sage.

Oetzel, J., Ting-Toomey, S., Yokochi, Y., Masumoto, T., & Takai, J. (2000). A typology of facework behaviors in conflicts with best friends and relative strangers. *Communication Quarterly, 48*(4), 397–419. https://doi.org/10.1080/01463370009385606

Oommen, D. (2017). A test of the relationships between host and home national involvements and the preference for intercultural conflict management styles. *Journal of Intercultural Communication Research, 46*(4), 314–329. https://doi.org/10.1080/17475759.2017.1329159

Pachankis, J. E., Hatzenbuehler, M. L., & Starks, T. J. (2014). The influence of structural stigma and rejection sensitivity on young sexual minority men's daily tobacco and alcohol use. *Social Science & Medicine (1982), 103 (Feb)*, 67–75. https://doi.org/10.1016/j.socscimed.2013.10.005

Parker, K., & Barroso, A. (2021). *In Vice President Kamala Harris, we can see how America has changed.* Pew Research Center. Accessed March 6, 2023, at https://www.pewresearch.org/fact-tank/2021/02/25/in-vice-president-kamala-harris-we-can-see-how-america-has-changed

Rahim, M. A. (2001). *Managing conflict in organizations* (3rd ed.). Quorum Books.

Rahim, M. A. (2002). Toward a theory of managing organizational conflict. *The International Journal of Conflict Management, 13*(3), 206–235. https://doi.org/10.1108/eb022874

Rahim, M. A., & Magner, N. R. (1995). Confirmatory factor analysis of the style of handling interpersonal conflict: First-order factor model and its invariance across groups. *Journal of Applied Psychology, 80*(1), 122–131. DOI: 10.1037/0021-9010.80.1.122

Rahim, M. A., Magner, N. R., & Shapiro, D. L. (2000). Do justice perceptions influence styles of handling conflict with supervisors? What justice perceptions, precisely. *International Journal of Conflict Management, 11*(1), 9–31. DOI: 10.1108/eb022833

Robbins, S. P., & Judge, T. A. (2014). *Organizational behavior* (16th ed.). Pearson.

Rogan, D., Hopkinson, G., & Piacentini, M. (2021). Relational dialectics: Researching change in intercultural families. *Qualitative Market Research, 24*(1), 47–62. https://doi.org/10.1108/QMR-03-2019-0051

Rogan, D., Piacentini, M., & Hopkinson, G. (2018). Intercultural household food tensions: A relational dialectics analysis. *European Journal of Marketing, 52*(12), 2289–2311. https://doi.org/10.1108/EJM-10-2017-0778

Rohrlich, B. F. (1988). Dual-culture marriage and communication. *International Journal of Intercultural Relations, 12(1)*, 35–44. https://doi.org/10.1016/0147-1767(88)90005-3

Rosenblatt, P. C., Karis, T. A., & Powell, R. D. (1995). *Multiracial couples: Black & White voices.* Sage. Rosenblatt.

Schmidt, W. V., Conaway, R. N., Easton, S. S., & Wardrope, W. J. (2007). *Communicating globally: Intercultural communication and international business.* Sage.

Silva, L., Campbell, K., & Wright, D. (2012). Intercultural relationships: Entry, adjustment, and cultural negotiations. *Journal of Comparative Family Studies, 43*, 857–870. https://doi.org/10.3138/jcfs.43.6.857

Tili, T. R., & Barker, G. G. (2015). Communication in intercultural marriages: Managing cultural differences and conflicts. *Southern Communication Journal, 80*(3), 189–210. https://doi.org/10.1080/1041794X.2015.1023826

Ting-Toomey, S. (1994). Managing conflict in intimate intercultural relationships. In D.D. Cahn (Ed.)., *Conflict in personal relationships* (pp. 47–77). Lawrence Erlbaum Associates.

Ting-Toomey, S. (2003). Managing intercultural conflicts effectively. In L. A. Samovar & R. E. Porter (Eds.), *Intercultural communication: A reader* (10th ed., pp. 373–384). Wadsworth/Thomson Learning.

Ting-Toomey, S. (2005). The matrix of face: An updated face-negotiated theory. In W. B. Gudykunst (Ed.), *Theorizing intercultural communication* (pp. 71–92). Sage.

Ting-Toomey, S., & Oetzel, J. (2001). *Managing intercultural conflict effectively.* Sage.

Tseng, W. S. (1977). Adjustment in intercultural marriage. In W. S. Tseng, J. F. McDermott, & T. W. Matetzki (Eds.), *Adjustment in intercultural marriage* (pp. 93-103). The University Press of Hawaii.

Yum, J. O. (1988). The impact of confucianism on interpersonal relationships and communication patterns in East Asia. *Communication Monographs, 55*(4), 374–388. https://doi.org/10.1080/03637758809376178

Chapter 14

The political context: How can we use communication to shape politics and culture?

Chapter objectives

After this chapter, you should be able to:

→ Understand and explain politics as cultural communication

→ Explain how politics and culture are interrelated

→ Identify examples of culture-based social movements

→ Understand the politics of immigration

→ Understand values for intercultural political leadership

Intercultural Communication for Everyday Life, Second Edition. John R. Baldwin, Alberto González, Nettie Brock, Ming Xie, and Chin-Chung Chao.
© 2024 John Wiley & Sons Ltd. Published 2024 by John Wiley & Sons Ltd.
Companion Website: http://www.wiley.com/go/baldwin2e

O n November 29, 2022, the U.S. men's soccer team was set to play Iran at the World Cup, hosted by Qatar. The games were already steeped in controversy, since FIFA (the governing body for international soccer) banned "One Love" wristbands that players planned to wear to protest discrimination against LGBTQ+ people in Qatar (Sullivan, 2022). The World Cup was taking place at a time of continuing protests in Iran, mainly led by women, against repressive laws and a deteriorating economy. To show solidarity with the protesters, the U.S. team briefly displayed on social media the flag of Iran with the symbol of the Islamic Republic removed. Iranian officials demanded that the U.S. team be expelled from the competition. However, the Iranian players also showed solidarity with the protesters by refusing to sing the Iranian national anthem during an opening match (Kiley, 2022). The United States would win the match 1–0.

All of this was taking place against a backdrop of international condemnation of Iran for supplying Russia with lethal drone weapons in its unprovoked war against Ukraine. To the U.S. players, their actions showed support for democratic ideals and for the repressed. To the Iranian government, the players' actions showed disrespect for Iran's sovereignty. Sometimes a soccer match isn't just a match.

POP CULTURE

Popular music is used in many cultures for political means, either to support the current government or ideologies, or to protest. In Brazil, for example, favela funk emerged from the poorest areas of Rio de Janeiro and represents an oppositional voice for the marginalized.

With classmates, develop a list of groups or singers from three different cultures who sing messages that are either mildly or overtly political. How effective do you feel their messages are, and why?

This chapter explores the nature of political communication and its implications for intercultural relations, civic engagement, and activism. We define political communication and explore two particular political domains that are especially relevant to intercultural relations. We also examine the nature of political leadership in international and diverse contexts and provide a leadership model that responds to the ever-increasing demands for dialogue and understanding.

Politics, culture, and communication: How do politics relate to culture?

Like culture, "politics" has many definitions. Most broadly defined, **politics** refers to the identification and public negotiation of competing interests. Like culture, politics presumes the creation and public sharing of meaning. Typically, we place politics in the realm of government. In democratic systems, candidates campaign for office and, if elected, politicians make laws, oversee the mechanisms of the state (agencies, services, taxation, etc.), and negotiate legislation with opposition parties. This is electoral politics. Civic engagement in the realm of government means knowing and following how government works, paying attention to political debates, and volunteering in efforts to help pass or defeat proposed legislation. In a single-party state like China, civic engagement means knowing the laws enacted by the central government and acting consistently with those laws. It means going to the website of the local party leaders and reading their posts. Above all, being engaged means acting virtuously to render assistance to others in need and to uphold order in the community.

In democratic systems, **communicative engagement** means participating in civic dialogue and making full use of expressive opportunities to influence deliberative democracy. Ideally, our participation has the potential to "convert society into a great community" (McKinney et al., 2005, p. 7). The person who practices communicative engagement seeks out opportunities to be heard on issues and is a critical reader and viewer of political messages.

There is another meaning to "politics." We will call this **politics 2.0** or cultural politics. Politics 2.0 refers to how social structures and institutions work to maintain their authority. This is what is called the "politics of consensus and consent" (Deetz, 1990, p. 46). Like White positionality in the United States (Whiteness, Chapter 9), politics 2.0 encompasses everyday actions that we regard as "natural" and "normal" that function to protect and advance the goals of dominant interests. When we renew a driver's license or pay taxes, we perform our consent to be permitted to drive and to have our income returned to the state or local government. When we use the term "American" when we really mean "a US citizen," or when we do not think of someone from Bolivia or Paraguay as "American," we uphold the notion that the United States is the true and only America and that everyone else in the Americas (North, Central, and South) does not have a claim to that name. Terms such as "gender politics," "identity politics," or "politics of the everyday" usually are directed at pointing out how we enact our consensus on these topics or how we attempt to disrupt consensus.

For example, the doctrine of American Exceptionalism plays out in athletic competition from high school to the professional conferences. The competitive and selective qualities of U.S. sports teams are thought to "mirror the values and beliefs of the dominant culture" (Miller, 1999, p. 189). Teams become synonymous with regional and national ideals, making team support an act of patriotism. Questioning a team name, for example, would be treasonous. Imagine, then, the challenges faced by Native American activists who for decades protested the names of teams such as the Cleveland Indians and the Washington Redskins. In the public imagination, the Native Americans "lost" the competition for the U.S. West, and as outsiders (the losers) had lost legitimacy (Miller, 1999, p. 191). By linking major league teams to such powerful influences as Manifest Destiny and American Exceptionalism, the teams protected their revenue stream against critical review by the already formed consensus of the public.

Yet change happens. After the 2020 murder of George Floyd in Minneapolis, the national pressure increased to remedy racial appropriations, and attention turned to major team names. In 2022, the Washington Commanders and the Cleveland Guardians took the field with new names. They shed their logos, which many saw as offensive to Indigenous peoples.

BREAK IT DOWN

What are some of your own practices—ways of talking, joking, dressing, shopping—that support dominant ways of thinking and acting? What are some practices that support alternative ways of thinking and acting? What is your agency to choose one or the other? To what extent can you undermine or resist dominant preferences that you disagree with?

Combining the notion of communicative engagement with politics 2.0, we can now see that participating in democracy is highly variable and problematic. Do people living in urban neighborhoods have the same opportunity to travel to a voting station on election day? Does a person who has been unemployed or is on a low income have the same opportunity as an affluent person to write an opinion letter to the local newspaper or to donate to a political candidate? Critical communicative engagement reflects upon the presence of dominant interests in our everyday practices and invents possibilities for disrupting practices that maintain inequity or hide exploitative interests. In intercultural contexts, we should attempt to identify "what conventional practices must be altered or expanded to allow for the discourse of the Other to be heard—and not only heard, but heeded" (McKerrow, 2000, p. 43). The next section illustrates these polar notions of politics by examining intercultural social movements.

Making change happen: What are some examples of successful social movements?

Quite often, intercultural communication is central to accomplishing political resistance and critique. Wide-scale, organized activism to advance social and political criticism and change is called a **social movement** (Stewart et al., 2007). While some movements may be "revivalist" and seek to reassert "an idealized past" (such as the Tea Party movement in the United States), many are "innovative" movements that seek to assert and implement new values and perspectives (p. 14). Innovative movements are most relevant to the formation of new intercultural relations.

Social movements are outside of established social institutions. Hence, one characteristic of social movements is that they are "uninstitutionalized collectivities." Social movements have belief systems that leaders and members can express with some conviction. Social movements define and pursue a moral good that leaders and members believe will make conditions better for people. Social movement messages are directed outward—to nonmembers (to gain new members or to gain support for change). Messages are also directed inward—to members (to maintain support and to mobilize members for action in support of goals). Finally, a movement has some sort of organization in order to maintain itself and mark progress toward its stated goals (Stewart et al., 2007, pp. 7–16).

While an understanding of social movements is important to placing a speech or text in a political and cultural context, another exciting concept also is available. As we learned in Chapter 9, **vernacular discourse** refers to locally produced meanings. It is "discourse operating within local communities" (Ono & Sloop, 1995, p. 20). Vernacular discourse is in the realm of politics 2.0 and allows us to examine the politics of the local and the local. Critical focus is upon marginalized communities and identities, and their interaction with the dominant interests because vernacular discourse "makes visible power relations among subjects" (Calafell & Delgado, 2004, p. 6). Since local meanings many times function persuasively to mediate relationships between marginalized and dominant communities, we also use the term **vernacular rhetoric**. This section examines the vernacular rhetoric of three innovative social movements that seek to address intercultural inequity.

The Green Belt Movement

Upon her death in the fall of 2011, Wangari Maathai may not have been a household name in the United States, but she was a world-famous activist known to millions. Former President Obama issued a statement that praised her work. The Green Belt Movement, he said, "stands as a testament to the power of grassroots organizing, proof that one person's simple idea—that a community should come together to plant trees—can make a difference, first in one village, then in one nation, and now across Africa" (The White House, 2011).

The Green Belt Movement (GBM; http://www.greenbeltmovement.org) began in Kenya in the 1970s. Maathai's goal was to empower the women of Kenya to protect the rural environment against degradation and misuse, by planting trees. The trees would provide windbreaks for schools and neighborhoods, prevent soil erosion, provide firewood for cooking, and allow a harvest of fresh fruit. Just as important, local women would learn new practices for planting and caring for the trees, and they would establish a new relationship with their local governments—a relationship based on mutual respect and equality (Maathai, 2004). In learning these new practices, the women would be critically engaged with their local government (Figure 14.1).

The GBM existed outside of official government programs and at times challenged the government. When the Kenyan government planned to replace Nairobi's central park with a building complex of offices and retail shops, Maathai objected, and filed a lawsuit to stop the development. The government threatened to outlaw the group and banished the organization to Maathai's home. The heavy-handed reaction by the government drew international support for Maathai and the building complex was abandoned (Bretton, 1998, p. 15).

Rhetorical communication was critical to the GBM. Maathai and her staff conducted workshops with the local women, which consisted of days of dialogue. The workshops led the women to reset their relationships with the land, their husbands, their government, and the future. Human rights advocate Frances Moore Lappé interviewed Maathai and asked about the persuasive power of the workshops. Maathai stated,

> Now that can take two days discussing, and that's when the personal transformation takes place. That's when people realize, yes, they may have been misled, but they have brains and they also can think. That's when we make a break, and from then on we are dealing with a different kind of person—very motivated, self-conscious, willing to make decisions, willing to go back to their communities and make a difference. (Lappé & Lappé, 2002, p. 186)

Figure 14.1 Professor Wangari Maathai, founder and advocate of the Green Belt Movement in Africa, stands up to hired security guards in the Karura Forest, Nairobi, Kenya, in April 1999. Source: Simon Maina/AFP/ Getty Images.

Eventually, Maathai mobilized more than 60,000 women to plant 20 million trees.

The basis of persuasion for the GBM is evident in the use of vernacular terms and knowledge. The slogan for the GBM was, "Save the Land Harambee." *Harambee* is the Swahili word that means "all pull together," and this word became the national slogan of Kenya's first president, Jomo Kenyatta (Maathai, 2004, p. 20). Maathai adapted the term to create an environmental mission and created a slogan that was recognized across the hundreds of communities in Kenya where the GBM recruited new members.

In addition to vernacular terms, vernacular knowledge also was valued by the GBM. When the foresters tried to teach the women about planting, they often used scientific terms and described complex procedures for planting. Again, demonstrating independence from existing institutions, the GBM eventually substituted the methods of the foresters with the methods developed by the women's ancestors. The women shared planting knowledge throughout their communities and became very innovative and resourceful. The foresters judged the women's methods unprofessional, but the GBM called the women "foresters without diplomas" (Maathai, 2004, p. 28).

The GBM lies at the intersection of three global movements—movements for women's empowerment, peace, and environmental protection. Maathai resisted patriarchy by providing a means for women to gain autonomy and change conditions in their communities. Maathai also considered violence and war as conflicts over resources. To improve the resources for all meant reduced conflict. Finally, creating a "greener" Africa allowed the continent to heal from decades of poor land use. The GBM clearly articulated its moral struggle against the forces of repression and exclusion. The GBM employed vernacular discourse and knowledge to gain members and to demonstrate a contrast to Western-educated politicians and foresters.

In 2004, Maathai was awarded the Nobel Prize for Peace. She continued to work for international awareness for women's agency and the environment. The GBM now has a goal to "Plant for the Planet" by extending its reach to additional countries. The GBM has enlarged its scope and become much more sophisticated. How the GBM will survive with the loss of its founder and charismatic leader remains to be seen, but the broader social movements in support of women, peace, and the environment continue.

What do you think? In this section, we are addressing leaders who have taken political action on issues specific to their regions and nations. Issues have included childcare, affordable healthcare, censorship, food security, rights to vote, and human trafficking. What are some pressing issues in your own area that need the action—from elected leaders as well as that of everyday citizens—to bring about change?

The immigrant rights movement

Among the most contentious issues confronting our global communities are struggles surrounding immigration and citizenship. Who enters a country, by what method, for how long and for what purpose, is a serious preoccupation in many parts of the world. It is serious because immigration ultimately involves questions of belonging and who becomes "one of us." Who belongs and who does not is political because the path to citizenship and entry into a community highlight particular interests of the community. The interests might include workforce demands, special relationships and agreements with other nations, humanitarian response to a crisis, or notions of national identity and pride. In this section, we will explore how these interests come into play in the U.S. immigrant rights movements.

Immigration is the entry into a country by a citizen of another country who then desires to remain in the country. A person (like a tourist) who enters a country with no intention of remaining is a non-immigrant (Chen, 2012, p. 264). Many of the conflicts around the world involve immigrants rather than non-immigrants. **Diaspora** refers to the movement of populations from one part of the world to another (Chapters 3, 12). This movement can be sudden, or it can occur over time. **Diasporic citizen** refers to a person who is a member of a group that has moved or been displaced. For example, in the 1940s and 1950s, thousands of people from mainland China and Taiwan immigrated to Central America seeking work. This created the Chinese diaspora in Panama (Siu, 2005). By nationality, the second- and third-generation descendants are Panamanian, but they remain diasporic citizens as they mediate the Chinese customs and values of their heritage with the equally meaningful Latino customs and values in Panama. Like the immigrant, "being diasporic means experiencing both identification with and displacement from both 'home' sites at once" (Siu, 2005, p. 11).

The common notion is that immigrant persons are legal or illegal. But it is not that simple. Like most identities, immigrant identities are contingent; that is, they are formed and understood in relation to a culture's values and history of immigration. Discourses on immigration and immigrant identities are shaped within "particular systems of inequality and domination" (Drzewiecka & Steyn, 2012, p. 2). While much of the debate on U.S. immigration policy falls into the realm of politics, the debate also is framed by politics 2.0!

The struggle over immigration policy and the humanitarian status of immigrants is unresolved throughout the world, and, if anything, it has grown worse over the last few years. It has been a dominant issue in major elections in France, Italy, the United Kingdom, and the United States (Edo et al., 2019), with right-wing parties winning several elections with opposition to immigration on their platforms. The COVID-19 crisis only intensified the problem, as politicians and pundits in many nations used COVID as a reason to bolster immigration restrictions. For example, Kurt Sengul (2021) outlines how right-wing populist Australian politician Pauline Hanson, building upon existing anti-Asian sentiment in Australia, wove together discourses of COVID- and immigrant-fear through on her Facebook page. The relationship between immigration, rhetoric, and attitudes is complex. For example, greater immigration in France is related to support for far-right candidates (Edo et al., 2019), and voters in Great Britain who favor Brexit (Britain's exit from the European Union) were more likely to also oppose immigration (Pickup et al., 2021)

However, in the United States, there have been concrete and opposing movements both in opposition to and in support of immigration at different times in history. Particularly after the attacks on the United States on September 11, 2001, there has been increasing attention on the U.S.-Mexican border. The calls to "secure our border" are now common in political discourse in the United States. But this discourse is also directed at people, namely the immigrants and migrant workers who are affected by new laws. In their study of the political rhetoric surrounding the passage of Proposition 187, the 1994 California law that withheld education and other benefits to undocumented persons, Kent Ono and John Sloop (2002) discovered that immigrants were depicted as human capital, criminal, immoral, and diseased (pp. 29–35), reminding us of the importance of cultural metaphors (Chapter 9). By 2007, the Congressional effort to reform national immigration policy failed and by the end of the decade the perception was that "behind every social ill lurks a brownskinned, illegal immigrant" (Powers, 2007, p. 13A).

As anti-immigrant rhetoric intensified, an oppositional social movement gained new strength (Figure 14.2). Its purpose was to create a counter-narrative that would frame the plight of the immigrants as a humanitarian issue. From March through May 2006, demonstrations involving

Figure 14.2 Protesters create a counter-narrative in support of immigrants.
Source: Emmanuel Dunand/ AFP/Getty Images.

hundreds of thousands were held in Dallas, Texas, Chicago, Illinois, Los Angeles, California, and Phoenix, Arizona. Disparate groups from labor unions to the Catholic Church supported the demonstrations (Pineda & Sowards, 2007). In many California cities, students walked out of classes and waved signs that read, "We are not criminals!" (Campo-Flores, 2006, p. 32). Farmers in agricultural states supported the movement, claiming that food supplies were jeopardized by the lack of farm workers. Activists like Enrique Morones acted locally. He founded Border Angels, a nonprofit organization that honored with white crosses those who had perished crossing the border, and volunteers assisted immigrants by placing water bottles in desert areas.

The movement organizers were able to reach across cultures to gain support from non-Latino immigrants. They studied the strategies of the anti-immigrant coalitions by following Stephen Valocchi's (2010) view that, knowing "how the dominant society frames an issue, then activists can use that knowledge in their own framing strategies" (p. 13). They drew upon the immigrant history of the United States to place the actions of those coming to the United States in a more favorable light. They also claimed the role of patriots, by waving the U.S. flag along with the flags of other nations (Pineda & Sowards, 2007).

As the Green Belt Movement and the immigration rights movement suggest, the effectiveness of a movement depends to a great extent on forming intercultural coalitions. The next section describes the leadership required to work across cultures.

The antiracism movement

The Black Lives Matter (BLM) movement was started by Alicia Garza, Patrisse Cullors, and Opal Tometi after the acquittal of the man who killed Black teenager Trayvon Martin in 2013. Over the next eight years, it became clear that the United States had a law enforcement problem. In the case of Ahmaud Aubery, a Georgia man killed while jogging, the United States had a vigilante problem as well. Instance after instance displayed a similar pattern: an unarmed Black resident is detained for a minor infraction, the resident questions or resists arrest, and the story ends in the death of the Black resident. In the case of Breonna Taylor, an EMS employee who was shot six times and died, the police entered the wrong apartment.

After the death of Floyd in May 2020 from the excessive force used by the police in Minneapolis (United States), which was captured graphically and heartbreakingly on video, protestors marched in cities big and small across the United States. After days of protests, Washington, D.C. Mayor Muriel Bowser declared 16th Street near the White House Black Lives Matter Plaza (Well, 2021). The vernacular quality of the protests was audible as marchers were directed to "say her name" and marchers would demand that local law enforcement officials "take a knee" in solidarity with the movement. Demonstrations also focused attention on anti-Asian hate crimes and anti-trans violence.

The antiracism movement is a broad-term movement that encompasses a variety of strategies and tactics to resist all forms of oppression, particularly race-based discrimination. The BLM website states that the movement "affirms the lives of Black queer and trans folks, disabled folks, undocumented folks, folks with records, women, and all Black lives across the gender spectrum" (Black Lives Matter, n.d.). Core to the antiracist movement is the conviction that thinking of yourself as not being racist is not enough to reverse centuries of racist history. You must be actively antiracist, which means calling out discriminatory acts at the interpersonal level, working in solidarity with (or speaking with) antiracist coalitions at the local level, and supporting social justice efforts at the national level.

Black intellectuals and academics have articulated a new awareness. Ibram X. Kendi provides a clear description of this awareness: "One endorses either the idea of a racial hierarchy as a racist, or racial equality as an antiracist. One believes problems are rooted in groups of people, as a racist, or locates the roots of problems in power and policies, as an antiracist" (Kendi, 2019, p. 9). Journalist Nikole Hannah-Jones created the "1619 Project" which was sponsored by the *New York Times*. This project was an effort to deliver a narrative of U.S. history in light of the legacy of slavery (Sreenivasan, 2019).

As with most things in politics 2.0, the antiracist movement, these efforts are not without opposition. At the University of North Carolina, trustees voted to deny tenure to Hanna-Jones, a vote the trustees subsequently reversed. But by then, Hannah-Jones, a Pulitzer Prize recipient, had decided to leave for Howard University (Jaschick, 2021). Residents in many school districts across the United States demanded that schools ban books that advocated for racial inclusion.

Being antiracist and relating to interculturality requires ongoing self-reflection. You may ask: What am I assuming about others in this situation? Who has privilege in this situation? How can I create shared power and equitable participation? Where am I and where are others after this conversation? A commitment to inclusion is hard work and means that we constantly learn about the struggles of others and we constantly reflect upon both our own interpersonal limitations and growth.

BREAK IT DOWN

An "ally" is someone from a dominant group (one with greater social power) who joins a struggle alongside members of a group to help them achieve greater social justice. Being an "ally" to a group that is marginalized or mistreated by a society is complicated, as there are dangers of doing "allyship" to meet one's own personal self-esteem needs or of being patronizing. Do your own research on being an "ally." What are tips that you can locate for someone who wants to be an ally for a group? If you want to be an ally of a group, see if you can specifically see what members of *that* group are looking for among those who would be allies. Share ideas of responsible "allyship" with your classmates or friends.

As we summarize these movements, we notice that some movements for social and cultural change gain enough momentum and become more formalized to the point that they are recognizable by name (and thus, in mainstream English, have their names capitalized)—The Green Belt Movement, Black Lives Matter, the Arab Spring. But many social movements remain informal, like the immigration movement. What we see is that social action, including that focused on issues of diversity and belonging, can vary in levels of formality and organization, in channels of social action, and, in formality of leadership.

Intercultural political leadership: What strategies can we use to bring about change?

From a communication perspective, **leadership** can be defined as a process of influencing a group of individuals to achieve a common goal (Northouse, 2013). Leadership occurs in a social context, and when members of a team are from differing cultural groups, there is the opportunity for intercultural interaction. Leadership, whether we are considering politics or politics 2.0, is a political act. Achieving a "common goal" implies broader interests. If you are leading a "dance marathon" in your community to raise funds for children ill with an incurable disease, what does this really mean? In the realm of politics 2.0, we might ask a few questions. Why are these funds necessary in the first place? Is it because not enough research is being conducted on this disease by corporate or government medical centers? Is it because the disease cannot be treated in a way that generates profit for pharmaceutical companies? Is it because adults can lobby government officials to direct research funds for adult diseases and children cannot? This section explores political transnational/intercultural leadership and the implications for our future interactions with others.

There are at least three unique elements to the leadership agenda of a co-cultural leader: two-pronged attention; dispelling negative stereotypes; and proof of self (Alire, 2001). Two-pronged attention is the awareness of the leader of the group as a whole and of other co-cultural group members. Dispelling negative stereotypes refers to the need for the leader to be aware of and counter any negative associations to the leader's race, nationality, or ethnicity that followers might bring to the situation. This is a task that a leader from the dominant culture will not need to address. The third element is proof of self; again, the leader from the dominant culture does not need to constantly maintain credibility to the followers. The co-cultural leader must be aware that some followers may continue to question the leader's decision-making. The leader must be mindful to reinforce credibility throughout the duration of the project (Alire, 2001).

Greta Thunberg: A leader for climate protection

Greta Thunberg is an example of a transnational co-cultural leader (Figure 14.3). They came to the world's attention at the age of 15. Thunberg began a school strike for climate protection and soon organized other students to follow. Thunberg gained notoriety for their forceful statements and relentless pressure on world leaders to act to mitigate climate change. They expressed two-pronged attention in frequent references to their age. At the 2019 UN Climate Action Summit, they stated: "I should be back in school, on the other side of the ocean. You have stolen my dreams and childhood with your empty words" (The Guardian, n.d.). They constantly position themselves as youth—the generation that will pay a future price for current inaction.

Figure 14.3 Greta Thunberg. Source: *Time Magazine*.

Thunberg dispelled the stereotypes of those who thought they were ignorant and naive or being exploited by special interests. One commentator referred to them as "a mentally ill Swedish child" (A Fox News guest called Greta Thunberg 'mentally ill,' 2019). Thunberg is on the Autism spectrum and considers her Asperger's syndrome her superpower (Teen climate change warrior, 2019). Thunberg considered her aspie identity a gift that allowed her to speak urgently to leaders without the politeness codes that can weaken the message.

Finally, Thunberg reinforced in their speeches that they are using scientific information that is commonly accepted. Also, they bolstered their credibility when they sailed across the Atlantic Ocean rather than to fly across and damage the atmosphere with jet emissions. In 2021, inspired by Thunberg, climate activists in 70 countries held demonstrations calling upon their national leaders to adopt climate protection policies. Thunberg's collectivist approach to healing the planet gained transnational support.

Servant leadership and Xiya Bastida

Leadership focuses on the achievement of group goals but we recognize that leaders accomplish individual goals as well. On a cooking competition show, a contestant might advance to a final only to be eliminated due to lack of time, a missing ingredient, or an unfavorable judge. But what if the approach were different? What if all the contestants and the judge had the same goal? What if the judge's goal were to serve the interests of the contestants only? This approach to leadership is known as **servant leadership**.

In his book, *The Case for Servant Leadership* (2008), Kent Keith summarized the key ideas of Robert K. Greenleaf, who originated the concept of the servant leader in the 1970s. Servant leaders "are motivated to make life better for others, not just themselves" (p. 10). They do not covet power; they empower others. Such leaders are humble and caring; they are good at building good relationships with others, and they are willing to learn from and be led by others. Cesar Chavez is mentioned in Chapter 9 as an extraordinary speaker who drew on Euro-American and Mexican influences to unionize migrant farmworkers in California. He dedicated his life to improving the working and living conditions of the farm workers. Yet he lived modestly. He spoke simply, yet directly and sincerely. He truly measured his success by the amount of improvement in the lives of the farmworkers. He and Dolores Huerta, the co-founders of the United Farm Workers, are examples of modern-era servant leaders (Sowards, 2012). Wangari Maathai, mentioned earlier in this chapter, is another example of a person who was dedicated to advancing the interests of women and their families, quite often at the expense of her own wellbeing.

In cultures that prize competition and individualism, the notion of being in a servant-like relationship with others is difficult to imagine. It is difficult to imagine this relationship within our home culture, let alone across cultures! Although meeting the expectations of servant leader is rare (and is often a subjective judgment), we can identify individuals who are selflessly reaching across cultures. One example is Xiye Bastida (Figure 14.4).

Figure 14.4 Xiye Bastida uses social media to persuade audiences.
Source: verdeyazul / https://verdeyazul.
diarioinformacion.com/quien-es-xiye-
bastida-la-nueva-greta-thunberg-hispana.
html / last accessed January 11, 2023.

Xiye Bastida has been called "America's Greta Thunberg" (Cimons, 2019). Growing up in Mexico, Bastida experienced the effects of extreme weather. They also learned from the Indigenous people that the natural world must be valued and protected. Their family moved to New York City, and soon Bastida was agitating for action on climate protection. They organized a student strike, called Fridays for Future, at their Manhattan school. At the age of 19, Bastida was speaking to world leaders and scolding them for not including members from the Global South at climate summits (Widdicombe, 2021). The Re-Earth Initiative promotes climate protection that values "inclusivity, accessibility, and unity" (Our Values, 2022). Re-Earth attempts to show awareness of the many different circumstances of the followers. Perhaps a follower cannot participate in a march due to a disability. Perhaps a follower does not have the income to afford environmentally friendly foods or light bulbs. Bastida and the co-leaders at Re-Earth acknowledge these circumstances and identities and adjust their messages accordingly. This model of service reveals a high degree of interculturality.

There are several elements to Bastida's narrative that are instructive for servant leaders in intercultural contexts:

1   Bastida is empathetic to the conditions of others, even those who experience climate change in other parts of the world.

2   She enters the social advocacy with curiosity, collaboration, and determination.

3   She draws from her environment to create innovative solutions to important problems.

4   She is motivated by a desire to serve.

What do you think? Oprah Winfrey has been honored for her philanthropic work. Millions of television viewers and magazine readers are informed and inspired by her views and actions, including establishing a leadership academy for girls in South Africa. At the same time, Winfrey has amassed great personal wealth. *Forbes* estimated in 2011 that Winfrey was worth $2.7 billion (O'Connor, 2011). Does Oprah qualify as a servant leader? Why or why not? If not, what other characteristics might demonstrate her to be a servant leader?

Summary

This chapter has described two notions of politics. One notion considers electoral politics and our civic obligation to be knowledgeable and to participate in democratic processes. This is political engagement. The second notion considers how dominant interests gain our consent as citizens by infusing our daily activities and practices with normalcy and nationalistic pride. This second notion—politics 2.0—leads to critical communicative engagement. Politics 2.0 asks us to understand co-cultures in relation to one another. What meanings and identities are privileged, and which are invisible? Who benefits from the invisibility or marginalization of certain co-cultures?

Living and acting with critical awareness is never an easy task. The reality for many of us is that, whether we live in a democracy or a single-party state, we support our political institutions; we accept the broad legal frameworks that constrain our actions, and we understand the utility of annual rituals like filing income taxes. At the same time, we have the capacity to critique and judge. We know—and so do our governments—that we have the capacity to resist. We might be driven by a sense of justice, or we might consider the welfare of those closest to us in our community, or perhaps we are driven by personal dissatisfaction. Resistance may come in different forms: founding a new political party, engaging in public protest against the "morality police" in Iran, defecting to another nation, or taking up arms against the state. Our relationships with our nations and cultures can be complicated and contradictory, and often we create a balance between loyalty and dissent. Exploring the two levels of politics described in this chapter allows us to be knowing actors in our communities.

This chapter also presented social movements as opportunities for intercultural interaction. The Green Belt Movement and the immigrant rights movement were successful because Wangari Maathai and immigrant rights activists were able to adopt vernacular (or local) meanings as they created their messages.

Finally, this chapter explored leadership as a political endeavor. Greta Thunberg worked against an entrenched attitude that burning fossil fuels was inevitable. Their public messages display the three elements for leaders who are people of color: two-pronged attention, dispelling negative stereotypes and reinforcing "proof of self," or credibility. Xiye Bastida was seen as a servant leader; that is, an individual who placed the interests of vulnerable human and animal populations before their own. Cesar Chavez and Wangari Maathai, other examples of servant leaders, might well have subscribed to Bastida's motto: "Imagine the future."

KEY TERMS

politics, 288
communicative engagement, 289
politics 2.0, 289
social movement, 290
vernacular discourse, 290
vernacular rhetoric, 290

immigration, 293
diaspora, 293
diasporic citizen, 293
antiracism, 294
leadership, 296
servant leadership, 298

Discussion questions

1   How do you participate in local and national politics? Are you as engaged as you would like? How is your participation guided by formal and informal rules?

2   Do you believe that you have more or fewer opportunities for political engagement than others?

3   What would motivate you to join a social movement? What risks would you take to advocate a cause you believed in?

4   Do you believe that you could lead a diverse group to accomplish a common goal?

5   Do you believe you could be a servant leader?

Action points

1   Conduct a Google search for Green Belt Movement and use Google Maps to examine the terrain of Kenya and surrounding countries. What environmental issues does your community face?

2   Using census data and other demographic information, determine the number of immigrants living in your community. Determine where they come from and what drew them to your community. What is the relationship between your community and immigrant populations? Welcoming? Hostile? Mixed?

3   See Xiye Bastida at https://www.xiyebeara.com What are their most current projects? What can you apply from their activism in helping your community?

For more information

Flores, L. A. (2003). Constructing rhetorical borders: Peons, illegal aliens, and competing narratives of immigration. *Critical Studies in Media Communication, 20*(4), 362–387. DOI: 10.1080/0739318032000142025

Griffin, R. A., & Calafell, B. M. (2011). Control, discipline and punish: Black masculinity and (in)visible whiteness in the NBA. In M. G. Lacy & K. A. Ono (Eds.), *Critical rhetorics of race* (pp. 117–136). NYU Press.

Holling, M. A., & Calafell, B. M. (2011). *Latina/o discourses in vernacular spaces: Somos de una voz?* Lexington Books.

Negrine, R. (2008). *The transformation of political communication: Continuities and changes in media and politics.* Palgrave.

Ngugi, T. W. (1986). *Decolonising the mind: The politics of language in African language.* James Curry Ltd.

Stevens, S. M., & Malesh, P. (2009). *Active voices: Composing a rhetoric of social movements.* SUNY Press.

References

A Fox News guest called Greta Thunberg 'mentally ill:' The network apologized. (2019). *Washington Post.* Accessed November 29, 2022, at https://www.youtube.com/watch?v=QzaQz5yYJHs

Alire, C. A. (2001). Diversity and leadership: The color of leadership. *Journal of Library Administration, 32*(3-4), 95–109. DOI: 10.1300/J111v32n03_07

Black Lives Matter. (n.d.). Accessed November 29, 2022, at https://blacklivesmatter.com/about

Bretton, M. J. (1998). *Women pioneers for the environment.* Northeastern University Press.

Calafell, B. M., & Delgado, F. P. (2004). Reading Latina/o images: Interrogating *Americanos. Critical Studies in Media Communication, 21,* 1–21. https://doi.org/10.1080/17513057.2011.627093

Campo-Flores, A. (2006). Immigration. *Newsweek,* April 10, pp. 30–38. Accessed July, 7, 2012.

Chen, H. (2012). Temporally legal: My traveling across borders of im/migration. In A. González, M. Houston, & V. Chen (Eds.), *Our voices: Essays in culture, ethnicity, and communication* (5th ed., pp. 263–269). Oxford University Press.

Cimons, M. (2019, September 19). Meet Xiye Bastida, America's Greta Thunberg. *PBS.* Accessed November 6, 2022, at https://www.pbs.org/wnet/peril-and-promise/2019/09/meet-xiye-bastida-americas-greta-thunberg

Deetz, S. (1990). Representation of interest and the new communication technologies: Issues in democracy and policy. In M. J. Medhurst, A. González, & T. R. Peterson (Eds.), *Communication and the culture of technology* (pp. 43–62). Washington University Press.

Drzewiecka, J. A., & Steyn, M. (2012). Racial immigrant incorporation: Material-symbolic articulation of identities. *Journal of International and Intercultural Communication*, 5, 1–19. https://doi.org/10.1080/17513057.2011.627093

Edo, A., Giesing, Y., Oztunc, J., & Poutvaara, P. (2019). Immigration and electoral support for the far-left and the far-right. *European Economic Review*, 115, 99–143. https://doi.org/10.1016/j.euroecorev.2019.03.001

Jaschick, S. (2021, July 7). Hannah-Jones turns down UNC offer. *Inside Higher Ed*. Accessed November 29, 2022, at https://www.insidehighered.com/news/2021/07/07/nikole-hannah-jones-rejects-tenure-offer-unc-job-howard-u

Keith, K. M. (2008). *The case for servant leadership*. The Greenleaf Center for Servant Leadership.

Kendi, I. X. (2019). *How to be an antiracsist*. New York: One World.

Kiley, S. (2022, November 29). Iran threatened families of national soccer team, according to security source. *CNN*. Assessed November 11, 2022, at https://www.cnn.com/2022/11/28/football/iran-soccer-family-threats-intl-spt/index.html

Lappé, F. M., & Lappé, A. (2002). *Hope's edge: The next diet for a small planet*. Jeremy P. Tarcher/ Putnam.

Maathai, W. (2004). *The Green Belt Movement: Sharing the approach and experience*. Lantern Books.

McKerrow, R. E. (2000). Opening the future: Postmodern rhetoric in a multicultural world. In A. González & D. V. Tanno (Eds.), *Rhetoric in intercultural contexts* (pp. 41–46). Sage.

McKinney, M. S., Kaid, L. L., Bystrom, D. G., & Carlin, D. B. (2005). The role of communication in civic engagement. In M. S. McKinney, L. L. Kaid, D. G. Bystrom, & D. B. Carlin (Eds.), *Communicating politics: Engaging the public in democratic life* (pp. 3–26). Peter Lang.

Miller, J. B. (1999). "Indians," "Braves", and "Redskins": A performative struggle for control of an image. *Quarterly Journal of Speech*, 85, 188–202. https://doi.org/10.1080/00335639909384253

Northouse, P. (2013). *Leadership: Theory and practice* (6th ed.). Sage.

O'Connor, C. (2011). Meet America's richest women (and not just Oprah and Meg). *Forbes*, September 22. Accessed July 7, 2012, at http://www.forbes.com/sites/clareoconnor/2011/09/22/forbes-400-meet-americas-richest-women-and-not-justoprah-and-meg.

Ono, K. A., & Sloop, J. M. (1995). The critique of vernacular discourse. *Communication Monographs*, 62, 19–46. https://doi.org/10.1080/03637759509376346

Ono, K. A., & Sloop, J. M. (2002). *Shifting borders: Rhetoric, immigration, and California's Proposition 187*. Temple University Press.

Our Values. (2022). *Re-Earth Initiative*. Accessed November 29, 2022, at https://reearthin.org/about

Pickup, M., de Rooij, E. A., van der Linden, C., & Goodwin, M. J. (2021). Brexit, COVID-19 and attitudes toward immigration. *Social Science Quarterly*, 102, 2184–2195. https://doi.org/10.1111/ssqu.13010

Pineda, R. D., & Sowards, S. K. (2007). Flag waving as visual argument: 2006 immigration demonstrations and cultural citizenship. *Argumentation and Advocacy*, 43(3-4), 164–174. https://doi.org/10.1080/00028533.2007.11821672

Powers, K. A. (2007). Immigrants become targets for all of society's ills. *USA Today*, August 29, p. 13A. Accessed August 29, 2012.

Sengul, K. (2021). Never let a good crisis go to waste: Pauline Hanson's exploitation of COVID-19 on Facebook. *Media International Australia*, 101–105. https://doi.org/10.1177/1329878X20953521

Siu, L. C. D. (2005). *Memories of a future home: Diasporic citizenship of Chinese in Panama*. Stanford University Press.

Sowards, S. K. (2012). Rhetorical functions of letter writing: Dialogic collaboration, affirmation and catharsis in Dolores Huerta's letters. *Communication Quarterly*, 60, 295–315. https://doi.org/10.1080/01463373.2012.669341

Sreenivasan, H. (2019, August 18). The 1619 Project details the legacy of slavery in America. *PBS NewsHour*. Accessed January 15, 2022, at https://www.pbs.org/newshour/show/the-1619-project-details-the-legacy-of-slavery-in-america

Stewart, C. J., Smith, C. A., & Denton, R. E., Jr. (2007). *Persuasion and social movements* (5th ed.). Waveland.

Sullivan, M. (2022, November 21) FIFA bans "One Love" armbands during World Cup Opening matches. *CBS Boston*. Accessed November 11, 2022, at https://www.cbsnews.com/boston/news/fifa-one-love-arm-bands-world-cup-us-wales

Teen climate change warrior. (2019). *CBS The Morning*. Retrieved November 29, 2022, from https://www.youtube.com/watch?v=BQ4rBLCpEeM

The Guardian (n.d.). *Greta Thunberg to world leaders: 'How dare you? You have stolen my dreams and Childhood.'* (Video). YouTube. https://www.youtube.com/watch?v=TMrtLsQbaok

(The) White House. (2011). *Statement by the President on the passing of Wangary Maathai*. Accessed March 30, 2011, at http://www.whitehouse.gov/the-press-office/2011/09/26/statement-president-passingwangari-maathai.

Valocchi, S. (2010). *Social movements and activism in the USA*. Routledge.

Well, J. Z. (2021, October 28). D.C.'s Black Lives Matter Plaza, created overnight, is now a permanent multi-million-dollar concrete installation. *The Washington Post*. Accessed December 9, 2022, at https://www.washingtonpost. com/dc-md-va/2021/10/28/black-lives-matter-plaza-dc

Widdicombe, L. (2021, December 27). How Xiye Bastida became a leader in the climate fight. *Vogue*. Retrieved June 6, 2022, from https://www.vogue.com/article/ xiye-bastida-climate-activist-profile. Accessed November 29, 2022.

Chapter 15

Intercultural communication in organizations: How does culture shape business and how is business culture changing?

Chapter objectives

By the end of this chapter, you should be able to:

→ Describe the impact on the corporate workplace and workers as a result of globalization

→ Discuss the strengths and limitations of globalization on world cultures

→ Outline specific dimensions of cultural difference that may impact organizational communication

→ Explain the views of business in a globalizing/glocalizing world

→ Explain corporate social responsibility and forms of CSR

Intercultural Communication for Everyday Life, Second Edition. John R. Baldwin, Alberto González, Nettie Brock, Ming Xie, and Chin-Chung Chao.
© 2024 John Wiley & Sons Ltd. Published 2024 by John Wiley & Sons Ltd.
Companion Website: http://www.wiley.com/go/baldwin2e

n today's globalized world, all of us are citizens of the global village. Therefore, we are encountering diversity on a daily basis, in a classroom, on a business trip, and at work. The authors have worked with around 24 students in each class for each semester. These students are by no means representative of all the countries in the world, but they create the impression of **diversity**, being of different genders, ages, cultures, sexual orientations, and so on. Are we aware of and ready for the challenges in the increasingly diversified classes and workplaces? Some might quote an old saying to the diverse classmates and coworkers: "When in Rome, do as the Romans do." We will begin our discussion about intercultural communication and organizations with the story about the adage.

The classic adage originated from Bishop Augustine. According to Michael Morris and colleagues (2014), history recorded that Augustine, Bishop of Milan was writing to Januarius, Bishop of Naples, with the above advice about an impending trip to their organization's headquarters in Rome. At the time, Christians in Rome fasted on Saturday, but Christians in other cities did not do so. To face the intercultural dilemma and avoid potential offense, Augustine suggested adapting to the local norm of fasting when they stayed in Rome and resuming their conventional norm when coming back home to Milan and Naples. Although Bishop Augustine adopted adaptation as a solution to the intercultural dilemma, people in today's increasingly globalized businesses and organizations face much more complex intercultural challenges.

Globalization is changing the ways of operation and means of communication in all organizations today. It is becoming more and more common for trans-national organizations to maintain international interactions with their clients over the telephone, by e-mail, via video-conference, or face-to-face. Globalization has also brought intercultural challenges at home. The workforces of organizations have been growing culturally diverse as a result of increased immigration, multiethnic identification, and multicultural policies and ideologies. Even managers of local enterprises need to learn about cultural differences in order to communicate and connect with their employees from various cultural backgrounds—and, as we note in Chapter 3, people need not come from different countries to have different cultures!

According to the U.S. Census Bureau (2020),

> The fastest-growing racial or ethnic group in the United States is people who are Two or More Races, who are projected to grow some 200 percent by 2060. The next fastest is the Asian population, which is projected to double, followed by Hispanics whose population will nearly double within the next 4 decades. (p. 6)

In contrast, "the only group projected to shrink is the non-Hispanic White population" (p. 7), which is supposed to decline from 198 to 179 million, despite overall national population growth. The population of the world overall will grow rapidly in developing countries while remaining stable or even decreasing in the developed countries. This is why Dani Rodrik (1997) noted, "The most serious challenge for the world economy in the years ahead lies in making globalization compatible with domestic social and political stability" (p. 2).

As a result, organizations today find it necessary to increase their cultural awareness and enhance their organizational communication competence to communicate correctly, effectively, and appropriately across cultural boundaries in this globally connected world. **Organizational communication** is a discipline within communication studies that focuses specifically on organizing behaviors across contexts. More commonly, this discipline explores the nuances of communication in organizations. Katherine Miller (2015) defines organizations as comprising five critical elements: (1) the existence of a social collective, which (2) occurs when a group of people work together to fulfill organizational and individual goals, by (3) coordinating activities, within (4) varied levels and nuances of organizational structure, while (5) simultaneously being embedded within an environment of other organizations. Communication is the glue that binds all the different organizational processes, systems, procedures, applications, interactions, and other shared realities together. The discipline of organizational communication has traditionally been U.S.-centered. In recent years, the scope of this discipline has traversed across cultures such as Brazil (Marchiori & Oliveira, 2009) and Germany (Theis-Berglmair, 2013). To help readers gain a better understanding of communication and intercultural communication in organizations and to enable organizations to think globally and act locally, we discuss intercultural communication in organizations from the aspects of globalization and its impacts, types of organizations and organizational cultures, cultural variations in organizations, organizations in a globalizing/glocalizing world, and intercultural communication across contexts in this chapter.

A global village: What is the impact of globalization on business?

History of globalization

For years, globalization has been a hot topic, and it shows no signs of going away anytime soon. Although it is still contested when and where globalization started, it is for sure the world is becoming smaller, and the effect is seen in all aspects of social life. This process can be termed as globalization, which has taken place quite many times and in different ways throughout human history. Globalization occurred with the trading routes between ancient China and Europe, in the contacts between India and its neighboring countries, and during the interactions and conflicts among Muslims, Jews, and Christians early in human history. History witnessed bigger scales of globalization with the rise of the Portuguese, Spanish, Dutch, and British maritime empires and their colonization in different parts of the world in the 16th and 17th centuries. Waves of globalization were facilitated and accelerated with the introduction of new modes of transport like railroads and steamships and telecommunications like radio and television in the 18th and 19th centuries. These waves of globalization revolutionized the world in major ways and became instrumental in maximizing the utilization of time and space. This trend was followed in the 20th century, with transportation becoming much faster and safer thanks to innovations in electronics and telecommunications. As a result, the world has been experiencing a drastic change with the advent of the Internet and mobile phones in the 21st century. Simply put, the world has become a "global village" (McLuhan, 1964, p. 6) as predicted by Marshall McLuhan, the guru of communication studies back in the 1960s.

Definitions of globalization

Globalization has been defined in various ways, and most definitions bear reference to the interconnectedness of political entities, economic relationships, and modes of communication. As the authors pondered how we could provide the most useful concepts of globalization by choosing from the hundreds of articles or books, we reflected on the story of the blind men who were attempting to describe an elephant. Although every blind man provided some descriptions about his part, each perspective alone was insufficient to understand the whole of the elephant. Our challenge of conceptualizing globalization is like the challenge of each of the blind men in describing the elephant with the added difficulty that the elephant is walking. There are various perspectives of globalization among different fields from traditional societies to modern societies. With economic relationships in focus, Paul Kennedy (1993) defined globalization "as primarily integrative structures," meaning the "local and national governments eventually cede control of policy to the global institutions such as the World Bank or the International Monetary Fund" (IMF) (p. 47). To the IMF, globalization is "the result of human innovation and technological progress" and "the increasing integration of economies around the world, particularly through trade and financial flows" (Clack, 2006, p. 4). *New York Times* columnist Thomas Friedman (1999) defined globalization as follows:

> It is the inevitable integration of markets, nation-states and technologies to a degree never witnessed before—in a way that is enabling individuals, corporations and nation-states to reach around the world farther, faster, deeper and cheaper than ever before and in a way that is enabling the world to reach into individuals, corporations and nation-states farther, faster, and deeper, cheaper than ever before. (pp. 7–8)

Friedman emphasizes the functions of globalization which integrate markets, nation-states, and technologies in such a way that individuals, corporations, and nation-states can be connected and reached in maximum scope, rate, and depth. Optimistic about the effects of globalization, Friedman urges active participation and integration into the globalization process.

With more and more individuals traveling to foreign countries or working in foreign companies and organizations, it is essential to know more about the cultures of foreign countries and endeavor to communicate well and work together. If individuals and organizations are unaware of cultural differences and do not know the efficient ways to get along and get business done, it can and does lead to poor performance and lost deals. **Culture** regulates how we think, feel, and behave, and it is expressed through our language and actions. For instance, our health is important to us, as it is to everyone around the world, but our definition of "health" and expectations about health and health care vary greatly (see, e.g., Witte & Morrison, 1995). Likewise, healthcare practitioners communicate and interact in distinct ways. When you are sick while traveling abroad, your expectations on health care processes and communication interactions with practitioners can be misunderstood or misinterpreted, and the context and culture differences can directly contribute to miscommunication, especially for the people who don't speak the language or/and understand the culture of the contexts/organizations. Since we are working and living in an interconnected global economy now, it is important that we fully understood the impacts of globalization on positive people relationships and lucrative business outcomes.

Impacts of globalization

Globalization does not just refer to an economic phenomenon. Its ripple effects reach all cultural aspects of any society in the world today. Ideas, customs, and cultural movements follow closely after the exchange of goods across national boundaries. Surely, globalization exerts its immediate and obvious impacts through both pros and cons. According to Batterson and Weidenbaum (2001), globalization:

1   accelerates economic growth by increasing the standards of living;

2   benefits consumers with higher income and lower-priced products and services;

3   increases employment and improves the working conditions of workers;

4   helps clean up and protect the environment;

5   helps developing nations with booming economies but also helps millions out of poverty;

6   helps protect human rights by linking economic freedom with political freedom;

7   fosters the growth of democratic governments throughout the world; and

8   guarantees the quality of life in terms of life expectancy, literacy, human health, leisure, and living standards.

In contrast, globalization also:

1   subjects many people to financial crisis and poverty in the name of corporate greed;

2   increases record corporate profits while the conditions of the poor continue to worsen;

3   shifts offshore jobs to developing countries with poor working conditions and abuses of workers' rights;

4   exploits local environments for corporate profits and contributes to global warming;

5   traps developing nations in debt and subjects millions of people to poverty;

6   supports a world trade in human bondage and slavery estimated in the millions;

7   threatens the sovereignty of nation-states with world trade and finance bodies; and

8   threatens public health, local economies, and the social fabric of farmers. (p. 18)

Globalization is no longer just a buzzword, as it was until just a few decades ago. It is our reality today. In many supermarkets, you will find vegetables, fruits, and other products from different parts of the world. In U.S. stores, we frequently see everything from mangoes to candy to asparagus to coffee that comes from countries like India, Belgium, Peru, and Nicaragua respectively. What a truly global eating experience (if you suspend judgment on the global footprint and method of growing)! Clothes that we shop for at retailers like Gap, Mango, Zara, or H&M are often manufactured in the developing world at extremely low costs but sold to consumers at highly marked-up prices. No wonder some stores can afford to have "80% off" sales—they are still making money even with those deep discounts!

What do you think? For a more detailed and critical view of how globalization affects our global community, please watch the video, *The New Corporation* freely available on the Internet with a reasonable request for donations for the creators and designers of the documentary (http://thecorporation.com). Watch some segments (or all 23 chapters on YouTube) and read the section below. What do you think are some strengths and advantages of globalization, for both global and local businesses and cultures?

Much has been written, said, and analyzed about globalization and its effects. While the more apparent changes brought about by globalization—such as the influx of foreign-made products into domestic markets, ease of travel, forging of cross-cultural business partnerships, and others—get written about frequently, one must wonder about what goes on behind this face of globalization. Have you ever wondered who the people behind these changes are, or what might be the circumstances under which they may have to work to please an ever-increasing and ever-demanding global clientele?

In his documentary, *The Other Side of Outsourcing*, New York Times reporter Thomas Friedman travels to Bangalore, India, to witness first-hand how globalization was occurring behind the scenes and how it was affecting the everyday people who make the lives in developed economies more comfortable and even possible. Communication scholars Mahuya Pal and Patrice Buzzanell (2008) examined the processes at a call center operation in Kolkata, India, and their implications for the employees. They found that call center employees actively negotiated and invoked strategic identities for themselves, even as they were involved in a cultural tug-and-pull, being Indian by day and assuming Western (U.S. American) names and identities by night when answering calls from customers (Figure 15.1).

A study by Jenny Chan et al. (2013) highlights the globalization of the electronics industry, specifically Apple, and the manufacturing workers the industry exploits in China. Specifically, Foxconn employees are overworked, underpaid, and there is an overall absence of fundamental labor rights. Another documentary, *The Corporation* (see "What do you think?," earlier), provides us with a unique lens through which to view apparel we buy because proceeds from the sale are said to benefit some deserving organization. Makers of the documentary investigate a popular celebrity's brand of clothing sold under the impression that a portion of the sale is being donated to a children's organization. They conduct similar investigations at sweatshops in Honduras, the Dominican Republic, and other parts of the developing world, and showcase the ugly face of global exploitation by large corporations.

Regardless of the many critical lenses through which we can view globalization, we have to admit that to run a corporation successfully at the global level, you need more than just good pricing strategies. Neuliep (2021) argues that hiring the right kind of people is critical to global success: "An understanding of cultural, microcultural, environmental, perceptual, sociorelational, verbal, nonverbal, and relational contexts of the native and host cultures increases the probability of being an effective and productive manager across cultures" (p. 398). He further declares that the growth (and success) of an organization in a foreign land depends unequivocally on effective communication.

Figure 15.1 Employees in call centers, such as this one in Bangalore, India, have to actively negotiate their identities as they interact daily with customers across national and cultural borders.
Source: Eric Lipman / The Library of Congress / Public Domain.

Figure 15.2 Katherine Miller's (2015) framework of utopian and dystopian effects of globalization.
Source: Miller, K. 2015 / Wadsworth

Utopian Effects	Dystopian Effects
Draws cultures closer together	Oppressive outcomes for inexpensive labor
Creates peace-loving, intelligent citizens	Risks for unemployment & outsourcing
Cooperation, goodwill	Individual & group resistance
Creates economic opportunities	Creates economic burden

Regarding organizations, globalization has demonstrated profound and far-reaching impacts, bringing about major organizational changes. According to Miller (2015), globalization has caused the time and space compression (space and time no longer connected, 24/7 connection and non-stop travel), enhanced people's sense of global consciousness (awareness of others' culture, attitudes, beliefs, and behaviors), and led to dis-embedded organizations and people (behavior and interaction often removed from local context). In addition to the above-mentioned effects, there are two proposed challenges and outcomes of globalization within organizational communication research and practices: convergence and divergence (Stohl, 2001). The convergence approach will consider how organizations might adapt their practices to "a global system that requires flexibility, responsiveness, speed, knowledge production, and knowledge dissemination" (Stohl, 2001, p. 325). In contrast, the divergence approach to the globalizing workplace tends to focus on the cultural distinctiveness found around the world. Furthermore, Miller (2015) suggested utopian and dystopian effects of globalization as below (Figure 15.2).

In brief, globalization has made way for free trade and business, and it has created cross-cultural communication between various parts of the world. On the one hand, globalization is making this world a better place to live in. It is improving the political scenarios in more and more countries, and it is resolving the social problems of poverty and unemployment. On the other hand, globalization is westernizing the local customs and values of the developing countries while modernizing those nations. The power imbalance may lead to linguistic, cultural, and traditional genocide if we do not keep a check on the disadvantages of globalization and let **diffusion** (the spread of ideas, behaviors, or artifacts from one culture to another) go wild. To embrace globalization and stay competitive, organizations need to adapt themselves to the trends of changes while dealing with the above five pairs of tensions. In addition, what makes communication effective will vary between cultures (see Chapter 12).

Cultural variability: How does culture shape the organizations?

Organizations in intercultural settings

With the corporate world becoming more and more interrelated and international, there has been a significant amount of literature on cross-cultural management. Cross-cultural management refers to "the study of the behavior of people in organizations located in cultures and nations around the world" (Adler, 1983, p. 226), focusing on the organizational behavior, especially interactions, of peoples across countries and cultures. For example, an older study comparing views of British and U.S. managers found some interesting differences. Both groups perceived American managers to be more direct and optimistic than the British managers. They also perceived the British to be more likely to avoid risks and to discuss issues longer than Americans before finding a workable solution to a problem (Dunkerley & Robinson, 2002).

However, much focus on international organizational communication has focused on Asia. According to Adler and colleagues (1986), "As the world enters the Pacific century, the differing impacts of Occidental and Oriental cultures on managerial interaction have become highly significant" (p. 306). They found that early research on cross-cultural management focused on 1) cross-cultural variance; 2) cultural determination; 3) convergence versus divergence; 4) intercultural interaction; and 5) synergy from cultural diversity. Most of the studies on Asian cultures have focused on Japan and a few on other countries like South Korea and China. (Indeed, Robert Shuter (1990, 2014) has argued that communication research has ignored large parts of the world, such as Africa and South America, by focusing on a small number of nations). Some studies found that Japanese managers and workers demonstrate a strong sense of identity with their work groups, an ethic of cooperativeness, a high dependence on the larger entity, a strong sensitivity to status, and active respect for the interests of individuals and for each individual as a person. Meanwhile, ethnic Chinese managers tend to honor a tight set of business rules, emphasizing hard work, thrift, and competitiveness, as well as a strong belief in Confucian familyism. Other studies found a long-range planning horizon, commitment to lifetime employment, and collective responsibility at the heart of the Japanese management system. The Chinese revealed a strong relationship between mind-sets and productivity, stressed equal sharing to such a degree that poor performance and good performance were rewarded equally, and became accustomed to the norm of avoiding standing out in any way. Yet, most of this research is based on Western theoretical models, which "fail to account for differences between Occidental and Oriental cultures and mind-sets" (Adler et al., 1986, p. 306).

Focusing on cross-cultural organizational behavior, Michelle Gelfand et al. (2007) found that culture was not the main focus in the studies on organizational behavior in the 1960s and 1970s. Existing studies were generally atheoretical, descriptive, and methodologically problematic, and organizational behavior theories were developed and tested on Western samples. It was with the advent of culture typologies (Hofstede, 1980; see Chapter 4) in the 1980s that scholars began studying national cultures to uncover the cultural boundaries of some Western organizational behavior models. Japanese models, such as quality control circles were among the research results. In the two decades around the year 2000, "cross-cultural theory and research have taken on the central role," and "a large wave of cross-cultural research was witnessed across all areas of the field" (Gelfand et al., 2007, p. 482). Scholars have since conducted major studies on dynamic cultural theory (Hong et al., 2000), organizational contexts (Aycan et al., 2000), and new taxonomies of cultural values (House et al., 2004), often using research methods that combine **emic** (or culture specific) with **etic** (or universal) perspectives on cultural differences (Jandt, 2021, see Chapter 4).

Finally, Littrell and Salas (2005) emphasized the reasons, purposes, and strategies of cross-cultural training in present-day organizations. Three reasons for continued cross-cultural training include the heavy financial losses associated with expatriate assignments, the lack of conclusive answers concerning the effectiveness of cross-cultural training, and the continuing diversity at the workplace. In order to improve expatriates' rate of success in their foreign assignments, cross-cultural training aims to equip the expatriates with the knowledge, skill, and attitudes needed for cross-cultural adjustment, effective on-the-job performance, and interactions with the host nationals. Seven strategies of cross-cultural training are listed:

1   didactic, providing factual information about the working conditions, living environ-
    ments, and cultural differences in the host countries;

2   attribution, developing attitudes and skills necessary for explaining the host national
    behavior from the host-culture point of view;

3   cultural awareness, educating the trainees about their own cultures so as to appreciate
    the differences between the home culture and host culture;

4   cognitive-behavior modification, assisting the expatriates in developing the habitual
    behaviors desired in the host culture;

5   interaction, making sure the incoming expatriates are learning from the expatriates
    whom they are replacing;

6   language, training those expatriates who will be immersed in a culture speaking a for-
    eign language; and

7   experiential, providing the expatriates with activities likely to be encountered during the
    foreign assignments and having them participate in the activities so as to learn by doing.

Types of organizations

Another issue to consider as we look at cultural variability in organizations is the structure or
type of organization. An **organization** is a social unit of people structured and managed to
meet a need or pursue some collective goals (Gardner et al., 2001). Typically, organizations
involve highly differentiated social systems, and individuals are divided into divisional units,
functional specialties, work groups, and status levels. Due to diversity, organization employees
have to "work competently with the expanding heterogeneity, including gender, age, race, religion, and ethnicity" (Barker & Gower, 2010, p. 296). According to Taylor Cox (1991), organizations can be classified into three types along a continuum based on the degree of employee
diversity: monolithic, plural, and multicultural. In a **monolithic organization**, the employees
are homogenous, with a limited number of minority employees. In a **plural organization**,
minority employees are moderate in number, but they generally hold lower-level jobs. In a **multicultural organization**, minorities should be represented at all levels of the organization, but
this is only an ideal so far. As a result, an increased focus on employee diversity, many schools
and workplaces have affirmative action plans in place, but they are often not enforced. Instead,
minority employees are pressed to assimilate into the mainstream culture or monolithic workgroups, while facing frequent prejudice and discrimination. Ideally, multicultural organizational
employees "have the best chance for treating workgroup members fairly, that is, respecting differences and valuing each person for special skills or knowledge" (Larkey, 1996, pp. 467–470).

  According to Miller (2015), many organizational types exist in today's world that were not
often considered in past decades such as nonprofit organizations, service organizations, nongov-
ernmental organizations (NGOs), virtual organizations, and **social organizations** (fraternities
and sororities). In addition, as a new way of organization, multinational companies result from
today's economic structures, which are turning global and adapting to the global economy.
Operating in two or more countries, **multinational companies** or organizations are economic and technical entities that tend to produce goods and services abroad. Different from
other organizations, multinational organizations usually have their employees composed of people from various geographical, religious, linguistic, and political backgrounds. To coordinate
routine activities and to keep their competitive edge in the global economy, organizations

including transnational ones make communication or intercultural communication the central means to devise, disseminate and pursue their organizational goals.

Many traditional organizations have flattened their structures since the 1980s (Kelleher et al., 1996). Traditionally, organizations followed the **hierarchical** structure of Taylor's (2006) theory, delegating authority in a pyramidal, hierarchical structure, with power concentrated primarily among the few individuals at the top. Research evidence suggests that hierarchical level and environment uncertainty may affect the communication behavior of organization members (Verma, 2013). Thus, senior managers usually take more part in conversations and meetings than lower-level managers under conditions of high uncertainty. To provide innovative, high-quality products, and instantaneous services to customer demands, more and more organizations have shifted authority downward and given employees increased autonomy and decision-making power. Team structures and network structures are typical examples. Team-structured organizations emphasize interpersonal relations by linking formal and informal group relations to influence an employee's behavior or performance. Independent or semi-independent organizations nowadays tend to choose network structures so that they can share resources, information, and manpower, and responsibility for joint projects. However, the types of structure most common or preferred will likely differ from culture to culture.

Cultural variations in organizations

Cultural differences are also called cultural variations. Many theoretical frameworks have been introduced in the study of cultural variations. Here, we focus on Hall's high- and low-context cultures and M-time and P-time orientations (see Chapter 8), and Hofstede's cultural dimensions (see Chapter 4), as a result of collective academic efforts. Although the cultural dimensions of Hall and Hofstede have been criticized for utilizing geographical borders between nation-states as boundaries for cultures, they still have some merit in discussing generalities of difference, as long as we keep in mind diversity within national cultures. Moreover, studies of communication practices and patterns today "still resonate with the cultural dimensions proposed decades ago" (Würtz, 2006, p. 276).

High- and low-context cultures First, context refers to "the information that surrounds an event," which is "bound up with the meaning of that event" (Hall & Hall, 2003, p. 200). On a scale from high to low context, the cultures in the world can be divided into **high-context cultures**, in which "most of the information is already in the person, while very little is in the coded, explicit, transmitted part of the message," whereas **low-context cultures** are those in which "the mass of the information is vested in the explicit code" (Hall, 1976, p. 79). It may be best not to think of this as a dichotomy, but as a continuum (or even contextual within cultures). In general, Japanese, Chinese, Arabs, and Mediterranean peoples belong to higher-context cultures while Americans, Germans, Swiss, and Scandinavians belong to lower-context cultures.

Polychronic time and monochronic time Based on his years of exposure to other cultures, Hall (1983) divided time orientations in various cultures into **polychronic time** or P-time and **monochronic time** or M-time. P-time refers to "the model of involvement in several things at once," while M-time means the time orientation in which "events are scheduled as separate items—one thing at a time" (p. 43). P-time orientation is more often observed in Mexico, Japan, China, and some Mediterranean countries. M-time orientation is usually witnessed among mainstream cultures in the United States, Canada, France, and north European countries.

While it is characteristic of organizational employees in P-time cultures to be oriented to people, those in M-time cultures are more oriented to tasks, schedules, and procedures. Thus, proper reporting can enable a P-time administrator to manage a surprising number of subordinates, but organizations run on the P-time model are often limited in size, which "are slow and cumbersome when dealing with anything that is new or different" (Hall, 1983, p. 46). M-time organizations can grow much larger than the P-time model, but the weaknesses of the M-time organization "lie in its blindness to the humanity of its members and extreme dependence on the leader to handle contingencies and stay on top of things" (p. 46).

There are caveats in the understanding of P-time and M-time orientations. While American time is mostly monochronic, which dominates the official worlds or business, government, and sports, etc., one finds P-time takes over at home, especially in those traditional homes where everything revolves around women. The Japanese are polychromic when looking and working inward to themselves, but they shift to the monochronic mode when they are dealing with the outside world. The French are "monochronic intellectually but polychronic in behavior" (Hall, 1983, p. 54). As noted in Chapter 4, the temporal focus might differ based on situational, urban-rural, ethnic, and other differences.

Six cultural dimensions Based on many studies, Hofstede and colleagues (e.g., Hofstede, 1991, 2001; Hofstede & Bond, 1988; Hofstede et al., 2010) have developed six cultural dimensions to explain cultural variations in the world. We introduced Hofstede's cultural dimensions in Chapter 4; therefore, here we point out the relevant research findings as they relate to organizational communication. Each country could be positioned through an index score on each of the six dimensions. One may find the index score of a particular country or in contrast with another country by going to the Hofstede Center at https://www.hofstede-insights.com/fi/product/compare-countries (Figure 15.3)

Figure 15.3 Hofstede Center shows index scores of Hofstede's cultural dimensions of four countries from around the world—Argentina, Canada, China, and Denmark.
Source: Adapted from https://www.hofstede-insights.com/fi/product/compare-countries

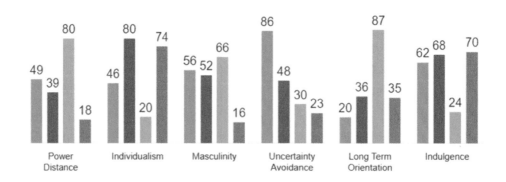

Power Distance (PD) refers to power inequality in a culture, which a group of people considers as normal. In high PD settings, hierarchies are exhibited, and employees are afraid of stating their opinions to their managers. In contrast, low PD cultures tend to view subordinates and supervisors as closer relationships, with level hierarchies in organizations. The second dimension, **Individualism versus Collectivism**, investigates how people value themselves and their groups/organizations. For instance, organizational goals are more important than individual goals in collectivistic cultures. The third dimension, **Masculinity versus Femininity**, refers to the gender roles in cultures. In highly feminine cultures, men and women are treated more equally; however, there may be a glass ceiling for females in highly masculine organizations. Hofstede (2011) focused on the traditional assignment of masculine roles to qualities such as assertiveness, competition, and toughness, and to feminine roles of orientation to home and children, people, and tenderness. **Uncertainty Avoidance** (UA), the fourth dimension, considers the culture's general orientation toward ambiguity. There are more formal rules and regulations in high UA settings. By contrast, low UA cultures tend to be more informal and focus more on long-range strategic matters. Simply speaking, a high UA culture prefers structured over unstructured situations.

In order to represent the range of cultural characteristics that Asian cultural members possess, Hofstede and Bond (1988) later provided a fifth cultural dimension, **Long-Term Orientation** (LTO) or Confucian work dynamics. LTO seems to play an important role in Asian countries. These countries are influenced by the Confucian philosophy for several thousands of years, representing essential Chinese traditional values such as hierarchical order of relationships, persistence, thrifty habits, and a sense of shame. In contrast to LTO, short-term orientation people's actions are driven by short-term results and the need for immediate gratification. Hofstede (2001) found that countries with high LTO believe a stable society requires unequal relations, where the family is the prototype of all social organizations. With their experience, older people (parents) have more authority and higher status than younger people do; men have more power than women do. Western countries, by contrast, are more likely to promote equal relationships, emphasize individualism, and find fulfillment through creativity and self-actualization. The last dimension is **Indulgence versus Restraint.** It is related to the gratification or control of basic human desires related to enjoying life. Indulgence scores are higher in Latin America, parts of Africa, the Anglo world, and Nordic Europe. Restraint is more frequently found in East Asia, Eastern Europe, and Muslim workplaces. In a "restraint" culture, there will be a clearer distinction between how an employee behaves with a peer as opposed to a superior, probably "muting" strong feelings in the presence of the superior or in a professional or class setting. In the "indulgence" culture, employees or students are encouraged to say what they feel on the occasion.

According to Hofstede Center Index scores, the U.S. American business culture, similar to but different from the Canadian score (provided in Figure 15.3) is characterized by low LTO (score: 26), moderate PD (score: 40) and UA (score: 46), and high masculine (score: 62), indulgence (score: 68), and individualism (score: 91). However, China has high PDI (score: 80), LTO (score: 87), and masculine (score: 69), and low indulgence (score: 24) and individualism (score: 20). Hofstede (1980) suggested that managerial styles can be traced to differences in cultural programming. For instance, Detelin Elenkov (1998) states that, since Russian managerial culture is identified by high PD and a strong collectivism, Russian employees expect an autocratic leadership style. In addition, he also claimed that American concepts of management that support participation in managers' decisions (low PD) and that allow subordinates to negotiate with one's employer (high individualism) are incompatible with the high PD and low individualism of Russian managerial culture.

Cultural bias in management theory

Research has shown that cultural values influence managerial behaviors (Hofstede, 1980; House et al., 2004). However, as stated earlier, the bulk of the management literature and theories reflect Western industrialized culture; even Hofstede's study (1980) used subjects from a large U.S. multinational corporation with a strong American culture. Thus, it is likely that most leadership theories and literature are culture-bound, reflecting U.S. values and beliefs. For example, both Leader-Member Exchange (LMX) theory and the original Path-Goal theory are based on an assumption that leadership consists of dyadic relationships between managers and workers. This assumption is clearly a reflection of the individualistic orientation of the dominant mainstream U.S. culture. In high PD cultures, there may be no personal relationship between leaders and followers.

In the USA, superior-subordinate relationships that foster independence and allow subordinates to experience autonomy and openness are generally accepted and preferred because of egalitarian norms (Hofstede, 1980). Accordingly, the LMX theory reflects this American cultural preference by stressing the reciprocal relationship between superiors and subordinates, as well as demonstrating a high degree of job autonomy for subordinates. However, in Asia, the relationships between superiors and subordinates are less open, and those fostering face saving are commonly preferred. In many countries, such as China, managers are expected to be paternalistic toward followers (Kim, 1994). Since paternalism involves dependence of followers on their managers for satisfaction of many of their personal as well as task-related needs, job autonomy, as recommended by the LMX theory, may truly violate Chinese cultural norms and values of low individualism.

In addition, according to one of the latest leadership theories—transformational leadership, effective management involves the exercise of individualized consideration toward followers. This Western managerial style may violate the cultural norms of highly collectivist cultures. The transformational theory also emphasizes the leadership style of intellectual stimulation, which encourages subordinates to be independent and to approach problems in new ways. This leadership behavior reflects the U.S. culture but may violate norms of dependency and conformity that characterize many other cultures such as the Japanese and Chinese cultures (Yokochi, 1989).

Organizational cultures: What is the "culture" of your organization?

Often, we think of cultures as nations or regions, but, as noted in Chapter 3, even families or organizations have culture. According to Thomas Whalen (2014), Roger Harrison first held the idea that organizations have cultures that can be identified, categorized, and managed. Stanley Davis (1984) coined the term **"corporate culture"** in the 1970s, and Andrew Pettigrew (1979) first used the term "organizational culture" in academic literature. The term was used to explain the economic successes of Japanese businesses that motivated their workers to nurture the commitment to a common set of core values, beliefs, and assumptions. Jeffrey Kerr and John Slocum (2005) defined **organizational culture** as a system of shared assumptions, values, and beliefs that show people what is appropriate and inappropriate behavior. These values have been found to have a strong influence on employee behavior as well as organizational performance (Ogbonna & Harris, 2000). According to Kelly Quintanilla and Shawn Wahl (2020), we will be able to understand organizational cultures by evaluating artifacts, rituals, language/jargon, and narratives/stories.

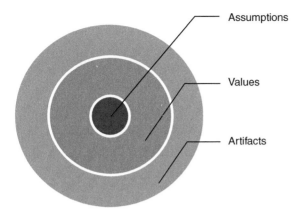

Assumptions

Values

Artifacts

Figure 15.4 Edgar Schein argues that three various markers can be seen as outer layer of an organizational culture "onion"
Source: Adapted from Schein, E. 1990.

We can think of the concept of organizational culture as existing along a continuum with the process approach at one end and classification approach at the other (Lim, 1995). The process approach follows Egdar Schein's (1990) model (Figure 15.4), in which culture consists of three levels: (1) artifacts, referring to the most visible and tangible aspects such as the physical, social, and environmental components of an organization; (2) values, meaning the deeply held beliefs or shared principles, standards, and goals that determine behavioral patterns within an organization; and (3) assumptions, representing the unconscious level of cultural or organizational beliefs about human nature and reality.

Six dimensions of organizational culture

The classification approach observes Geert Hofstede's (1980, 2001) model of cultural dimensions, summarized below (see also Chapter 4). Based on their studies (Hofstede et al., 1990), scholars have determined six dyadic dimensions of organizational cultures, that "describe the larger part of the variety in organizational practices" (Hofstede, 2011, pp. 19–21):

→ *Process-oriented vs. results-oriented.* Process-oriented cultures are dominated by technical and bureaucratic routines while results-oriented cultures by a common concern for outcomes. Associated with the culture's degree of homogeneity, there were vast differences in the study participants' perceptions among different levels in process-oriented cultures, but almost everybody perceived their practices in about the same way in results-oriented cultures.

→ *Job-oriented vs. employee-oriented.* Job-oriented cultures assume responsibility for the employees' job performance only while employee-oriented cultures assume a broad responsibility for their members' overall wellbeing. Hofstede et al. (1990) argue that this orientation is part of a culture and not just a choice for an individual manager.

→ *Professional vs. parochial.* Professional members, who are usually highly educated, identify primarily with their profession whereas parochial members derive their identity from the organization they work for. This dimension is also known as the "local vs. cosmopolitan" or internal versus external frame of reference.

→ *Open systems vs. closed systems*. This dimension refers to the common style of internal and external communication and to the ease with which outsiders and newcomers are admitted. Empirical evidence of systematic difference shows that organizational cultures also contain elements from national cultural differences.

→ *Tight vs. loose control.* This dimension deals with the clarity and enforcement of formal and informal rules within an organization, including the degree of formality (e.g., of clothing) and punctuality within the organization, based on the function of the organization's application of technology.

→ *Pragmatic vs. normative.* The last dimension describes the degree of flexibility or rigidity in dealing with the environment, especially the customers. This dimension measures the degree of customer orientation, which has been extensively researched in the marketing literature. Specifically, a more pragmatic organization is market-driven; the normative organization is focused on following ethical guidelines above all else.

What do you think? Think about a specific organization that you belong to. This might be a club, workplace, class cohort, sports team, or religious organization (e.g., a mosque, temple, or church). On the tensions above, where do you see your organization (e.g., are rules strongly enforced and understood, or is your organization more flexible?)? Using ideas from earlier chapters, what are some of the expected behaviors in your organization (Chapter 4)? What are some of the organizational stories people tell (e.g., about heroes or failures) (Chapter 7)? What sorts of prejudices are played out formally or informally in your organization (Chapter 6)? Finally, what underlying meanings or values do these things reveal about your organization?

Factors that influence organizational cultures

Organizational culture is usually influenced by the following factors: (1) the diversity of the workforce, such as the proportion of local nationals, expatriates, and third-country nationals; (2) the policy compatibility between the home country and the host country organization; (3) the length of time the subsidiary has been in operation; (4) the ownership structure of the subsidiary, like sole ownership or shared ownership; (5) the degree of national cultural distance among network members; (6) the level of constraining government regulations such as mandatory employee quotas; and (7) the relative strategic importance of the subsidiary perceived by the home country management (Griffith & Harvey, 2000).

These factors explain why cross-cultural communication with employees overseas involves complex and vexing problems. For a better understanding of organizational cultures, David Griffith and Michael Harvey (2000) provide the following perceptual mapping of competing organizational cultural values:

In Figure 15.5, flexibility means the level of **decentralization**, control means the level of **centralization**, internal means maintaining existing cultural systems, and external means adapting to the local or home country cultural systems. The vertical axis illustrates the organizational preference towards the level or degree of flexibility/control dimension. The horizontal axis illustrates the internal/external dimension of organization culture. The four quadrants illustrate the generic orientations characterizing organizational cultures depending on the structure and cultural focus of an organization's market strategy.

Figure 15.5 Griffith et al. provide perceptual mapping of competing organizational cultural values. Source: Griffith, D. A., & Harvey, M. G. 2000 / With permission of SAGE Publications.

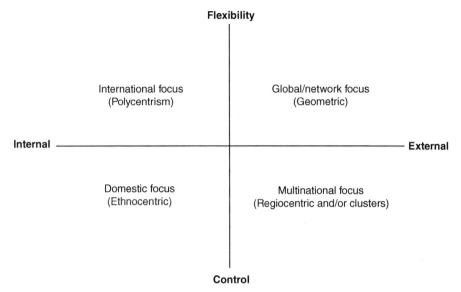

Corporate social responsibility: How can organizations make a difference?

Corporate social responsibility (CSR): What is it?

In today's fast-paced, money-grabbing, success-hungry, highly competitive global business environment, how much should organizations worry about being socially responsible? The question is itself meaningless since organizations can no longer afford to remain silent spectators to the many concerns that abound in society. In addition, since international governing bodies such as United Nations and the World Bank have little formal authority over organizations' actions, the past several decades have called for the development of norms—social expectations for proper behavior rather than laws and regulations enforced by government authorities. That is, the sets of norms are attempts to shape corporate behavior in ways nations cannot (Mumby & Kuhn, 2018). **Corporate social responsibility** (CSR) refers to the obligatory services and practices organizations should provide to their global communities as a gesture of symbiotic gratitude. According to Andreas Rasche and colleagues (2017), CSR is "the integration of an enterprise's social, environmental, ethical, and philanthropic responsibilities toward society into its operations, processes and core business strategy in cooperation with relevant stakeholders" (p. 6). Dennis Mumby and Timothy Kuhn (2018) add that "CSR is an alternative (and pragmatic) way to regulate the conduct of private companies in a globalized economy" (p. 346).

Forms and cases of CSR

Perhaps our best understanding of what CSR is will come from looking at some of the different forms that it can take. The first type of CSR is the organizations with greening initiatives that include organizations' development of environmentally friendly products and efforts to avoid producing environmental disasters. A second form is when companies practice social accounting to assess the costs and benefits of their activities in the hope of accomplishing not merely economic outcomes but social justice and environmental responsibility as well. The third form of CSR is based on the evaluations and recognition of organizations' ethical behaviors (CSR ratings) by independent civic organizations, the consulting firms, and the business press (Mumby & Kuhn, 2018).

Many websites now provide lists of the top socially responsible corporations, with the reasons for their assessments (See "What do you think" below). For example, the Donorbox website provides a list of 14 companies, each socially responsible for a different reason. These include:

→ Ben and Jerry's ice cream: The company donates U.S.$.05 for every one-pound tub sold to charity, especially issues involving social justice.

→ IKEA furniture: IKEA promotes environmental sustainability by using "sustainable" materials (cotton, wood, etc.). The company seeks to be using only recycled or renewable materials by 2030.

→ Indigo Reach partners with various organizations to promote "female empowerment, environment, and heritage." They have helped empower over 64,000 women, educate over 47,000 children, and plant over 40,000 trees.

→ Coca-Cola: This corporation donates at least 1% of annual profits to charity, partnering with campaigns such as Arwa's "Price of Water," which worked to provide clean drinking water to refugees in the Middle East.

Corporate social responsibility is not new, but it is growing in popularity. Just as today, Wal-Mart, Apple, NASCAR, and other organizations are pushing back against U.S. laws that discriminate against LGBTQ+ individuals, Coca-Cola historically threatened to move its base from Atlanta, Georgia when local business leaders were boycotting a dinner to honor Martin Luther King, Jr., an Atlanta native who had recently won a Nobel Peace Prize ("The Time Coca Cola got White Elites…", 2015). The threat ended the boycott—and the dinner sold out. In the same way, organizations around the world are turning their attention to social responsibility, such as Assisi Garments, of India, which produces fair-trade clothing using organic materials (Figure 15.6).

To relate the CSR concepts to Hofstede's dimensions, Husted (2005) proposed that egalitarian, individualist, and feminine values tend to constitute green or sustainable values, and Costa Rica is an example. Costa Rica is low in masculinity and low power distance, and it has used considerable resources in its social and institutional capacity for environmental sustainability.

What do you think? Do some research to find examples of what corporate social responsibility is. Then look up the most responsible companies in your country or in the world. How strong is the corporate social responsibility of the companies that provide your favorite products or services? Can you think of examples where companies who are socially responsible in some ways commit social abuses in other ways? Is it possible for companies to put on a show of corporate responsibility without a true commitment to societal causes?

Figure 15.6 Assisi Garments, of Tirupur, India, creates fair-trade garments from organic materials for distribution around the world. Source: Joerg Boethling/Alamy Stock Photo

Intercultural organizing and communication for civic engagement

In recent years, organizational communication scholars have encouraged activities that take their work from theory to social change and civic engagement. On one hand, employees can organize against unfair organizational policies, as demonstrators in China did to protest Apple, Inc. policies they claimed included child labor and 24-hour workdays (Moore, 2012). On the other hand, there is also the rise of an entire type of organization directed at civic engagement. Organizational scholar Laurie Lewis (2005) observes that the rise of the civil society sector, which is also known as the nonprofit sector or the third sector, is a global phenomenon. Engaging in our communities, local or international, while remaining mindful of cultural nuances, can lead to personally enriching experiences for the scholar-practitioner, and mutually beneficial collaboration partners, and the collective social worlds we cohabit. By communicating ideas, engaging in dialogue, encouraging multiple perspectives, examining tensions that may para-doxically inspire communication (Ganesh & Zoller, 2012), and fostering collaborative networks and relationships, as students and scholars of intercultural organizational communication, we are empowered to serve our global communities. At the same time, as mindful communicators, we need to develop other-centered capacities capable of cultural intelligence and sensitivity.

Alexandra Murphy, of DePaul University, created an effective U.S.-based partnership with Kenyan NGOs to address family-based HIV/AIDS education curriculum (Murphy, 2012). Because U.S. funds provide the resources for the partnership, the desire for a successful outcome of collabo-rative efforts creates dialectics of social discourse and political appropriateness, and dilemmatic norms of culturally sensitive education and information dissemination protocols. Culturally moti-vated to using direct communication to problem-solving, the U.S. partners had to learn to adapt to the Kenyan partners' style of using strategic counter-spaces and a form of silent communication to exert indirect power, while the Kenyans had to learn to understand U.S. styles of communicating in order to make the partnership work. Murphy recommends that in international intercultural social engagement activities, partners reassess communicative acts of exclusion, silence, and agenda-set-ting in the context of power relations. This engagement includes a self-awareness, on the part of the people involved, of their own positions and advantages in the collaboration, as well as cultural values they might be imposing on the other. As Miller (2015) claimed, it is increasingly common for individuals with needs and goals to come together in organizations known as cooperatives that are often motivated by a concern for democracy, social justice, and environmental and global responsibility, and all the cooperatives need intercultural communication competence (see Chapter 12).

Summary

This chapter began with an introduction to globalization and its impacts. Globalization connects people and organizations all over the world. It affects every aspect of our daily life and influences the business world both positively and negatively. Organizations, especially those aiming at the international markets, need to be fully aware of the double-edge sword effects of globalization, understand their own strengths and weaknesses, and then try to fit in while looking at the big picture. What followed was a discussion about the major types of organizations and organizational cultures preceded by a brief literature review of the researches on organizations in intercultural settings. Finally, we closed by considering ways that organizations can engage the community for social good, giving types and cases of both organizations and individuals who are making a difference. The important point to remember is that intercultural communication is especially important for success in international organizational contexts. Communication is essential to organizing, and organizing without communication is simply non-existent.

KEY TERMS

diversity, 305
globalization, 305
organizational communication, 305
culture, 307
diffusion, 310
emic, 311
etic, 311
organization, 312
monolithic organization, 312
plural organization, 312
ticultural organization, 312
social organizations, 312
multinational companies, 312
high-context cultures, 313

low-context cultures, 313
polychronic time, 313
polychronic time, 313
individualism versus collectivism, 315
masculinity versus femininity, 315
uncertainty avoidance, 315
long-Term orientation, 315
indulgence versus restraint, 315
corporate culture, 316
organizational culture, 316
decentralization, 318
centralization, 318
corporate social responsibility, 319

Discussion questions

1   How would you apply the definition of organizational communication used in this chapter to understanding the role of communication in organizations in your own culture?

2   Define globalization as you understand it. What is the history of globalization in your culture? How does this phenomenon affect your life, personally and professionally? Now

pick a foreign country of your choice and research how globalization started affecting that country.

3 Are the concepts of the old and new social contract applicable in your culture? How are forms of employment in your culture similar to or different from the discussion here?

4 This chapter highlights the differences between cultures. What are our similarities? There are almost eight billion of us cohabiting on this Earth today. What are the common pan-cultural concerns and issues that affect us collectively and as world citizens?

Action points

1 Divide students into groups of three or four. Instruct groups that they have to create an organizational culture model (Schein's Onion Model can be the base for their model) based on the characteristics of a selected organization. Each group has to write at least three examples for each level. Then ask them to discuss: a) Why is it important to understand the values of the organization? b) How do you feel about the organizational culture of the organization in relation to its multicultural workforce? and c) After completing this activity, do you think that your organization embraces the idea of a multicultural perspective of organizational culture? Yes or No? Justify your claim.

2 Ask students to look at the qualities in the Intercultural Exercise (Lambert & Myers, 2005) and describe the most important quality in the workplace, and why they chose it. Then, ask them to identify the most difficult quality to practice in organizations, and why. Discuss how using these qualities make the difference by relating back to the lecture material. In addition, invite students to consider using intercultural communication skills in the workplace, so that they can be more effective in their roles (Qualities in the Intercultural Exercise: To be persistent; To learn from interacting; To respect other cultures; To be aware of stereotypes; To be aware of one's own limitations; To be aware of one's own culture; To tolerate ambiguity; To relate to people; To be able to communicate well; To be non-judgmental; To practice empathy; To be flexible; To listen and observe; To adjust based on others' reactions).

3 Pretend you are considering developing a business in a foreign country. First, pick a country with which you want to do business. Then, read and research online, the different business/professional etiquettes that might challenge your own cultural values and mannerisms. Brainstorm ideas on how to approach business dealings in this new culture. For example, for businesses to develop and grow successfully in many parts of Latin America, one needs to establish a strong network of connections with decision-makers. Business cannot be rushed and you really need to get to know your potential future business collaborates on a personal basis first; only when a comfortable level of trust and friendship is established may the business topic be raised. If you are not from Latin America, these practices may seem unprofessional or time-consuming. However, these are accepted as a normal part of doing business in this part of the world.

4 How does your culture define diversity? In the United States, diversity is collectively understood as differences in race, gender, sexual orientation, social class, national origin, religious affiliations, and (dis)ability status. How do the diverse workgroups in your culture work together in an organization? What are the tensions and issues that are most important to an inclusive organizational culture in your country?

5 Read the dialogue below and find out the type or types of organizational cultures the people in the conversation find themselves in:

Director   : "Why don't you purchase Software A instead of Software B?"

Dr. Tyma   : "Sir, Software A is outdated while Software B is far advanced."

Director   : "But the approval for Software B will take time, while I have to show on papers that the lab has been established." (Note: The tone here is non-cooperative and of an accusation. Obviously, it will create a defensive climate. A climate of control implies that the senior's view is the only valid one. What if the director said the following?)"O.K. In that case you make a proposal, explaining the advantages of Software B over Software A and let us forward the proposal."

For more information

Aquire, S. (2022, August 26). 14 best socially responsible companies that are making impact. *DonorboxBlog*. Accessed December 7, 2022, at https://donorbox.org/nonprofit-blog/best-corporate-responsibility-companies

Bardhan, N., & Weaver, C.K. (Eds.). (2011). *Public relations in global cultural contexts*. Routledge.

McIlrath, L., Lyons, A., & Munck, R. (Eds.). (2012). *Higher education and civic engagement: comparative perspectives*. Palgrave-Macmillan.

Moran, R.T., Harris, P.R., & Moran, S. V. (2011). *Managing Cultural Differences: Global leadership strategies for cross-cultural business success* (8th ed.). Butterfield-Heinemann.

Varner, I., & Beamer, L. (2011). *Intercultural Communication in the Global Workplace* (5th ed.). McGraw-Hill.

Wiseman, R. L., & Shuter, R. (Eds.). (1994). *Communicating in Multinational Organizations*. Sage.

References

Adler, N. J. (1983). Cross-cultural management research: The ostrich and the trend. *Academy of Management Review, 8* (2), 226–232. https://doi.org/10.2307/257749

Adler, N. J., Doktor, R., & Redding, S. G. (1986). From the Atlantic to the Pacific century: Cross-cultural management reviewed. *Journal of Management, 12 (2)*, 295–318. https://doi.org/10.1177/0149206386012002

Aycan, Z., Kanunggo, R. N., Mendonca, M., Yu, K., Deller, J., Stahl, G., & Kurshid, A. (2000). Impact of culture on human resource management practices: A ten country comparison. *Applied Psychology: An International Review, 49*(1), 192–221.

Barker, R. T., & Gower, K. (2010). Strategic application of storytelling in organizations: Toward effective communication in a diverse world. *Journal of Business Communication, 49*, 295–312. https://doi.org/10.1177/0021943610369782

Batterson, R., & Weidenbaum, M. (2001). The pros and cons of globalization. *Center for the Study of American Business, Washington University in St. Louis*. Accessed December 9, 2022, at https://openscholarship.wustl.edu/mlw_papers/175/

Chan, J., Pun, N., & Selden, M. (2013). The politics of global production: Apple, Foxconn, and China's new working class. *New Technology, Work, and Employment, 28*(2), 100–115. https://doi.org/10.1111/ntwe.12008

Clack, G. (2006). The challenges of globalization. *eJournal of USA, 11*(1), 1–5.

Cox, T. H., Jr. (1991). The multicultural organization. *Academy of Management Executive, 5(2)*, 34–47. https://doi.org/10.5465/ame.1991.4274675

Davis, S. M. (1984). *Managing corporate culture*. Harper & Row.

Dunkerley, K. J., & Robinson, W. P. (2002). Similarities and differences in perceptions and evaluations of the communication styles of American and British managers. *Journal of Language and Social Psychology, 21*. https://doi.org/10.1177/026192702237956

Elenkov, D. (1998). Can American management concepts work in Russia? A cross-cultural comparative study. *California Management Review, 40*(4), 133–156. https://doi.org/10.2307/41165968

Friedman, T. (1999). *The Lexus and the olive tree: Understanding globalization.* Farrar, Straus & Giroux.

Ganesh, S., & Zoller, H. (2012). Dialogue, activism, and democratic social change. *Communication Theory, 22*, 66–91. https://doi.org/10.1111/j.1468-2885.2011.01396.x

Gardner, M. J., Paulsen, N., Gallois, C., Callan, V. J., & Monaghan, P. G. (2001). Communication in organizations: An intergroup perspective. In W. P. Robinson & H. Giles (Eds.), *The new handbook of language and social psychology* (2nd ed., pp. 561–584). John Wiley & Son.

Gelfand, M. J., Erez, M., & Aycan, Z. (2007). Cross-cultural organizational behavior. *Annual Review of Psychology, 56*, 497–514. https://doi.org/10.1146/annurev.psych.58.110405.085559.

Griffith, D. A., & Harvey, M. G. (2000). Executive insights: An intercultural communication model for use in global inter-organizational networks. *Journal of International Marketing, 9*(3), 87–103. https://doi.org/10.1509/jimk.9.3.87.19924

Hall, E. T. (1976). *Beyond culture.* Anchor.

Hall, E. T. (1983). *The dance of life: The other dimension of time.* Doubleday and Company.

Hall, E. T., & Hall, M. R. (2003). Key concepts: Understanding structures of culture. In M. G. Serapio & W. F. Cascio (Eds.), *Readings and cases in international management: A cross-cultural perspective* (pp. 151-162). Sage.

Hofstede, G. (1980). *Culture's consequences: International differences in work-related values.* Sage.

Hofstede, G. (1991). *Culture and organizations: Software of the mind.* McGraw-Hill.

Hofstede, G. (2001). *Culture's consequences: Comparing values, behaviors, institutions, and organizations across nations* (2nd ed.). Sage.

Hofstede, G. (2011). Dimensionalizing cultures: The Hofstede model in context. *Online Readings in Psychology and Culture, 2*(1), 1–25. https://doi.org/10.9707/2307-0919.1014

Hofstede, G., & Bond, M. H. (1988). The Confucius connection: From cultural roots to economic growth. *Organizational Dynamics, 16*(4), 4–21. https://doi.org/10.1016/0090-2616(88)90009-5

Hofstede, G., Hofstede, G. J., & Minkov, M. (2010). *Cultures and organizations: Software of the Mind* (3rd ed.). McGraw-Hill.

Hofstede, G., Neuijen, B., Ohayv, D. D., & Sanders, G. (1990). Measuring organizational cultures: A qualitative and quantitative study across twenty cases. *Administrative Science Quarterly, 35*, 286–316. https://doi.org/10.2307/2393392

Hong, Y., Morris, M. W., Chiu, C., & Benet-Martinez, V. (2000). Multicultural minds: A dynamic constructivist approach to culture and cognition. *American Psychology, 55*, 709–720. https://doi.org/10.1037/0003-066X.55.7.709

House, R. J., Hanges, P. W., Javidan, M., Dorfman, P., & Gupta, V. (Eds.). (2004). *Culture, leadership, and organizations. The GLOBE study of 62 societies.* Sage.

Husted, B. W. (2005). Culture and ecology: A cross-national study of the determinants of environmental sustainability. *Management International Review, 45*, 349–371.

Jandt, F. E. (2021). *An introduction to intercultural communication: Identities in a global community* (10th ed.). Sage.

Kelleher, D., McLaren, K., & Bisson, R. (1996). *Grabbing the tiger by the tail: NGO's learning for organizational change.* Canadian Council for International Cooperations.

Kennedy, P. (1993). *Preparing for the twenty-first century.* Random House.

Kerr, J., & Slocum, J. W. (2005). Managing corporate culture through reward systems. *Academy of Management Executive, 19*, 130–138. https://doi.org/10.5465/AME.2005.19417915

Kim, U. (1994). Significance of paternalism and communalism in the occupational welfare system of Korean firms: A national survey. In U. Kim, H. C. Triandis, C. Kagitcibasi, S. C. Choi, & G. Yoon (Eds.), *Individualism and collectivism: Theory, method, and applications* (pp. 251-266). Sage.

Lambert, J., & Myers, S. (2005). *Trainer's diversity source book: 50 ready-to-use activities, from icebreakers through wrap ups.* Alexandria, VA: Society for Human Resource Management.

Larkey, L. K. (1996). Toward a theory of communicative interactions in culturally diverse workgroups. *Academy of Management Review, 21*, 467–470. https://doi.org/10.2307/258669

Lewis, L. (2005). The civil society sector: A review of critical issues and research agenda for organizational communication scholars. *Management Communication Quarterly, 19*, 238–267. https://doi.org/10.1177/0893318905279190

Lim, B. (1995). Examining the organizational culture and organizational performance link. *Leadership and Organizational Development Journal, 16*(5), 16–21. http://dx.doi.org/10.1108/01437739510088491

Littrell, L. N., & Salas, E. (2005). A review of cross-cultural training: Best practices, guidelines, and research needs. *Human Resource Development Review, 4*, 305–334. https://doi.org/10.1177/1534484305278348

Marchiori, M., & Oliveira, I. L. (2009). Perspectives, challenges, and future directions for organizational research in Brazil. *Management Communication Quarterly, 22*, 671–676. https://doi.org/10.1177/0893318909332070

McLuhan, M. (1964). *Understanding media.* Gingko Press.

Miller, K. (2015). *Organizational communication: Approaches and processes* (7th ed.). Wadsworth.

Moore, M. (2012, January 27). Apple 'attacking problems' at its factories in China. *The Telegraph.* Accessed September 2, 2012, at http://www.telegraph.co.uk/technology/apple/9043924/Apple-attacking-problems-at-its-factories-in-China.html

Morris, M. W., Savani, K., Mor, S., & Cho, J. (2014). When in Rome: Intercultural learning and implications for training. *Research in Organizational Behavior, 34*, 189–215. https://doi.org/10.1016/j.riob.2014.09.003

Mumby, D. K., & Kuhn, T. R. (2018). *Organizational communication: A critical introduction.* Sage.

Murphy, A. G. (2012). Discursive frictions: Power, identity, and culture in an international working partnership. *Journal of International and Intercultural Communication, 6*, 1–20. https://doi.org/10.1080/17513057.2012.740683

Neuliep, J.W. (2021). *Intercultural communication: A contextual approach* (8th Ed.). SAGE.

Ogbonna, E., & Harris, L. (2000). Leadership style, organizational culture and performance: Empirical evidence from UK companies. *International Journal of Human Resources Management, 11*, 766–788. https://doi.org/10.1080/09585190050075114

Pal, M., & Buzzanell, P. (2008). The Indian call center experience: A case study in changing discourses of identity, identification, and career in a global context. *Journal of Business Communication, 45*(1), 31–60.

Pettigrew, A. (1979). On studying organizational culture. *Administrative Science Quarterly, 24*, 570–581. https://doi.org/10.2307/2392363

Quintanilla, K. M., & Wahl, S. T. (2020). *Business and professional communication: KEYS for workplace excellence* (4th ed.). Sage.

Rasche, A., Morsing, M., & Moon, J. (2017). *Corporate social responsibility: Strategy, communication, governance.* Cambridge University Press.

Rodrik, D. (1997). *Has globalization gone too far?* Institute for International Economics.

Schein, E. (1990). Organizational culture. *American Psychologist, 45*(2), 109–119. https://doi.org/10.1037/0003-066X.45.2.109

Shuter, R. (1990). The centrality of culture. *Southern Communication Journal, 55*, 237–249. https://doi.org/10.1080/10417949009372792

Shuter, R. (2014). The centrality of culture in the 20th and 21st centuries. In M. K. Asante, Y. Miike, & J. Yin (Eds.), *The global intercultural communication reader* (2nd ed., pp. 48–57). Routledge.

Stohl, C. (2001). Globalizing organizational communication. In F. M. Jablin & L. L. Putnam (Eds.), *The new handbook of organizational communication: Advances in theory, research, and methods* (pp. 323–375). Sage.

Taylor, F. W. (2006). *The principle of scientific management.* Cosimo Classics.

Theis-Berglmair, A. M. 2013. Why organizational communication has not gained a foothold in German-speaking communication studies – Until now: An historical outline. *Management Communication Quarterly*, Online First. https://doi.org/10.1177/0893318912470078

The time Coca-Cola got White elites in Atlanta to honor Martin Luther King, Jr. (2015, April 4). *NPR.* Accessed December 7, 2022, at https://www.npr.org/sections/codeswitch/2015/04/04/397391510/when-corporations-take-the-lead-on-social-change

U.S. Census Bureau. (2020). *Current population survey.* Washington, DC: GPO. Retrieved from, Accessed December 7, 2022, at http://www.census.gov

Verma, P. (2013). Relationship between organizational communication flow and communication climate. *International Journal of Pharmaceutical Sciences and Business Management, 1*(1), 63–71. Accessed March 6, 2023 at https://www.academia.edu/5368651/Relationship_between_Organisational_Communication_Flow_and_Communication_Climate_

Whalen, T. B. (2014). Utilizing the social transaction theory of social ontology to understand organizational culture change. *Journal of Business & Economics Research, 12*(1), 37–42. https://doi.org/10.19030/jber.v12i1.8375

Witte, K., & Morrison, K. (1995). Intercultural and cross-cultural health communication: Understanding people and motivating healthy behaviors. In R.

Wiseman (Ed.), *Intercultural communication theory* (pp. 216–246). Sage.

Würtz, E. (2006). Intercultural communication on websites: A cross-cultural analysis of websites from high- context cultures and low-context cultures. *Journal of Computer-Mediated Communication,*

11(1), 274–299. https://doi.org/10.1111/j.1083-6101.2006.tb00313.x

Yokochi, N. (1989). *Leadership styles of Japanese business executives and managers: Transformational and transactional.* United States International University.

Conclusion

R eaders come to a book like this with different reasons and from different backgrounds. Some are students, others business professionals; readers come from around the world or represent diverse cultural backgrounds from within a nation. You might have opened this book with many cultural experiences on your life record, or you might be someone who thinks they have never had a true "intercultural" interaction. Some may have been looking for practical work solutions, and others for ways to integrate culture into social change and civic engagement. Many readers are already involved in civic and political engagement, and others have not yet found or made the opportunity for such engagement.

We see several themes that run through this book. The first is that we all have choice to respond to our surroundings, yet not all choices are equal. Each of us is constrained by birth, age, ability, location, family, and so on. Thus, we live a life between choice and constraint. We feel that cultural knowledge gives us more choice over our actions: we realize how much of what we do is cultural, so have more choices to go against the norm, if we choose to do so, or to go with the norm, but embracing the beauty of culture, rather than passively floating through life, "culturally" speaking.

We framed the book largely in terms of civic and political engagement, because we feel that civic life is important for citizens, regardless of where you live. There are many reasons to be involved in our communities and world. Our goal has not been to persuade you in any particular direction regarding political issues, though we would be naïve or deceptive if we told you that we do not have our own perspectives. We hope that you find the book helpful for engaging civically in the world around you.

At the same time, we live in a material world, with school, job, and relationships. So, although we wanted to focus on social action, we also hope you learned more about relationships, consumption, and production of media, the global workplace, cross-cultural adjustment and competence, and other practical issues. So, we sought to make the book practical both professionally and civically.

There is a lot to learn about culture. Message production and consumption are complex, with language and nonverbal elements interacting to accomplish many tasks, from expressing feelings to giving directions. We have focused on some specific contexts and aspects of using language, such as rhetoric. And increasingly, we cannot separate our use of language and nonverbal behavior from our understanding of media messages and social media, so we have included

Intercultural Communication for Everyday Life, Second Edition. John R. Baldwin, Alberto González, Nettie Brock, Ming Xie, and Chin-Chung Chao.
© 2024 John Wiley & Sons Ltd. Published 2024 by John Wiley & Sons Ltd.
Companion Website: http://www.wiley.com/go/baldwin2e

discussion of those here as well. Messages—mediated and face-to-face—are impacted by and impact many things: our own identities, our social contexts, our educational and organizational contexts, and, increasingly, global issues and structures.

However, we have highlighted that media and face-to-face messages can be best understood if we look at underlying ideas upon which they are built. These underlying ideas from one perspective might be things such as cultural values and the beliefs and norms that intersect with those values. We have introduced (and evaluated) several frameworks of such values; but if you travel abroad or work with people of a specific group or culture, the information here should serve only as a springboard into your own investigation of specific cultures. We all continue to learn all our lives about differences and similarities that unite us. From a different perspective, our face-to-face and mediated communication are also built upon underlying systems of ideas— "ideologies". And in every society, these sets of ideas struggle together, as groups seek prestige and power to define terms. We hope that awareness of the existence of these ideas and how they are maintained, negotiated, and at times manipulated will make you a more responsible user and producer of messages.

Finally, we hope that throughout this book you have found the delight in understanding others and ourselves that has driven us, as authors, to investigate the areas of culture and communication that create a rich fabric as our experiences are woven together with those of other backgrounds. We welcome your insights and thoughts on the book, as we continue to build each other up and sharpen each other for the task of making this a more harmonious and equitable world for all.

Glossary

Accommodating (yielding): A conflict approach in which one party gives in to the requests or demands of the other

Acculturation: The process of learning another culture, and one's sense of identification with that culture—in part or whole—either through moving to live in that culture or through two cultures living side-by-side in the same geographical space

Activism: Involvement that includes participation in the political system

Adjustment: Broadly defined, the process one goes through changing one's behavior and adapting psychologically in transition to another culture

Adjustment stage: The third stage of the U-curve, in which travelers feel a growing sense of understanding and being able to live and succeed in the new culture

Affordances: The functions or "action possibilities" of a (social) medium that allow users to do specific things with/through that medium

Agency: The degree of choice we are aware of having in a particular situation

Alienated approach: An approach to returning home from another culture in which the traveler becomes overly critical or bitter about the home culture

Ally: Someone from one group, often a dominant group, who advocates, supports, or works with people from another group, often a marginalized group, for social justice

Altruism: The notion of doing good for someone, even a stranger

Antiracism movement: a variety of strategies and tactics to resist oppression, particularly race-based discrimination

Anxiety: Feelings of uneasiness, tension, or apprehension that occur in intercultural interactions

Appreciation: The attitude and action of not only accepting a group's behaviors, but also seeing the good in them, even adopting them, and actively including the individuals of a group

Arbitrator: A neutral, objective, third party who can resolve a conflict based on the facts of the conflict situation presented to her or him

Argot: Language used by those in a particular underclass, often to differentiate themselves from a dominant culture (e.g., prostitutes, prisoners)

Arms-length racism: A form of racism in which we might be friendly toward people of other races, but want to keep them at a distance, such as not having them as neighbors, friends, or romantic partners

Assimilation: Giving up one's own culture to adopt another; that is, accepting both behaviors and underlying ways of thinking

Asylum seeker: Someone who is seeking legal protection from the new state, rather than simply moving there because of conditions of strife

Attitude: A disposition to relate to things, actions, or people in certain ways

Attribution: A process by which we give meanings to our own behavior and the behavior of others

Authoritarian theory: A theory of mass communication where the media is controlled entirely by the government

Avoiding (withdrawing): A conflict approach in which individuals prefer to simply avoid confrontation with the offender or may be afraid of consequences resulting from a direct confrontation of the issue

Axiology: A set of assumptions about the role of values in research

Backchanneling: Verbal and paralanguage cues used to indicate we are listening to another communicator

Intercultural Communication for Everyday Life, Second Edition. John R. Baldwin, Alberto González, Nettie Brock, Ming Xie, and Chin-Chung Chao.
© 2024 John Wiley & Sons Ltd. Published 2024 by John Wiley & Sons Ltd.
Companion Website: http://www.wiley.com/go/baldwin2e

Background phase: The initial phase of negotiation, in which parties assess their position, consider what they know of the other parties, and plan out their communication language

Basso's hypothesis: A hypothesis by anthropologist Keith Basso, upon observing use of silence among the Apache, that people may use silence to respond to situations of uncertainty

Behavior valence: In expectancy violation theory, the positive or negative evaluation we give to a behavior that violates our expectancies

Belief system: A set of interrelated beliefs, including values, world view, norms, and mores of a culture

Belief: An assumption that someone has about the nature of something; a cognition (thought) about the connection between two or more concepts

Biculturalism/integration: An approach to acculturation in which travelers or minority members, rather than unlearning their culture, become able to negotiate well both culture of origin and dominant culture

Breadth (of self-disclosure): In social penetration theory, the number of topic areas about which we self-disclose

Categorical imperative: An ethical approach in which there is a clear right or wrong, regardless of culture or circumstance, based on logic

Categorization: The mental process of grouping things, attributes, behaviors, and people into like clusters

Centralization: An organizational structure in which decision-making is made by a small number of organizational members, typically at the top of the organizational structure. See also "Flexibility"

Channel: The medium through which a message travels from an information source to a destination

Chronemics: The conceptualization and use of time

Civic engagement: Involvement in the community, regardless of politics

Co-cultural communication: Communication between people of different groups within a larger, dominant culture

Co-cultural group: A group or culture that exists within the same space as other groups or cultures, sharing some aspects of a dominant culture

Code-switching: Changing linguistic forms of speech, whether between registers, between elaborated or restricted codes, or between languages

Collaborating (integrating): A conflict approach in which parties seek to maximize their own rewards while also facilitating the meeting of the goals of the other party

Color blindness: A strategy for reducing prejudice in which people attempt to ignore "race" or ethnicity in social interaction

Communication accommodation theory: A theory that predicts how people adjust their communication in certain situations, the various factors that lead to such changes, and the outcomes of different types of changes

Communication appropriateness: Following rules of a context or relationship in communication

Communication competence: A combination by which a communicator is both effective and competent

Communication effectiveness: The ability to accomplish our desired tasks through communication

Communication for social change/developmental communication: Communicative efforts to bring more development to other communities

Communication ritual or Conversational episode (CE): A portion of a conversation that has a distinct beginning and ending

Communication system: The set of signs and symbols we use to transfer ideas, emotions, or impressions to others

Communication: The process of creating and sending symbolic behavior and the interpretation of behavior between people

Communicative engagement: Participating in civic dialogue and being fully aware and expressive in public deliberation

Communicative ethic: See dialogic ethic

Communicator reward valence: In expectancy violation theory, the perceived reward or punishment that we think we can receive from a person who violates our expectancies

Competing (dominating): A "zero-sum" conflict approach in which one party is concerned primarily with meeting their own goals, seeking to win the conflict regardless of cost to the other party

Compromising (conceding): A conflict approach in which each party makes concessions, giving up some goals to achieve others

Conflict: A difference in values, processes, expectations, or results—real or perceived, and related to interpersonal relations or decision-making content— between two people or groups

Confucian work dynamism: A cultural orientation based in Confucian philosophy that values respect for tradition, thrift, persistence, and personal steadiness—that is, a long-term pragmatism

Connectivity: The networked structure among social media users

Connotation: The set of feelings an individual associates with a particular word

Constitutive approach: A view of social reality that suggests that we create social reality through communication, rather than culture, sex, and race merely predicting how we communicate

Contact cultures (high- and low-contact cultures): Cultures that differ in the degree to which members tend to seek more sensory input during face-to-face interaction through various nonverbal channels

Contact theory: A theoretical approach that suggests contact between people of antagonistic groups can, under the right conditions, reduce intolerance between groups

Control: An aspect of a "centralized" organization in which decisions are made by a small group of people and there are predetermined appropriate paths of communication between organizational members

Convergence (1): The process of changing our behavior to be more like that of the person with whom we are speaking

Convergence (2): An approach to globalization that emphasizes the need for organizations to adapt their practices to a global marketplace

Convergency: The combination of the forms and functions of information, media, electronic communication, and electronic computing

Conversational episode (CE) or communication ritual: A portion of a conversation that has a distinct beginning and ending

Corporate culture/organizational culture: A set of values and assumptions that is shared by an "organization" that guides organizational members' behaviors

Corporate social responsibility: The obligatory services and practices organizations should provide to their global communities as a gesture of symbiotic gratitude

Crisis stage: The second stage of the U-curve, in which travelers go through a period of stress, often feeling a need to complain or withdraw, with symptoms of stress, fatigue, powerlessness, depression, or even psychosomatic sickness

Critical perspective: An approach to research with assumptions that social inequalities and injustice exist and that research and theory should seek to address these

Critical race theory (1): A perspective that analyzes how social systems (e.g., law, education, marketing, housing) favor Whites over those of other groups

Critical race theory (2): A movement to change the legal system away from oppression and an unjust treatment of racial and ethnic minorities.

Cross-cultural adaptation/sociocultural adjustment: One of two dimensions of adjustment, referring to one's sense of fitting in and ability to negotiate the culture (such as accomplishing tasks); some writers use "adaptation" more broadly to refer to the process one goes through in adjusting to another culture, be that psychological adjustment, ability to negotiate the culture, or assimilation

Cultural communication: Research that involves comparative studies between cultures

Cultivation theory: A theory that posits a shift in an individual's behavior and beliefs based on their media consumption

Cultural calamity: A large-scale event, often beyond the control of people, that shapes nearly every aspect of culture

Cultural communication: The study or practice of communication in a single culture

Cultural identity: A person's sense of connectedness to a "culture" as that person defines it (e.g., the shared values, beliefs, and norms of a group, or a specific heritage of origin)

Cultural imperialism: The view that global media are the purveyors of certain cultural and political—usually Western—values to the exclusion of others in the weaker countries of the world

Cultural myth: A narrative that is popularly told to teach preferred ways of behaving

Cultural pluralism/multiculturalism: A response in which a dominant cultural group allows an immigrant or minority group to maintain both group and new/dominant culture identities

Cultural relativism: An approach to ethics and social research that states that we should not make moral or ethical judgments upon other cultures and that each culture should determine for itself what is right

Cultural values: Values held by the majority of members of a given culture

Culture shock/cultural adjustment: A sense of anxiety experienced in a new culture, usually over a longer period of time, as a result of losing a sense of the expected social cues one has in one's own culture

Culture: The way of life of a group of people, including symbols, values, behaviors, artifacts, and other shared aspects, which continually evolves as people share messages; and is the result of struggle between different groups who share different perspectives, interests, and power relationships

Datafication: The ability to quantify many social aspects into data

Decentralization: An organizational structure in which decision-making is shared among members of different levels of the organization. See also "Flexibility"

Deculturation: The process of unlearning one's own culture when one lives for an extended period of time in a different culture

Denotation: The relatively objective dictionary-type definition of a word

Depth (of self-disclosure): In social penetration theory, the intimacy of detail that we self-disclose

Derived ethic: An ethical approach developed by looking across cultures to find the ethical beliefs that are similar in all cultures

Developmental communication/communication for social change: Communicative efforts to bring more development to other communities

Dialectic/dialectical tension: A tension between opposing "poles" or aspects of a relationship in which both ends of each tension are always present, both contradicting and completing each other

Dialectic: For Aristotle, the rigorous methods for testing competing claims used by scientists and other experts

Dialogic ethic: An ethical approach in which we converse directly with people of other cultures before affirming ethical stances that involve those people

Diaspora: Where the people of one geographic area and group spread out across many different cultures

Diasporic citizen: A person who is a member of a population that has moved or been displaced

Differentiated and undifferentiated codes: Language codes characterized by more (or less) levels of difference between speech registers, depending on the person with whom we are speaking

Diffusion: The spread of artifacts, behaviors, and ideas across a group or culture or between groups or cultures

Diffusion: The spread of ideas, behaviors, or artifacts from one culture to another

Digital activism: Political participation done through social media, such as sending messages, promoting campaigns, or organizing protests

Digital Blackface: The online practice of appropriating Black images/bodies/sounds by non-Black people for playful purposes

Digital divide: When different groups of people have unequal access to electronic media, including hardware, technology, or software

Digitality: How all the information and content on social media is digitalized and converted into digital form, which allows all kinds of mathematical operations

Directive: In speech acts theory, speech used to influence the behavior of another person

Discourse (1): A unit of language greater than one sentence (e.g., telling a story, giving a description, chit chat, interview)

Discourse (2): Practices, messages, and concepts linked together to portray a particular idea: the way that a notion is described in terms of other ideas in society (e.g., the discourse of beauty)

Discrimination: Treating someone differently because of the group to which they belong

Discursive elements of language: Elements of language use linked to a broader pattern of meaning

Disintegration approach: An approach to social media in which cultural minorities or immigrants into a culture are marginalized

Display rules: Cultural rules about the display of emotion, indicating when, to whom, in what context, and how much we should show certain emotions

Distributive, or positional negotiation: Negotiation that involves competitively pushing for our own goals and agenda with little regard to the other party

Divergence (1): When we highlight our own communication style when talking with people from other groups to mark it as different from our communication

Divergence (2): An approach to globalization in which workplace characteristics, even of the same company, may vary from culture to culture

Diversity: The unique backgrounds, personality, life experiences, and beliefs of individuals—a combination of differences (gender, age, culture, sexual orientation differences, etc.)

Division: The different beliefs and ways of interacting that potentially lead to intercultural conflict

Echo chamber (1): In information environment in which people tend to receive and pay attention to news and opinions from those who already share their perspective

Echo chamber (2): When people pay attention only to certain media, often as filtered through the feeds provided to them in their social media

Efficacy, self-efficacy: A belief that we can accomplish a task to which we set ourselves

Elaborated code: A way of speaking in which people spell out the details of meaning in the words in a way that those outside of the group can understand them

Emblem: A gesture that has an explicit verbal translation that is known among most members of a group

Emic approach: An approach to researching culture in which researchers seek to set aside their own understandings and understand a culture's meanings or behaviors from the perspective of the culture

Enculturation: The process of learning one's own culture

Epistemology: A set of assumptions about knowledge and what counts as data

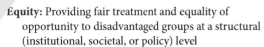

Equity: Providing fair treatment and equality of opportunity to disadvantaged groups at a structural (institutional, societal, or policy) level

Essentialism: Treating cultures as if everyone in the culture is the same ("monolithic") or that the culture is unchanging ("static")—that is, treating a culture as if it has a constant and unchangeable "essence"

Ethical egoism: An ethical approach in which we make choices based simply on what seems good or beneficial to us, without regard for others

Ethics: How we judge the rightness or wrongness of our interactions with others

Ethnic cleansing: The attempt to remove a population by murder or forced deportation from a country or area of a country

Ethnicity: A sense of shared history and geographical ancestry, usually along with other markers, such as culture, language, or religion

Ethnocentrism: A perception in which people see their group as the center of everything, possibly superior to others, using their group or culture as a reference to judge other groups

Ethnography of communication: A method of research and writing that involves detailed observing, usually involving interaction with people, to understand the lives of a group of people

Ethnophaulism: A racial slur, or name for another group

Etic approach: An approach to researching culture in which researchers start with a framework or theory developed outside of cultures and apply it to cultures, for example, to compare cultures on some dimension

Everyday racism: See subtle racism, microaggressions

Exacting style: A communication style in which speakers give information as necessary

Exaggerated style: A communication style in which speakers use language not so much to describe reality precisely, but to embellish upon it (e.g., exaggeration, metaphor)

Exclusion: A response in which a dominant cultural group simply negates the existence of an immigrant or minority group, having no relations with them

Exogamy: Marrying outside of one's perceived group, as opposed to *endogamy*, marrying within one's group

Expatriate: A noncitizen worker who lives in a country for an indeterminate length of time

Expectancies: Expectations for nonverbal and verbal behavior based on our culture, our personal preferences, and our knowledge of the other communicator

Face: The image that people want others to have of them in interaction

Faux pas: A mistake we make in our own or another culture; a breach of etiquette that brings embarrassment to self or others

Feedback: Some sort of verbal or nonverbal response, to the sender

Feminism: A social movement to ensure that women are treated equally to men.

Feminist standpoint theory: The consideration of the lived (and unique) experiences of women, as influenced by unequal power relations in society

Filter bubble: An information bias in which people receive information on social media based on (and sometimes limited to) the media platform's algorithm, geared to the sorts of sources the individual has already accessed on that platform

Flexibility: An aspect of "decentralized" organizations in which control is decentralized, allowing more openness of information exchange between different members of the organization

Formal time: A time reference to a specific time on the clock

Framing: The practice of presenting information, especially in the news media, through a particular ideological lens

Fundamental attribution error: An error of perception in which we overestimate the role of personal characteristics in someone else's behavior and do not place as much weight on context

Gender: Socially constructed cultural and social expectations based on biological sex

Globalization: The complex interconnections between business, political, and cultural systems across cultural and national boundaries

Golden mean: An ethical approach in which people avoid extreme positions, or choose the middle road in making ethical choices

Guilt: A negative emotion that entails personal responsibility for a wrong committed

Guilt culture: A culture in which people are more likely to be motivated by a sense of remorse when they behave badly, based on a sense of personal responsibility

Haptics: Nonverbal behavior involving touch

Hate crime: An act of open discrimination, vandalism, physical or sexual abuse, or other harmful behavior (including "flaming" behaviors on Internet video and news sites) that is based on group belonging

Heavy viewers: People who watch more than 15 hours of television a week

Hegemonic masculinity: An image of how men are "supposed to" act, which stems out of an oppressive, systemic discourse which privileges certain characteristics as "normatively masculine"

Hegemony: Some form or level of control over another group, such as political, cultural, or economic power; how the powerful keep their power in a society, largely by making their (dominant) ideologies seem commonsense, taken-for-granted and not worthy of questioning

Heterogeneity: The dissimilarity between people (including gender, age, race, religion, and ethnicity) in a given group (as opposed to "homogeneity")

Heterosexism: A system of images, policies, and collective thought that privileges heterosexual relationships and marginalizes or disenfranchises those in homosexual relationships

Hierarchical: An organizational structure with power concentrated primarily among the few individuals at the top

High culture: The activities and expressions that represented what people believed to be moral and intellectual refinement (opera, theater, museums)

High-context culture: A culture in which meaning is more often implicit, that is, inside of the communicators, because they know what to expect based on the circumstance and on role and status relationships

Homophobia: An irrational fear of someone who is lesbian or gay

Honeymoon stage: The first stage of the U-curve, in which travelers feel a time of happiness and excitement as they first arrive at a new culture

Humanistic perspective: A perspective to research that assumes that humans are unique from other aspects of the natural world, such as through their cognitive abilities, ability to make choices, or symbolic nature

Humanistic principle: An ethical approach that states that we should treat others well and not do anyone harm

Hybridity (1): The blending of cultural elements from two or more cultures, such as when a portion of a diasporic group moves to a single region and cultures influence each other; the blend is usually favored or directed by the group with more power

Hybridity (2): The view that cultures are inherently mixed, and not pure, because they are formed through histories of borrowing, copying, and mutual influencing

Hybridized cultural identity: A cultural identity that emerges from a virtual community composed of diverse people

Hyperexplanation: A form of convergence Whites often use with Blacks or members of other minority groups

(U.S.), including repetition and simplified grammar and word choice

Hypertextuality: The networking function of information technology that allows a large quantity of information to freely move around within a series of interconnected nodes in the network

Identification: When communicators connect their perspective to that of another; the opposite of division

Identity politics: The practice of laying claim to an identity in order to help ourselves integrate into our communities and fit into parts of our social world; how groups with these identities vie for various types of power—social status, economic power, the power to define social norms, and so on

Ideology: A system of meanings and assumptions that each of us holds to assist us in making sense of the social world as well as our role and function in that world

Immediacy: Verbal and nonverbal behaviors that show warmth, liking, and affiliation

Immigrant: Someone who travels to another culture, with intent to stay permanently

Immigration: The entry into a country by a citizen of another country, who then desires to remain in that country

Implicit bias: Prejudices that are beyond our awareness or intention but still have the potential to impact our behavior

Inclusion: Creating a climate, through words, actions, and policy, where people of diverse groups feel welcome and feel that they can participate fully

Indigenous framework: An approach that allows everybody to create and share their own content to promote diverse ways of understanding the production of meaning-making on social media

Individualism/collectivism (I/C): A culture's orientation toward the self in relation to others; the degree to which a culture values individual (or nuclear family) goals and belonging, or adherence to the needs and goals of important in-groups

Individuation: When we see a person as an individual, rather than simply as a member of a group

Indulgence-restraint: A cultural orientation that differs between self-expression and indulging in behaviors at the moment versus engaging in behavior appropriate to the situation or role-relationships (see "propriety")

Informal time: Time references that refer to more vague expressions of time than formal time, such as "after a while," "later," and so on

In-groups: Those groups to which we see ourselves belonging

Innovation/invention: When someone within a culture derives or creates a new artifact, behavioral practice, or idea

Instrumental and affective styles: Whether communication is more goal-directed (instrumental) or emotional and expressive (affective)

Instrumental value: A characteristic, trait, or "mode of conduct" that people in a culture hold to be important for reaching societal goals

Integration stage: The final stage of the U-curve, in which a traveler reaches a more or less stable identity, taking on the new culture as her or his own

Integration/biculturalism: An approach to acculturation in which travelers or minority members, rather than unlearning their culture, become able to negotiate well both culture of origin and dominant culture

Integrative, or principled negotiation: Negotiation that uses collaborative strategies and consciously considers the needs and expectations of the other party to develop mutually satisfying ends

Interactivity: Social media's interactive function that provides users opportunities to produce and reproduce information content during interactions

Intercultural adaptation: see cross-cultural adaptation

Intercultural communication competence: A communicator's ability in another culture both to reach task completion and to do so while also following the appropriate rules of the situation

Intercultural communication: Communication between people of two different cultures in which cultural differences are large enough to impact the production or consumption of messages

Intercultural Conflict: Interaction between people of different cultural groups in which there is explicit or implicit tension because of different norms, beliefs, values, processes, desired outcomes, etc.

Intercultural rhetoric: attempts at gaining cooperation in which at least two cultural rhetorical traditions meet

Intercultural transformation: A process in which, through adapting to new culture(s), communicators gain new ways to think, act, and feel beyond our culture of origin

Intergroup communication: Communication in which perception of the other person as a group member becomes important, regardless of real cultural differences

Intermarriage: Marriage between people of perceived out-groups regardless of the grounds—religious, cultural, racial, and so on

International communication: Often interchangeable with intercultural communication; sometimes refers specifically to national media systems and the role of culture in shaping those systems

Interpersonal communication: Communication between specific individuals (as opposed to sending a message to a mass public); in the model of communication, interacting with people as individuals as opposed to members of groups

Interpretive approach: A perspective to research in which researchers provide a holistic interpretation of a behavior or text in its context, often admitting that it is the researcher's interpretation, rather than assuming it as a fact

Intersectionality: The multiple identities each person has; none of those identities are any more or less important than any other; they all work together to construct identity.

Intolerance: Any thought, behavior, policy, or social structure that treats people unequally based on group terms

Invention/innovation: When someone within a culture derives or creates a new artifact, behavioral practice, or idea

Jargon: A vocabulary used by people within a specific profession or area (such as rugby players, competitive online gamers, or mine workers)

Kinesics: Body movement, including gestures, stance, gait (how we walk), posture, and facial expressions of emotion

Kuan-hsi: An aspect of Chinese relationships that refers to the use of and developing of relationships as a social resource—similar to *wasta, palanque, blat, clout,* and the *jeito brasileiro*

Language: A system of verbal, nonverbal, and visual symbols that a group pieces together to share meaning

Lasswell's model of communication: An approach to media effects that consider the variables of source, content, channel, and audience

Law: A norm or rule that has been codified—that is, made formal by a government, with punishments established for violation

Leadership: a process of influencing a group of individuals to achieve a common goal

Libertarian theory: A theory of mass communication wherein no one has control over the media and an individual can publish whatever they want

Long-term orientation: See Confucian work dynamism

Low/popular culture: The everyday activities and expressions of people

Low-context culture: A culture in which people place more meaning in the "explicit code;" that is, in the words themselves

Maintenance: When we make no changes in behavior when speaking with other individuals or people in other groups

Mansplaining: A form of overaccommodation in which men "talk down" to women, such as by giving unnecessary details or speaking in a condescending or patronizing manner

Marginality: A state in which sojourners or minority members end up not identifying with either the new or original culture, often ceasing to want any interaction

Masculinity/femininity: A cultural orientation that describes how the culture orients toward rules of men and women, including how rigid or flexible gender roles are and whether the culture is more direct and goal oriented or relational and face-saving

Mean world syndrome: An effect of consumption of media (in cultivation theory) in which heavy viewers of televised media develop a more violent view of social reality than is actually the case

Media conglomerates: The small handful of media companies that own the majority of the world's media content

Media frames: A concept that describes how media suggest the issues and controversies surrounding the story

Mediator: A neutral third party that tries to resolve disputes with reason and compromise instead of more aggressive measures

Melting pot approach: A response in which a dominant cultural group expects an immigrant or minority group to lose its own cultural identity to become like the dominant culture

Message: A set of symbols—words, sounds, or images—placed together to represent some meaning

Meta-ethic: An overarching guideline of behavior toward other people, which either can or should be applied to people in all cultures

Metaphor: A verbal expression in which an item that is well known is associated with another item that is less well known

Metaphorical archetype: A metaphor deeply embedded in cultural use and highly persuasive in public discourse

Microaggressions: Everyday expressions of intolerance that people of non-dominant racial, sex, gender orientation, and other groups must live with, which are often too subtle to even notice, but which become part of the fabric of one's life

Migrant: Someone who has moved voluntarily or involuntarily for short or long periods of time

Miscegenation: The marrying of individuals across racial or ethnic lines

Monochronic culture: A culture in which people tend to do one task at a time

Monochronic time: The time orientation in which events are scheduled as separate items—one thing at a time

Monolithic organization: Highly homogenous organizations that identify with one country and consist of one dominant cultural group

Moral exclusion: An ethical approach in which people apply a different standard of conduct to outgroups than they do to members of their own group

Morality: How someone judges a behavior is right or wrong, good or bad

More: A very strong norm, with negative social results for violating it

Morpheme: The smallest unit of sound that adds distinct meaning to a word, such as root words, prefixes, suffixes, or, in some language, verb or noun endings

Multicultural organization: An organization with minorities represented at all levels of the organization

Multicultural person: A person who, through multiple cultural experiences, is able to negotiate various cultures easily, living between or beyond cultures

Multiculturalism/cultural pluralism: A response in which a dominant cultural group allows an immigrant or minority group to maintain both group and new/dominant culture identities

Multinational/multicultural organizations: Organizations that typically identify with one nationality but do business in several countries

Mutual intelligibility: The common meanings and interests people share in order to understand each other, necessary for identification

Narrowcast media: Media created for a specific audience rather than a general one

Nationalism: A pride in and/or loyalty to our own nation

Negative face: A desire to be seen as autonomous or independent of others

Negotiation: A form of decision-making that involves multiple parties with competing interests, yet with a reason to work those interests out together through exchanging information

Neo-tribe: A group with shared values and behaviors that are based on an interest group, such as fandoms or people with particular hobbies and interests that include sets of expectations and behaviors

Noise: Physical or psychological interference that keeps the receiver from receiving the message as sent

Norm: An expectation for behavior with a moral component

Nuclear family: A family composed of the parents (father and mother) and their children

Objective culture: The artifacts that a culture produces

Oculesics: A culture's use of eye behavior, particularly gaze

Ontology: A set of assumptions about the nature of reality

Organization: A group of people that work in some form of structure to meet a goal

Organizational communication: A subset of the communication discipline that analyzes how people work together in groups through communication to meet a common goal

Organizational culture/corporate culture: A set of values and assumptions that is shared by an "organization" that guides organizational members' behaviors

Orientalism: An ideology in the West (i.e., White, Judeo-Christian Europe, and its former colonies) by which the Orient (especially Asia and the Middle East) becomes a mirror image of what is inferior and alien to the West

Outcome phase: The last phase of negotiation, the culmination of all the events and communicative behaviors that comprised the conflict negotiation process

Out-groups: Groups with which we do not associate or cooperate

Overaccommodation: Converging too much or in ineffective ways

Paradigm: A way of seeing or making sense of the world

Paralanguage/paralinguistics: Characteristics of voice and vocalization that are neither verbal nor strictly nonverbal, including rate of speech, volume, intonation, pronunciation, tone of voice, sighs, laughter, grunts

Particularist ethical approach: An ethical approach that assumes what is right or wrong in human conduct may vary based on different contexts, cultures, or situations

Patriarchy: A system of male-based power, in which men have authority or dominance (formal and/or informal) over women

Peace principle: An ethical approach that treats the human spirit as the basis for a universal ethics

Phoneme: A distinct sound in a language, such as the way particular consonants or vowels are pronounced in a language (including tones, clicks, etc.)

Phonology: The way that sounds tend to occur together within a language

Platform: A media system or service that provides media to an audience

Platformization: The interaction of individuals and meeting of individual needs through media platforms; the domination in the media market of large companies who sell and control media "platforms" through which individuals interact

Plural organization: An organization with a moderate number of minority employees, but with those employees typically holding lower-level jobs

Political correctness: An attempt to change communication through terminology and references—the avoiding of words, images, or actions that marginalize or put down other groups or people that belong to those groups

Political engagement: Involvement that includes participation in the political system

Politics 2.0: How social structures and institutions work to maintain their authority; how these structures gain our consensus on their legitimacy, and how they gain our consent to control how we live

Politics: The identification and public negotiation of competing interest

Polychronic culture: A culture in which people may prefer to do multiple tasks at the same time

Polychronic time: The model of involvement in several things at once

Popular/low culture: The everyday activities and expressions of people

Popularity: The level of renown or admiration held by a certain person, topic, or organization

Positive face: A desire to be seen as competent or included/liked by others

Postcolonialism: A field of study that looks worldwide at problems created by colonization, seeking to bring awareness to these problems and provide empowerment to those harmed by colonial relations

Postmodernism: An approach to social reality that suggests that meanings are created by the discourses in which they are placed, thus rejecting the idea that there are universal, overarching theories, as well as the idea of unified cultures, groups, or disciplines

Power distance: A cultural orientation that describes the degree to which social inequality is accepted in a culture, especially if those in the lower status groups accept that inequality as just and natural

Pragmatics: The aspect of language that deals with how we accomplish tasks with language, such as the ways we might make a request in different contexts or the type of action an utterance is trying to accomplish (e.g., joke, insult, hint); see speech acts theory

Prejudice: An attitude in which we seek to avoid someone or are hostile toward that person because of the attitudes we hold toward the person's group

Proactive approach: An approach to returning home from another culture in which the traveler sees the good and bad in both the host and home culture, taking in her or his identity portions of both

Process phase: When the actual negotiation, collaborative engagement, or competition occurs between the parties

Process: As it refers to communication, the ongoing creation, sending, receiving, and interpretation of a message, often including feedback provided to the sender and the role of the message in the ongoing relationship or social system

Programmability: Social media's ability to direct what users are able to do with the media, influencing their contributions

Propinquity: Physical closeness between people, and by contrast, virtual closeness, that implies increased contact

Propriety: Engaging in the proper behavior for the proper relationships or situation; saying what is right in different social and relational contexts, as well as saving and giving face

Prosody: The vocalic shaping of utterances, including pitch, volume, tempo, tone, and rhythm

Proxemics: The use of interpersonal distance behavior, including territoriality

Psychological adjustment: One of two dimensions of adjustment, referring to one's psychological wellbeing or emotional satisfaction (often measured by looking at travelers' level of depression)

Public Sphere: Any area of social life where discussion of public opinion occurs

Race: Supposed biological differences between groups, but influenced by social and political considerations

Racism: An action (or thought or communicative behavior) toward another person based on the person's perceived racial belonging, possibly with societal power held by the group of the perpetrator

Reality: The actual object we perceive in our environment (as it relates to language)

Receiver: A device or instrument through which a destination source decodes or interprets a signal received from an information source

Reciprocity: A practice of giving and receiving from others—can include material things, such as gifts, or information, such as in self-disclosure

Redlining: A practice in which banks avoid giving mortgages to people wanting to purchase in certain neighborhoods or to people of different ethnic or racial groups

Redneck racism: A form of racism in which one clearly feels one's group is (racially) superior to other groups; often expressed in clear statements of superiority, racial slurs, and so on

Refence: Allow someone from another group into one's circle of friends or relations, but see that person as an exception to the general feelings or stereotypes one has of that person's group

Reference: The thought image in our mind that either perception of reality or attention to a symbol brings about

Refugee: Someone who travels outside of her or his country either by force or because of violence, oppression, or threat to freedom or life in one's own land, often based on reasons of group belonging (e.g., race, sex, ethnicity, political affiliation, tribal group)

Register: A form of speaking within a language that includes level of formality in terms of pronunciation, word choice, grammar, terms of direct address, etc.

Relationship: A connection between two or more individuals in which they have both rights and responsibilities toward each other beyond what would be expected in interaction with strangers

Remediation: Doing something concrete to make up to the injured party for a wrong or embarrassment

Resocialized approach: An approach to returning home from another culture in which the traveler sheds the foreign culture and adopts totally to the culture of origin

Restricted code: A way of speaking or "code" used by people who know each other well, including grammar, word choice (such as jargon or argot), and so on

Return culture shock/return cultural adjustment: The process of going through a period of stress when one returns home from a stay in another culture

Rhetoric/rhetorical action: Inducing cooperation through the use of symbols and meanings; for Aristotle, a practical art that seeks to discover the appropriate means for persuading an audience

Rhetorical communication: A message that is planned and adapted to an audience or multiple audiences

Rhetorical tradition: The historical and social influences and ethnic practices that inform a speaker's message

Ritual view of media communication: A view that includes transmission but adds the notion of our understanding of the way our world is portrayed and confirmed in media

Romeo and Juliet effect: When a couple feels it must be stronger due to societal or family pressure (that is, blaming problems on family and society)

Rule: A prescription or cultural belief about which behaviors are appropriate in certain situations

Sapir-Whorf hypothesis: The "linguistic relativity" view of language, which states that the language of a culture dictates the very way that people within that culture can think

Script: A set of cultural rules regarding expected behavior that include expectations of who does what (actors, roles), and any expected sequence of actions in a communication routine

Secondary baby talk: A form of convergence younger people sometimes use with older people, including higher pitch, simpler grammar, use of "we," and so on

Secular culture: A culture in which life problems and solutions are seen in terms of science and human ideas

Segregation: A response in which a dominant cultural group intentionally or unintentionally separates immigrant or minority groups into their own communities

Selective adaptation: A pattern by which an immigrant or minority group chooses some aspects of the dominant culture to adopt but maintains other aspects of the original culture

Selective attention: The idea that we only pay attention to certain things, often impacted by what we hold to be important, as well as our negative or positive expectations

Selective perception: A mental process through which biases shape how we interpret the stimuli in our environment

Selective recall: A mental process through which we only remember certain things that conform to our expectations or biases

Self-construal: A psychological notion of how strongly we see ourselves independent from others or connected to others

Self-disclosure: revealing things about ourselves to someone else, specifically things that would not normally be known by the other and about which there is at least some risk of sharing

Selflessness: A consideration of the needs of the other

Self-serving (or egocentric) attribution bias: An error of perception in which we give meanings to the behaviors of others and ourselves that protect our self-concept

Semantics: The area of language study that refers to word meanings and lexical choice (the number or type of words available to describe something)

Semiotics: A cross-disciplinary approach that looks at how meaning is conveyed through "signs"

Sender: In the explanation of the communication process, the source or creator of a message

Servant leadership: A style of leadership that places the needs of the followers first

Sex: Biological make-up that distinguishes what kinds of sexual organs and genetic characteristics an individual is born with

Sexism: A system of ideas, images, laws, beliefs, and practices that work against women in the favor of patriarchy

Shame culture: A culture in which people are motivated more by a sense of social obligation or duty, and are more likely to act in a way to protect the honor or "face" of their group

Shame: In cross-cultural communication research, a negative reflection upon one's group experienced as a result of one's behavior [Note: This differs from a common psychological definition of the term]

Sign systems: When different codes are placed together in a text to give meaning

Sign: The combination of the signified and the signifier and the relationship between them

Signified: An object or idea that is represented by a sound or image; part of a "sign"

Signifier: The sound or image that represents a concept or thing; part of a "sign"

Silence: Refraining from speech; in a context of non-response to group-based oppression, a possible form of intolerance

Similarity-attraction hypothesis: A research proposition that the more similar we are to people, the more we will grow to like them

Social capital: A concept referring to investment in community, including social organization, trust, networks, a sense of citizenship, and norms

Social construction: The notion that concepts, such as race, gender, or our identities, are created through communication in the context of our social world, histories, and relationships

Social drama: A conflict that arises when a community norm or rule is violated

Social identity: Our self-perception in terms of roles (e.g., student/teacher), relationships (e.g., enemy, brother/sister, lover), or groups to which we belong (e.g., religious, racial, national)

Social identity theory: A theory that suggests that how we see ourselves is closely tied to how we see the groups to which we belong; that when we interact with others, we identify them based on personal terms, expectations, and membership in groups; and that we compare groups against our own

Social media: Websites and phone applications that allow media users to develop networks and interact with others

Social movement: Wide-scale, organized activism to accomplish social change

Social penetration theory: A theory of relationship growth that suggests that self-disclosure is what causes people to grow closer together

Social responsibility theory: A theory of mass communication where the media acts as a watchdog to the government, working to inform the public in an unbiased manner, while still working to keep people safe by censoring some news

Social scientific research: Research that typically seeks to make claims that apply to most people ("generalizing" claims) using systemized methods that allow for counting and statistical analysis

Social system: A set of individuals, groups, and institutions within a society often working toward a specific function, and the relationships between them

Sociocultural adjustment/cross-cultural adaptation: One of two dimensions of adjustment, referring to one's sense of fitting in and ability to negotiate the culture (such as accomplishing tasks)

Sojourner: Someone who travels to another culture for a longer term, but with intent to return home

Solidarity (relational distance): The degree of familiarity and/or intimacy we have with another person

Soviet theory: A mass communication theory that was prevalent in the Soviet Union

Speaking with: Being an ally to a community; advocating the interests of a community along with its members

Speech acts theory: A perspective that looks at the types of actions people accomplish with speech

Speech code: The system of symbols, meanings, assumptions, and norms for communication adopted by a group of people

Speech codes theory: A theory of communication that considers the uniqueness of the speech codes (ways of speaking) in each community

Speech community: A group of people that shares a common speech code

Spirit(ual) (or sacred) culture: A culture in which there is more of a sense of presence of the spiritual or divine in everyday life

Stereotype: An oversimplified, often unvarying attribute assigned to a group or to a person because that person is a member of a group

Stigma: A lack of social acceptability of a group or person, sometimes to the point of shame or disgrace

Stress-adaptation-growth dynamic: An approach to cross-cultural adjustment that suggests that adjustment is cyclical: one feels stress from the new culture, but adapts to that stress, leading to new ways to act, think, and feel

Subjective culture: The thought elements of a culture, such as values, beliefs, attitudes, norms, and world view that are shared by a group of people

Subtle racism/prejudice: An intolerance that one still holds toward another person because of the group to which the person belongs, but that is expressed in difficult-to-notice ways

Succinct style: A communication style in which speakers use understatement or silence, giving less detail in a situation than the other styles

Sweatshops: Factories, often in developing nations where there is inexpensive labor

Symbol: A sound or visual representation of the reality

Symbolic annihilation: When groups and cultures are underrepresented or represented in troublesome manners, such as trivialization or condemnation, especially in media

Symbolic ethnicity: When people represent their ethnicity through signs or symbols, even if they have mostly assimilated into a dominant culture

Symbolic racism: A set of ideas expressing negative feelings toward minority members in a culture, which are embedded in other symbols or behind political attitudes

Symbolic: A characteristic of communication that describes how images, words, sounds, or nonverbal behaviors serve to represent something else

Syntax: The structural order of words or grammar within a sentence

Systemic prejudice: Inequality of access, opportunity, reward or punishment based on group belonging

Taboo: A norm so strong that cultural members may not even talk about it

Terminal value: An end-state or desired outcome of action for individuals

Territoriality: How a person or group perceives of and marks territory

Tolerance: The application of the same moral principles and rules, caring and empathy, and feeling of connection to human beings of other perceived groups

Transactional: A characteristic of communication that describes the way in which both partners produce and consume the messages of the other; that is, it is the give-and-take between two or more people in message exchange

Transmission model of communication: A view of media in which media are believed to impart, send, give, or *transmit* information from sender(s) to receiver(s), through a fairly linear process

Transmitter: A device or instrument, including media or human voice and body, that we use to transfer symbols to represent some meaning

U-curve: A model of adjustment where one arrives in a new culture excited and well-adjusted, goes through a period of crisis, and then adjusts to the new culture

Ultimate attribution error: An error in perception that blends fundamental and self-serving attribution biases in which we give different meanings to the failures and successes of others than to our own

Uncertainty avoidance: A cultural orientation that describes the degree to which a culture accepts or dislikes uncertain and ambiguous situations; the general orientation of a group of people to clarity of structure

Uncertainty reduction theory: A theory of relationship growth that states that the better we can predict and explain the behaviors of another person, the more relationships will grow

Uncertainty: One's ability to explain or predict the behavior of another person

Universal values: A set of values that some research suggests exist in all cultures to some degree

Universalist ethical approach: An approach to ethics in which the same principles of right or wrong or morality are applied to all cultures

Utilitarianism: An ethical approach based on what is practical by determining the greatest benefit for the greatest number of people

Value: An idea or priority that a person (or culture) holds to be important and that serves as a guide for behavior

Vernacular discourse: Local meanings produced by marginalized communities that (1) affirm community membership and (2) critique power relations with the dominant culture

Vernacular rhetoric: The persuasive use of vernacular discourse

Virtual community: A group of individuals who connect across geographic boundaries through the Internet, especially through social media and who feel a sense of commonality and cohesion

Virtual culture: A culture that has emerged, or is emerging, from the use of computer networks for communication, entertainment, and business

Virtuality: The phenomenon that social media form a virtual space and a virtual community that crosses all the boundaries of human society

Voluntarism: The notion of giving our own time to a charitable organization

W-curve: A curve describing a process adjustment, both sojourning abroad and coming home

World view: A set of assumptions or cognitions about humans and their place in the cosmos, including things such as the purpose of humans, the nature of deity, the relative position of humans to nature and the rest of the cosmos

Xenophobia: A fear of things different; here, specifically, a fear of groups besides our own

Index

Page locators in *italics* indicate figures. This index uses letter-by-letter alphabetization.

Intercultural Communication for Everyday Life, Second Edition. John R. Baldwin, Alberto González, Nettie Brock, Ming Xie, and Chin-Chung Chao.
© 2024 John Wiley & Sons Ltd. Published 2024 by John Wiley & Sons Ltd.
Companion Website: http://www.wiley.com/go/baldwin2e

Printed and bound by CPI Group (UK) Ltd, Croydon, CR0 4YY

31/08/2023

08107149-0001